Gero Guttzeit
The Figures of Edgar Allan Poe

Buchreihe der ANGLIA/
ANGLIA Book Series

Edited by
Lucia Kornexl, Ursula Lenker, Martin Middeke,
Gabriele Rippl, Hubert Zapf

Advisory Board
Laurel Brinton, Philip Durkin, Olga Fischer, Susan Irvine,
Andrew James Johnston, Christopher A. Jones, Terttu Nevalainen,
Derek Attridge, Elisabeth Bronfen, Ursula K. Heise, Verena Lobsien,
Laura Marcus, J. Hillis Miller, Martin Puchner

Volume 56

Gero Guttzeit

The Figures of Edgar Allan Poe

Authorship, Antebellum Literature, and Transatlantic Rhetoric

DE GRUYTER

For an overview of all books published in this series, please see
http://www.degruyter.com/view/serial/36292

Zugl.: Gießen, Univ., Diss., 2014

ISBN 978-3-11-063527-0
e-ISBN (PDF) 978-3-11-052015-6
e-ISBN (EPUB) 978-3-11-051818-4
ISSN 0340-5435

Library of Congress Cataloging-in-Publication Data
A CIP catalog record for this book has been applied for at the Library of Congress.

Bibliografische Information der Deutschen Nationalbibliothek
Die Deutsche Nationalbibliothek verzeichnet diese Publikation in der Deutschen Nationalbibliografie; detaillierte bibliografische Daten sind im Internet über http://dnb.dnb.de abrufbar.

© 2018 Walter de Gruyter GmbH, Berlin/Boston
This volume is text- and page-identical with the hardback published in 2017.
Druck und Bindung: CPI books GmbH, Leck

♾ Printed on acid-free paper
Printed in Germany

www.degruyter.com

Meiner Tochter Lenja Sophia

Contents

Acknowledgements —— IX

Abbreviations —— XI

Note on the Text —— XIII

Introduction —— 1
    The Problem of Poe —— 1
    Rhetoricizing Poe —— 9

Part I Authorship, Antebellum Literature, and Transatlantic Rhetoric

1 Towards a Rhetoric of Authorship: Theoretical, Poetical, and Performative Figures of the Author —— 21
1.1   The Figures of the Author —— 22
1.2   Theoretical, Poetical, and Performative Figures of the Author —— 32

2 "Under the Ban of the Empire of Literature": Print Culture, the Rise of the Author, and the Transatlantic Dispersal of Rhetoric, 1776–1849 —— 54
2.1   The Author, Rhetoric, and the Emergence of Literature —— 55
2.2   The Effects of Poetry from the New Rhetoric to Romantic Aesthetics —— 64
2.3   "How to Write a Blackwood Article": Transatlantic Antebellum Cultures of Print and Rhetoric —— 77

Part II The Figures of Edgar Allan Poe

3 "Letters of Recommendation": The Transatlantic Poet-Critic between the Rules of Rhetoric and Romantic Aesthetics —— 89
3.1   The Poet-Critic in the "Letter to B—" —— 92
3.2   The Rules of Rhetoric and Doggerel Aesthetics —— 104

4 The Genius Rhetorician: The Rhetoric of "The Philosophy of Composition" —— 124

4.1 Poe, Dickens, Godwin and the Question of Writing Backwards —— 124
4.2 From "The Philosophy of Composition" to *The Philosophy of Rhetoric* —— 129
4.3 The Poetical Madness of Composition —— 139
4.4 Godwin's Autocommentary —— 141
4.5 Figuring the Rhetorical Poet-Critic in Times of Romanticism —— 145

5 "The Ingenuity of Unravelling": Abductive Powers and Rhetorical Inventors in the Tales of Ratiocination —— 148

5.1 The Author's and Detective's Creative and Resolvent Powers —— 149
5.2 Author and Detective as Rhetorical Inventors of Truth —— 162

6 The Jingle-Man and the Damned Rhetorician: Poetry, Elocution, and the Political Rationale of Verse —— 172

6.1 Poe and the Failure to Distinguish Between Poetry and Rhetoric: A Short Reception History —— 173
6.2 The Elocutionary Production of Beauty: Style and Performance in "Ulalume" —— 177
6.3 "A Well Understood Poetical License": The Politics of Performance in "The Rationale of Verse" —— 187

7 "The Only Proper Stage for the Literary Histrio": Delivery and its Dangers in the Antebellum Cultures of Rhetoric and Print —— 196

7.1 "Stand and Deliver": Poe's Boston Lyceum Appearance and its Aftermath —— 201
7.2 "The Characteristics of a Popular Performer": Acting Against "Loss of Breath" —— 208
7.3 "X-ing a Paragrab": Technological Delivery, Anastatic Printing and Crossing Out the Author —— 218

Concluding Remarks —— 223

Works Cited —— 226

Index of Names —— 250

Index of Subjects —— 253

Acknowledgements

> Only those voices from without are effective which can speak in the language of a voice within.
>
> Kenneth Burke, *The Rhetoric of Motives* (1969: 39)

Some of Poe's overtly metatextual tales – such as "Manuscript Found in a Bottle" in 1835 and "The Purloined Letter" in 1844 – appeared in an annual publication called *The Gift: A Christmas, New Year, and Birthday Present*. This is quite fitting in that the very origins of this book lie in a Christmas present in 1998 but also in that I have been given so much by my teachers, colleagues, friends, and family, to all of whom I would like to give thanks. I could not have written, perhaps authored, this book without them.

At the University of Siegen, I was introduced to Anglophone literatures and ancient languages by Nancy Bunge, Werner Deuse, K. Ludwig Pfeiffer, and Brigitte Pichon. My interest in the rhetorical connections between Scotland and the United States originated during the Masters programme in creative writing at the University of Edinburgh, while I was discussing my own fledgling literary attempts with, among others, Rajorshi Chakraborti and Mati Kaim. Thank you.

At Gießen, where most of the work on this project was completed, I would like to thank my *Doktorvater* Ingo Berensmeyer, who introduced me to authorship studies and supported me from the earliest to the latest stages of the book. I am also indebted to my second supervisor Annette Simonis, who taught me comparative literature, and to the other members of my dissertation committee Wolfgang Hallet and Andreas Langenohl. For their help, a bed to crash on or one *Hanjer* too many, thank you, René Dietrich, Julia Faisst, Tobias Gabel, Mirjam Horn-Schott, Frank Ipgrave, Tim Kurtzweil, Reinhard Möller, Alexander Scherr, Jutta Weingarten, and Katharina Zilles. First and foremost, I wish to thank Natalya Bekhta and Daniel Hartley for countless hours of discussions about rhetoric, poetics, dialectics, and narratology, for reading my work and helping me write, for their critical acuity and for their deep friendship.

Beyond Gießen, I am grateful to my colleagues and friends at Ghent University, where I researched and taught as part of the *Research on Authorship as Performance* (RAP) project, in particular Maaheen Ahmed, Sean Bex, Gert Buelens, Marysa Demoor, and Debora Van Durme as well as my colleagues on the journal *Authorship* Yuri Cowan and Jasper Schelstraete. At De Gruyter, my thanks go to the editors of the Anglia Book series and my in-house editors, Ulrike Krauß and Katja Lehming. I also wish to express my gratitude to the many colleagues who offered a forum or commented themselves on the project, among whom are Heinrich Detering, Christoph Ehland, Emron Esplin, Monika Fludernik, Margarida Vale de Gato, Jerome McGann, James Phelan, Sean Moreland, Jeffrey A. Savoye, Oliver Scheiding, and Alexandra Urakova.

Thanks are also due to the institutions and individuals who generously supported my work: above all, to the German National Academic Foundation, the *Studienstiftung*, that supported me as an undergraduate and as a postgraduate student, both at home and abroad. To the International Graduate Centre for the Study of Culture and the International PhD Programme *Literary and Cultural Studies*, in particular their director, Ansgar Nünning. To Susan Jaffe Tane and the Poe Museum Richmond.

Thank you for supporting me whenever the going got tough: Jakub Limanowski. Norman Hammel. Laura Prehl. And to my parents Elke and Helmut, my brother Karl, and my wife Miriam: Danke! You are my voice within.

Abbreviations

CT	*Critical Theory: The Major Documents* (edited by Stuart and Susan Levine)
CW 1–5	*The Collected Writings of Edgar Allan Poe* (edited by Burton R. Pollin)
E&R	*Essays and Reviews* (edited by G. R. Thompson)
ERK	*Eureka* (edited by Stuart and Susan Levine)
LTR I-II	*The Letters of Edgar Allan Poe* (3rd edition edited by John W. Ostrom, Burton R. Pollin, and Jeffrey A. Savoye)
MTC 1–17	*The Complete Works of Edgar Allan Poe* (The Monticello Edition edited by James A. Harrison)
PMS	*Poems* (The Collected Works of Edgar Allan Poe edited by T. O. Mabbott)
T&S	*Tales and Sketches* (The Collected Works of Edgar Allan Poe edited by T. O. Mabbott)

Note on the Text

I wish to thank the New York Public Library for permission to cite the autograph letter signed Charles Dickens to Edgar A. Poe, March 6, 1842 (Berg Coll MSS Dickens). The Henry W. and Albert A. Berg Collection of English and American Literature. The New York Public Library. Astor, Lenox and Tilden Foundations.

An earlier version of parts of chapters 1.1 and 2.1 appeared as "Authorship in Literary Theory and Fiction: Writing on Writers" in *Key Concepts and New Topics in English and American Studies*. Edited by Ansgar Nünning and Elizabeth Kovach, 115–34. Trier: Wissenschaftlicher Verlag Trier 2014.

An earlier and shorter version of chapter 2.2 appeared as "From Hearing to Overhearing? Eloquence and Poetry, 1776–1833" in *Anglistentag 2013 Konstanz. Proceedings of the Conference of the German Association of University Teachers of English* 35, 261–270. Trier: Wissenschaftlicher Verlag Trier 2014.

An earlier version of chapter 4 appeared in German as "Writing Backwards? Autorpoetik bei Poe und Godwin" in *Theorien und Praktiken der Autorschaft*. Edited by Marcus Willand and Matthias Schaffrick, 377–402. Berlin: de Gruyter 2014.

Introduction

No other author has haunted literary studies quite like Edgar A. Poe. He was called "a stumbling block for the judicial critic" by T. S. Eliot (1949: 327), and Shoshana Felman claimed that "[i]n the history of literary criticism no other poet has engendered as much disagreement and as many critical contradictions" (1988: 133). No matter whether critics took the stance of supporters or detractors, Poe has occupied "an anomalous position in both the old and new canons of antebellum American writing" (J. G. Kennedy and Weissberg 2001: xiii). At the same time, Poe has been crucial to the development of the modern author, as a writer and critic who was "very conscious of the revolutionary nature" (Genette 1997: 368) of his poetical ideas. In current Poe studies, Poe's anomalous position tends to be explained and interpreted via recourse to the paradigm of American antebellum print culture: the strongest studies take Poe to be a "pivotal figure" (McGann 2013a: 245) who is "singularly representative" (J. G. Kennedy 2013: 9) of an antebellum literary culture that is first and foremost a culture of print (McGill 2003).

My suggestion in this book is to reconceptualise the emergence of antebellum literature from the complex interplay between print culture and what I call the contemporary *culture of rhetoric*, building on the work of Gregory Clark and S. Michael Halloran (1993) and James Perrin Warren (1999). Its fundamentally transatlantic character has been demonstrated by Nan Johnson (1991), Winifred Bryan Horner (1993) and Susan Manning (2002, [1990] 2009, 2013). Concepts, strategies, and performances informed by the transatlantic nexus of early nineteenth-century rhetoric play a central role in what made Poe crucial for modern authorship, particularly in his critical writings, his literary works, and his lectures. This book discusses the many figures of the author as they appear around, in, and through Poe's textual and discursive practices, and shows that they are better understood by turning to the history of transatlantic rhetoric. In so doing, it also demonstrates that rhetorical theory offers new ways of conceptualising authorship beyond the long nineteenth century.

The Problem of Poe

"In regard to the work of an already famous or infamous author," Poe himself wrote in 1845, general opinion makes up "a species of critical shadow that fully answers, nevertheless, all the purposes of a substance" (E&R 372). Indeed, Poe's oeuvre has posed fundamental interpretative problems ever since the beginnings of scholarly engagement with his works in the later nineteenth century, which is further complicated by the fact that it "invites impossible attempts to say everything at once" (Tally 2014: 5). For a long time, Poe was viewed, in the words of one of his own poems, as a writer "Out of Space – out of Time" (PMS 344). While Poe studies have acknowledged this "problem of Poe," as Vernon Louis Parrington called it in 1927 ([1927] 1987: 58), it is only recently that the picture of a displaced and untimely Poe has been redrawn.

Over the course of the past decades Poe's image has been fundamentally altered by scholarship that focuses on his relation to the emerging literary market of the antebellum United States and its corresponding print culture.[1] Shawn Rosenheim and Stephen Rachman consolidated the early phase of the (neo)historicization of Poe in their edited collection, *The American Face of Edgar Allan Poe* (1995), stating that he was "always both in and out of his time" (1995: xx; cf. Whalen 1992). Significantly, they pointed out that many of what were perceived as postmodern features of Poe's writing emerged out of Poe's relation to the medial conditions of antebellum literature (xx). The interrelation between Poe's writings and the American capitalist publishing industry was foregrounded by Terence Whalen in his study of *Edgar Allan Poe and the Masses* (1999), who depicts Poe as "a writer who was both product and portent of an emerging mass culture;" or, in Poe's own words, "a poor devil author" under the "horrid laws of political economy" (ix).[2] Critical attention to the American publishing industry was further focused by Meredith McGill's study of the circulation of literary texts through unauthorized reprintings in a system that had no international copyright agreement in place. In *American Literature and the Culture of Reprinting* (2003), she argued that Poe's work redefined "authorship not as origination

---

[1] This is not to disregard earlier approaches that offer insight into Poe and authorship. The definitive survey of Poe scholarship is Scott Peeples' *The Afterlife of Edgar Allan Poe* (2004). Peeples traces three earlier phases of Poe's critical reception before the current one: 1) the debate about Poe's place in American literature between 1849 and 1909, 2) Poe and Psychoanalysis, and 3) Poe's reception from Early Formalism to Deconstruction (Peeples 2004: ix). The first stage is mainly of historical interest, though it had a lasting impact on the popular image of Poe: Poe's literary executor, Rufus Griswold's, villainising obituary and temperance advocates' use of his alcohol problems in cautionary tales (Peeples 2004: 6) were met by defences by friends and followers such as Sarah Helen Whitman and, of course, Charles Baudelaire (albeit on very different grounds). This stage was particularly marked by attempts to appropriate Poe as a national American writer and, in particular, a Southern writer (Peeples 2004: 21).

[2] The phrase "poor devil author" is in "Some Secrets of the Magazine Prison-House" (E&R 1036), and "the horrid laws of political economy" is to be found, among other places, in his 1841 review of Dickens' *Old Curiosity-Shop* (E&R 211). Cf. also Kevin Hayes' study of *Poe and the Printed Word* (2000).

but as manipulation, a practice defined by interruption, inconsistency, and uncertainty, not mastery" (186). In current research, Poe has thus become a figure and figurer of antebellum print culture.

The emphasis on Poe as a figure of print culture has been complemented with investigations into the "socio-historical Poe" (Peeples 2004: 93), particularly with regard to mass culture, race, and gender. Jonathan Elmer's study *Reading at the Social Limit: Affect, Mass Culture, and Edgar Allan Poe* (1995) traced the dialectic between Poe's figuration of mass cultural artefacts and his own status as a symptom of mass culture; Poe's work makes visible what Elmer calls "the social limit," a boundary that "is less between the democratic individual and the sovereign people than it is internal to both simultaneously" (Elmer 1995: 19).[3] Authorship in the sense of attribution studies was central to the debate on Poe's racism, as it centred on the anonymous apologist essay "Slavery," better known as the "Paulding-Drayton Review," which appeared in the *Southern Literary Messenger* during Poe's stint as an editor ("Slavery" 1836). By now it is almost certain that it was written by pro-slavery author and judge, Nathaniel Beverley Tucker (Whalen 1999: 111–146).[4] The publication in the magazine, owned by Thomas Willis White and edited by Poe, remains an example of what Terence Whalen calls "average racism," a term that has become something like a consensus view (Whalen 1999: 111), though some critics have argued that "Poe's writings actually seem to destabilise the whole notion of a black-white binary divide" (A. Smith 2013: 65).[5] In *Gender and the Poetics of Reception in Poe's Circle* (2004), Eliza Richards investigated the social authorship of Poe and female writers in his circle "in an antebellum literary culture that valued poets as performance ar-

---

[3] For a pathbreaking rereading of Poe in terms of nationalism, cf. J. Gerald Kennedy's *Strange Nation: Literary Nationalism and Cultural Conflict in the Age of Poe* (2016), which appeared too late to be considered here.
[4] Cf. also the case for Poe's authorship in Rosenthal (1974) and the refutation in Ridgely (1992).
[5] Race is of special importance with regard to Poe as is Poe to issues of race, as Toni Morrison argued in her discussion of Poe's novel *The Narrative of Arthur Gordon Pym of Nantucket* (1838): "No early American writer is more important to the concept of American Africanism than Poe" (Morrison 1992: 32). As Scott Peeples explains it, "the prevailing assumption seems to be that race is always in the unconscious of his work, although it rises into clear view in a large handful of texts dealing with mastery, servitude, and revolt" (Peeples 2004: 103; cf. J. G. Kennedy and Weissberg 2001). Following Leon Jackson, Peeples is also careful to stress that, while certainly most prominent, the debate on Poe and race should not be limited to representations of African Americans but also further the discussion of the portrayals of other ethnic groups such as Native Americans (Peeples 2004: 107). The debate about Poe and race initially turned around the moral evaluation of the author Poe as a racist but has now reached a point where Poe is viewed as a crucial point of intersection of the discourses about race in antebellum America.

tists and celebrities as well as geniuses" (E. Richards 2004: 2). Rather than as a representative of the (male) genius, Richards reads the author 'Poe' as "a reversal or mirroring of the type of the poetess; he is a figure to which the transactions among a circle of poets is ascribed" (E. Richards 2004: 3).[6] Recent Poe studies have thus located Poe at crucial nodes of the social, political, and technological networks of antebellum print culture and the American nation.

The image and concept of Poe's authorship have changed from a displaced and untimely Poe to a Poe deeply immersed in the American print culture of his time and as a "pivotal figure" within it (McGann 2013a: 245): Poe's life and works are now regarded as indicative and, indeed, representative of the contradictions and processes of antebellum literary culture. This contrasts with earlier phases of criticism particularly insofar as they might be said to understand the author Poe not in terms of authorship in general but as a relatively singular entity: either – albeit determined by its unconscious – as a psyche in psychoanalytic approaches[7] or – despite the emphasis on the intentional fallacy – as the poet-cre-

---

[6] As Eliza Richards argues elsewhere, "[w]omen are everywhere and nowhere in Poe studies" (E. Richards 2000: 10). Poe's autodiegetic tales are virtually always narrated by men who project their fears upon women and subject them to "the objectifying, even murderous powers of the male gaze" (Person 2001: 141). The group of tales most often analysed is the one that features eponymous dying women and consists of "Berenice," "Eleonora," "Morella," and the story Poe thought his best, "Ligeia"; among others, Cynthia Jordan, Leland S. Person, Colin (Joan) Dayan, and J. Gerald Kennedy have analysed the stories' depiction of "gendered power relations" and "the question of whether Poe endorses or exposes the misogynist fantasies that create the central conflicts" (Peeples 2004: 45). In a special issue of *Poe Studies* in 1993, Dayan argued that "Poe does not sustain the eternal polarities, but instead analyzes the slippage in too convenient oppositions, the reversibility of all concepts, and ultimately, the confounding of men and women" (Dayan 1991: 1). Many of Poe's poems fit his (in)famous critical dictum that "the death [...] of a beautiful woman is [...] the most poetical topic in the world" (CT 65), the indebtedness of which to "Western poetry's most important illusion of transcendence: the Dantean myth of Beatrice" has recently been suggested by Jerome McGann (2014b: 187).
[7] The second stage of Poe criticism that Peeples distinguishes is dominated by psychoanalytic approaches to Poe's texts, which can be viewed as falling into a pre-Lacanian and a post-Lacanian phase. One of the most famous psychoanalytic studies of literature, Marie Bonaparte's *Edgar Poe: Étude psychoanalytique* (1933; first translated as *The Life and Works of Edgar Allan Poe*, 1949), established the importance of Poe's childhood trauma of losing his mother at the age of two, an argument that still underpins one of the most important biographies, Kenneth Silverman's *Edgar A. Poe: Mournful and Never-Ending Remembrance* (1991). While it has become clear that "Poe's tales can have psychological depth without necessarily being all about Poe himself" (Peeples 2004: 41), the connections between creativity and neurosis made so prevalent by early psychoanalytic theory also influenced discussions of autonomous and heteronomous aspects of authorship. While the discussion about madness and method of the artist in its clinical form has more or less subsided, sanity and insanity served as an important metaphorical

ator of an oeuvre in the new criticism.[8] In deconstructionist approaches, the emphasis on the linguistic and fictional self-reflexivity present in so many of Poe's texts was still paired with an interest in Poe as a single author, albeit as one of difference and contradiction.[9] In a certain respect, it is only with neohistoricist approaches that the singular author Poe really dwindles in importance, while at the same time authorship in general becomes more important. What distinguishes the current phase of Poe studies from earlier ones is its attention to the relation between authorship and larger paradigms of meaning such as na-

---

field to explain literary authorship, particularly in the romantic age. Lacan's "Seminar on the Purloined Letter" (given in 1955, published in 1957, and translated into English in 1972) deals with the two scenes of observation that inform the tale and their relevance for his notions of the real, the imaginary, and the symbolic (cf. the text and a survey of the argument in Muller and Richardson 1988; cf. also Peeples 2004: 54–61; for the relation between Lacanian psychoanalysis and rhetoric, cf. Lundberg 2012). Derrida's response in "The Purveyor of Truth," in which he argued that Lacan had constructed a privileged position for himself as analyst, moved the debate to the question of reading and the symbolic order in general; it elicited responses by many critics such as Shoshana Felman and Barbara Johnson (collected in Muller and Richardson 1988). In a way that few, if any, other narratives have done, Poe's final Dupin story thus initiated a debate about reading as well as language and the symbolic in general.
8 Peeples suggests to view the development from early formalist to deconstructivist approaches as one phase (2003: 90). Whilst the preference for short forms, the dismissal of didacticism, and the use of irony made Poe an attractive writer to New Critics, the popularity of his genres, the mechanical appearance of his writing, and the equivocal morals of his fiction made him problematic (Peeples 2004: 64; cf. the discussion of Aldous Huxley's and Yvor Winters' attacks on Poe's poetry in chapter six). Allen Tate, Edward Davidson, Harry Levin, and Richard Wilbur replaced the unconscious unity of the author as conceptualised by psychoanalytic critics with a notion of a specific system of thought at the core of Poe's writings. Neocritical work on Poe remains important, particularly because it problematised the periodisation of Poe with regard to late Romanticism and early Modernism.
9 In contrast to neocritical unity, deconstructionist approaches emphasized difference in Poe: Poe's riddles, hoaxes, codes, wordplay, and the mixture of critical and creative aspects in his writing are among the things that led to "articulations of Poe as proto-deconstructionist" (Peeples 2004: 85). Language, writing, and self-referentiality in Poe are examined in studies by J. Gerald Kennedy on *Poe, Death, and the Life of Writing* (1987), Michael J. S. Williams on *A World of Words* (1988), and Dennis Pahl on *Architects of the Abyss* (1989) – discussions that play into questions of Poe's presentation of authorship within literary texts. Poe as the inventor of the detective story, discussed in chapter five, was also central to John T. Irwin's studies on *American Hieroglyphics* (1980) and *A Mystery to a Solution: Poe, Borges and the Analytic Detective Story* (1994). As Paul Hurh has recently argued, "Poe initiates a move that we would now call deconstruction" (Hurh 2015: 117).

tionalism,[10] political economy, and social identity issues connected to race, gender, and class.

As of today, the attempts to resolve the problem of Poe have reached an enormous number,[11] and Poe studies has been a burgeoning field for many decades. A steady flow of journal articles is emerging not only from the two Poe journals, *Poe Studies* and the *Edgar Allan Poe Review*; the number of texts on Poe can be estimated by a search for the occurrences of "Poe" in publication titles in the MLA International Bibliography: between 1990 and 2015, "Poe" was mentioned in the titles of 1,071 texts, which equals roughly one scholarly publication on Poe every nine days. Poe is not only the "The Figure of Mass Culture" as whom Jonathan Elmer (1995: 1) has so aptly described him, but has also become a figure of intense academic interest.

Yet what Jerome McGann has recently called "the vexed cultural status of Edgar Allan Poe" nonetheless remains (2014a: 148). This vexed status is a result not only of Poe's resistance to critical paradigms such as the American Renaissance or the New American Studies, but also of his image in popular culture, his role in literary history, and the inherent contradictions of his writings. Poe's position between 'high' and popular culture is partly a result of the appropriations of Poe which still partake in the "Poe legend" or "Poe myth" of "a perfectly archetypal horror writer" (Perry and Sederholm 2012: 1). Poe's role in literary history is complicated by the fact of his importance for the emergence of modern French poetry; this has led to a picture of Poe primarily as a precursor of modernism, most famously sketched by T. S. Eliot (1949). Eliot discussed "the art poétique of which we find the germ in Poe, and which bore fruit in the work of Valéry" (Eliot 1949: 342). Eliot and others such as Patrick Quinn, in *The French Face of Edgar Allan Poe* ([1957] 1971), established the master narrative of Poe as a precursor of modernity, justified to a large extent by his influence on Baudelaire, which can, indeed, hardly be overestimated.[12] The other main periodising concept that has been used to interpret Poe is that of (dark) Romanticism (Thompson 1974; Shucard 1990: 108–109). A seminal reading of Poe as a romantic was proffered by Edward Davidson in *Poe: A Critical Study* (1957), who viewed Poe as

---

10 This goes hand-in-hand with ongoing research on Poe's international and global appeal. Cf. Esplin and Gato (2014) on Poe and translation and Esplin (2016) on Poe in Spanish America. For a reading of Eliot's and other American critics of the French Poe in terms of transatlanticism, cf. Filippakopoulou (2015).
11 The number of edited collections of scholarly essays dedicated to Poe over the last five decades is approaching fifty (Kopley 2013: xiii, xv–xvii), and there were roughly forty biographies in 2004 already (Peeples 2004: 41).
12 Cf. e.g. Baudelaire ([1857] 1969).

a romantic with an "artistic mind delighting in its destruction" (Davidson [1957] 1973: 47). The case for the importance of romantic irony to an understanding of Poe's writings was made by G. R. Thompson, in *Poe's Fiction: Romantic Irony in the Gothic Tales* (1973). The question of whether Poe is a late Romantic or Proto-Modernist has remained the central issue with regard to periodising Poe's works in terms of literary history, yet neither option does justice to Poe's inheritance of earlier traditions stemming from the late eighteenth century, one of which – the Gothic – is a generally acknowledged source for Poe's tales. Lastly, the 'problem' of Poe is a result of what his contemporaries already recognized as contradictions and tensions within his work itself, which James Russell Lowell famously epitomized in the passage on Poe in *A Fable for Critics*: "Three fifths of him genius and two fifths sheer fudge,/[...]/Who has written some things quite the best of their kind,/But the heart somehow seems all squeezed out by the mind" (1848: 59; cf. Rosenheim and Rachman 1995: x). The multiple receptions of Poe thus have their origins in the contradictions of Poe's writing and in the many faces of the author himself.

One of the reasons why Poe is relevant beyond the specific field of Poe studies is his importance for literary and cultural history in general and the history of authorship and rhetoric in particular. Poe's theories, texts, and performances stand at the threshold of modernity and emerge out of momentous changes to authorship, literature, and rhetoric. Just like the critical shadow "Poe" is very elusive, the term "authorship" itself is hard to grasp beyond such definitions as the one in the Oxford English Dictionary as "[t]he person who originates or gives existence to anything" (OED s.v. author n[1]). Depending on the specific definition of literary authorship, it might be said to have been central in virtually all of Poe studies or, alternatively, it might be restricted to the extra-literary historico-economic conditions of authorship, as has been very much the case in recent debates. Three paradigmatic conceptions of Poe's authorship from recent work will illuminate insights and blind spots in Poe studies that are illustrative of typical approaches to authorship.

A basic distinction in current approaches to the problem of Poe that rely on specific notions of authorship can be made between more contextualist and more textualist approaches. A paradigm for contextualism is the collection *Edgar Allan Poe in Context* (2012), edited by Kevin J. Hayes, which consists of thirty-seven essays organised into five major types of context: geographic, social, and publishing contexts as well as literary and (pseudo-)scientific contexts (Hayes 2012: v–vii). In the preface, Hayes explains the rationale of the volume: "Though Edgar Allan Poe is the subject of this book, the chapters do not provide in-depth critical explications of his writings. Instead, each chapter provides a general overview of its subject and uses whatever pertinent Poe writings –

verse, fiction, reviews, essays – to suit" (2012: xv). While the list of contexts includes literary contexts as one among many, it appears that the author Poe has been dissolved in(to) his context(s), quite in keeping, of course, with many author-critical strands of contemporary theory, even though such an approach might lead to the desire to "get reacquainted with the Poe who used to be described as 'out of space, out of time'" (Elmer 2003: 132).

To speak of contextualist and textualist approaches is of course to simplify drastically, but textual matters do figure strongly in Poe studies. Take, for example, Richard Kopley's argument in the collection, *Poe Writing/Writing Poe* (2013), edited by Kopley and Jana Argersinger. In the preface, Kopley writes that the book "concerns Poe's response to his reading and his larger world, as well as later writers' response to Poe" (Kopley 2013: xiii). The expressed methodology of close readings informed by historical contexts is complemented by categories for the understanding of literary authors such as "achievement and influence," and the philological reconstruction of legible and uncorrupted texts, which Kopley formulates and illustrates with Poe's story "Some Words with a Mummy": "if we ascribe any personal resonance to the historian whom Poe's mummy describes [...] – a fellow who is to be embalmed, then brought back to life after five or six hundred years to discover his great book wholly obscured by the errors that critics have made, requiring that he totally rewrite the book [...] – then let us hope that with this book [the collection *Poe Writing*], at least, we are leaving the returning Poe a relatively clear oeuvre – and little rewriting required at all" (2013: xv). The image of Poe returning from the grave and finding himself and his works truly represented aptly encapsulates the different notion of authorship at the heart of the enterprise Kopley suggests: one of preservation and evaluation. The two collections thus instantiate two different conceptions of authorship: one that is based on the dissolution of the author into context – a death of the author –, and one that is based on preservation and evaluation – encapsulated in the return of the author from the grave. Both are fitting figures of the author, not only in Poe studies but also in authorship studies.

If one of the tasks of authorship studies is to make such implied conceptions of authorship explicit, it needs to answer the question of "how to relate individual cases and models to their wider context(s) or media settings" (Berensmeyer, Buelens, and Demoor 2012a: 9). A recent explicit theorisation of the relation between the author Poe and antebellum US culture is the result of the project that formed the basis of the collection *Edgar Allan Poe and the Remapping of Antebellum Culture* (2013), edited by J. Gerald Kennedy and Jerome McGann. Here, the emphasis – following on from Meredith McGill's suggestion of the antebellum "culture of reprinting" – is on interlinking the author Poe with antebellum print culture. As Kennedy explains in the introduction, within antebellum print culture, Poe would "figure not as the unrecognized Master Genius, but rather as a shrewd, peripatetic author-journalist whose circulation in what he called 'Literary America' epitomized the ploys and practices of a horizontal culture of letters sustained by proliferative redistribution" (2013: 2). Kennedy clarifies that the interest in the author Poe is not one of context or evaluation but that Poe is a paradigmatic case for the study of antebellum print culture: "His involvement in the magazine world and print culture, in the politics of reputation, in the problem of copyright, in the dilemma of [Northern and Southern] sectionalism, in the cultural rivalries among eastern cities, and in his ceaseless promotion of 'Independence, Truth, [and] Originality' in American literature make him singularly representative of the practical realities of antebellum literary production" (J. G. Kennedy 2013: 9).[13] Rather than thinking of Poe's importance as a representatively singular author, Kennedy suggests looking at him as a singularly representative author – representative of antebellum literary culture that is, at heart, a culture of print. My suggestion in what follows is not only to remap antebellum print culture through Poe but also to examine Poe's various figures of the author such as the transatlantic poet-critic, the genius rhetorician, the detective, and the elocutionist in light of the contemporary culture of rhetoric, the emergence of literature, and the rise of the romantic author.

Rhetoricizing Poe

The well-known slogan of dialectical thought is "Always historicize!" (Jameson 1981: 9), and it has been suggested that rhetorical studies should "Always rhetoricize!" (Wetherbee 2015: 282). The purpose of this book, then, is the project of rhetoricizing Poe. What calls for such a project is not only the relevance of the culture of rhetoric for antebellum literary culture, but the central and virtually overlooked role that rhetorical concepts, strategies, and performances play in Poe's authorship. Poe's discourses are demonstrably, if subtly, determined by rhetorical theories and practices of the late eighteenth- and early nineteenth centuries. 'Rhetoricizing Poe' then refers not only to the systematic approach to his discourses that this book will adopt but also to the centrality of rhetoric to Poe's own conceptions and practices of authorship – particularly to his view of literature in terms of effect: in other words, Poe is a rhetoricizing author.

---

[13] The phrase "Independence, Truth, Originality" is from Poe's March 30, 1844 letter to James Russell Lowell, in which he lays out the principles of his coveted own journal (LTR I: 432 = LTR-173).

While previous research on Poe and rhetoric has been comparatively scarce and isolated, several studies on related issues provide some of the materials for the project of rhetoricizing Poe, especially with regard to Poe's criticism. Building on Margaret Alterton's seminal study on the *Origins of Poe's Critical Theory* ([1925] 1965), Robert D. Jacobs argues, in *Poe: Journalist and Critic* (1969), that eighteenth-century British – and particularly Scottish – treatises in rhetoric and criticism form the decisive critical "matrix" (Jacobs 1969: 3–34) for Poe's literary theories. While Jacobs stressed the importance of Poe's Southernness for his rhetoricity (like McLuhan 1944), there emerges – if taken together with Alterton's and Michael Allen's work (1969) – a picture of the Scottish face of Poe. A polemical account of rhetoricity in Poe's critical writings was given by Ulrich Horstmann (1975), who argues that Poe aimed to nullify the advances of romantic literary theory by "re-rhetoricizing poetry" (14; my translation), yet the force of Horstmann's argument is hampered by an unquestioning belief in what Jerome McGann (1999 [1983]) has described as the romantic ideology. Another, more recent German study by Patrick Full examines the opposition of the fancy and the imagination in Poe's critical writings and also usefully, if briefly, points to the importance of the Scottish rhetorician George Campbell's *Philosophy of Rhetoric* (2007: 77–78). John A. Dern (2001, 2013) has pointed out rhetorical strategies in tales such as "The Cask of Amontillado" and "Never Bet the Devil Your Head." The most exhaustive treatment of Poe's relation to rhetoric to date is Brett Zimmerman's monograph on *Edgar Allan Poe: Rhetoric and Style* (2005), which mainly consists of a 200-page catalogue listing the rhetorical figures found in Poe's writings. While Zimmerman offers analyses of argumentative structures in such overtly rhetorical tales as "The Tell-Tale Heart," his study evinces the kind of meticulousness in its classification of linguistic schemata that has often been used as an argument against rhetoric, narrowly conceived as the analysis of mere style. While some attention has been paid to Poe's own practice as a lecturer,[14] very few studies have examined Poe's connection to contemporary oratory and the elocutionary movement. What is lacking is an investigation into Poe's singular representativeness for the interrelations of the literary and rhetorical cultures of his time.

The period in which Poe was writing and speaking was crucial for the rise of the romantic author and for the emergence of the modern Western idea of literature as aesthetic, creative or imaginative writing with its concurrent separation of canonical and popular literature (R. Williams 1985: 186–187). Political, economic, and technological developments culminated in the fundamental reorgan-

---

[14] Cf. the essays discussed in chapter seven.

ization of literature, poetry, and rhetoric, and in their ultimate specializations. In the late eighteenth and early nineteenth centuries, "the *writer* bec[ame] an *author*" (Woodmansee 1984a: 429), and the romantics defined what was to remain the modern notion of the author: the romantic theory of authorship "may be said to account for everything that is commonly or conventionally taken to be implied by talk of 'the author'" (Bennett 2005: 56). In Poe's time, the developments connected to the industrialisation of print are one of the key factors in these momentous shifts. What has not been sufficiently recognized is the emergence of the modern idea of literature from the complex interplay of print culture and what I shall call the antebellum culture of rhetoric, many aspects of which have been described by other critics as a "culture of eloquence" (Warren 1999) or an "oratorical culture" (Clark and Halloran 1993).

This antebellum culture of rhetoric is particularly noteworthy since the emergence of literature and the rise of the author coincided in most European countries with what is often called the fall, death or disappearance of rhetoric (Sutton 1986, Knape 2013: 1). However, in the United States this process took longer than in Europe (Berlin 1996: xiv), and rhetoric remained a stronger force in theory, politics, and literature until the middle of the nineteenth century. To grasp the unevenness of these transatlantic developments, I suggest to speak of the *dispersal of rhetoric* in chapter two. Even today, compared to other Western, particularly non-Anglophone, nations, the United States has a particularly strong rhetorical tradition that focuses on communication rather than tropes and figures (Ong 2010; G. A. Kennedy 2005: 364).

In the antebellum culture of rhetoric, eloquent performance was at the core of political, social, religious, and literary culture, as evidenced, for instance, in contemporaries' emphasis on "vocal culture" (Kidd 1857; Murdoch and Russell 1845) and the epoch's self-description as a "golden age of oratory" (Parker 1857). Rhetorical texts formed the basis of collegiate education from the late eighteenth through the first half of the nineteenth century (Johnson 1991; Berlin 1996: xiv) and undergirded the popular lecture movement that was institutionalised in the Lyceum lecture system (Ray 2005; Wright 2013). The Lyceums came to be a place "where group identifications could become meaningful through behavioral patterns, through recurring rhetorical acts" (Ray 2005: 7) and were, in Ralph Waldo Emerson's enthusiastic formulation, hailed as "the true Church of the coming time" (Emerson 2001: 48).

The importance of the culture of rhetoric can hardly be overestimated. Significantly, it was often 'literary' authors who played a role in this culture of rhetoric such as Emerson (Railton 1991: 23–49; Thompson 2007; Voelz 2010: 62–104), Margaret Fuller (Kolodny 1994), Herman Melville (Short 1992), Frederick Douglass (Blight 1998; A. Adams 2014: 21–32), and, of course, Edgar Allan

Poe. In his standard account of the emergence of English as a field of study, Gerald Graff opposes the oratorical culture inside early nineteenth-century colleges to "the literary culture outside" (2007: 35), which was rightly criticized by Clark and Halloran; they argue that "[t]he culture outside during the early years of the nineteenth century was not 'literary' in our sense of that term, but oratorical" (1993: 3).

The basis of antebellum rhetorical theory and practice lay in the various transatlantic traditions of the "New Rhetoric" (Howell 1971: 441–694) transported to the United States from the British Isles; chiefly Scottish but also Irish and English rhetorical theory remained highly influential in the United States in the nineteenth century (Johnson 1991; Manning 2002, [1990] 2009, 2013). It consisted of four major traditions: stylistic or belletristic rhetoric; the elocutionary movement or elocutionist rhetoric; epistemological rhetoric; and (neo)classicist rhetoric (Howell 1971; Berlin 1984; Johnson 1991: 14–15). Treatises by the Scottish New Rhetoricians such as George Campbell and Hugh Blair influenced both prominent English and American rhetoricians such as Richard Whately and John Quincy Adams as well as a myriad of handbook writers. These texts exerted a continuous influence in the United States up until the mid-nineteenth century, giving shape and content to the antebellum culture of rhetoric and influencing the literary authors at work within it. Hence, rather than subsuming Poe under the heads of dark Romanticism or Proto-Modernism, I shall locate his writings in the historical situation of the transatlantic continuum of the British-American New Rhetoric.

The antebellum period, then, sees the interconnected developments of the emergence of modern literature, the transatlantic dispersal of rhetoric, and the rise of the romantic author, the specific combination of which is the key to the perennial problem of Poe. By inheriting and retaining rhetorical ideas about literary production, most prominently in his emphasis upon the centrality of effect, Poe is at odds with the (late-)romantic age. In other words, the problem of Poe is, partly, a symptom of the romantic dispersal, repression, and transformation of rhetoric; his status as something like a literary anachronism is a direct correlate of his use of rhetoric, which – with the rise of the romantic author and the emergence of modern literature – was itself becoming an anachronism. As a result of the transatlantic dispersal of rhetoric, Poe appears particularly anachronistic if viewed from a European perspective, but less so in the United States, in which rhetoric remained vital for a longer time as part of the antebellum culture of rhetoric. Hence, the guiding historical hypothesis of this book is that Poe's critical theories, his literary writings, and his authorial performances evince a rhetorical understanding of literature and its contexts at a time when rhetorical discourse was in the process of becoming separated from poetical discourse.

Yet the relevance of rhetorical traditions also goes far beyond the individual case of Poe. While there is no way of answering the problems made urgent by authorship theory with a study of a single author, such a case study can illuminate the general literary situation of a period. The categories of rhetoric are particularly applicable to the antebellum United States because of the prevalence of its culture of rhetoric, yet these or similar rhetorical categories are not limited to historical periods in which rhetoric remains a potent cultural force: as systematic categories, they are important for the analysis and interpretation of literary texts in other periods. Because rhetoric has a history of two-and-a-half millennia and yet remains relevant as a theoretical position in our own time, a rhetorical position always has to be what one might call a combination of historicized theory and theorized history.

Consequently, my examination of Poe in terms of the history of rhetoric is complemented in systematic terms with the development of a theoretical rhetoric of authorship that delineates what I term *figures of the author*. This concept is meant to encompass both the figurational activities of the author and the resulting products and performances, or what one might call, echoing Stephen Greenblatt's terminology, the author's fashioning of discourse and the author's self-fashioning. Greenblatt's seminal chiasmatic dialectic is doubly relevant since its original definition includes rhetoric as the "chief intellectual and linguistic tool" of Renaissance self-fashioning: "It [rhetoric] offered men the power to shape their worlds, calculate the probabilities, and master the contingent, and it implied that human character itself could be similarly fashioned, with an eye to audience and effect" (Greenblatt 1980: 162). The concept of figures of the author goes beyond the chiasmus of the author's fashioning of discourse and the author's self-fashioning in attempting to grasp the peculiar dialectic between the autonomous aspects of the author as figurer of discourse and self on the one hand, and, on the other, the heteronomous aspects of the author as figured by the historical situation, that is, the way in which the author is figured by her or his context.

The various figures of the author can then be internally divided according to their dominant aspect into theoretical, poetical and performative figures, in line with a fundamental rhetorical distinction, which originates in Aristotle and Quintilian and is reasserted in modern positions such as Richard McKeon's architectonic notion of rhetoric. As the example of Poe makes clear, authorship is primarily a matter of producing literary texts, but it cannot be regarded solely as such, since authorship also involves reflecting upon this production and staging oneself as a producer. The **theoretical dimension** of the figures of the author relates to the self-conceptions authors develop in response to the concepts and models of authorship that are present in their own historical situation. By contrast, the **poetical dimension** of the figures of the author concerns the interrelated activities of invention, arrangement, and stylization, which either become visible only as traces of activity in the resulting poetical product, or, are self-reflexively foregrounded within the poetical text (as, for example, via the use of metafictional characters). Finally, the **performative dimension** of the figures of the author refers to the rhetorical operations of memory and performance and, more generally, to stagings of the authorial self, not only in such settings as public readings, but also in theatrical contexts in other media. All three dimensions are present in *every* figure of the author. In other words, the dimensions are what Karl Bühler, in his theory of language, refers to as "phenomena of dominance, in which one of the three fundamental relationships [...] is in the foreground" (2011: 39).[15] Which dimension happens to be dominant at any one time is a result of the particular situation to which the discourse or performance responds.

The resulting model of rhetorical theory, poetics, and performance makes it possible to modernise a variety of rhetorical categories such as the triad of the effects of discourse (informing/*docere*, entertaining/*delectare*, moving people to action/*movere*) and the five classical stages of production (invention/*inventio*, arrangement/*dispositio*, style/*elocutio*, memory/*memoria*, performance/*actio*), which can then serve as a heuristic framework for the analysis and interpretation of authorship in its culturally specific dimensions. The fusion of the concept of the 'figures of the author' with the three major rhetorical aspects of authorship thus yields the major areas of interest of this book: the theoretical, poetical, and performative figures of the author as we find them around, in, and through Poe.

Developing a theoretical rhetoric of authorship – that is, a rhetoric designed to understand, rather than to practise, literary production – offers sophisticated tools to unite the contextualist approaches currently dominant within Poe studies (and beyond) with aspects of literary textuality. Rhetoric is one of the aptest methodological means for responding to the renewed interest in the figurative qualities of literary texts in the wake of such movements as the New Formalism (Theile and Tredennick 2013, Bogel 2013, C. Levine 2015), while, at the same time, retaining the focus on their specific power as instances of persuasive discourse in particular historical situations. Rhetoric, in Kenneth Burke's seminal formulation, examines critical and literary texts as both "*strategic*" and "*stylized* answers" to the questions posed by historical situations (1973c: 1).

---

15 As Jürgen Habermas phrases it, Bühler puts forward "the general thesis that language represents a medium [...] that *simultaneously* serves three different, although internally related, functions" (Habermas 1998: 277; my emphasis). In chapter two, I demonstrate how Bühler's model itself follows rhetorical distinctions.

Rhetoric itself was and is a discourse that has continuously and consistently engaged with the question of the relation of discourse in general and poetical discourse in particular, especially in the antebellum period. The opposition of the two that continues to this day, for instance in the battles between departments of rhetoric and literary studies in the United States, is a regrettable one that should be overcome. As Gerald Graff rightly comments: "the long-standing split between literature and composition [...] has been disastrous for *literary study itself*" (2007: xvii–xviii).

* * *

This book is divided into two parts. In order to meet the dual requisite of historicized theory and theorized history and to lay the groundwork for other studies of the interrelations between rhetoric and authorship, the first part of the book contains one systematic and one historical chapter. Employing the fundamental rhetorical distinction between theory, poetics, and performance, the second part then examines Poe's theoretical, poetical, and performative figures of the author. Compared to the United States with its dozens of PhD programmes in rhetoric, there is little rhetorical research in English departments in Germany beyond that in Early Modern studies, and chapter one attempts to contribute to remedying this on an abstract level. Readers primarily interested in Poe might hence want to begin reading with chapter two.

Chapter one offers prolegomena towards a theoretical rhetoric of authorship. Building on the debate about the death and the return of the author in recent critical theory, I establish in detail the notion of the figures of the author via recourse to ancient and modern rhetorical theories of figuration, persuasion, and situation. As the fundamental concept of a theoretical rhetoric of authorship, 'figures of the author' should be understood as the processes and products of authors' persuasions and figurations that respond to particular historical situations. This general concept is then diversified via recourse to the fundamental distinction of the rhetorical arts and sciences into theory, poetics, and performance. This move is central since it allows for the possibility of integrating and reinterpreting two of the central categorical systems of rhetoric as a heuristic framework for the analysis of figures of the author: first, the three types of effect – the cognitive (*docere*), ethical and gentle emotional (*delectare*), and political and strong emotional effects of a discourse (*movere*) – are interpreted as rhetorical conceptions of the literary situation as a communicative situation and thus as constitutive of theoretical figures of the author. Secondly, the division of poetical and performative figures of the author is based on a reinterpretation of the five stages of production as authemes sensu Harold Love. As processes shared by rhetoric and poetics in the classical system, invention, arrangement, and style (*inventio, dispositio, elocutio*) can thus be refashioned as historically informed poetical figures of the author such as inventor, arranger, and stylizer. Similarly, the final two stages memory and delivery (*memoria* and *actio/pronuntiatio*) are interpreted as informing figures of the author that inscribe authorship into cultural memory through performance.

Chapter two – the historical chapter – compares and critiques the familiar narratives of the romantic rise of the author and the fall of rhetoric against the background of the emergence of the modern concept of literature. Discussing theories of rhetoric and poetry from the New Rhetorical treatises of George Campbell and Richard Whately to the romantic aesthetics of Thomas De Quincey and John Stuart Mill, I demonstrate that the separation of poetical and rhetorical discourse was a key factor in the emergence of romantic authorship and that this separation was, crucially, discussed in rhetorical terminology based on the triad of effects. The continuing relevance of this triad is particularly visible in the United States, for instance in William Cullen Bryant, but also in Poe. Broadening the scope from these definitions of poetry to the general conditions of authorship in America, I examine American antebellum literary culture in terms of the transatlantic interrelations between the culture of print and what I call the antebellum culture of rhetoric, thereby also laying the groundwork for future studies of this broader historical situation. The historical chapter ends with a discussion of Poe's satirical tale "How to Write a Blackwood Article" as one of the most paradigmatic transatlantic examples of the inextricably intertwined cultures of print and rhetoric.

Part II then uses the systematic concepts and the analysis of the historical situation to reconstruct the fundamentally rhetorical character of Poe's writings and performances. Taking up the opposition between rhetorical and romantic positions with regard to the definition of poetry and its transatlantic connections from chapter two, chapter three compares Poe's "Letter to B—" with its romantic sources in the works of Coleridge and Wordsworth. Poe's appropriation of these sources is paradigmatic for his cultural situation as he appropriates elements of Romanticism in order to figure himself as a transatlantic poet-critic, a figure of the author that would otherwise not have been available to him. Yet at the same time, he rejects those elements in the romantic sources that do not fit his rhetorical system of effects which is already, even in this early text, beginning to take shape. I trace the emergence of this system of effects in Poe through a study of "The Letter to B—" as a Horatian art of poetry, with which it shares not only its classification of effects but also its distinctive form as a letter. The second half of the chapter includes the first discussion of Poe's explicit definitions of rhetoric, which are interpreted against the background of the New Rhetoric. What can be seen in a variety of Poe's critical writings is an opposition between Poe's uses of a rhetorical rule-based craft of the author and an emphatic concept of genius based on romantic aesthetics, which Poe consciously rejects.

The fourth chapter discusses Poe's most famous critical text, "The Philosophy of Composition," his autocommentary on "The Raven." Resituating it in a debate with Charles Dickens about an earlier autocommentary by William Godwin, I reconstruct the common rhetorical ground on which Poe and Godwin develop their theoretical figures of the author. I demonstrate for the first time that Poe's central theory of effect is a restatement of the rhetorical triad of effects and interpret its connections to the New Rhetoric, particularly its epistemological strand in George Campbell. Taking into consideration both the theoretical and poetical aspects of Poe's figure of the author in the text, I give a new answer to the questions surrounding the text by viewing it as Poe's response to his historical situation as a writer under the conditions of the romantic split between rhetorical and poetical discourse.

Chapter five examines the foremost examples of Poe's poetical figures of the author, his ratiocinative detectives, such as the Chevalier C. Auguste Dupin. By making use of the concepts of rhetorical invention and inventors as developed in chapter one, I show how Poe's poetical figure is striated by theoretical interests in the co-functioning of the creative and analytical faculties of the author. My reconstruction of the meaning of rhetorical and poetical invention is based on Charles Sanders Peirce's concept of abduction as a third, and specifically rhetorical, type of inference other than deduction and induction, to which we find a precursor in Poe's *Eureka*. In order to effect the impression of real or apparent truth on the audience, Poe structures his tales of ratiocination according to the rhetorico-logical form of the abductive inference. Thus, I argue, in establishing a new genre, Poe also invented an innovative poetical figure of the author as detective.

The final two chapters examine the performative dimension of Poe's figures of the author with particular reference to the elocutionary movement. Chapter six stands at the intersection between poetical and performative figures of the author, since it investigates Poe's figuration of authorship – through style and performance – in his poetry. It reconstructs major critical responses to Poe as a poet such as Emerson's epithet of the jingle-man and contrasts them with a reading of "Ulalume" in terms of contemporary elocutionary theory. In similar fashion, in an interpretation of Poe's much-maligned critical text, "The Rationale of Verse," I show how the essay is fundamentally an attempt to constitute a performative figure of the author. This figure is the result of intra-American and transatlantic cultural and political tensions that emerge in such performative dimensions of poetry as its elocution.

The final chapter reconstructs the performative and dramatic aspects of Poe's figure of the literary performer – the *histrio* – by employing rhetorical concepts for the analysis of delivery in various media. The first section examines Poe's own practice as a lecturer with particular attention to his famous appearance at the Boston Lyceum in the context of what I call the antebellum market of eloquence. The examination of Poe's virtual failure on this stage is complemented with a discussion of the figure of the author as a popular performer in Poe's satire "Loss of Breath." The final section analyzes Poe's figurations of some of the medial conditions of antebellum literature as it emerged in the interplay of the cultures of print and rhetoric.

The final pages suggest some potential avenues for future research on authorship, antebellum literature, and transatlantic rhetoric that take the theoretical and historical insights of this book beyond the figures of Edgar Allan Poe.

Part I **Authorship, Antebellum Literature, and Transatlantic Rhetoric**

1 Towards a Rhetoric of Authorship: Theoretical, Poetical, and Performative Figures of the Author

> The success of an author's rhetoric does not depend on whether he thought about his readers as he wrote; if 'mere calculation' cannot insure success, it is equally true that even the most unconscious and Dionysian of writers succeeds only if he makes us join in the dance.
> Wayne Booth, *The Rhetoric of Fiction*, 1983: xiv

In beginning this sketch of the basic principles and concepts of a theoretical rhetoric of authorship, it is worthwhile to revisit the one of the major beginnings of contemporary authorship theories. There is an illustrative – perhaps a symptomatic – coincidence between the author and rhetoric in Roland Barthes' writings in the late 1960s. Barthes wrote his seminal "La mort de l'auteur" in 1967 and first published it in an English translation in 1968 in the short-lived American art magazine, *Aspen*. Two years later in 1970, issue no. 16 of the journal *Communications* was dedicated to "Recherches rhétoriques," and Barthes contributed his well-known overview of ancient rhetoric, "L'ancienne rhétorique: aide-mémoire" (Barthes 1970), which was based on his 1964/1965 lectures on the history of rhetoric. Barthes' crucial essay on authorship, then, is framed by his engagement with rhetoric. At first glance, Barthes' texts on authorship and rhetoric even seem to represent a reversal of the familiar narratives of the death of rhetoric and the birth of the author in the eighteenth and nineteenth centuries, which are discussed in the next chapter. While Barthes attempted to establish *écriture* and relegate rhetoric to the "rank of a merely historical object" (Barthes [1970] 1988: 93), still it seems that, if Barthes killed the author in 1967, he also lent a maieutic hand in the re-birth of rhetoric in 1970, albeit as a daughter of a "new semiotics of writing" (Barthes [1970] 1988: 11). As the example of other critics such as Gérard Genette shows,[1] to a certain extent, Barthes' critique of the author is indeed contemporaneous with a major reconception of rhetoric within French thought: in terms of the history of critical thought, the death of the author met the re-birth of rhetoric. My attempt in this part of the book is similar to the reconstructive purpose of Barthes' *aide-mémoire*, yet also differs substantially, first and foremost in making rhetoric the chief theoretical instrument to conceptualise the author.

This task is complicated by the diverse state of the field of authorship studies and the fact that categories of authorship play a role in law, technology, the

---

[1] On the relation between rhetoric and French semioticians more generally, cf. Abbott (2006).

media, and the sciences as well as philosophy, literature and culture in general.² One of the conclusions that can be drawn from the German debate is a non-exhaustive typology of authorship concepts that includes the aspects of authorship as intention, inspiration, competence, individuality, authority, style, copyright as well as gendered and collective authorship.³ In order to meet the dual requisite of historicized theory and theorized history outlined in the introduction, this first part of the book on the rhetoric of authorship contains one systematic and one historical chapter. Complemented in chapter two with an historical reconstruction of the rise of the author, this first chapter builds a heuristic framework for the analysis of authorship, which is based on a fundamental rhetorical triad that distinguishes theoretical, poetical, and performative figures of the author. These dimensions, in turn, will be diversified via recourse to the rhetorical theories of the three classes of the potential effects of discourses (part of the theoretical dimension), the three rhetorical-poetical processes of invention, arrangement, and style (poetical dimension), and the final two processes of memory and performance (performative dimension). The result of these diversifications will be a rhetorically informed theory of the author as both figurer and figured that can be applied to theoretical, poetical, and performative activities and products.

1.1 The Figures of the Author

The Deaths and Returns of the Author

Like the critical shadow of Poe that continues to haunt the dominant paradigms of American studies, the category of the author has disappeared from and returned to literary studies many times, long after its modern inception in the idea of the romantic genius. If viewed from a distance, the development of authorship theory over the course of the twentieth and twenty-first centuries evinces an oscillation between arguments pro and contra. In other words: the deaths of the author have always been intimately connected with the returns of the author and vice versa. The debates about the author should thus not be reduced to the poststructuralist critique and its affirmations or refutations, since the rele-

---

2 Cp. e.g. the diverse topics treated in the open access journal *Authorship* (ISSN: 2034–4643) <http://www.authorship.ugent.be>, 2011-

3 I translated and adapted these categories from Jannidis et al. (1999: 7) and a later encyclopaedia entry by one of the group, Matías Martínez (2008: 45).

vant discussion begins much earlier with such concepts as the New Critical "intentional fallacy" and Wayne Booth's "implied author."[4]

Nevertheless, Roland Barthes' argument in "The Death of the Author" remains the best example of an absolute anti-intentionalism.[5] Joining his critique of God and Man with a fundamental critique of the Author, Barthes claimed that the meaning of the text does not emanate from a god-like authorial subject but that it is constituted in the act of reading, as the famous last lines of the essay show: "we know that to give writing its future, it is necessary to overthrow the myth: the birth of the reader must be at the cost of the death of the Author" (Barthes [1968] 1977: 148).[6] To back up his attack on what is basically a romantic and religious idea of the author, Barthes contrasts the *Author-God*, the Author with a capital 'A,' whose voice determines all meaning, with the *scriptor*, a writer who is not imbued with authority and who is "born simultaneously with the text, is in no way equipped with a being preceding or exceeding the writing" ([1968] 1977: 145).

The arguments against using a concept of the author as a category of interpretation, which Barthes epitomizes (rather than Focault's historicist argument that is discussed in chapter two), were countered in debates about the "Return of the Author" in literary and cultural scholarship of the 1980s and 1990s. The proponents of a return to the author have emphasized 1) the gap between author-critical theories and practices of interpretation, 2) the possibility of authorial readings that complicate rather than simplify texts, and 3) the inevitability of the problem of authorship.[7]

---

4 I have traced this oscillatory development in more detail in Gutlzeit (2014a, 118–126), on which my following arguments on Barthes and the German debate on authorship are based.
5 The debate about the author's intention has not only been fought in literary studies but also preoccupied the analytic philosophy of art for some time. At the risk of simplification, one might summarise the positions as lying between the extremes of 'actual intentionalism' and 'anti-intentionalism,' with intermediate positions of 'hypothetical' and 'partial intentionalism' (for some central arguments, cf. Stecker 2005). My own position is closest to Paisley Livingston's definition of partial intentionalism: "authorial intentions figure in [the determination of the work's meaning], yet combine with other factors, such as features of the finished text, artefact, or performance, and aspects of the historical and artistic context in which the work was created" (Livingston 2005: 142).
6 As mentioned before, the text was first published in English in the short-lived art magazine *Aspen*. Cp. also the French version in Barthes (1994).
7 Important texts for the Anglophone and German-speaking debate are collected in S. Burke (1995) and Jannidis et al. (2000). Love (2002) and Bennett (2005) provide useful introductions to the field. Cf. the essential monographs by Stillinger (1991) and S. Burke ([1992] 2008) and edited volumes and special issues by Woodmansee and Jaszi (1994), Jannidis et al. (1999), Detering (2002), Donovan, Fjellestad, and Lundén (2008), Berensmeyer, Buelens, and Demoor (2012b), Schaffrick and Willand (2014).

In his seminal reconstruction of the debates within French thought that led to the critique of the author in the 1960s and its translation into British-American academia,[8] Seán Burke diagnoses a "massive disjunction [...] between the theoretical statement of authorial disappearance and the project of reading without the author" ([1992] 2008: 165). The most striking evidence of this has been produced by Simone Winko (2002). Analyzing a wide selection of academic articles in German studies, she found that a critical stance against the author in an article did not mean that the practices of interpretation in the same article corresponded to this theoretical stance but evinced the same argumentative recurrence to the author as the producing instance of the text (Winko 2002: 353). Interpretations that expressly rely on the author in one way or another are often rejected as biographical or 'biographistic' approaches that *necessarily* reduce literary texts to the lives of their authors, as Jannidis et al. (2000: 24–25) point out.[9] In place of such a simplifying rejection, Burke offers a more complex picture of the tension between authorial individuality and the generalising tendency of theory:

> The question of the author tends to vary from reading to reading, author to author. [...] A theory of the author, or of the absence of the author, cannot withstand the practice of reading, for there is not an absolute *cogito* of which individual authors are the subalternant manifestations, but authors, many authors, and the differences (in gender, history, class, ethnology, in the nature of scientific, philosophical, and literary authorship, in the degree of authorship itself) that exist between authors – within authorship – defy reduction to any universalising aesthetic [...] the essential problem posed by the author is that whilst authorial subjectivity is theoretically unassimilable, it cannot be practically circumvented ([1992] 2008: 183).

Authorship, for Burke, is thus a condition of interpretation that varies in its importance from reading to reading and from situation to situation. The problem of authorship thus calls neither for a dismissal nor an apotheosis of the author, but is to be approached as that which varies in accordance with the type of authorship and historical situation under consideration.

---

[8] Cf. S. Burke ([1992] 2008: 8–18, 183–184, and passim). The first of three editions of *The Death and Return of the Author: Criticism and Subjectivity in Barthes, Foucault and Derrida* was published in 1992.

[9] Jannidis et al. argue that "taking the author into consideration when interpreting a literary text does not mean that the interpretation degenerates into naïve biographism" (1999: 24–25; my translation).

Figuring the Author

This emphasis on the historicity and situatedness of authorial readings cannot serve as a justification for altogether foregoing any systematic attempt to categorize different concepts of authorship. Indeed, the challenge of thinking the author seems to be to conceptualise authorship in terms of both heteronomous constraints and autonomous freedom, to analyse both the cultural impossibilities and individual powers of the writer. Such a systematic attempt is made in the following typology of author functions taken from Ingo Berensmeyer, Gert Buelens, and Marysa Demoor (2012a: 14), which is partly based on my own earlier reading of German critic Heinrich Detering's typology of authorship models:[10]

	heteronomy	autonomy
weak	author as originator and communicator of texts, tied to rules and conventions	author as creator of immaterial 'work' that is materially represented in the text
strong	Barthes' 'scripteur': writer as merely a textual function, a compiler	author as absolute ruler over the work and its meaning, a genius

The typology distinguishes not only between autonomous and heteronomous aspects of authorship, but also between weak and strong notions of these two aspects. The strong notions encompass Barthes' *scriptor* and *Author-God*, while the two weak notions view the author as a *producer* of a literary *text* and a *creator* of a literary *work* with all their respective corroborating evaluations. All four concepts are to be understood not as idealised types but as points on a scale the exact location of which can only be determined by an investigation of the specific historical situation in which the model, concept, or idea appears. Both weak and strong notions of authorship can be accommodated within a theoretical rhetoric of authorship premised upon what I call 'figures of the author,' a concept that grasps the general dialectic between the heteronomous and autonomous sides of both the author's fashioning of discourse and the author's self-fashioning.[11]

---

[10] Detering's model, a contribution to the discussion at the German Studies DFG Symposium in 2001, can be found in Polaschegg (2002: 322–323). My development of the conceptual oppositions can be found in Guttzeit (2010: 28–30 and passim).

[11] Lucille Kerr, in *Reclaiming the Author: Figures and Fictions from Spanish America* (1992), uses a similar concept, yet does not conceptualise it rhetorically: she "aims to examine the figure of the author as one of the concepts about which the Spanish Americans talk as they do literature." Kerr reflects particularly on "the possible relationship between the analysis of implied or fictional author-figures and the consideration of the empirical authors assumed to be responsible for their invention" (Kerr 1992: viii). Another more or less prominent use of the term of which I am aware is as a chapter title that is not defined in Chartier (1994: 25–60). Similar concepts include

The term 'figure' has a long rhetorical and interpretive history. 'Figure' (Lat. 'figura') is etymologically related to *fictor*, a Latin word that covers meanings similar to the Greek ποιητής/poietes (and which is also the root of 'fiction'), as becomes obvious in an early use by the scholar Varro in his work on the Latin language: "the *fictor* 'image-maker,' when he says '*Fingo* "I shape"' puts a *figura* 'shape' on the object" (Varro 1938: 244–245 = 6.78). Originally meaning 'plastic form,' it was used as the translation for the Greek rhetorical term σχῆμα/schema and became a major concept in rhetoric and poetics. The combined sense of plasticity and formedness pertains to both the author's fashioning of texts as well as her or his self-fashioning, since both remain highly volatile cultural processes. The intimate connections between the notion of the *figure* and interpretation were famously delineated by Erich Auerbach (1984). Although the Christian, theological mode of figural interpretation used in late Antiquity and the Middle Ages is not directly relevant for all historical epochs, Auerbach's reconstruction of 'figura' as a rhetorical concept in his classic essay of the same name illuminates the term's flexibility and scope. 'Figure' developed through Varro, Lucretius, and Cicero to its canonical formulation in the ninth book of Quintilian (Auerbach 1984: 12–21). Quintilian famously distinguished between *tropes* as single words that are not used in their proper meaning (such as metaphor) and *figures* which can be composed from the proper meanings of words (2001d, 11–34 = 9.1).[12] Auerbach explains the difference and its implications thus: "The aim of a figure is not, as in all tropes, to substitute words for other words; figures can be formed from words used in their proper meaning and order. Basically all discourse is a forming, a figure, but the word is employed only for formations that are particularly developed in a poetic or rhetorical sense" (1984: 26). This ties in with

---

"figures of speech" in Raymond J. Wilson's study of *American Writers and the Literary Marketplace from Benjamin Franklin to Emily Dickinson* (1989) and "figuring authorship" (Newbury 1997): Michael Newbury speaks of "figurative comparisons between writing and other sorts of work" (1997: 11), suggesting a notion of rhetoric as simile and/or metaphor in Aristotle's sense of a shortened simile but he does not deal with the rhetorical tradition in antebellum America. In French studies, Jérôme Meizoz has established the concept of the "postures of the author" that authors can assume within a Bourdieuian literary field. His emphasis on the inevitability of the presentation of the authorial self is particularly pertinent: "On the stage of the enunciation of literature, the author can introduce and express her- or himself only as endowed with a persona, a posture. Moreover, the work is also a self-image offered to the public" ("Sur la scène d'énonciation de la littérature, l'auteur ne peut se présenter et s'exprimer que muni de sa persona, sa posture. Par ailleurs, l'oeuvre constitue aussi une image de soi proposée au public"; Meizoz 2007: 19; my translation). In the continuing German debate on the staging of authorship ("Autorschaftsinszenierung"), emphasis is now being placed on authorial 'forms of the subject' understood as 'subjectification strategies' (Kyora 2014).

12 Quintilian further distinguishes between figures of thought (34–96 = 9.2) and figures of speech (2001d, 96–163 = 9.3).

Nietzsche's thesis that "[w]hat is usually called language [Rede] is actually all figuration" (Nietzsche 1989: 25). In such a view, rhetoric is an unfolding of the figurative possibilities of language or speech *in toto*. As Nietzsche argued, "the *rhetorical* [die *Rhetorik*] *is a further development*, guided by the clear light of the understanding, of *the artistic means which are already found in language*" (Nietzsche 1989: 21).

One of the most pertinent exemplifications of the dialectic between the author as figurer and figured has been developed by Jonathan Elmer in his study of Poe's relation to mass culture. Elmer argues that "Poe both theorizes and exemplifies 'the figure of mass culture,' a phrase in which the ambiguity of the genitive (both subjective and objective) marks the trace of the social limit, that disjunctive relay point between any individual's figuration of mass culture and mass culture's figuration of the individual" (Elmer 1995: 21). Poe is thus both a fashioner of mass culture and being fashioned by it: "For if he offers us a rich imagination of the mass culture of the day – a view of the democratic "mob," a sampler of most of the popular and mass literary forms of antebellum magazine culture – he is also, and equally, imagined by mass culture: he is, in fact, its symptom." (Elmer 1995: 21). Taking into consideration Poe's relevance to mass culture up until the present day, Elmer sees at work in and around Poe a dialectic of figurer and figured, and it is this dialectic which makes Poe exemplary of the figures of the author.

Taken together, Quintilian's notion of the rhetorical figure, Auerbach's explication of it, and Elmer's view of Poe's relation to mass culture enable us to define the term 'figures of the author.' The term captures the dialectic between autonomous and heteronomous aspects of the author's figuration, and it also encompasses the rhetorical and poetical products that are usually the basis for the ascription of literary authorship. Understood as a subjective genitive, it refers to the figurational activity of the author that results in poetical and rhetorical products. Understood as an objective genitive, it refers to the many shapes of the author, i.e. the author's image that is produced partly by herself and her products, but also, and often more decisively, by the historical situation that determines the possibilities of becoming an author in the first place. Authors produce figures and are simultaneously produced as figures: they are both figurers and figured. The interplay of these two is the object of a theoretical rhetoric of authorship.

Figuration, Persuasion, Situation

The rhetorical concept of figuration unfolds its full explanatory power only when it is viewed in conjunction with its complementary notion of persuasion. Hence, I want here to embed my notion of the 'figures of the author' in other important aspects of the rhetorical tradition that are not immediately related to figuration itself, namely persuasion and situation. I. A. Richards' conception of rhetoric as "a study of misunderstanding and its remedies" ([1936] 1971: 3) might very well be applied to the subject of rhetoric itself and its history of two-and-a-half millennia. Nevertheless, one of rhetoric's foremost historians, George A. Kennedy, writes: "[i]t has become a commonplace of the history of rhetoric to speak of two traditions": "the Aristotelian, which stresses the logical side of the subject, and the Isocratean, emphasizing the literary aspects of rhetoric" (2007: 14).[13] Rhetoric-as-persuasion is based on Aristotle's famous conception of rhetoric as the counterpart to dialectic: as the "ability, in each [particular] case, to see the available means of persuasion" (Aristotle 2007: 37 = 1355b).[14] The modern tradition of rhetoric-as-figuration is often traced to Nietzsche's thesis that language *per se* is rhetorical,[15] but it has ancient classical Greek and Latin predecessors besides Isocrates and his (likely) teacher Gorgias. For instance, Quintilian argues that "if we compare the older language with our own, almost everything we say now is a Figure" (2001d: 97 = 9.3.1).[16] The duality of figuration and persuasion is

---

[13] Cf. also Vickers (1988b), G. A. Kennedy (1999), Knape (2000a). The best one-volume overview of the state of research in the history of rhetoric is Gaillet and Horner (2010). On rhetoric in the Middle Ages, the Renaissance, and the eighteenth-century, cf. Murphy (1974), Mack (2011), and Howell (1971), respectively. For nineteenth-century British, American, and transatlantic rhetoric, cf. chapter two.

[14] The tradition of persuasion is in no way less influential than that of figuration. For example, Cicero's definition of the first duty of the orator was to speak so as to convince: "primum oratoris officium esse, dicere ad persuadendum accommodate" (1942: 96–97 = 1.31.138). Critics who view rhetoric as persuasion often espouse neo-Aristotelian positions such as the Tübingen school (Gert Ueding, Joachim Knape), the Chicago School of Criticism (Richard McKeon, Wayne Booth) and their successors working in the field of rhetorical narratology today (James Phelan, Peter Rabinowitz). Beyond literary studies, the notion of persuasion has been used in the rhetoric of science (Alan G. Gross, Herbert W. Simons, Deirdre N. McCloskey) and in the anthropological 'rhetoric culture project' (cf. my review of one of the central collections of the project in Guttzeit, 2012). The most prominent rhetorical theory focused on argumentative persuasion is Chaïm Perelman and Lucie Olbrecht-Tyteca's *New Rhetoric* ([1958] 1969), a project that is continued in many ways today by Michel Meyer. Cf. also Stephen Toulmin's work, particularly Toulmin ([1958] 2003).

[15] "[L]anguage is rhetoric, because it desires to convey only a doxa [opinion], not an epistēmē [knowledge]" (Nietzsche 1989: 23). Cf. Kopperschmidt (1994).

[16] Humanist and Renaissance texts such as Erasmus' *De Copia* (1512) and Enlightenment rhetorics such as Giambattista Vico's build an historical bridge from ancient rhetoric to the interests of literary critics and philosophers in the twentieth century, for example, in the so-called four master tropes metaphor, metonymy, synecdoche, and irony, usually attributed to Vico and reconceptualised by Kenneth Burke (1969a: 503–517). The systematic and historicist possibilities inherent in such distinctions are apparent, for instance, in Roman Jakobson's generalisation of metaphor and metonymy as the two axes of language, or in Hayden White's use of the master tropes to analyse forms of histor-

relevant both systematically and historically. This will become apparent time and again in later chapters, for instance in the mixture of persuasive and figurative aspects that affects Poe's theoretical figures of the author or in his famous character Chevalier C. Auguste Dupin, whose quality as a poetical figure of the author depends on aspects of persuasive rhetoric such as the abductive inference.

The relevance of the opposition between figuration and persuasion has often been noted within literary studies. Northrop Frye argued that, while seemingly "psychologically opposed to each other," "ornamental rhetoric is inseparable from literature itself, [...] which exists for its own sake" and that "[p]ersuasive rhetoric is applied literature, or the use of literary art to reinforce the power of argument" (Frye [1957] 2000: 245). The same opposition is construed by Paul de Man as that of "two incompatible, mutually self-destructive points of view," linking to the basic opposition in J. L. Austin's speech act theory:[17] "[t]he aporia between performative and constative language is merely a version of the aporia between trope and persuasion that both generates and paralyzes rhetoric and thus gives it the appearance of a history" (1979: 131). There seems little use today in assigning to rhetoric and all utterances such endless aporia, but de Man's take, like Frye's, is indicative of a paradoxical tension between persuasion and figuration, which is discussed by Jonathan Culler:

> [O]ne might claim that rhetoric was at one time the art of inventing appropriate formulations and organizing them so as to produce the desired effect of the whole; at another time rhetoric was an inventory of devices or conventional figures which threaten to entrap and limit a writer unless he go beyond them or give them new life by a creative or innovative use. It is far from clear, however, that we have here two separate historical realities, and

---

ical thinking in the nineteenth century. Cf. e. g. Jakobson (1987b). White posits "four principal modes of historical consciousness on the basis of the prefigurative (tropological) strategy which informs each of them: Metaphor, Synecdoche, Metonymy, and Irony" (1973: xi). Cf. also the work of the Groupe μ (Dubois and et al. 1981). Deconstructionists such as Jacques Derrida, Paul de Man, and J. Hillis Miller extended and transformed the rhetorical doctrines of figurative speech, though the deconstructionist take on rhetoric often met with harsh criticism from more traditional rhetoric scholars. Cf. Brian Vickers exemplary refutation of "the reduction, fragmentation, and misapplication of rhetoric" in de Man in Vickers (1988a: 40), which became the final chapter of Vickers (1988b: 435–479). Albeit very different in scope, the generalisation of figuration also appears in conceptual metaphor theory from George Lakoff and Mark Johnson to Mark Turner's work in cognitive rhetoric. In different ways, then, all these thinkers have proposed extensions and transformations of the rhetorical doctrine of figurative speech, ones which transcend the doctrine of figures of speech as the mere dress of thought to establish figuration as a fundamental condition of discourse.

17 Cf. J. Austin (1973). The similarities between Austin's language theory and rhetoric are apparent. As Joachim Knape comments tersely: "What Austin [...] posits as the *pragmatic turn* in the philosophy of language, has been self-evident to rhetoricians for two-and-a-half-thousand years" ("Was Austin [...] als *pragmatic turn* der Sprachphilosophie postuliert, ist für Rhetoriker seit zweieinhalbtausend Jahren selbstverständlich"; Knape 2000b: 118; my translation).

if we wish to account for the possibility of rhetoric taking either of these forms at a given moment in history, we would be well advised to keep the two sides of the paradox together, as components of a paradoxical definition. (1978: 607–608)

Culler's suggestion of keeping the two aspects together is certainly to the point. Yet his 'solution' not to attempt to resolve the opposition also leaves something to be desired. My suggestion of, if not resolving the paradox, then at least of better understanding it, entails the introduction of another central rhetorical term, namely that of the situation.

Persuasion and figuration always appear as aspects of historical instances of discourse production and reception that rhetoric understands as situational. As Lloyd Bitzer explained in a seminal essay: "rhetorical discourse comes into existence as a response to a situation, in the same sense that an answer comes into existence in response to a question, or a solution in response to a problem" (1968: 5). There has been disagreement with regard to the elements of the situation, as Bitzer distinguishes them,[18] yet this does not impair his general thesis: "Not the rhetor and not persuasive intent, but the situation is the source and ground of rhetorical activity – and [...] of rhetorical criticism" (1968: 6).[19] Both rhetorical discourse and rhetorical criticism arise as complex responses to particular historical situations, and, ideally, rhetorical criticism itself is aware of its own intricate situation in history.

All three elements of persuasion, figuration, and situation are conceptually integrated with one another in Kenneth Burke's "The Philosophy of Literary Form," in which the concepts of *situation* and *strategy* provide the central frame, a frame which Burke would later develop into the dramatistic pentad.[20] In the essay, Burke defines both critical and imaginative texts as strategic responses to specific historical situations:

> Critical and imaginative works are answers to questions posed by the situation in which they arose. They are not merely answers, they are *strategic* answers, *stylized* answers. [...]

---

[18] Bitzer distinguishes "three constituents of any rhetorical situation: the first is the *exigence*; the second and third are elements of the complex, namely the *audience* to be constrained in decision and action, and the *constraints* which influence the rhetor and can be brought to bear upon the audience" (1968: 6).
[19] The major problem with Bitzer's conception is that he does not conceive of the complex historical interplay between discourse-producers and situations; it appears as if there were a one-to-one relationship between one (ontologically given) situation and one appropriate response (Bitzer 1968: 11). For further criticism, cf. e.g. Vatz (1973).
[20] This is obvious from a footnote in K. Burke (1973c: 106). For Burke's most influential version of the pentad, cf. K. Burke (1969a).

> [I]n so far as situations overlap from individual to individual, or from one historical period to another, the strategies possess universal relevance. (1973c: 1)

Burke thus integrates the texts into the development of history and views them as translatable across time periods, while at the same time connecting their individual and collective dimensions, making them possible objects of systematic analysis. The fact that he names them *strategic* or *stylized* answers is an echo of the two aspects of persuasion and figuration, which he views – as the syntactic parallelism makes clear – as equal. Burke's argument thus opens up the possibility of viewing persuasive and figurative aspects within the framework of rhetorical actions that respond to questions posed by historical situations.

While conceived as a general theory of literature as symbolic action,[21] Kenneth Burke's suggestions accord with Seán Burke's conclusion at the end of his study of *The Death and the Return of the Author:* namely, that as a solution for dealing with the author in critical practice, one should adopt "the middle way of situated authorship" because "[s]o far from consolidating the notion of a universal or unitary subject, the retracing of the work to its author is a working-back to historical, cultural and political embeddedness" ([1992] 2008: 194).

Finally, this helps to specify the definition of the key concept at the heart of the theoretical rhetoric of authorship as I conceive it: *figures of the author* should be understood as the processes and products of authors' persuasions and figurations that respond to particular historical situations. The example of the inspiration of the romantic genius – the foremost modern model of the author – might illustrate the import of this rhetorical point of view. As Kenneth Burke put it more generally in his analysis of the role of rhetoric "in all *socialization*," if the author "does not somehow act to tell himself (as his own audience) what the various brands of rhetorician have told him, his persuasion is not complete. Only those voices from without are effective which can speak in the language of a voice within." (K. Burke 1969b: 39). In a rhetorical analysis, then, the inspiration of the romantic author is a rhetorical monologue in the language of a voice that was, at one point, outside, but has now become an inner voice. As such, it is a response to a certain historical situation with all its conflicts and competing viewpoints. At the same time, however, rhetoric also views the situation as transformable through symbolic action. In other words, in one sense, authors only come into being as responses to historical situations, yet in another sense,

---

[21] Cf. Jameson's critique (1978a, 1978b) and Burke's response to it (1978) in *Critical Inquiry.* Their positions are contrasted from a rhetorical perspective in Wetherbee (2015).

they also attempt to shape them through the twin processes of rhetorical-poetical persuasion and figuration.

Ideally, such a definition makes a rhetoric of authorship an example of what Steven Mailloux regards as the strength of rhetorical approaches in general: "a near perfect instrument [...] for overcoming the now artificial distinction between textual and extra-textual interpretive approaches," since "[r]hetoric is both inside and outside the text, and constitutive of the distinction between the two in particular historical situations of performance and criticism, production and interpretation" (2000: 21). Such a rhetoric of authorship, then, would make good on the claim of being a combination of historicized theory and theorized history. Grounded in a specifically rhetorical understanding of figuration, persuasion, and situation, this rhetoric of authorship can make use of the rich storehouse of concepts and metaphors that the rhetorical tradition offers. Hence, in the second half of this chapter, I suggest several divisions of the figures of the author, according to the specific types of activity and discourse that are involved in cultural phenomena of literary authorship. The most fundamental of these divisions is the one between theory, poetics, and performance.

1.2 Theoretical, Poetical, and Performative Figures of the Author

Although from diametrically opposed ends of the spectrum of literary theory, two of the strongest supporters of rhetoric in literary studies have been the French narratologist Gérard Genette and the British Marxist Terry Eagleton. In his call for an unrestricted rhetoric, Genette argues that rhetoric should become a theory of all discourse and no longer be restrained to metaphor theory alone: "a metaphorics, a tropology, a theory of figures, does not relieve us of general rhetoric, still less of that 'new rhetoric' (as it might be called), which we need [...] and which would be a semiotics of discourses. Of all discourses" (1982: 121).[22] Eagleton comments that ancient rhetoric, "saw speaking and writing not merely as textual objects, to be aesthetically contemplated or endlessly deconstructed, but as forms of *activity* inseparable from the wider social relations between writers and readers, orators and audiences, and as largely unintelligible outside the social purposes and conditions

---

[22] Genette also mentions a general rhetoric in his quasi-Platonic dialogue towards the end of his monograph on the architext. With the architext, rhetoric shares the quality of being "above, beneath, around the text" but, like all the other terms suggested, Genette also rejects "rhetoric, or theory of discourse, which overarches everything way up high" (1992: 83–84).

in which they were embedded" (Eagleton 2008: 179).[23] Genette and Eagleton end their arguments on strikingly similar notes. Eagleton concludes his sub-chapter on "Politics and Rhetoric" in *How to Read a Poem* (2008) thus: "The slogan of a radical literary criticism, then, is clear: Forward to antiquity!" (16). Genette concludes his article on "La rhétorique restreinte" with a quotation from Verdi's *Falstaff* that suggests turning to ancient sources will lead to progress: "Torniamo all' antico, sara [sic] un progresso" (1982: 121). What follows shall heed their advice in translating crucial rhetorical distinctions from antiquity into concepts for the analysis and interpretation of figures of the author.

In his *Handbook of Literary Rhetoric*, Heinrich Lausberg explicates one of the major schemes for distinguishing the ancient disciplines of knowledge (τέχναι, *artes*, *scientiae*), which is based on the type of action the person with such knowledge would perform and the kind of artwork that this action would result in: "If the focus is [...] upon the action performed (*opus* [...]) a tripartite classification of the *artes* is arrived at, corresponding to the **degrees of concreteness** of the *opus*" (Lausberg 1998: 5 = §10): the most concrete poietical arts, the less concrete performative arts, and the least concrete theoretical arts.[24] The origin of this distinction lies in Aristotle's tripartite division of fundamental types of knowledge, which distinguishes between theoretical knowledge (ἐπιστήμη θεωρητική/*episteme theoretike*), practical knowledge (ἐπιστήμη πρακτική/*episteme praktike*), and poietical knowledge (ἐπιστήμη ποιητική/*episteme poietike*).[25] Rather than separating only praxis and theory as modernity is wont to do (take Eagleton's [2008: 180] definition of rhetoric as covering "both the practice of effective discourse and the science of it"),[26] Aristotle and the rhetorical tradition after him assume that there is a fundamental

---

23 In *How to Read a Poem* (2008), Eagleton also makes the case that literary criticism faces "an alarming situation. [...] If most of its practitioners have become less sensitive to literary form, some of them also look with scepticism on the critic's social and political responsibilities. [...] In both ways, then, literary criticism is in danger of breaking faith with its origins in classical rhetoric" (16).

24 Of the three major possibilities for rendering the meaning of ποιητική/*poietike* into English, 'poetic,' 'poetical,' and 'poietical,' the latter is best suited to draw attention to the distinctive Greek meaning of 'productive.' In the other chapters of the book, I use the more old-fashioned alternative to 'poetic,' namely 'poetical,' to mean the domain that is introduced in this section as 'poietical' or 'productive.'

25 Cf. the passages in the *Metaphysics* (Aristotle 1995a: 1619 = 1025b21–26; 1995a: 1681 = 1064a10–16). The Aristotelian distinction of the τέχναι/*artes*/*scientiae* was later inherited and used not only as a general classification of human knowledge, but also as a mode of intrarhetorical distinction, most prominently by Quintilian in his *Institutio Oratoria* (Quintilian 2001a: 397 = 2.18.1–3).

26 On the historical opposition of theory and practice, cf. Lobkowicz (1967) and Bernstein ([1971] 1999).

difference between the knowledge involved in how to think something, the knowledge of how to perform something, and the knowledge of how to make something. In a seminal essay in rhetorical studies, the philosophical mentor of the Chicago school of criticism, Richard McKeon, makes this distinction the basis for his call for rhetoric as "an architectonic art, an art of structuring all principles and products of knowing, doing, and making" ([1971] 2005: 198), yet it can also function more specifically as the architectonic principle of a rhetoric of authorship.

If we understand rhetoric as a general science of discourse that is primarily practical (πρᾶξις), but also includes the analysis (θεωρία) and the production of discourse (ποίησις), it can function as a heuristic frame of reference for its sister art of poetics. The classification thus results in a revitalisation of the ancient concept of poetical discourse as something that is the result of a productive activity, the ποίημα/poiema as a result of ποίησις/poiesis.[27] It also views this poietical activity in the context of theoretical and performative activities, thus offering a heuristic framework for analysing and interpreting the figures of the author in different symbolic contexts and historical situations. The example of Poe makes this clear; what makes Poe relevant for literary and cultural history is foremost his poetical production: his poems, tales, and novels. At the same time, however, this activity and its products do not fully define his authorship; in similar fashion, it is a result of his theoretical activity, as it emerges in his criticism, and of his performative activity, for instance, in his lectures. As the later chapters will show, these activities intermesh considerably, leading to various figures of the author such as the transatlantic poet-critic, the genius rhetorician, the detective, and the elocutionist. Beginning with the poietical dimension, authorship can thus be conceptualised as a phenomenon that emerges in the irresolvable interrelatedness of all three dimensions. If the aim is to analyze figures of the author in their larger cultural implications, it is both poetics and rhetoric – both as a theoretical science and performative art of discourse – that are required. Authorship as a rhetorical phenomenon is, as Aristotle's, Quintilian's, and McKeon's division shows, a phenomenon of knowing, making, and doing.

In keeping with the spirit of Genette's and Eagleton's advice, the remainder of this chapter introduces some of the most fundamental rhetorical distinctions belonging to the theoretical, poetical, and performative dimensions of the figures

---

[27] By virtue of its semantic connections in Greek, such a poietical domain includes the original attribute of authorship that is evinced in ποιητής, the Greek word for the 'maker' of drama or poetry, or the Scottish appellation for a poet, *makar*. The term also helps to foreground the semantic component of activity in the notion of 'fiction' which is usually understood as an object today: Latin 'fingere' denotes a poietical activity, meaning 'to form, shape, fashion,' as discussed in the introduction of 'figure' above.

of the author: 1) the three types of effect of a discourse – *docere, delectare*, and *movere* – are interpreted as aspects of the literary situation viewed as a communicative situation, 2) the first three stages of production – invention, arrangement, and style – are conceptualised as constituting figures of the author that are shared by rhetoric and poetics, and 3) the final two stages of production – memory and delivery – are interpreted as informing figures of the author that inscribe authorship into cultural memory through performance.

Theoretical Figures of the Author: Instruction, Entertainment, Agitation

In its most fundamental sense, a theoretical figure of the author is an answer to Foucault's famous question, *What is an author?* Or more precisely, *How can one think the author?* Potential answers to this question can be more figurative (as in Barthes' concept of the author as a dead person) or predominantly persuasive (as in Foucault's notion of the author as a function of discourses). The theoretical dimension of literary authorship is difficult to subdivide, since it is self-reflexive: in other words, an author's 'individual' theory potentially includes all that can be covered by a general theory of authorship.[28] Philip Sidney, Samuel Taylor Coleridge, Edgar Allan Poe, Christine Brooke-Rose, Toni Morrison, David Lodge, Margaret Atwood, or Salman Rushdie would be good examples of poet-critics who developed explicit theoretical work alongside their poetical and performative activities. Yet often the theoretical dimension is also left implicit, and it is only certain quasi-theoretical presumptions that guide the author without their necessarily having consciously reflected upon them. Even in such cases, however, someone who aspires to become or be an author necessarily has to have some, no matter how indistinct, idea about what an author is, which can thus be analyzed as an implicit theoretical figure of the author.

The elementary assumption of rhetorical theories of authorship – that is, their basic theoretical figure of the author – is that the author is a communicator in a situation that is irreducibly defined by the positions of the author(s), the audience, the discourse, and what the discourse is about. Within this communicative situation, the author is viewed as the producer of certain effects on an audience through her discourse. These effects correspond to fundamental aspects of the speech situation and

---

28 For contemporary reconceptualisations of such issues of plagiarism-as-authorship, cf. Horn (2016).

are traditionally divided into cognitive (*docere*), ethical and gentle emotional (*delectare*), and political and strong emotional effects (*movere*).²⁹

Beginning with Aristotle, rhetoric thus offers an inclusive theory of the basic communicative situation that includes a rhetorician's potential to inform the audience about something (λόγος/*logos*), the ethos of the speaker (ἦθος/*ethos*), and the appeal to the audience (πάθος/*pathos*), all viewed as technical means for speakers to communicate what they intend to the audience.³⁰ The most diversified ancient terminology for the ends or effects of discourse can be found in the Roman rhetoricians. According to Quintilian, on whose terms I shall rely as general descriptions, persuasion (*persuadere*) can be divided into informing, instructing or "giving information" (*docere*); entertaining, delighting, "pleasing" or "conciliating" (*delectare* or *conciliare*); and arousing emotions, moving people to action or "appealing to the emotions" (*movere*).³¹ While the terms employed for the triad vary, the shades of meaning of each term can be taken as indicative of the dimensions the three types of effect encompass.³² The overall effect or end of rhetorical discourse, persuasion, is thus distinguished into three major possible effects of discourse.

In the eighteenth century, the formative period of rhetorical theory up until the middle of the nineteenth century, one of the major inheritors of this triad is the Scottish rhetorician George Campbell, a major proponent of the epistemological tradition, in his *Philosophy of Rhetoric* (1776). Modifying the Roman rhetoricians' distinction of the three degrees of persuasion, he reinstitutes persuasion itself as a fourth dimension, and, in a characteristic move, assigns each dimension a specific mental faculty: "All the ends of speaking are reducible to four; every speech being intended to enlighten the understanding, to please the imagination, to move the passions, or to influence the will" (Campbell [1776] 1988: 1). It was Campbell's and similar contemporary versions of the rhetorical triad that would be influential not only for definitions of rhetorical discourse but also for

---

29 Cp. Knape 2000b: 110–113.
30 For a short overview of positions in antiquity, cf. Lausberg (1998: 113–118 = §§ 256–258) and Schirren (2008). Aristotle writes: "Of the *pisteis* provided through speech there are three species; for some are in the character [ēthos] of the speaker, and some in disposing the listener in some way [pathos, GG], and some in the speech [logos] itself, by showing or seeming to show something" (Aristotle 2007: 38 = 1356a)
31 Quintilian (2001e: 313 = 12.10.59). The translations quoted are Russell's.
32 The terms fulfil a variety of functions, e.g. being used to distinguish between the more familiar three levels of rhetorical style (Quintilian 2001e: 313 = 12.10.59), which Russell translates as "plain," "grand," and "intermediate." On the relation between Aristotle's *ethos* and Quintilian's *delectare*, cf. Lausberg (1998: 114–116 = §257.2).

the definition of literary and poetical discourse. As I argue in later chapters, its inheritors include John Stuart Mill, William Cullen Bryant, and Edgar Allan Poe. It would be a mammoth task to trace the various guises assumed by the triad of effects throughout Western history, so I present here in tabular form the bare minimum of what I perceive to be the central stages in its development up to the late eighteenth century with one outlook onto the twentieth century. What is not sufficiently emphasized even within rhetorical studies is that this rhetorical triad is the equivalent of modern day communication models. To exemplify this, I add – as one particularly pertinent example – the dimensions of Karl Bühler's organon model of language to the table, which illuminates the earlier rhetorical distinctions and vice versa.³³

	Docere	Delectare	Movere	(Persuadere)
Aristotle	Logos	Ethos	Pathos	
Quintilian	Docere	Delectare	Movere	(Persuadere)
Antonio Minturno³⁴	Probare	Delectare	Movere	
Philip Sidney³⁵	'show the way'	'give a sweet prospect'	'intice a man to enter'	
George Campbell	Enlighten the understanding	Please the imagination	Move the passions	(Influence the will)
Karl Bühler³⁶	Representation	Expression	Appeal	

---

33 For links to Roman Jakobson's communication model and Charles W. Morris' theory of signs, cf. Knape (2000b: 113).
34 The Italian poet-critic Antonio Minturno (1500–1574) is a good candidate for being the first in the Renaissance to explicitly apply the rhetorical triad of effects to poetry. Mixing Cicero's and Quintilian's terms, Minturno writes in book 3 of *De poeta* (1559) that it is the duty of the tragic poet "ut probet, ut delectet, ut moveat" (1559: 179). The triad would thus become a staple of the renaissance ideal of the poet-orator and appeared in Sir Philip Sidney, John Rainolds, Henry Peacham, Thomas Wilson, and others (Müller 1993: 226–228).
35 Wolfgang G. Müller argues that, in applying the triad of effects of *docere*, *delectare* and *movere* to poetry, Sidney equates rhetoric and poesy to claim that the poet is better equipped to achieve these effects than representatives of the other arts and sciences (1993: 226): "Nowe therein of all Sciences [...] is our Poet the Monarch. For he dooth not only shew the way [*docere*], but giveth so sweete a prospect into the way [*delectare*], as will intice any man to enter into it [*movere*]" (Sidney 2011: 25).
36 The situation Bühler bases his model on is the paradigmatic situation of rhetorical theory: the speech situation. Bühler stresses that the meaning of a sound only emerges in the interplay of three factors: sender; receiver; and objects and states of affairs, which correspond to the semantic functions of expression, appeal, and representation (2011: 35).

As becomes particularly obvious from the comparison with Bühler's semantic functions of the word, all the earlier interpretations of the rhetorical triad attempt to grasp the basic communicative situation between producers and recipients of discourse about the world. The difference lies in the fact that rhetoric views all aspects of discourse as potential means for the discourse-producer to influence an audience, whereas Bühler's model attempts a neutral description of the interrelations between the elements. Thus Bühler's "expression" of "inner states" is conceived as more heteronomous than Aristotle's definition of *ethos* as only those elements of the speaker's personality that influence the audience in an artistic way. Bühler's dimension of appeal is the one that is generally recognized as the rhetorical dimension (even by Bühler himself),[37] yet as the rhetorical triad makes clear, rhetoric developed categories for the other dimensions as well. In short, whereas most people associate only Bühler's appellative aspect with rhetoric, rhetoric encompasses all three semiotic aspects.

As I explained at the beginning of this section, theoretical figures of the author are particularly difficult to categorize because of their self-reflexivity. One model that must enter the discussion at this point is M. H. Abrams' scheme of the possible orientations of criticism, since it maps – by way of a Luhmannesque 're-entry' – the coordinates of the communicative situation to the artistic situation. Abrams argues that "[f]our elements in the total situation of a work of art are discriminated and made salient, by one or another synonym, in almost all theories which aim to be comprehensive" ([1953] 1971: 6). Abrams links these four aspects of the situation of the work of art to orientations of criticism, classifying theories accordingly into theories that are primarily objective (focussing on the work), expressive (artist), mimetic (universe), and pragmatic (audience).

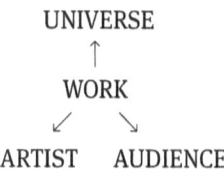

Figure 1: M. H. Abrams' diagram of the total situation of the work of art ([1953] 1971: 6)

The rhetorical triad of effects offers an important clarification of Abrams' well-established terms. As visualised in his diagram, the author appears to be simply

---

[37] In what he calls "the thesis of the three functions of language in simplest terms," Bühler identifies rhetoric with "appeal in language," lyric poetry with expression, and epic poetry and drama with representation (2011: 39).

one of the elements of the situation, yet concepts of the author – like concepts of the other elements – are only meaningful in relation to all of the other elements of the situation. Hence, when one of the other elements changes, the notion of the author also changes. For example: when neoclassical theory stressed the mimetic aspect of literature, this corresponded with a concept of the author as a representer (sensu Bühler) of nature, and, even more specifically, as an instructor (in the sense of *docere*) of truths about nature.

Even in twentieth- and twenty-first century authors, in whom rhetorical terminology can no longer be assumed to be a direct influence, the fundamental aspects of the speech situation of communicator, audience, discourse, and topic of discourse are irreducible. Commenting on "the rhetorical stance," Wayne Booth finds that this stance "depends on discovering and maintaining in any writing situation a proper balance among the three elements that are at work in any communicative effort: the available arguments about the subject itself, the interests and peculiarities of the audience, and the voice, the implied character, of the speaker." (Booth 1963: 141). As applied to fictional narrative, the scheme corresponds to what James Phelan has called "the recursive relationships among authorial agency, textual phenomena, and reader response" (1996: 19), in which any narrative is understood as "a rhetorical action: an author's attempt to harness all the resources of storytelling for the purpose of a set of effects (cognitive, emotional, ethical) in an audience" (2010: 243).

Generally, when they are viewed as theoretical figures of the author, the rhetorical effects appear as functional roles of the author, for example as the orator's duties in Cicero.[38] Joachim Knape's distinction of the "communicator functions" of "informator," "elocutor," and "orator"[39] (2000b: 113) is a systematic account of such roles.[40] While Knape does not make it explicit, the "Informator" corresponds to the effect of *docere*, the "Elokutor" to *delectare*, and the "Orator" to *movere*. Authors, Knape rightly points out, "want to act autonomously in all three functions": "They want and need informational freedom, i.e. they want to be allowed to invent messages (right of fiction), they want creative freedom,

---

38 They are "formulated variously as *probare/docere, conciliare/delectare*, and *movere/flectere* and repeated throughout the Ciceronian canon (*De oratore* 2.182, 310, 3.104; *Orator* 69; *Brutus* 185, 276; *De optimo genere* 3)" and are "central to his rhetorical theory" (Baumlin 2001: 269).
39 My translation of Knape's three "Kommunikatorfunktionen": "Informator," "Elokutor," and "Orator" (Knape 2000b: 113).
40 Knape rightly insists that, from the perspective of rhetoric, "although functionally differentiated, every human being [is] simultaneously informator, elocutor, and orator in communication" ("jeder Mensch [ist] in der Kommunikation zugleich, wenn auch funktional getrennt, Informator, Elokutor und Orator") (Knape 2000b: 114; my translation).

i.e. to be allowed to develop unusual structures in a text (right of form), and they want oratorical freedom, i.e. to be allowed to communicate their own messages (right of action)."[41] Whilst these general theoretical figures of the author always have to be analyzed with reference to particular historical situations, they also offer the possibility of grouping authorial roles more generally according to the dominant rhetorical function. Thus a prevalence of the rhetorical function of *docere* would mean that the author is regarded primarily as an instructor about nature or society (as in, for instance, the Renaissance poet-orator and the Victorian sage, respectively). If the rhetorical function of *delectare* dominates, the author is seen mainly as an entertainer (as, for example, twenty-first century popular fiction writers such as Dan Brown). An emphasis on the function of *movere* would mean that the author is viewed in the first place as an agitator (e.g. in muckraking novelists such as Upton Sinclair). These theoretical figures of the author as instructor, entertainer, or agitator do not exhaust the dimensions of the triad, yet can be viewed as paradigmatic examples of them.

Poetical Figures of the Author: Invention, Arrangement, and Style

The theoretical aspect is only one of three major dimensions of the figures of the author. As concepts for the poetical and performative dimensions I shall adopt the rhetorical terminology for the five stages of the production of a discourse, the first three of which are shared by rhetoric and poetics (*inventio, dispositio, elocutio*), while the final two (*memoria, actio/pronuntiatio*) are specifically rhetorical. The first three terms denote an author's activities in the production of a discourse: these figurational activities can either become visible only as traces of activity in the resulting poetical product, or, they can be self-reflexively foregrounded within the poetical text (as, for example, via the use of metafictional characters). Thus the poetical aspects of a figure of the author concern the interrelated activities of invention, arrangement, and stylization, but they might also appear in fictional characters that depict rhetorical inventors (as for example, in the heroization of rhetorico-poetical invention in Auguste Dupin, as discussed in chapter five); arrangers (as in the excessively rational arrangement of the murderer "The Tell-Tale Heart" that is structured according to the classical *arrange-*

---

[41] Authors "wollen mit allen drei Funktionen souverän umgehen": "Sie wollen und brauchen informatorische Freiheit, d.h. sie wollen Mitteilungen auch erfinden dürfen (Fiktionsrecht), sie wollen gestalterische Freiheit, d.h. eventuell auch ungewohnte Strukturen im Text entfalten dürfen (Formrecht) und sie wollen oratorische Freiheit, d.h. sie wollen eigene Botschaften vermitteln dürfen (Handlungsrecht)" (Knape 2000b: 115; my translation).

ment of a speech),⁴² or stylizers (as in the character of Mr Blackwood in "How to Write a Blackwood Article," discussed at the end of chapter two).

Few concepts are as useful for the conceptualisation of the poetical and performative aspects of figures of the author as Harold Love's concept of "authemes," a term that explicitly opposes what Jack Stillinger (1991) aptly calls the myth of solitary genius. Love defines it thus: "The term 'authorship' [...] will not therefore denote the condition of being an originator of works, but a set of linked activities (*authemes*) which are sometimes performed by a single person but will often be performed collaboratively or by several persons in succession" (2002: 39). According to his conceptualisation of the stages of production of a text, Love distinguishes precursory, executive, declarative, and revisionary authorship (40–50). These authorial "linked activities" are geared towards the interests of attribution studies, but Love also notes as the earliest attempt to distinguish authemes the already-mentioned five rhetorical arts, canons, or offices (*officia, partes rhetorices*). While somewhat truncated, Love's description of the rhetorical stages of production as activities of authorship is worth quoting at length:

> There have been many attempts to distinguish the activities involved in authorship. An influential early one was Quintilian's breaking down of the tasks of an orator into *inventio, dispositio, elocutio, memoria* and *pronuntiatio*. In still earlier times there were Athenians who would provide a citizen with a written speech that could be memorised and delivered in the Agora as his own. This meant that the first contributor would do the *inventio, dispositio*, and *elocutio* and a second the *memoria* and *pronuntiatio*, which, in the specialised field of oratory, were by no means the easiest bits. But even when Demosthenes, say, performed all these five stages himself, the distinction between them would still exist, along with subsidiary ones such as that by which the oration was built from structural modules, each following its own rules and precedents. (2002: 39)

Love speaks of this distinction as a thing of the past, but this is more an indication of a lack of interdisciplinary exchange than a factual description. The five rhetorical canons are still present in contemporary rhetorical theory and pedagogy, especially in the United States, where they are used in the fields of composition and communication.⁴³ As Winifred Bryan Horner observes, "[r]hetorical systems often called 'new' have never quite given up the classical canons, arguing either for or against them." While "[r]hetoric has historically evidenced a tendency to reduce itself largely to one or two of its canons," "the classical canons

---

42 Cf. Zimmerman (2005: 28–50).
43 Cf. the 'classic' example Corbett and Connors (1999). Cf. e.g. also Horner (1988). On the general reception of ancient rhetoric in contemporary American rhetorical studies, cf. Welch (2013).

have persisted over the years." She concludes that "[a]ll of them [...] are necessary for a full understanding of a communication act, whether it be written, spoken, electronic, or some combination of any or all of these" (Horner 1993: ix).

While there are earlier versions, for instance in Aristotle,[44] the canonical form of the five rhetorical arts hearkens back to the first Roman rhetorical treatise, the anonymous *Rhetorica ad Herennium*, for a long time presumed to be written by Cicero. What is remarkable is that, in the formulation in the *Ad Herennium*, the phases of production are attributed to the orator as faculties: "The speaker, then, should possess the faculties of Invention, Arrangement, Style, Memory, and Delivery" (Caplan 1964: 7 = 1.2.3).[45] The *Ad Herennium* thus evinces what Thomas Schirren calls an example of that "focus on the author which has to place the theory of the five canons in the centre of any rhetorical theory" (2008: 622; my translation).[46] Right from its codification, the stages of production are thus inherently connected to the speaker as author. The later Roman tradition, however, would interpret the stages not as faculties but as arts that were part of the overall system of rhetoric.[47] Most rhetoricians agreed with Quintilian's already-mentioned summary of the five parts of rhetoric:

> The system of oratory, as a whole, according to most authorities, and the best of them, consists of five parts: Invention, Disposition, Elocution, Memory, and Delivery or Performance (both terms are in use). Every utterance, at any rate every one by which some meaning is expressed must have both content [*res*] and words [*verba*]. If it is brief and limited to a single sentence, it may need nothing else; but longer speeches do require more. For it is not only what we say and how we say it that matters, but also in what sequence: Disposition is therefore essential. Now we shall not be able to say all that the subject demands, nor put everything in its proper place, without the help of Memory: so this will be the fourth part.

---

[44] Aristotle distinguishes εὕρησις/heuresis (invention), which he discusses in the first two books of the *Rhetoric* as well as λέξις/lexis (style), τάξις/taxis (arrangement), and ὑπόκρισις/hypokrisis (delivery), which he discusses in book three.

[45] The individual definitions are as follows: "Invention is the devising of matter, true or plausible, that would make the case convincing. Arrangement is the ordering and distribution of the matter, making clear the place to which each thing is to be assigned. Style is the adaptation of suitable words and sentences to the matter devised. Memory is the firm retention in the mind of the matter, words, and arrangement. Delivery is the graceful regulation of voice, countenance, and gesture" (Caplan 1964: 7 = 1.2.3)

[46] "Es ist diese Autorzentrierung, die die Theorie von den Produktionsstadien der Rede ins Zentrum jeder rhetorischen Theorie stellen muss" (Schirren 2008: 622).

[47] It is worth remarking in passing that the technical terms both for the triad of discourse effects and the five stages of production veer between duties of the producer, *officia oratoris*, and arts or parts of rhetoric, *artes* or *partes rhetorices*, thus evincing either an agent-oriented or a system-oriented definition.

But a Delivery which is unbecoming, either in voice or gesture, spoils the whole thing and virtually destroys it. So the fifth place has to be given to Delivery. (2001b: 22–25 = 3.3.1–3)[48]

The first three arts concern the stages of production that are the same in the production of rhetorical and poetical discourse: *inventio, dispositio,* and *elocutio* can thus be reconceptualised as concepts for the analysis of poetical figures of the author. Such an idea is also in keeping with the history of rhetoric, as becomes obvious in the very term ποιητής/poietes. While the literal and 'literary' meaning of ποιητής is well-known and often quoted in literary studies, it is remarkable that its rhetorical meaning is virtually always neglected. The two primary meanings of ποιητής are "*maker*" and "*workman*," while the two secondary meanings are "*composer of a poem, author*" and "*author*" of a speech" as opposed to the "deliverer of it" (Liddell, Scott and Jones 1940, s.v. ποιητής). The first three rhetorical stages of production, invention, arrangement, and style, were thus applied to the production both of poetical and rhetorical discourse, to the common ancestry of which the two figurative meanings of ποιητής are a testament.[49]

The distinction of these rhetorical and poetical aspects is usually based on the central notion of μίμησις/mimesis in Aristotle's *Poetics*.[50] As Lausberg puts it, "in the field of language, both [rhetoric and poetics] (rhetoric in any case in its parts, *inventio, dispositio, elocutio* [...]) are certainly poietic arts" (1998: 19 = §35). The difference between the two consists in their central focus: while poetics is (in ancient, Renaissance, and neo-classicist conceptions) based on a mimesis of reality (mimetic *sensu* Abrams), rhetoric is focused on the effect on the audience (pragmatic *sensu* Abrams). Lausberg clarifies the distinction thus: "The poet

---

48 To chart the transformations of these five rhetorical arts over time would in effect mean to write a history of rhetoric. Cf. e.g. Booth (2004: 23–38). What unites many of these developments is the negation of the possibilities of rhetorical *inventio* to arrive at truth and the corresponding reduction of all of rhetoric to the canon of *elocutio* as mere lists of figures of speech. Cf. e.g. Walker (2000), Ong ([1958] 2004).
49 Another case in point is Jeffrey Walker's revisionary history of the ancient rhetorical tradition that was from its very beginning poetic, as he demonstrates: "what came to be called rhetoric was neither originally nor essentially an art of practical civic oratory— rather, [...] it originated from an expansion of the poetic/epideictic domain, from 'song' to 'speech' to 'discourse' generally" (2000: ix).
50 On Aristotle's crucial notion of mimesis, the imitation or representation of action, cf. Schmitt (2008: 119–125). Stephen Halliwell, in his 1995 translation of the *Poetics*, leaves the term untranslated (Aristotle 1995c). Cf. also Halliwell (1998).

also of course wields influence over the audience, but in the way characteristic of poetry, through μίμησις" (1998: 19 = §35).[51]

The fact that mimesis is the classical point of distinction between rhetorical and poetical discourse leads straight to the implications of the first stage of production, *inventio*. It is perhaps the most complicated and contested of rhetorical terms,[52] but its two major English translations give an indication of the productive tension inherent in it. 'Invention' and 'discovery' point towards its characteristic mixture of the production of something new and the seeking out of something that has already been thought: "while English distinguishes between *invention*, which brings into existence something new, and discovery, which finds what is already there, both Latin and Greek use the same word, *inventio* or *heurein*, for both" (Watson 2001: 389). In rhetorical *inventio*, the borders between the two are fluid, such that Lausberg describes *inventio* as a "process of exhaustive productivity" (Lausberg 1998: 119 = §260).[53] For our purposes, the crucial aspect of *inventio* is that what makes the author an inventor in the rhetorical sense is a combination of 'finding what is already there' and 'bringing into existence something new.' As we shall see in chapter five, it is precisely this dialectic of invention which lies at the heart of the abductive inference – a rhetorical type of inference that leads to a new insight – according to which Poe structures his tales of ratiocination.

---

[51] At the same time, Aristotle explicitly connects the *Rhetoric* to the *Poetics* and vice versa at several points, most crucially in his discussions of the presentation of thought, of delivery, and, of course, of style and in particular metaphor. Cf. Aristotle 2007: 92 = 1372a; 195 = 1403b; 197 = 1404a; 198 = 1404b; 199 = 1404b, 200 = 1405a, 248 = 1419b; Aristotle 1995b, 2330–2331 = 1456a-b. In many other instances, the connection is implied as, for instance, in the discussion of pity (Aristotle 2007: 139 = 1385b). What is more, Aristotle also conceives of tragedy in terms of its effect on the audience in the central term of κάθαρσις/katharsis. As Jeffrey Walker demonstrates, rhetoric can similarly be thought of as "an art of shaping and guiding an audience's *pathê* toward a *katharsis* of particular moods/intentionalities in practical judgments/actions" (2008: 85). For the relation of Aristotle's poetics and rhetoric viewed from the perspective of the 'death of rhetoric,' cf. Ricoeur (1996).

[52] The scope of invention is far too large to do it justice here. A good overview is given by Watson (2001). Cf. also Lausberg 1998: 119–208 = §§260–442.

[53] The way that rhetoric has traditionally analyzed this relation is via the theory of τόποι/*topoi*, *loci*, or commonplaces. The term has a variety of meanings that can be divided roughly into a material understanding and a formal understanding, though the two aspects constantly intersect. Material topoi are excerpts and selections, usually quotations, from other texts that are regarded as worthy of storage. In contrast, the formal meaning of topoi is that of "search formulas" (Lausberg 1998: 171 = §373) or "ratiocinative procedures, or 'places,' 'common' to a range of disciplines of inquiry or lines of investigation" (A. Moss 2001: 119).

1.2 Theoretical, Poetical, and Performative Figures of the Author — 45

The second rhetorical art, that of arrangement, is closely interlinked with that of invention; they "are inextricable" in the classical system (Fahnestock 1996: 34). This is clear from the fact that the common structure of a discourse is often used as a heuristic device in invention. While Aristotle distinguishes two to four parts and Cicero seven, in various places (R. Enos and Fahnestock 2001: 41–43), the most common structure has six parts, each with a distinctive persuasive function.[54] The translation "arrangement" covers only one of the meanings of the Greek τάξις/taxis and Latin *dispositio*. Other translations into English include "disposition," "order," and "method," and contemporary rhetoricians "pursue similar issues under the rubric of 'form,' part of genre theory and analysis" (Fahnestock 1996: 35).

Disposition thus lends itself most obviously to literary application in matters of generic form. For instance, Heinrich F. Plett has demonstrated the rhetorical conceptualization of poetic genres in the Renaissance (Plett 2004: 151–78). Kenneth Burke's conception of form as progressive, repetitive, conventional, or incidental is a modern development of rhetorical arrangement (1968: 124). As one example of the progressive type of "a perfectly conducted argument," Burke names "the form of a mystery story, where everything falls together, as in a story of ratiocination by Poe" (1968: 124). In similar fashion, the generic form of the tale of terror falls under the category of *dispositio*, and both forms – like genres in general – are relevant for the definition of authorship – and in this case, particularly in terms of autonomy and heteronomy: on the one hand, the tale of ratiocination reaffirms the power of reason to discover the reasons of horror and thus to dispel its binding charm, thereby reconstituting the order that was lost when the crime happened. On the other, Poe's tales of the grotesque, his Gothic fantasy-pieces from "Metzengerstein" and "The Fall of the House of Usher" to "The Tell-Tale Heart" present what Allen Tate saw as the reason for Poe's status as "the transitional figure in modern literature," namely that Poe "discovered our great subject, the disintegration of personality" (Tate 1952: 461). The representation of subjectivity in "The Tell-Tale Heart" is particularly telling in this regard, since it presents the narrator's mad argument in a rhetorically highly structured speech. Taking into consideration the relation between poetic madness

---

54 Cf. also Quintilian (2001b: 179 = 4 prooemium 6). Fahnestock explains their distinctive functions: "The *exordium* predisposes the audience to the speaker and topic. The *narration* reprises the facts of the case [...] The *partition* identifies the precise point at issue and predicts the parts of the argument to come in what we would now call metadiscourse. The *confirmation* gives the supporting arguments, and the *refutation* attacks the opposition. These two sections switch places depending on whether the speaker accuses or defends. Finally the *peroration* summarizes the case and makes a final appeal to the audience's emotions." (Fahnestock 1996: 33; my emphasis). The six-part form also varies between rhetorics (Lausberg 1998: 120 = § 261), but some functions have apparently remained similar until the five-part essay in college composition.

and the romantic imagination (Burwick 1996), Poe's text can be read as a metafictional representation of the madness of the narrator in a way that foregrounds the author as an autonomous arranger.[55] The two genres – detective fiction and the tale of terror – present paradigmatic configurations of reason and madness, of autonomy and heteronomy, configurations that have in a similar way been used to describe models of authorship. Hence, critics' evaluation of Poe's critical texts such as "The Philosophy of Composition" often depend on the *literary* genre with which the critic combines the reading of Poe's essay.[56] As an autheme, disposition covers rhetorical and poetical structures on macro-, meso-, and microlevels, and can serve as a starting-point for the analysis of the relation between literary authors as arrangers of literary as well as rhetorical form.

The array of rhetorical concepts pertaining to the third rhetorical art, that of *elocutio* ("style" or "elocution") is larger than that of any other art. In Aristotle's broadest use of the term, the difference between εὕρησις/heuresis and λέξις/lexis is the distinction between the 'what' and the 'how' of the discourse.[57] One of the most influential categorizations internal to *elocutio* are the levels of style,[58] the terms for which vary greatly but are reducible to three: the plain, or low style, the middle style, and the grand, or high style.[59] While these are often hypostatized, Quintilian, among others, makes it clear that they are con-

---

[55] What is crucial to "The Tell-Tale Heart" is that the rhetorical structure of the text remains intact, indeed becomes overly foregrounded. Tate speaks of "the superimposed order of rhetoric" in this context (Tate 1952: 461), yet, rather than being superimposed, the rhetorical structures are integral to the overall effect of the tale – no matter whether we interpret them in straightforwardly rhetorical terms (Zimmerman 2001) or rhetorico-legal terms (Wall 2013).

[56] This tendency applies to "The Philosophy of Composition" as discussed in chapter four but also, for example, to *Eureka*, as is indicated by Leon Howard's "Poe's *Eureka:* The Detective Story that Failed" (1972).

[57] G. A. Kennedy translates: "The next subject to discuss is *lexis*; for it is not enough to have a supply of things to say but it is also necessary to say it in the right way" (Aristotle 2007: 194 = 1403b15). Cf. Lausberg 1998: 215 = §455.

[58] Other central concepts for the analysis of style include the four qualities, among which the well-known *ornatus* (often couched in the almost proverbial metaphor of the 'dress of thought') is only one. They most often consist of grammatical correctness (Latinitas) and the three rhetorical categories clarity (perspicuitas), ornament (ornatus), and appropriateness or propriety (aptum/decorum). Cf. Lausberg 1998: 216 = §458 and Müller 2001: 745–746. The system of all figures and tropes can be organised according to the four categories of change: Quintilian distinguishes changes by addition, by omission, by transposition, and by substitution (Quintilian 2001a: 143–145 = 1.5.38–39).

[59] Variations are given in brackets: the plain, or low style (*genus subtile/ tenue/ gracile/ humile*), the middle style (*genus medium/ modicum/ mediocre/ moderatum*), and the grand, or high style (*genus grande/ grave/ vehemens/ sublime*). This list is compiled from Lausberg 1998: 472–477 = §1079 and Müller (2001).

nected to the types of discourse effect and have to be adapted to each situation.[60] The individual tropes and figures between which rhetorical treatises and handbooks distinguish are far too numerous to list here, but the implications of a broad conception of figuration have already been outlined above.

Understood as an autheme, style is that operation which remains most similar in rhetorical and poetical production: while syntax and word choice are the most obvious objects of the author's stylizations, even rhythm, metre, and rhyme, often conceived as the sole domain of lyric poetry, strongly figure as "phonological figures" in classical and modern rhetoric.[61] Like invention and arrangement, the operation of stylization can also be metafictionally represented – this might range from the parody of speech styles (which we often find in Poe) to the actual representation of a fictional writer's attempts to compose stylistically apt or beautiful texts (as discussed in the example of "How to Write a Blackwood Article" in chapter two).

A theoretical rhetoric of authorship thus finds ample resources for the discussion of the poetical figures of the author in the schema of the first three arts of rhetoric, especially if they are interpreted as figures of the author. That the three phases of production, or authemes, that are shared by rhetoric and poetics can be interpreted as defining possible roles or operations is in some ways already apparent from their early codification as faculties of the speaker in the *Rhetorica ad Herennium*. The writer as inventor, the writer as arranger, and the writer as stylizer are only the most obvious of such figures of the author, but even in the skeletal state in which the rhetorical arts have been presented here, one can see how emphasis on specific authemes changes historically and how these authemes are transformed.

Performative Figures of the Author: Performance and Memory

Memory and performance are the final two rhetorical stages of production, and, as classically conceived, they clearly belong to the performative arts. Performative figures of the author refer not only to the rhetorical operations of memory and performance but also to all stagings of the authorial self – in such settings as public readings, but also in theatrical contexts in other media. In my sketch of some of the central categories of these terms, I deviate from the standard order, as laid out in the *Ad Herennium*, beginning with performance and ending with

---

60 The common assignation is of the plain style to *docere*/informing, the middle style to *delectare*/entertaining, and the grand style to *movere*/moving the audience. Cf. Lausberg 1998: 471 = §1078.
61 Cf. Plett (2010: 97–146). For a reinterpretation of style, especially in its modern guises, as the basic category of poetics, cf. Hartley (2016).

memory rather than vice versa, in order to show some of the possibilities of reinterpreting the classical art of memory in medial terms.

The basic rhetorical concept of *praxis* is one of a domain in which the speaker or writer can act with the guidance of 'scientific' and artistic principles and processes. As we saw earlier, for Quintilian, and indeed for most of the classical tradition, the whole of rhetoric is ultimately an art and science of praxis. Rhetorical discourse remains incomplete if it is not pronounced, not put into action, not delivered to an audience. While all rhetorical distinctions find their meaning in the communicative interplay between producer/s and recipient/s of discourse about the world, the rhetorical tradition, particularly in the later eighteenth and early nineteenth centuries, has developed an especially rich vocabulary for discourse-as-performance. This highly complex and medially variable phase of production is usually referred to in English as "delivery," sometimes as "action" or "presentation," yet its meaning might better be grasped as encompassing the manifold meanings that are connoted in our time in the (non-Classical) term *performance*.

It goes without saying that the primary model for delivery in antiquity was the speech, and hence delivery was viewed mainly as the bodily performance of discourse. Its importance might be illustrated by an anecdote that both Cicero and Quintilian relate about Demosthenes: when asked by someone what was the most important part of rhetoric, Demosthenes named delivery as the most important thing, and then he also named it the second and the third most important thing, at which point the person stopped asking (Quintilian 2001e: 87–89 = 11.3.6). Two of the major aspects of oral delivery, voice and gesture, were already subtly subdivided in Cicero, Quintilian, and others. Following Aristotle, ancient Greek rhetoricians had used the term ὑπόκρισις/hypokrisis that denoted play-acting on a stage and also already implied the contemporary English meaning of 'hypocrisy.' Latin had two terms for the final rhetorical canon: it was called either *actio* or *pronuntiatio*, two terms which name the two sides of 'acting' (gesture) and pronouncing (voice) a speech (Quintilian 2001e: 84–183 = 11.3). That the fifth canon also includes the outer appearance of the orator becomes apparent in Quintilian's detailed discussions of dress and hairstyle (Quintilian 2001e: 157–163 = 11.3.137–149). Awareness of norms, fashions, and customs, not only in speech but also in gestures and outer appearance is a necessity: thus all aspects of the orator's embodied performance are relevant to the purpose of the discourse.

What all rhetoricians agree upon is that the orator's delivery is related to the arts of the poet and the actor. Aristotle goes so far as to argue that "[i]t is plain that delivery has just as much to do with oratory as with poetry" (Aristotle 1995d, 2238 = 1403b). While poetic recitation might be the speciality of a reciter or rhapsodist, poets can also fulfil that role for their own or others' poetry. Both oratory and recitation are closely linked to acting, and the similarities between the orator, the poet, and the actor can be analysed by the application of the terminology of rhetorical delivery.

Perhaps the key element of rhetorical performance that also applies to the poet and the actor is what might be called the dialectics of affection. Roman rhetoricians, Quintilian in particular, argue that an orator has to bring himself into a similar emotional state to the one he intends to produce in the audience, or he will not be able to convince them: the self-affection of the orator is the necessary precondition for the affection of the audience. As Quintilian formulates it in his detailed discussion in book six: "The heart of the matter as regards arousing emotions [...] lies in being moved by them oneself" (Quintilian 2001c: 59 = 6.2.26). It is the very same rhetorical dialectics which governs Horace's demand that the poet has to feel emotions himself in order to make the audience feel them: "If you would have me weep, you must first feel grief yourself" ("si vis me flere, dolendum est/primum ipsi tibi" (Horace [1926] 1945: 459 (ll. 102–3)).

Little attention was paid to delivery in the Middle Ages,[62] and the Renaissance also pales in comparison with the enormous amount of rhetorical work on delivery in the eighteenth and early nineteenth century, when the ancient conceptions were reformulated under the different medial conditions of print-capitalism (Anderson 2006: 37–46). Not only was there renewed attention to delivery as embodied performance, but there was also a change in meaning as the categories of delivery were reformulated in order to accommodate the different mediality of print culture. As Kathleen Welch has it, "[w]ith the medium of print, delivery comes to focus on presentation, typeface, [and] ways of reading" (2001: 218). Its redefinition would thus, via ways of reading, also affect ways of writing literature, as can be shown, for instance, with regard to Poe's "Ulalume" or "The Bells."[63]

The importance of rhetorical delivery was particularly visible in the writings of the so-called elocutionary movement,[64] which crossed the Atlantic from Ireland and Great Britain. As I demonstrate in chapter six, this furnished the background for Poe's thinking about versification and poetry. The writings of elocutionists such as Thomas Sheridan, John Walker, and Gilbert Austin were modified and adapted to the American situation by writers like William Russell,

---

62 In this paragraph I rely mostly on Welch (2001).
63 Cf. the discussion in chapter six.
64 Also called "elocutionist rhetoric." The standard treatment is still Howell (1971): 145–258. Despite its contemporary importance, elocutionary rhetoric has been portrayed pejoratively or simply neglected, even within rhetorical studies, as Nan Johnson points out (1991: 13); one recent exception is Sloane (2013) who maintains that elocutionist rhetoric resurfaced as the core of the New Criticism.

Benjamin Rush, and James Edward Murdoch. Echoing Quintilian's account, Russell maintained in his *American Elocutionist* (1844) that public address, "as a combination of speech and action, directs itself to the mind, through the ear and the eye. Regarded as an art, it consists, accordingly, of two parts, – elocution, or the regulated functions of the voice, – and gesture, or the proper management of the body" (Russell 1844: 199). While part of the general developments in the New Rhetoric of the eighteenth and nineteenth centuries, the elocutionary movement was also a tradition in its own right.

Medial shifts such as the one to mass printing tend generally to lead to a focus on problems of delivery. Our contemporary situation is a case in point, since, as a result of the contemporary shift towards multimedia environments on the internet, rhetorical research on delivery is once again on the rise. As Ben McCorkle puts it, "rhetorical theorists are extending our body-centric notion of delivery so that it no longer deals exclusively with the vocal or gestural aspects of an oration but also with the medium, design elements, or paratextual features of non-oratorical artifacts" (2012: 2). Hence, contemporary rhetoric usually regards delivery "spoken, printed, or electronically transmitted [...] as the synthesizing act of rhetorical composition" (Sloane 2001: 800). The changes of the information revolution are thus somewhat similar to the historical role of the printing press as an agent of change *sensu* Elizabeth Eisenstein. Both have a fundamental impact on the understanding of delivery.

Understood as an autheme, delivery foregrounds the medial dimension of discourse in such settings as authorial public readings, in which the author acts as speaker *sensu stricto*. The most prominent contemporary example with Poe is certainly Charles Dickens.[65] But it also applies to the final phase of discourse production under the conditions of print culture, in which rhetorical possibilities are intricately connected to problems of the materiality of communication. Indeed, the interrelation between performance and the materialities of communication has been at the centre of literary and cultural research for some time, as K. Ludwig Pfeiffer's argument shows: "We have come or (looking at the ancient Greeks as one example) reverted to dynamic contexts of *performance* (which may attract or disappoint) and to meaning *effects* (which may be fascinating or misleading but hardly right or wrong)" (1994: 2). Ultimately, the rhetorical concept of *actio* integrates oratorical and non-oratorical performance as one phase in the production of discourse, thus opening up potential avenues of research on the medial interconnectedness of discourse and performance. Poe engaged with performative aspects of both print and speech in various gen-

---

[65] Cf. the discussion in chapter six, Dickens (1975), and Adams (2014).

res ranging from his own lectures to his tales, poems, and criticism, as chapters six and seven demonstrate.

Memoria is, somewhat ironically, in many ways the most elusive of the five arts. Its integration as the fourth of five production phases in the *Ad Herennium* and other rhetorical handbooks has led to a truncated conception of it as the mere memorizing of the speech for its performance. If it were simply a matter of learning by rote for situations in which it is demanded that one speak without written prompts, then memory would easily become superfluous, once this situation of primary orality disappeared.[66]

Yet the role of memory, even in the classical system, is far broader. The other four arts are "futile," Quintilian argues, unless "held together, as it were, by this animating principle" (2001e: 59 = 11.2.1):

> All learning depends on memory, and teaching is in vain if everything we hear slips away. It is this capacity too that makes available to us the reserves of examples, laws, rulings, sayings, and facts which the orator must possess in abundance and have always at his fingertips [...] Even impromptu eloquence rests [...] on this same power of the mind. [...] Memory [...] acts as a sort of intermediary, and hands on to Elocution what it receives from Invention" (2001e, 59–61 = 11.2.1–11.2.3)

Quintilian's description oscillates between the two major meanings of memory as natural and as artificial, as does much of the rhetorical tradition, since the two terms can hardly be thought adequately independently of one another. Both natural and artificial memory are mediators between the other four phases of production, but they have the strongest connection to invention: as "the guardian of all the parts of rhetoric," writes the author of the *Ad Herennium*, memory is the "treasure-house of the ideas supplied by Invention" (Caplan 1964: 205 = 3.16.28), clearly linking the commonplaces of invention to *memoria* and vice versa.[67] The basic conception of artificial memory, as the book presents it, is that it consists of 'places' and 'images': "artificiosa memoria ex locis et imaginibus" (Caplan 1964: 208 = 3.16.29).[68] Orators are to develop series of pla-

---

[66] I am taking the term 'primary orality' from Walter J. Ong (2013: 133–134).
[67] For a reconstruction of the basic concept of artificial memory, it is best to turn to this anonymous handbook, since "all attempts to puzzle out what the classical art of memory was like must be mainly based on the memory section of *Ad Herennium*" (Yates [1966] 1999: 5).
[68] Given its intermedial function, the explanation of memory given in the *Ad Herennium* is, hardly surprisingly, based on the analogy of memorizing and writing: "Those who know the letters of the alphabet can thereby write out what is dictated to them and read aloud what they have written. Likewise, those who have learned mnemonics can set in [loci] what they have heard, and from these [loci] deliver it by memory. For the [loci] are very much like wax tablets

ces/loci in a distinct order that they can reuse for different speeches and then place individual images that refer iconically either to things or words in these places. Artificial memory is thus a highly complex figurative process between natural memory and a quasi poetical imagination, sharing characteristics such as the use of figurative images with rhetorical performance.

The basic principle of mnemotechnics, as the art of memory is sometimes called, has remained quite stable up to the present day. As in the case of the commonplace book, its heyday was during the Renaissance, in which intricate memory palaces and memory theatres became cultural means and obsessions, often with occult underpinnings (Yates [1966] 1999). William E. Engel (2012) has demonstrated the relevance of such memory conceptions for Poe and Melville, as they were mediated by early modern arts of memory.

What becomes visible in the history of *memoria* is that rhetorical theory offers an art of memory that has larger theoretical and cultural implications. As William N. West puts it, "[t]he study of memory encompasses not just ideas of memory at a particular historical moment, but entire regimes of memory, ways of privileging certain types of knowledge, certain values, certain ideas, beliefs, symbols—in short, an entire cultural ethnography coalesces around the apparently innocuous ability to remember the past" (2001: 484). The dimensions of communicative and cultural memory have recently been the focus of much research, especially in Germany, inaugurated by Jan Assmann's adaptation of Maurice Halbwachs' theories of memory (Assmann [1992] 2007; 2008).[69]

Rhetorical *memoria* is a key element in conceptions of authorship, not only in terms of the individual, but also in terms of those cultural institutions that inaugurate and defend specific topoi or topics as relevant. If we regard the *topoi* as the communicative and authoritative basis of literary institutions, as Frauke Berndt suggests we should, such institutions would include both the canon and the author (Berndt 2005: 43).[70] In terms of its wider implications, *memoria* thus becomes an instrument for thinking the relation between author and canon. Considered as an autheme, it can be viewed as indicative of authors' his-

---

or papyrus, the images like the letters, the arrangement and disposition of the images like the script, and the delivery is like the reading" (Caplan 1964: 209 = 3.17.30) In Caplan's (1964) otherwise excellent edition, the choice of "background" as a translation for "locus" is infelicitous, since it obscures the links to the topics of invention. I shall either speak of 'places' or use one of the classical terms, and have replaced "background/s" in this quotation accordingly.

69 For an overview and a detailed bibliography of the connections between rhetorical topoi and research on cultural memory, cf. Berndt 2005: 48–52. For the links between rhetorical *memoria* and Pierre Nora's "lieux de mémoires", cf. Den Boer (2008).

70 On rhetorical 'topoi'/topics, cf. Bloomer (2001).

torically situated difficulties with, and strategies for, inscribing themselves (and other authors) into cultural memory, especially in the shape of the canon. As an age of canon formation and the emergence of new concepts of authorship, the antebellum culture of rhetoric was an important stage in the adaptation and transformation of the performative rhetorical arts, and institutions such as the Lyceum played a central role when it came to performative figures of the author. As I show in chapters six and seven, Poe, in particular, would struggle with precisely these problems of the author, while, in the process, producing ingenious stagings of authorship in various media.

* * *

To conclude, rhetoric not only offers categories for the understanding of poetical processes and products but also integrates this poetical knowledge into a larger framework of communicative and literary theory as well as memory and performance in speech, writing, and other media. If the aim of contemporary authorship studies is to examine authorship as cultural performance in its media settings, as Berensmeyer et al. argue (2012a), then literary authorship is as much a category of poetics as it is of rhetoric.

The theoretical rhetoric of authorship as I conceive it distinguishes between theoretical, poetical, and performative figures of the author. These figures are rhetorically structured processes and products of authors' fashioning of both discourse and themselves as well as of the cultural topoi on which they base their own discourses. Figures of the author exist only in a continuum with the autonomy and heteronomy of the thinking, writing, and performing subject in particular historical situations – in this particular case, the American antebellum culture of rhetoric.

This heuristic framework is one that can only be made fruitful by its application to particular historical situations. Like any theory, this one is ultimately a system of *topoi*, or, in Kenneth Burke's term, a "terministic screen," a conceptual system that "[w]e *must* use [...], since we can't say anything without the use of terms; whatever terms we use, they necessarily constitute a corresponding kind of screen; and any such screen necessarily directs the attention to one field rather than another" (K. Burke 1973b: 50). How the terministic screens of rhetoric changed historically, in what ways they intersected with the history of the author, and to what extent they were present in the rhetorical culture of the antebellum United States is the subject of the following chapter.

2 "Under the Ban of the Empire of Literature": Print Culture, the Rise of the Author, and the Transatlantic Dispersal of Rhetoric, 1776–1849

[I]n more than one period, and in none perhaps more decidedly than our own, the very name of Rhetoric has been put under the ban of the empire of literature; and the sentence has been justified by misrepresentations both of the purposes of the art, and of the works which result from it. [...] We hear truth, good taste, and eloquence, severally spoken of as the antithesis of rhetoric.

William Spalding, *Treatise on Rhetoric*, 1839: 276

In the conclusion to his seminal monograph on *Transatlantic Insurrections: British Culture and the Formation of American Literature, 1730–1860*, Paul Giles suggests that the doubled Wilson in Poe's "William Wilson" (1839), which portrays both Wilsons' upbringing in England, is indicative of the transatlantic fissures between Britain and the United States. Giles explains the problem of Poe as a result of his evasion of the political opposition in the United States between "a genteel, postcolonial conformity and an aggressive American chauvinism" by delineating "an aesthetics of reversal, where the normative and the deviant, the familiar and the *unheimlich*, are always sliding into each other, continually complicating each other's existence" (Giles 2001: 191).

In the same year that Poe published his transatlantic Gothic tale of one Wilson's rebellion against the other, the Scottish writer and academic William Spalding published his *Treatise on Rhetoric*, lamenting the newly established empire of literature. A protégé of Francis Jeffrey, the long-time editor and virtual godfather of the *Edinburgh Review*, Spalding would become Regius Professor of Rhetoric and Belles Lettres at the University of Edinburgh a year later. The motto evinces a deep unease in the rhetorical tradition at the changes that are affecting the realm of culture. Spalding's treatise understands them through the use of rhetorical terminology such as antithesis, but, even more crucially, connects it to the emergence of what we still know today as literature. Put under the ban of the empire of literature, rhetoric appears to have become the antithesis of eloquence, one of its synonyms: a rebellious doubling of similarly momentous impact as the one depicted in Poe's tale.

My approach here is to sketch the development of how literature established its reign over rhetoric, and how this process related to the rise of the romantic author. The history of the relation between rhetoric and poetry, literature's ancestor, testifies to the fact that transatlantic rhetoric is one of the keys to understanding both authorship and literature in the period. By revisiting and interrelating the familiar master-narratives of the rise of the author and the fall of rhetoric, the emergence of literature can be read as partly a result of the struggles between rhetoric and poetry reaching back to the eighteenth century. The history of rhetoric around 1800 is thoroughly transatlantic, and the antebellum United States was characterized by the pervasive influence of belletristic rhetoric, the elocutionary movement, epistemological rhetoric, and (neo)classicist rhetoric as developed by the British, in particular Scottish, New Rhetoricians. A reconstruction of their influence on contemporary rhetorical and literary culture, in which rhetorical treatises, poetical texts, and oratorical practices circulated widely, will thus complement the current scholarly emphasis on antebellum print culture. It was precisely out of the inextricably intertwined cultures of print and rhetoric that Poe's theoretical, poetical, and performative figures of the author would develop.

2.1 The Author, Rhetoric, and the Emergence of Literature

Like Barthes' attack on the author as a category of interpretation, the crucial historicist impetus to the critique of authorship also emerged in the French debate about intertextuality, writing, and authorship in the late 1960s.[1] In contrast to Julia Kristeva and Roland Barthes, Michel Foucault conceptualised the author as a variable function of discourse and examined the conditions of the discourse about the author, moving the debate from that of the author as a systematic category of interpretation to the problem of the historical development of the author. In "What is an Author?" ("Qu'est-ce qu'un auteur?" 1969), Foucault pointed out the "classificatory function" (Foucault 1984: 107) of the author's name and distinguished between discourses that have an author function and those which do not. Its major traits are:

> (1) the author function is linked to the juridical and institutional system that encompasses, determines, and articulates the universe of discourses; (2) it does not affect all discourses in the same way at all times and in all types of civilization; (3) it is not defined by the spontaneous attribution of a discourse to its producer, but rather by a series of specific and complex operations; (4) it does not refer purely and simply to a real individual, since it can give rise simultaneously to several selves, to several subjects – positions that can be occupied by different classes of individuals (113)

---

[1] For a more detailed discussion of authorship theory and the birth of the author, cf. my article Guttzeit (2014a: 116–26), on which the following reconstruction of the rise of the author is based. For a discussion of the importance of Julia Kristeva's concept of intertextuality for the poststructuralist critique of the author and a discussion of Harold Bloom's ([1973] 1997) concept of the anxiety of influence, cf. Horn (2010: 332–334, 335–336).

For Foucault, the author exists in a cut, in a space in between the historical writer and the narrator such that there is a multiplicity of personal roles involved inside and outside the text. He argues that: "It would be just as wrong to equate the author with the real writer as to equate him with the fictitious speaker; the author function is carried out and operates in the scission itself, in this division and this distance" (112). All discourses which have the author-function evince this "plurality of self" (112). The only instance where Foucault admits something like the originality traditionally attributed to authors is in thinkers like Karl Marx and Sigmund Freud, whom he views as examples of "'founders of discursivity'" (114). Yet, for Foucault, the author remains "a certain functional principle by which, in our culture, one limits, excludes and chooses" (119). While not free of contradictions (S. Burke [1992] 2008: 86–91). Foucault's calm insistence on the historical variance of the author concept could furnish the basis for research that aimed at examining authorship as an historical phenomenon.

The Rise of the Author

The impetus of Foucault's argument was taken up by scholars such as Martha Woodmansee and Mark Rose who illuminated the politico-economic and legal conditions of the modern, or more precisely, romantic emergence of the author. As Andrew Bennett writes, "recent studies in the history of authorship suggest that the 'modern' configuration of authorship is related to developments in legal, political, economic, commercial and other discourses, to the spread of and innovation in print technology and to changes in the legal constitution of literary ownership and commercial society" (2005: 56). Analyzing late eighteenth-century German writers' responses to the emerging literary market, Woodmansee argued that "critical concepts and principles as fundamental as that of authorship achieved their modern form" in an "interplay between legal, economic, and social questions on the one hand and philosophical and esthetic ones on the other" (1984a: 440). Woodmansee has repeatedly stressed, also in collaborative articles with law professor Peter Jaszi, that "the modern regime of authorship, far from being timeless and universal, is a relatively recent formation – the result of a quite radical reconceptualization of the creative process that culminated less than 200 years ago in the heroic self-presentation of romantic poets" (Woodmansee and Jaszi 1994: 2–3).[2]

---

[2] Cf. also their edited collection on intellectual property with Mario Biagoli (Biagioli, Jaszi, and Woodmansee 2011).

The major result of this historicist research in the wake of Foucault has rightly become a commonplace: no single period has influenced modern conceptions of authorship more than the late eighteenth and early nineteenth centuries.³ When German and English Romantics developed the notion of original genius, they effectively gave birth to the author. Like many concepts still in use today, such as 'literature' itself or the 'novel', the concept of the 'author' was developed in an era of momentous socio-economic, political, and cultural changes. The American and French revolutions, the beginnings of industrialisation, ongoing secularisation and the further development of liberalism and individualism conjoined with the aforementioned emergence of the capitalist marketplace, the rise of printing technologies, and the institution of copyright law.

In terms of intellectual history, works like Edward Young's *Conjectures on Original Composition* (1759) and Karl Philipp Moritz's "An Attempt to Unify All the Fine Arts and Sciences under the Concept of That Which Is Complete in Itself" ([1785] 2012) developed an understanding of literary production in stark contrast to the image of the poet as a competent artisan that had dominated neoclassicism and other earlier periods. Such 'proto-romantic' thoughts were taken up by the romantics in Germany and Britain and elsewhere. "The Romantic theory of authorship," writes Andrew Bennett in his monograph, *The Author*, "may be said to account for everything that is commonly or conventionally taken to be implied by talk of 'the author'" (2005: 56).⁴

The key legal development that accompanied the emergence of the author – namely, copyright – had ties both to political censorship and to the literary market. Examining the history of copyright before and after the first copyright law, the Statute of Anne (1710), Mark Rose maintains that "the notion of the author

---

3 For recent work on authorship in the eighteenth century, cf. Hammerschmidt, Guttzeit, and Buelens (2015).
4 This becomes especially clear if we look back beyond the hiatus between the neoclassical and the romantic author. Antiquity developed a rich vocabulary for different aspects of the writer such as the 'learned poet' (*poeta doctus*). The major systematic opposition of the autonomous writer and the heteronomous writer took the form of two well-known terms: the *poeta faber*, meaning the poet as artisan, and the *poeta vates*, the poet who is inspired (or enthused) by the gods. Put in very broad terms, the medieval writer was thought of more as a copyist relying on authorities sanctioned by the Catholic Church, rather than being an author himself, as is shown, for instance, by the then prominent practice of the commentary. In the Renaissance, writers and thinkers became once again interested in the lives of individual artists and writers, as works like Giorgio Vasari's *Lives of the Most Eminent Painters, Sculptors, and Architects* (1550) evinced, but for English and American literature and culture none of these changes compares to the birth of the romantic author. Cf. Guttzeit (2014a: 116–117).

[...] as a cultural formation [...] is inseparable from the commodification of literature" (1993: 1). For Rose, what makes the modern author "is proprietorship; the author is conceived as the originator and therefore the owner of a special kind of commodity, the work" (1).

This economic and legal background partly explains the increasing emphasis on originality in eighteenth- and nineteenth-century Romanticism. Before Romanticism, neoclassical poets and critics such as John Dryden, Alexander Pope, and Samuel Johnson, in a mimetic theory of literature sensu Abrams, had stressed the importance of technique and of generally accepted truths (understood as 'nature' but also connected to Aristotelian ideas of the philosophical character of the drama). The most frequently quoted example is Alexander Pope's characterisation of wit, one of the central traits of the poet, in his *Essay on Criticism* (1711): "*True Wit* is *Nature* to Advantage drest/What oft was *Thought*, but ne'er so well *Exprest*" (1961: 272–273 = lines 297–98).[5] In accordance with ancient and Renaissance rhetorical and poetical thought, Pope and others did not define poets by their creative powers or their capacity to discover new and original thoughts, but – broadly conceived – viewed them as artisans whose words aptly phrase self-evident truths or worlds that the poet had created (as in Philip Sidney).[6]

As the importance of originality for the definition of the poet increased, so the importance of craft decreased, and it was supplanted by an emphasis on the inspired expression of a unique individual. Inspiration no longer came from outside, from the gods as in antiquity or what neoclassicism thought of as 'nature', but from inside the genius:

> as [moments of inspiration] are increasingly credited to the writer's own genius, they transform the writer into a unique individual uniquely responsible for a unique product. That is, from a (mere) vehicle of preordained truths – truths as ordained either by universal human agreement or by some higher agency – the *writer* becomes an *author* (Woodmansee 1984a: 429)

At the end of this trajectory, it was the inner life of the poet that was to be expressed in literature – and not generally accepted truths *sensu* Pope. The most frequently quoted example of this is William Wordsworth's claim in the preface to the later editions of *Lyrical Ballads* (1798/1800) that "Poetry is the spontane-

---

[5] The editors E. Audra and Aubrey Williams (Pope 1961: 272) rightly link this to Quintilian's principle of observing nature and then following it: "naturam intueamur, hanc sequamur" (2001c: 380–381 = 8.3.71)

[6] Cf. the editors' arguments on Pope's relation to rhetoric in the introduction to the Essay on Criticism (Pope 1961: 212–22).

ous overflow of powerful feelings: it takes its origin from emotion recollected in tranquillity" (1991: 251).

Overall, then, the romantic author was defined as an inspired male individual who created original literature by expressing his own inner nature. Shakespeare and Goethe came to be seen as the pinnacle of literary genius in Britain and Germany respectively, and their genius was absorbed into national(ist) historical narratives. Not only does the romantic model of authorship still inform the everyday understanding of the author, but it also remains one of the focal points of debate in literary and cultural theory. One of the least researched aspects in the field is the historical interrelation with rhetoric.

Rhetoric: Fall, Suppression, Dispersal?

The rise of the author coincided with what is often called the fall of rhetoric, as the eighteenth and nineteenth centuries saw the decline of rhetoric as a university discipline and as a field of knowledge. As Joachim Knape writes: "In most European countries, the study of rhetoric as a formal subject disappeared from university curricula in the 18th and 19th centuries, replaced by the various branches of philology and other disciplines in the humanities" (2013: 1). In the United States this process took place later than in Europe (Berlin 1996: xiv) and rhetoric in general remained a stronger force in theory, politics, and literature. In both Europe and the United States, the (partial) disappearance was the result of a longer-running process, of which the transformation of rhetorical thought into psychology is a striking example. Daniel Gross has reconstructed the rhetorical history of the concept of emotions in which affects central to political rhetoric came to be naturalised in psychology: "overtly political rhetoric in the context of the English Civil War was transformed into an implicit epistemology in the Age of Sensibility and beyond" (Gross 2006: xiv). As was the case with other aspects of rhetorical knowledge, which became the basis of modern criticism or aesthetics, for example, this process was one of dispersion and reduction: "Seventeenth-century political rhetoric [...] became a generalized psychology thereafter, and passions that were once overtly rhetorical, such as anger, pride, and humility, now quietly gird the Western system of belief that emotion is hardwired to the human nature we all share equally" (Gross 2006: xiv). Thus concepts of rhetorical character were being transformed as certain sciences such as psychology took on their modern shape in the seventeenth and later centuries.

With regard to literature, the romantic conceptions both of the author and of poetry were central in the process of the marginalisation of rhetoric. At the end of this process, rhetoric came to be understood as a theory of the merely figurative dress of thought, and ceased to be viewed as a theory of communication.[7] In the romantic age, the concept and practice of poetry changed fundamentally as rhetoric-as-communication was transformed into rhetoric-as-mere-style. Since High Romanticism regarded neoclassicist poetry as a language without connection to authenticity or originality, it consequently redefined poetry in terms of the poet's expression of feeling, as essentially an uncommunicative communication. This mirrors some of the general characteristics of romantic ideology, as Jerome McGann has analysed it: "The polemic of Romantic poetry [...] is that it will not be polemical; its doctrine, that it is non-doctrinal; and its ideology, that it transcends ideology" ([1983] 1999: 69–70).

The upheaval created by this major shift to the author and away from rhetoric can hardly be overstated, since these two processes are central with regard to the emergence of the very concept of *literature* in "the process of cultural reorganization that attended the transition from feudal to capitalist society in the early nineteenth century" (White 1997: 21). *Literature* replaced older terms such as *poetry* and younger terms such as *belles lettres* to become one of the central terms in what Raymond Williams aptly described as the "modern complex of **literature**, *art*, *aesthetic*, *creative* and *imaginative*" (1985: 186). In *Keywords*, Williams mapped out the central semantic shifts in the term that are indicative of larger developments in social and cultural history. Beginning as a late medieval and Renaissance "isolation of the skills of reading and of the qualities of the book," which was connected to the arts of grammar and rhetoric, *literature* is reinterpreted in Romanticism, at the precise time when the strong concept of the author emerges. *Literature* replaces the older term, *poetry*, which was still connected to notions of *poiesis* (in the sense discussed in chapter one):

> Then **literature** was specialized towards *imaginative writing*, within the basic assumptions of Romanticism. It is interesting to see what word did service for this before the specialization. It was, primarily, *poetry*, defined in 1586 as 'the arte of making: which word as it hath alwaies beene especially used of the best of our English Poets, to express the very faculty of speaking or wryting Poetically' (note the inclusion of speaking). (R. Williams 1985: 186–87)[8]

Williams goes on to explain why literature was most likely, semantically, to emerge as the new general term, stressing the relation of writing and speaking:

---

[7] On rhetoric and communication, cf. chapter one and Guttzeit (2016); on style as the dress of thought, cf. chapter six.
[8] The Renaissance quote is from William Webbe's *A Discourse of Englishe Poetrie* (1586).

2.1 The Author, Rhetoric, and the Emergence of Literature — 61

> It is probable that [the] specialization of *poetry* to verse, together with the increasing importance of prose forms such as the NOVEL [...], made **literature** the most available general word. It had behind it the Renaissance sense of *litterae humanae*, mainly then for secular as distinct from religious writing, and a generalizing use of *letters* had followed from this. *Belles lettres* was developed in French from [the mid-seventeenth century]; it was to narrow when *literature* was eventually established. *Poetry* had been the high skills of writing and speaking in the special context of high imagination; the word could be moved in either direction. **Literature**, in its [nineteenth-century] sense, repeated this, though excluding speaking. (R. Williams 1985: 187)

Williams repeatedly stresses the exclusion of speaking in the emergence of literature. While *poetry* or *poesy* still meant an art of both writing and speaking for the Renaissance writer, this changed in the age of print culture and the literary period of Romanticism. Indeed, one might say that the birth of writing in the sense of *literature* occurred at the cost of speaking.

The same is true of the discipline of rhetoric that was conceived of as a general theory of both spoken and written discourse before its (temporary) "fall" (Booth 2004: 26) in the nineteenth century. There have been a variety of suggestions as to how one should understand this development of rhetoric in the eighteenth and nineteenth centuries: as the "death" (Sutton 1986), the "end" (Bender and Wellbery 1990), the "transformation" of rhetoric (Till 2004), or the "long goodbye" to rhetoric (Uhlig 2012). A common way of narrating this development was espoused by Paul Ricoeur, which is the all more striking because of Ricoeur's engagement with the complexities of Aristotelian rhetoric and poetics, particularly metaphor and mimesis: "Rhetoric died when the penchant for classifying figures of speech completely supplanted the philosophical sensibility that animated the vast empire of rhetoric, held its parts together, and tied the whole to the *organon* and to first philosophy" (Ricoeur 2003: 9). Here, Ricoeur clearly takes the position of philosophy rather than rhetoric in its own right and only looks at its development in France (rather than in the US, for instance). What is even more telling is Ricoeur's rhetorical strategy of personifying rhetoric as someone with an almost inexplicable penchant for classifying. In this abbreviated version of rhetoric's demise, rhetoric itself becomes the major agent in "reducing *itself* [...] to one of its parts" (Ricoeur 2003: 9; my emphasis). Such an abstract account forecloses rather than invites the possibility of a reconstruction of the cultural history of rhetoric.

In contrast, viewing the development of rhetoric in larger socio-economic, political and cultural contexts, Hayden White's summary of the nineteenth-century developments as a process of the "suppression of rhetoric" is far more suggestive. Put very briefly, White's thesis is that rhetoric was excluded from the spread of literacy in the nineteenth century and remained a theory of and for the elites, whom it furnished with a theory of political discourse. In a passage worth quoting at length, he explains why what he calls the suppression of rhetoric was a condition for the emergence of literature:

> before the invention of 'literature' in the nineteenth century, rhetoric effectively served as a science of speaking, writing, and reading on the basis of which instruction in their processes of production could be – and was – provided. This is why the suppression of rhetoric was a necessary precondition for the separation of literary from other kinds of writing, the constitution of 'literature' as the virtual antithesis of mere literacy, and the establishment of the myth of the unteachability of the latter as against the teachability of the former. [...] [T]he terms *literacy* and *literature* [...] belong to the same process of a general reorganization of culture as that which attends the establishment and integration of the nation-state, the transition from an 'estate' to a 'class' organization of society, the advent of corporate capitalism, and the transformation of the masses from subjects into citizens capable of taking their place as functionaries in a system of production and exchange for profit rather than use. The separation of what had formerly been called belles lettres from the general domain of 'discourse,' of which it once had been considered to be a branch or department, and its elevation to a new status for the designation of which the term *literature* was coined, were effects of this process of cultural reorganization. From that point on, literature would be regarded as a kind of writing, the value of which lay in part precisely in its differentness not only from speech but also from the kind of writing that would henceforth be considered to be merely literate. (White 1997: 22–23)

The exclusion of speaking from literature, which Williams traced, is thus mirrored in, if not identical with, the exclusion of rhetoric from the domain of 'true' literature. White's framing of the development is especially useful, since it does not focus on technology, in this case, print technologies, as most other accounts of the antebellum situation tend to do. He unfolds the emancipatory dangers of rhetoric as a body of knowledge intimately connected to power over others, making clear why the connection of rhetoric to power is not a thing of aristocratic regimes of the past, but continues to be relevant in democratic societies.

In contrast to isolated accounts of the fall, death, decline, or end of rhetoric, White thus suggests a grounding of the nineteenth-century development of rhetoric in the political, social, and economic developments of the time. While his view of the suppression of rhetoric is certainly polemical, he is also careful to stress that this does not entail the complete eradication of rhetorical knowledge, but rather that the political elites of the nineteenth century transformed rhetorical knowledge to retain its use for elites alone and not for the masses because as a discipline rhetoric "claims also to know the secret of practical speech, speech in its active, conative, and political uses, speech as an instrument of power and rule" (1997: 28). Rhetoricians Andreea Ritivoi and Richard Graff agree in viewing the rise of literature and the end of rhetoric as central aspects of the emergence of the humanities curriculum in the nineteenth century: "the rise of Literature did influence major developments in humanities instruction in institutions of higher education, developments that did little to accommodate traditional rhetoric" (Ritivoi and Graff 2008: 945). The institutional development of rhetoric in the nineteenth century is explicable as a result of changing social power relations.

The fate of rhetoric was thus closely tied to the rise of literature and aesthetics in general, as romantic and utilitarian aesthetics isolated the poetical text and turned it into a literary one.[9] The philosophical discipline of aesthetics was itself one of the major transformations of rhetorical knowledge, as the abundance of rhetorical categories in A. G. Baumgarten's *Aesthetica* (1750) demonstrates.[10] In John Poulakos' (2007: 335) words, one might say that the discipline of aesthetics emerged "[f]rom the depths of rhetoric." The process of aestheticization in the nineteenth century included the sacralization of the literary text as against the mundane rhetorical text that was crucial for the foundation of the discipline of English, as James Berlin argued: "English studies was founded on a set of hierarchical binary oppositions in which literary texts were given an idealized status approaching the sacred." Against these newly defined literary works, "rhetorical texts and their production were portrayed as embodiments of the fallen realms of science and commerce and politics, validating in their corrupt materiality the spiritual beauties of their opposite" (Berlin 1996: xiv).[11] One of the inevitable results of this sacralization was the idea that the production of poetical texts could not be taught in the way that mundane 'rhetorical' writing could be.[12] As White delineates the decisive link between rhetoric and poetry in the nineteenth century: "Rhetoric claims to know the secret of the mode of expression called poetical, and this is why, from the standpoint of

---

9 Cf. White (1997: 28). For the most extensive discussion, especially of the German idealist origins of the ideology of the aesthetic, cf. Eagleton (1990). For a re-affirmation of aesthetic categories cf. Loesberg (2005).
10 Cf. the full Latin-German edition in two volumes Baumgarten (2007).
11 Besides the aestheticization of literature, White also points to the strategies of the feminisation of literary writing and its reinterpretation as a luxury by utilitarian thinkers (White 1997: 24–25; 23). For Poe's response to utilitarian thinking about literature, cf. the discussion in chapter three.
12 One of the best examples is the institutional resistance to creative writing programmes, particularly in Germany. Creative writing programmes came to be of paramount importance for American post-World War II writing (McGurl 2009). The programmes were adopted in the UK from the 1970s onwards, and Germany – with a couple of exceptions – still retains a particular resistance to such programmes (Glindemann 2001).

the modern ideology of aestheticism, it had to be suppressed" (1997: 28), or, in other words, this is how rhetoric came under the ban of the empire of literature.

The situation in the United States is particular in two regards, because the rhetorical tradition has been especially strong ever since the revolutionary era. Hence, my suggestion is to view the relation between the fall and suppression of rhetoric in Europe and the ongoing importance of the culture of rhetoric in the US as a situation of dispersal. For one, the dispersal of rhetoric happens later than in other Western countries, as scholars such as Nan Johnson and James Berlin have pointed out: "rhetoric served as the very core of the college curriculum in the United States until the late nineteenth century, as it in fact had in most Western societies up to the end of the eighteenth century" (Berlin 1996: xiv). Another factor, peculiar to the antebellum period, is the presence of rhetorical concepts and practices in the culture of rhetoric, which, while not as all-encompassing as that of the earlier heydays of rhetoric in antiquity or in the Renaissance, remained a pervasive aspect of the culture. What is similar to other Western countries, however, is the replacement of poetry as the encompassing term for what then came to be known as literature and its empire.

2.2 The Effects of Poetry from the New Rhetoric to Romantic Aesthetics

In order to trace the dispersal of rhetoric and the replacement of 'poetry' by 'literature' in more detail, the second section of this chapter is devoted to a comparison of eighteenth-century rhetorical accounts of poetry with accounts that are indicative of the specialisation of poetry in romantic and utilitarian accounts contemporary with Poe. These accounts are a testament to the emergence of *literature* in the way that Williams and White have analysed it, a development that also entails a reinterpretation of rhetorical discourse as *eloquence*. This process is epitomized in John Stuart Mill's metaphorical summary of the change from poetry as something that is heard to something that is overheard. The larger critical development in which this transformation of poetry stands moved from the British New Rhetoric of the eighteenth century to romantic aesthetics. The most striking thing about these discussions is the continuing relevance of rhetorical terminology based on the triad of the effects of discourse (as discussed in chapter one), especially in the United States.

The explicit critical efforts between the 1770s and the 1830s to define the borders between poetry and what the period calls "eloquence" – according to Spalding spoken of as the antithesis of rhetoric – are part of the process of the dispersal of rhetoric and the rise of the author and literature.[13] This period of change can be bookended by the first publication of the Scottish New Rhetorician George Campbell's *The Philosophy of Rhetoric* in 1776 on the one hand, and by John Stuart Mill's famous 1833 essay "Thoughts on Poetry and Its Varieties," on the other. In Campbell and Mill we find diametrically opposed positions which are traces of a central development in the theory of the relation between rhetoric and poetry that is crucial for the question of the emergence of literature and the decline of rhetoric.[14] American conceptions of the relation of rhetorical and poetical discourse of the same time, most notably by William Cullen Bryant, also evince a strong continuity of rhetorical thinking about poetry that contrasts with Mill's negation of the audience. The debate, which is shaped by other thinkers and writers such as Richard Whately and Thomas De Quincey, evinces a general characteristic that is crucial for Poe's times: while rhetoric is ostensibly opposed to poetry, this opposition is still framed in terms which are themselves highly rhetorical. While Campbell's and Mill's positions are diametrically opposed they both use the same rhetorical vocabulary to articulate their arguments.[15] The debate between them centres on one of, if not the, most fundamental of all rhetorical categories: the effect of discourse on the recipient.

Hearing Poetry in George Campbell

When it comes to the distinction between rhetorical and poetical discourse around 1800, the crucial element is the audience. Of the rhetorical theorists, George Campbell is the most explicit on this score: for him, rhetoric is all about the effect on the audience that the speaker or writer attempts to achieve.[16] The first chapter of his *The Philosophy of Rhetoric* opens thus:

> In speaking there is always some end proposed, or some effect which the speaker intends to produce on the hearer. The word *eloquence* in its greatest latitude denotes, 'That art or talent by which the discourse is adapted to its end.' ([1776] 1988: 1)

---

[13] Cf. Engell (1995), which is a revised version of Engell (1989: 194–219). The importance of the term "eloquence" is already given in earlier times, especially the Renaissance, yet its interpretation changes significantly in Romanticism. Cf. e.g. Skinner (1996) on Hobbes.
[14] The following argument on the development in Britain is based on my Anglistentag 2013 paper "From Hearing to Overhearing? Eloquence and Poetry, 1776–1833" (Guttzeit 2014b).
[15] This is representative of a certain continuity of rhetoric in Romanticism under the surface. Cf. Bialostosky and Needham (1995).
[16] General studies of Campbell include Suderman (2001) and Walzer (2003). For an overview of the research on Campbell, cf. particularly Walzer (2003: 127–138).

Rhetorical discourse is thus not at all restricted to an orator speaking, but encompasses all purposeful human communication. For Campbell, rhetoric is "the grand art of communication, not of ideas only, but of sentiments, passions, dispositions, and purposes" ([1776] 1988: lxxiii).[17] Necessarily, the focus on effective discourse goes hand in hand with a focus on the audience: "The necessity which a speaker is under of suiting himself to his audience, both that he may be understood by them, and that his words may have influence upon them, is a maxim so evident as to need neither proof nor illustration" ([1776] 1988: 102).

While Campbell is working in the empiricist tradition of rhetorical theory from Adam Smith to Hugh Blair,[18] the scope of his project is unique: his *Philosophy of Rhetoric* initiates the epistemological tradition in that he conceives rhetoric as a universal art of communication grounded in empirical observations of successful oratorical and writerly practice. As Arthur Walzer phrases it, "Campbell never intended to produce a handbook. His work is a theory, involving an account of belief relevant to a theory of rhetoric" (2003: 137). Campbell's project is thus not a practical rhetoric, but an examination of the interrelation between rhetorical theory and the Enlightenment philosophy of the human, as theorised especially by David Hume: a science, not an art.[19]

Campbell's central theoretical move, however, is representative of rhetorical theory far beyond the eighteenth century, since it applies the rhetorical triad of the ends or effects of a discourse, including the general end of *persuadere*. As we saw in chapter one, Campbell takes the triad of *docere*, *delectare*, and *movere*, and, in line with a Humean distinction,[20] assigns each function a specific mental faculty: "All the ends of speaking are reducible to four; every speech being intended to enlighten the understanding, to please the imagination, to move the passions, or to influence the will" ([1776] 1988: 1). Different versions of this

---

17 Walzer explains that this definition, which Campbell also uses in his *Lectures on Systematic Theology and Pulpit Eloquence* (1807), was developed by Campbell together with Alexander Gerard (Walzer 2003: 39). Gerard is the author of the *Essay on Genius* (1774), who redefined the rhetorical canon of invention as a (teachable) associative process (Larsen 1993).
18 Its main philosophical guarantors are Francis Bacon and David Hume. For an overview cf. Bevilacqua (1968).
19 Campbell himself conceived of the development of rhetoric as having four stages, the third being the art and the last the science (Campbell [1776] 1988: lxxxiv). Cf. the discussion in chapter four and Bevilacqua (1968).
20 Walzer explains: "Though the general inspiration for linking faculties with discourse types was *The Advancement of Learning* [...], the particular faculties that Campbell identifies are not exactly Bacon's. The faculties listed here—understanding, imagination, passions, and will—are the same as those listed by Hume in the *Enquiry*, though the list is fairly common" (Walzer 2003: 40)

scheme would be used to define poetry not only by rhetoricians in the wake of Campbell but also by John Stuart Mill, William Cullen Bryant, and, as I shall argue in part II, Edgar Allan Poe. For now, the focus is on drawing out some of the general characteristics of such rhetorical definitions of poetry around 1800.

How does poetry fit into the rhetorical system in Campbell's *Philosophy of Rhetoric?* For Campbell, poetry mainly has the end of pleasing the imagination and moving the passions, but it can also fulfil the other functions. For Campbell, poetry is one kind of rhetorical discourse (here he uses the synonymous term "oratory"), a view for which he argues as follows:

> Poetry indeed is properly no other than a particular mode or form of certain branches of oratory. [...] [T]he direct end of the former, whether to delight the fancy as in epic, or to move the passions as in tragedy, is avowedly in part the aim, and sometimes the immediate and proposed aim, of the orator. The same medium, language, is made use of; the same general rules of composition, in narration, description, argumentation, are observed; and the same tropes and figures, either for beautifying or for invigorating the diction, are employed by both. ([1776] 1988: lxxiii)

That Campbell subsumes poetry under rhetorical discourse is no surprise, since he understands rhetoric as a general theory of communication. The argument for this subsumption is clearly one of the unity of the two, albeit not as equal partners: rhetorical and poetical discourse have similar ends, the same general and particular means, and follow the same rules. The governing discipline, however, is rhetoric. For Campbell, poetry is first and foremost a kind of rhetorical communication in the traditional genres of epic, drama, and satire.[21] It is capable of an Aristotelian type of poetic truth,[22] but its main appeal is to please the imagination, while it can also move the passions and, to an extent, move the will and enlighten the understanding. Like all rhetorical discourse, it is made for produc-

---

21 The third genre that Campbell distinguishes is not lyric poetry as renaissance and romantic conceptions of the generic triad would have comprehended it, but satire, which figures the poet as reasoner (Campbell [1776] 1988: 22). In a section entitled "Words considered as Sounds," he discusses onomatopoeia and other phonetic devices. Based on Alexander Pope's precept that the sound be made an echo to the sense, he examines examples chiefly from Pope and Milton in terms of how they imitate aspects of reality. He discusses the imitation of sound, motion, size, difficulty and ease, and the agreeable, establishing a typology of possible representative functions of the sound of words (Campbell [1776] 1988: 317–333).
22 Campbell speaks of "general truths regarding character, manners, and incidents. When these are preserved, the piece may justly be denominated true, considered as a picture of life; though false, considered as a narrative of particular events." ([1776] 1988: 33).

ing an effect on an audience through particular linguistic means. Like all rhetorical discourse, poetry is written to be heard.

Whilst published in the year of the American Revolution, Campbell's treatise had its strongest influence in the nineteenth century, particularly in the American antebellum culture of rhetoric. Students at British and American universities thus regularly came in contact with a rhetorical theory of poetry, the institutional background of which I shall outline in more detail below.

Campbell's continuing influence in Britain is evidenced by the last major treatise of the New Rhetoric: in 1828, responding mainly to Campbell, Richard Whately, the English Archbishop of Dublin, wrote *Elements of Rhetoric*, a work that was to be reviewed by Thomas De Quincey. Whately is acutely aware of the different possibilities of how to think the relation of rhetoric to poetry: he states that "some writers have spoken of Rhetoric as the Art of Composition, universally; or, with the exclusion of Poetry alone, as embracing all Prose-composition" (1828: 4).[23] In contrast to Campbell's general theory of communication, however, Whately views rhetoric as an "off-shoot from Logic": Logic is a monologic process of investigation, whereas rhetoric is "*Argumentative Composition*" (Whately 1828: 6) responsible for "*conveying truth* to others" (Whately 1828: 23).[24]

Whately's somewhat implicit definition of poetry consists essentially of three elements. His discussion builds on Campbell's argument for the truth of fictions and enlarges it with the notion of plausibility as one kind of probability, thus tying poetry to persuasion in an Aristotelian way (1828: 39). The second aspect of poetry he mentions is feeling: "The art of addressing the feelings [...] does not belong exclusively to Rhetoric, since Poetry has at least as much to do with the branch" (1828: 29–30). The third aspect besides plausibility and feeling is style, which he discusses in connection to the elegance of the argumentative composition: "Nor are the considerations relative to Style and Elocution confined to argumentative and persuasive compositions" (1828: 30). For Whately, poetry is thus an art of addressing the feelings by means of plausibility and style.

Whately's *Elements of Rhetoric* is a link to romantic conceptions of rhetoric, since it was reviewed, or rather used as a springboard, by Thomas De Quincey: he takes a decisive leap towards Mill's argument in what he himself called an "excursive review" of Whately's book. It first appeared in December 1828 in *Blackwood's Magazine*, not only one of the most important British literary jour-

---

[23] Douglas Ehninger reprinted the seventh British edition of 1846, which is augmented, in Whately ([1828] 1963). In order to chart the chronological development, I cite the second edition of *Elements of Rhetoric* (1828) in this section.
[24] It should be noted in passing that, despite this stated restriction, Whately in fact discusses a plethora of topics in science, philosophy, and religion.

nals but also one of the most widely received and copied in the United States by many readers, including Poe. De Quincey's verdict connects Whately with Campbell: "Dr Whately's is incomparably the best book of its class, since the days of Campbell's *Philosophy of Rhetoric*" (1828: 908).

Despite this connection, there are enormous differences between De Quincey and his more traditional rhetorical presursors. De Quincey no longer speaks about poetical discourse in the way that Campbell and Whately did, by connecting it to truth and plausibility. While he also discusses poetry, he is much more concerned with the notion of probability in the context of argumentation, discussing the notion of the enthymeme at great length.[25] De Quincey diagnoses the circulation of two contemporary ideas of rhetoric: "one of which is occupied with the general end of the fine arts; that is to say, intellectual pleasure" (1828: 885). In this department of intellectual pleasure, De Quincey finds the highest rhetorical powers in the works of poets from Philip Sidney to John Milton. The other idea concerns the bad public image of rhetoric: this idea "applies itself more specifically to a definite purpose of utility" (1828: 885), a utility that De Quincey would 'clarify' in later editions: "utility, viz., fraud" (1862: 22).

The decisive distinction De Quincey makes is one between eloquence and rhetoric in terms of the key romantic opposition between authenticity and artificiality, which are no longer to be viewed as identical as they were in Campbell. What De Quincey does is to separate rhetoric and eloquence by taking up William Wordsworth's definitions of poetry, to the extent of echoing his very phrases:

> By Eloquence, we understand the overflow of powerful feelings upon occasions fitted to excite them. But Rhetoric is the art of aggrandizing and bringing out into strong relief, by means of various and striking thoughts, some aspect of truth which of itself is supported by no spontaneous feelings, and therefore rests upon artificial aids. (1828: 888)

Artificial aids versus spontaneous and powerful feelings, aggrandizing versus overflow: De Quincey inherits many of the romantic oppositions, confirming to some extent M. H. Abrams's distinction between the expressive theories of Romanticism which focus on the author in contrast with the pragmatic theories of neoclassicism that focus on the audience. The dialectics of affection and self-affection, as posited by Quintilian (discussed in chapter one), is now regarded as articifial rather than artistic. As Wellek phrases it, rhetoric in De Quincey is

---

[25] In Aristotle's *Rhetoric*, the enthymeme is the "rhetorical syllogism" paired with the paradigm as "rhetorical induction" (Aristotle 2007: 40=1356b).

defined as "unemotional mental pyrotechnics" ([1965] 1966: 113).²⁶ Hence, De Quincey's response to Whately is crucial, since he romanticises eloquence and claims it as the right kind of rhetoric.

The romantic transformation of the understanding of poetry thus occurs at the same time as the redefinition of rhetoric. There is a development from Campbell's universal theory of rhetoric which includes poetry, to Whately's connection of poetry and feeling, and to De Quincey's reinterpretation of rhetoric as being opposed to eloquence. This process of gradual reduction or restriction reaches its apex in John Stuart Mill's notion of poetry as discourse that is overheard. Mill's position is crucial for and representative of the momentous changes affecting rhetoric, poetry, and literature in the romantic and postromantic age.

Overhearing Poetry in John Stuart Mill

The opposition of eloquence and poetry in terms of the effect on an audience is nowhere as obvious as in Mill's essay, "Thoughts on Poetry and its Varieties" (1833). Later, in *A System of Logic* (1843), Mill would in fact define rhetoric along similar lines to Whately: "The sole object of Logic is the guidance of one's own thoughts: the communication of those thoughts to others falls under the consideration of Rhetoric, in the large sense in which that art was conceived by the ancients" ([1843] 1974: 6).²⁷ Yet "Thoughts on Poetry" reads, in many ways, like a response to the distinction between rhetoric and poetics by the New Rhetoricians, and its central metaphor has become a locus classicus of the relation between poetical and rhetorical discourse as understood by Romanticism.

In the section on the question of "What is Poetry?", Mill deals with the differentia specifica of poetry in contrast to other aspects of literary texts, comparing it at first to narrative and description.²⁸ The last aspect from which Mill believes he must distinguish poetry – and the one that he dwells on the longest – is that of eloquence. Mill writes:

> Poetry and eloquence are both alike the expression or utterance of feeling. But if we may be excused the antithesis, we should say that eloquence is *heard*, poetry is *over*heard. (Mill [1833] 1981: 348)

---

26 Wellek ([1965] 1966: 113) also discusses the resulting contradictions of De Quincey's conception of rhetoric for his notion of a "literature of power."
27 Cp. the discussion of Poe's explicit definition of rhetoric in chapter three.
28 In his argument for poetry as a kind of oratory, Campbell says "the same general rules of composition, in narration, description, argumentation, are observed" (Campbell [1776] 1988: lxxiii)

While focusing on feeling, Mill is more than aware of the rhetorical tradition and its classification of effects. "Eloquence," writes Mill, echoing neorhetorical classifications of effects, "is feeling pouring itself out to other minds, courting their sympathy, or endeavouring to influence their belief, or move them to passion or to action" (Mill [1833] 1981: 348–349).

The similarities between Mill's and Campbell's enumerations of functions are striking. Both classifications are apparently based on the rhetorical triad of effects. As explained earlier, *persuadere* is not usually conceived as a fourth effect in ancient sources but as the ultimate effect to which the three others are subordinated. Its meaning, however, corresponds quite closely to Campbell's and Mill's fourth categories:

Types of effect	Docere	Delectare	Movere	(Persuadere)
Campbell's faculties	Understanding	Imagination	Passions	Will
Campbell's ends of discourse	Enlighten the understanding	Please the imagination	Move the passions	Influence the will
Mill's ends of eloquence	Endeavouring to influence other minds' belief	Courting other minds' sympathy	Move other minds to passion	Move other minds to action

In accordance with his attempt to ground rhetoric in a Humean science of man, Campbell also interprets the types of effect in terms of their corresponding faculties.[29] The differences between Campbell's and Mill's possible ends of discourses are few, yet telling: in every aspect, Mill inserts the phrase "other minds" (or "their") as if to stress an orientation towards an audience – which, for Campbell, goes without saying. In other words, while rhetorical conceptions assume the presence and importance of other persons in any communicative act, Mill's conception of eloquence is so solitary to begin with that he needs to add the reference to other persons. In terms of content, Mill's possible ends of discourse seem to differ only with regard to the imagination: Campbell's 'pleasing the imagination' is set against 'courting other minds' sympathy.'[30] Whatever the

---

[29] While historically specific in its form, this conceptual oscillation between function of discourse and mental faculty repeats itself in the history of rhetoric, for instance in the *Ad Herennium*, as I argued in chapter one.

[30] The link between the two might lie in the concept of the sympathetic imagination. As Walter Jackson Bate argued in a seminal essay, the sympathetic imagination was one of the key ideas taken over from the eighteenth century Common Sense School (which more or less includes the New Rhetoricians) by Romantic authors and critics. Epitomizing Alexander Gerard's *Essay on*

precise origin of Mill's "sympathy," the systematical similarities to Campbell outweigh the differences by far.

There is, however, one key difference: Campbell and Mill disagree in their general definitions. Campbell views all rhetorical discourse as a relation of ends and means, defining eloquence as "That art or talent by which the discourse is adapted to its end" (Campbell [1776] 1988: 1). This is where the difference in frameworks lies, since Mill's definition speaks of "feeling pouring itself out" (Mill [1833] 1981: 348).

For Mill, even rhetorical discourse thus lies strangely outside the relation of ends and means. And this holds even more true for his definition of poetry: "Poetry is feeling, confessing itself to itself in moments of solitude, and embodying itself in symbols, which are the nearest possible representations of the feeling in the exact shape in which it exists in the poet's mind" (Mill [1833] 1981: 348). While the poet is central in Mill's definition, it is striking that he is so only in the sense of a space where poetry can happen. It is personified feeling that is engaged in solitary confession and embodies "itself" in romantic symbols. Because of its figurative character, the theoretical figure of the author that Mill establishes veers towards complete heteronomy. Poetry is a soliloquy that hardly even requires the poet, let alone an audience.

Mill tempers this extreme personification somewhat in his explanations, but he retains an absolute negation of dialogicity, of any audience whatsoever:

> when [the poet] turns round and addresses himself to another person; when the act of utterance is not itself the end, but a means to an end—viz. by the feelings he himself expresses, to work upon the feelings, or upon the belief, or the will, of another,—when the expression of his emotions, or of his thoughts tinged by his emotions, is tinged also by that purpose, by that desire of making an impression upon another mind, then it ceases to be poetry, and becomes eloquence (Mill [1833] 1981: 349)

Overhearing presupposes a discourse that is audible. Consequently, Mill thinks of all poetry as a soliloquy, born in the inner life of the poet and 'untinged' by the rules of art. As part of romantic ideology, this view is long-lived. What is more, Mill, who was of course no literary critic, is here the purer romantic than Wordsworth, who was more open about some of the rhetorical dimensions of his poetry. In the Preface to *Lyrical Ballads*, for instance, Wordsworth states that his habits of meditation formed his feelings in such a way that his poetical

---

Genius (1774), Bate writes: "The creative imagination, under the influence of a passion prompted in the poet by sympathetic identification, comprehends and then fuses into a concrete totality all that gives birth to that passion and serves as vent to it" (1945: 154).

descriptions "will be found to carry along with them a *purpose*. If in this opinion I am mistaken I can have little right to the name of a Poet" (1991: 237).

Nevertheless, Mill's statement was by no means singular but encapsulates in unusually pure form the tendency to redefine poetry and with it rhetoric and literature in the early nineteenth century. Originally appearing in the journal *Monthly Repository*, Mill's text indicates a turning point in the development of romantic aesthetics, as he finalises the supplanting of rhetoric by eloquence and wholly excludes poetry from the realm of ends and means, which will become one of exclusive utility – an example of the suppression of rhetoric *sensu* Hayden White. At the same time, the terms in which Mill does so show his indebtedness to rhetorical terminology, and represent an instance of what we might call, with White, the "rhetoric of anti-rhetoric" (White 1997: 27) – a rhetoric that pretends to be unrhetorical. If we leave this British debate on the relation of poetical and rhetorical discourse a little earlier than Mill's somewhat final statement and cross the Atlantic, as all of the texts discussed here also did, then we find sources that testify to the continuity of rhetorical ideas of poetry as something heard in the antebellum United States.

The Rhetorical Effects of Poetry in William Cullen Bryant

There is a tradition of viewing poetry and eloquence in the United States that keeps alive the rhetorical framework that was so prominent in Campbell. As I shall argue in part II, Poe partakes in this tradition, yet its most explicit embodiment comes even earlier in William Cullen Bryant's "Lectures on Poetry." While also informed by romantic ideas about the symbol, Bryant's four lectures on poetry, held at the New York Athenaeum in April 1825,[31] were steeped in the rhetorical tradition. Bryant acknowledges that there is a distinction between poetry and eloquence, but it seems to him "that it consists solely in metrical arrangement": "Eloquence is the poetry of prose; poetry is the eloquence of verse" (Bryant 1884: 13). Bryant is a romantic to the extent that he distinguishes eloquence from "mere persuasiveness" and identifies eloquence with "those appeals to our moral perceptions that produce emotion as soon as they are uttered," but it is rather a matter of romanticizing the rhetorical process than negating the connection between rhetoric and poetry. For him, the orator is "himself affected with

---

[31] It might be mentioned in passing that the New York Athenaeum later merged with the New York Society Library, where Poe gave his lectures on "The Poets and Poetry of America" and "The Universe" in 1845 and 1848, respectively.

the feelings he would communicate," which echoes Quintilian's dialectics of self-affection, and if "the same man go[es] to his closet and clothe[s] in numbers conceptions full of the same fire and spirit, [...] they will be poetry" (Bryant 1884: 13). When it comes to the relation of nature and art in the attainment of authorship, Bryant level-headedly negates the Latin antithesis of *poeta nascitur, orator fit* with a Quintilianesque insistence on the interdependence of the two: "The maxim that the poet is born and the orator made is a pretty antithesis, but a moment's reflection will convince us that one can become neither without natural gifts improved by cultivation" (1884: 13). Despite his emphasis on passions and feeling, he comments that "[t]o write fine poetry requires intellectual faculties of the highest order, and among these, not the least important, is the faculty of reason" (Bryant 1884: 11). In its comparison of rhetoric and poetry, Bryant's position evinces some similarities to Mill's, yet, in a crucial contrast, the emphasis is on the similarities between the two language arts: the figure of the author is that of a poet-rhetorician or rhetorician-poet.

What is more, Bryant's definition of poetry is couched in the term "offices" and relies on the rhetorical tripartition of effects: "There is no question that one principal office of poetry is to excite the imagination, but this is not its sole, nor perhaps its chief, province; another of its ends is to touch the heart, and [...] it has something to do with the understanding" (Bryant 1884: 8). Bryant specifies that the production of fitness, symmetry, and congruity according to principles of taste "gratifies the understanding" (Bryant 1884: 11). Bryant thus distinguishes three principal offices of poetry that correspond to the rhetorical dimensions, leaving out the genuinely rhetorical overall aim of persuasion to action: poetry is to excite the imagination (*movere*), to touch the heart (*delectare*), and to gratify the understanding (*docere*).

How deeply ingrained the interest in the distinction between rhetorical and poetical discourse was in the antebellum culture of rhetoric can be seen in a university essay (a "theme") from November 1830 by the later orator and abolitionist, Wendell Phillips, written during his days as an undergraduate at Harvard.[32] Phillips writes: "Is not poetry rather that excitement of the feelings that ends in itself, – is it not affective, sublime indeed, but somewhat abstract? While Eloquence is the same feelings urged forward to action, excited by intense, perhaps often personal, instinct" (qtd. in Warren 1999: 9). Warren rightly comments that "Phillips distinguishes between the two by distinguishing their respective ends or effects" (Warren 1999: 9). Rather than negating the audience in poetry as

---

32 The text was found and is discussed by Warren (1999: 8–10). The text is part of a collection, *Themes and Dissertations*, bound by W. Phillips himself, of his undergraduate essays at Harvard.

Mill does, Phillips defines rhetoric positively as aiming at action. This and the other themes that Phillips and his fellow students wrote as undergraduates at Harvard suggest the wide-spread consciousness of the problem of the empire of literature over rhetoric as well as some of the differences and similarities in its proposed solutions on both sides of the Atlantic.[33]

The discussion of the functions or offices of poetry is directly relevant for the contemporary theoretical figures of the author. Indeed, in the romantic age the poet and the orator were faced with a similar problem when it came to figuring themselves in public in relation to their audiences. Often, this came close to the strategies of what Baldassare Castiglione, in his famous rhetorical handbook for the Renaissance courtier, called *sprezzatura*. Such a "rhetoric of anti-rhetoric" (White 1997: 27), as we saw it in Mill, has its topos in the principle that art is about hiding art: *ars est celare artem*.[34] Both in the neorhetorical treatises and De Quincey's text there is an awareness of the danger of a rhetorical speech being recognized as such and thereby losing its effect. As Campbell writes: "To [...] profess an intention to work upon their [the audience's] passions, would be in effect to tell them that he [the orator] meant to impose upon their understandings, and to bias them by his art, and consequently, would be to warn them to be on their guard against him" (Campbell [1776] 1988: 23). In De Quincey, the identification of rhetoric with an elevated diction leads to the same loss of credibility: "A man is held to play the rhetorician, when he treats a subject with more than usual gaiety of ornament" (1828: 885). Therefore, it is a necessity to hide the artistry involved in speaking. In this regard, Whately explicitly compares the poet to the orator: "A Poet, a Statesman, or a General, &c., though extreme covetousness of applause may mislead them, will, however, attain their respective Ends, certainly not the less for being admired as excellent, in Poetry, Politics, or War: but the Orator attains his End the better the less he is regarded as an Orator." (Whately [1828] 1963: 211–12). In Whately's take on the topos, poets, politicians, and generals do not have to hide their art, while the orator always needs to *celare artem*. Judging from the relation of romantic poets to rhetoric and conscious artistry, it appears that Whately was wrong here. In the romantic age, the danger of betraying signs of artifice instead of sincerity, of wanting to be heard rather than overheard, was not greatest for the orator, but for the poet.

---

33 For a list of similar themes, cf. Warren (1999: 9–10).
34 Or: artis est artem celare, as Campbell has it: "Nothing is better founded than the famous aphorism of rhetoricians, that the perfection of art consists in concealing art" (Campbell [1776] 1988: 23). Ancient topoi include e.g. Quintilian (Quintilian 2001a: 303=2.5.8).

To conclude the discussion of the development from rhetorical poetics to romantic aesthetics, we can say that "from hearing to overhearing" epitomizes the shift in the theory of the relation between rhetoric and poetics that remained in force as part of romantic ideology. Mill's metaphorical distinction is a result of the romanticising redefinition of *eloquence* in terms of the overflowing expression of feeling, as found in De Quincey. Whately's *Elements of Rhetoric*, with its strict distinction between logic and rhetoric and its corresponding focus on style and expression, represents a movement in rhetoric itself towards late-romantic theory, which essentially negates Campbell's general theory of communication and his notion of poetry as something that is to be heard. In the antebellum US, however, we find a strong continuing tradition of thinking about poetry in terms of the rhetorical triad of effects, of which William Cullen Bryant's "Lectures on Poetry" and Wendell Phillips' and others' themes at Harvard University are examples.

The development of poetry from something that is heard to something that is overheard is one of the key developments towards the emergence of literature in the sense that Raymond Williams and Hayden White understand it. Poetry is reinterpreted against the background of romanticising transformations of rhetoric. Literature in the modern sense is thus not only a result of technological shifts from speech to print: it emerges at the point when poetry is in the process of being de-rhetoricized. In what might appear paradoxical, this process continues to draw on rhetorical terminology such as the triad of effects, particularly in the antebellum culture of rhetoric. It is this force field of tensions between rhetorical and poetical discourse, between eloquence and poetry, out of which definitions of literature emerge in the early nineteenth century.

This is immediately relevant for contemporary figures of the author, since the poet's figure is in the process of shifting from someone who talks to someone for some purpose to someone who talks to himself: the reasoning public speaker in Campbell and Bryant contrasts sharply with the overheard solitary genius in Mill. These two are then the dominant conceptions of authorship in and through (or against) which authors such as Poe had to develop their theoretical conceptions of authorship.

How this theoretical opposition between the figures of the poet as someone who speaks to an audience for a purpose and someone who speaks only to himself appeared within the broader antebellum culture, will become clear through a reconstruction of the inextricable interplay between the cultures of print and rhetoric. In the final section of this chapter, these broad outlines are first reconstructed and then examined in one of their paradigmatic literary appearances in Poe's "How to Write a Blackwood Article."

2.3 "How to Write a Blackwood Article": Transatlantic Antebellum Cultures of Print and Rhetoric

Antebellum authorship emerges in a highly complex historical situation in which an increasing number of the American cultural elite demanded a genuinely American literature. Antebellum literature as a whole stands at the beginning of consumer capitalism and mass culture in the United States, as a new middle-class readership emerged into existence. Many studies have stressed the existence of a differentiated audience, usually thought of in terms of 'high' and 'low,' or the 'few' and the 'many' (as in Allen 1969). Poe himself was also aware of this: while he frequently spoke disparagingly of "the rabble" (e.g. E&R 103, 304, 574), he attempted to appeal both to the "popular and the critical taste" with "The Raven" (CT 62).[35] Terence Whalen argues that the capitalist logic of the emerging literary market functioned as the mediating entity between such different conceptions: "Poe's relation to [his audiences] was mediated by a third entity who acted as the embodiment of capital itself [...] the Capital Reader [, ...] a personification of the peculiar logic that accompanied the new publishing industry" (1999: 9–10). While Whalen's concept of the Capital Reader has been criticized (McGill 2001: 143), there is general agreement that the connection between capitalist market and print culture was crucial for the conditions of antebellum authorship.[36]

In this historical constellation the characteristic medium and technological agent of change was the magazine, which was essentially transatlantic in character. Due to the absence of an international copyright law, American magazines often consisted of reprintings from British magazines, and pirated editions of British authors were one of the economic cornerstones of antebellum culture. Meredith McGill has stressed the ubiquity of such practices, coining the term "culture of reprinting" to describe this transatlantic situation (2003). Indications of these processes in Poe include his advocacy of a copyright agreement (E&R 1036) and his obsession with plagiarism, particularly in the so-called little Longfellow war (E&R 696–777).

With these newly emerging phenomena of readership and medium, the American development of authorship instantiates most of the general characteristics of the rise of the author in England, France, and Germany. The pioneering effort in the field was made by William Charvat (1968), and, as Michael Newbury rightly maintains, "Charvat's central points – that the emergence of copyright protection, an expanded reading public, and increasingly sophisticated ways

---

35 Cf. Railton (1991: 132–151)
36 Cf. e.g. J. G. Kennedy (2013: 2).

of printing, marketing and distributing texts fostered a change in the relations between writer, publisher, and reader – remain indisputable" (1997: 3).[37] Newbury's study *Figuring Authorship in Antebellum America* (1997) expands on Charvat's work by exploring the relation of the rhetorical construction of authorship to other forms of labour. He criticizes the structuring of the literary field on such grounds as "generic distinctions," "gender exclusivity" or "affiliations with particular intellectual strains and philosophical schools," arguing that these structurings "ignore that writing is one form of work among many" (1997: 4). His suggestion is to read "other modes of labor as figures for writing;" thus, historically, he argues "figuring authorship became a way of defining writing's place within a newly arranged hierarchy of labor as well as a way of ordering the increasingly complex literary profession itself" (Newbury 1997: 5). Consequently, Newbury is not interested in the explicit and implicit traditions of rhetoric in antebellum America but rather in how one form of labour is used as a kind of Aristotelian metaphor for another form of labour. How writing as labour diversified and also entered spheres where it was no longer recognized as labour is investigated by Leon Jackson. Jackson posits the existence of a multiplicity of "specific authorial economies [...] from the most intimate and private of exchange practices to the most public" (Jackson 2008: 7–8). He names patronage, charity, gift exchange, and writing competitions as some of the alternative cultural settings in which authors could thrive (Jackson 2008: 8).

What comes out clearly in all recent studies is the overcoming of the romantic narrative by stressing the constant interconnection of the author and the marketplace. Rather than simply viewing the solitary or unrecognised genius as fighting against the marketplace – a gesture most familiar to students of Poe from Baudelaire's classic stylization of Poe as the *poète maudit* par excellence[38] – the genius and similar notions of authorship come into being precisely as a legitimation strategy on and for the market. Hence, there is agreement on the centrality of print technology and the emerging literary marketplace for antebellum literary authorship.

Adding to this insistence on the role of the print marketplace and its corresponding culture when it comes to definitions and performances of authorship, I posit the inextricable interplay between print culture and contemporary rhetorical culture.[39] Antebellum culture was steeped in rhetorical performances of all

---

[37] Cf. also Raymond J. Wilson (1989), Michael Newbury (1997), and David Dowling (2009).
[38] Cf. e.g. Baudelaire ([1857] 1969).
[39] In the case of Early American culture of the late eighteenth century, this interplay was analysed by, for instance, Jay Fliegelman. Cf. his study of rhetorical thoughts and practices in the case of Thomas Jefferson (Fliegelman 1993).

kinds such from the popular lecture to the private act of writing. Glorified by Edmund Parker in 1857 as *The Golden Age of Oratory*, scholars have found evidence of a vibrant rhetorical culture at the heart of antebellum politics, religion, education and literature. According to James Perrin Warren (1999), there are a variety of factors which make antebellum America what he calls "a culture of eloquence." He traces aspects of it in religion, in every-day life, and, particularly, in politics, citing as examples the focus on the sermon in the Congregational Churches of New England; opportunities for public speaking in the North and the South that mirrored the traditional three genres: "forensic, political, and celebratory speaking create three large and varied arenas in which the public address flourished"; and the emergence of "some of the most renowned orators of American history, the most celebrated being the trio of Calhoun, Clay, and Webster" (Warren 1999: 11). Even more important areas, however, were the popular lyceum movement and liberal arts education in the college system. Founded by Josiah Holbrook in 1826, the lyceum movement – as one of the first initiatives in adult education – grew quickly, and by the mid-1840s, according to Warren, "as many as four thousand communities had a lyceum or some similar society" (1999: 11). The appeal of the lyceums has recently been described as "cosmopolitan" (Wright 2013). The most visible aspect of the lyceum movement was the popular lecture, which was dominated by white male speakers in the early period: Henry David Thoreau, Ralph Waldo Emerson, Edgar Allan Poe, and many others all became a part of the antebellum public lecture system; later, African American orators such as Frederick Douglass and female speakers such as Susan B. Anthony, Elizabeth Cady Stanton and Anna Dickinson also rose to prominence in the system.

Education in antebellum colleges was based on rhetorical theory, poetics, and practice. At the heart of this oratorical culture were rhetorical analysis, theme writing, classroom performances, and oral exercises in "disputation, declamation, forensic oration, and the like" (Clark and Halloran 1993, 1).[40] Literary and debating societies as well as literary magazines took rhetorical thinking beyond the classroom, and textbooks like Blair's *Lectures on Rhetoric and Belles Lettres*, Caleb Bingham's *Columbian Orator*, and John Quincy Adams' *Lectures on Rhetoric and Oratory* had a formative influence "on the generation that reached maturity between 1825 and 1860" (Warren 1999: 10–11): that is, on Poe's generation.

As we saw earlier in this chapter, the antebellum culture of rhetoric is partly a result of the romantic reinterpretation of rhetoric as eloquence but it is at the

---

40 Cf. Warren (1999: 10) and Graff (2007: 36–51).

same time a testament to the continuing importance of New Rhetorical thought in the United States up until 1850. During Poe's lifetime, American rhetoric was defined by the transatlantic connection to Scotland; the most important force in Early American education in language, speech, and writing and in other college subjects was British and especially Scottish rhetoricians, as many scholars have argued.[41] Nan Johnson summarises this influence in terms of rhetorical theory:

> Nineteenth-century rhetoric relied substantially on Campbell and Blair's innovations and on the subsequent extension of their revisions by Richard Whately in *Elements of Rhetoric*. In theoretical terms, the nineteenth-century tradition can be understood as executing a refined synthesis of those theoretical commitments that promoters of the New Rhetoric were the first to combine: a philosophical approach to rhetoric that examined the nature and aims of rhetoric in terms of the processes of the 'mental faculties'; the view that the study of rhetoric applies to all major forms of communication, oral and written; an aesthetic/ethical commitment to the critical study of rhetorical theory and the development of taste; and a neoclassical approach to rhetoric as the art of adapting discourse to purpose, audience, and occasion (1991: 19–20)

This theoretical influence is also crucial for the emergence of English as an academic discipline and for the emergence of modern criticism. The Regius *Chair in Rhetoric and Belles Lettres* at the University of Edinburgh that Hugh Blair occupied from its establishment in 1762 to his retirement in 1784 might be said to be the first professorship in what was solidified over the course of the nineteenth century as "English studies." The foundational character of the discipline becomes apparent in Lord Kames' rechristening of the field of rhetoric as *criticism*. As Neil Rhodes explains, the term 'rhetoric' was beginning to fall into disfavour and replaced by Kames with 'criticism': "Kames's *Elements of Criticism* appeared in 1762, going through eleven editions to 1839, and it may fairly be said to have established the nomenclature up to the present day" (2008: 30). Despite Kames' replacement of 'rhetoric' with 'criticism,' the New Rhetoricians, according to James Engell, "are, prior to the twentieth century, the most important and cohesive group of critics in English": "[t]he appeal of their lectures and volumes, often used as texts on both sides of the Atlantic, lasted into Queen Victoria's reign" (1989: 195). If understood in terms of rhetorical invention, i.e. as a process that both relies on something already in existence and that at the same time produces something original, the contributors to *The Scottish Invention of English Literature* have substantiated their claim that the Scottish New Rhetoric established the ground for the development of English as a discipline (Crawford [1996]

---

[41] The most detailed institutional account is in Court (2001).

2008). In the antebellum United States in particular, New Rhetorical theory of Scottish origin was the basis of university education in rhetoric and poetics.

What is more, the New Rhetoricians extended their influence well beyond the theoretical disciplines. Their rhetoric informed politics, education, and literature both in Britain and the United States. The late Susan Manning pointed out that "[j]ust about every major figure of the Revolutionary era was directly or indirectly taught by Scots," naming as examples John Adams, Benjamin Rush, and Thomas Jefferson. Similarly, the "next generation internalised self-consciousness about 'correctness'" from the rhetorics and grammars that were adapted in the US from British models: "Poe, Hawthorne, Emerson, and Thoreau all learned its lessons of correctness" (Manning 2002: 246).[42]

As a reason for this kind of influence, Manning and other scholars have pointed to the similarities in Scotland's and America's relation to England. Scots and Americans "both suffered from a colonial inferiority complex" and as a result of this "experienced a revival in nationalism," as Winifred Bryan Horner argues: "Both countries were seeking a voice," "Scotland in fear of losing its identity while taking on an English identity and the United States as a struggling new nation in the New World" (Horner 1993b: 172).

These processes are of paramount importance in the development of the concept of literature as *English* literature: a study of the vernacular as opposed to classical languages that developed at the same time in transatlantic connections between Scotland and the United States. As Horner writes of the specifically linguistic reasons for these transatlantic rhetorical connections:

> The study of English literature developed within the rhetoric course simultaneously in Scotland and the United States primarily during the 1800s. [...] It was a new and eagerly adopted idea in the Scottish and American universities but one eschewed by the English universities until well into the twentieth century. This fact is easy to understand against the social and political backdrop of Scotland and the United States. [...] Students from these countries, so recently provincials, felt that they were basically second-rate and spoke a dialect inferior to the London standard. To become more 'English' they wanted to know and understand the literature of England and speak and write the London standard. Their English courses, which included both composition and rhetoric, were a way to reach this goal. (1993b: 181)

---

[42] This is nowhere as obvious in Poe as in "The Rationale of Verse." That this influence is not restricted to correctness, will become apparent in part II of the book. In particular, my argument in chapter six posits the relevance of the transatlantic elocutionary movement for linguistic and specifically poetic performance in Poe and beyond through an analysis of "The Rationale of Verse."

All of these influences combined with the result that the New Rhetoric and its accompanying Common Sense philosophy were formative in the emergence of American 'literary' authorship.[43] Though these authorial roles have so far only been examined in isolation, there are a number of individual studies that point to this connection. Because of his career as a lecturer, Emerson is a prime example of rhetorically conceived authorship and Susan Manning points out connections between Emerson's essays and George Campbell's rhetorical 'science of man.'[44] Caleb Bingham's *Columbian Orator* was formative for Frederick Douglass (Blight 1998). The importance of Blair's rhetoric for Herman Melville's writings was outlined by Bryan C. Short (1992). Thoreau studied Blair, Campbell, and Whately under Edward Tyrell Channing at Harvard (Woodlief 1975).[45] As Wylder (1971) and Lindberg-Seyersted (1968) have argued, even the works of the supposedly most private of American poets, Emily Dickinson, were influenced by Ebenezer Porter's and Richard Whately's rhetorics.

Besides the rhetorical treatises and handbooks such as Campbell's, Blair's, and Whately's, another main transatlantic channel for rhetoric were the many (often Scottish) magazines such as the *Edinburgh Review* and *Blackwood's Edinburgh Magazine*, all of which flooded the American market in authorized and unauthorized reprints. The reviews were already enormously influential in Britain so that, in 1809, Byron famously counter-attacked "Scotch reviewers" that were attacking – and not only in his eyes – "English bards." The Scottish reviewers similarly attacked American literature, as is evinced by Sydney Smith's oft-quoted question in an 1820 review, a question which vexed many American literati in the early nineteenth century: "In the four quarters of the globe, who reads an American book?" (Smith 1820: 79).

Nevertheless, these magazines would meet few more eager readers than the self-declared magazinist Edgar Allan Poe.[46] In Poe criticism, *Blackwood's Edinburgh Magazine* was established early on as one of the major sources of Poe's critical theory and his Gothic tales (Alterton [1925] 1965; Jacobs 1969; Allen

---

[43] The classic study of the interrelation of common sense philosophy and early American views of fiction is T. Martin (1961).

[44] Susan Manning writes: "Emerson's essays embody a central aspiration of the Scottish Enlightenment 'Science of Man': to reunite, as the rhetorician George Campbell put it, the 'sometimes unnaturally separated' 'natural relation between the sciences and the arts, like that which subsists between the parent and the offspring'" (Manning 2002: 252). The quotation is from Campbell ([1776] 1988: lxix).

[45] Cp. also the educational and argumentative importance of Blair and especially Whately for Margaret Fuller (Kolodny 1994: 362).

[46] On Poe as a magazinist, cf. e.g. Parks (1964). For Poe's reading of Blackwood tales, cf. McMullen (2010).

1969). While *Blackwood's* was one of the major transatlantic channels for German and English Romanticism, many of the critical texts that Poe read and studied continued to be informed by earlier ideas from Scottish Enlightenment rhetoricians. For the remainder of this chapter, I shall sketch some of these relations as they appear in one particularly pertinent result of some of the transatlantic connections just outlined, namely Poe's satire "How to Write a Blackwood Article" (1838/1845).

Authorship, Rhetoric, and Transatlanticism in Poe's "How to Write a Blackwood Article"

If "William Wilson" engages with transatlantic tensions between Britain and the United States implicitly, then Poe's satire "How to Write a Blackwood Article" (1838/1845) faces the cultural challenge head-on – by reflecting on and parodying the transatlantic critical and literary relations between the potential ally Scotland and the United States. What makes it particularly relevant is that it features a literal death of the author as a result of a rhetorically modulated transatlanticism. The story consists of two interconnecting parts, the first of which describes the main character Psyche Zenobia's instruction by Mr Blackwood in how to write a sensational tale for the magazine; in the second, "A Predicament," she depicts her own paradoxical death resulting from an attempt to experience that kind of sensation that would furnish the material for the tale. While the two texts were published separately in Poe's collection of *Tales of the Grotesque and Arabesque* in 1840, they fit together as frame narrative to embedded narrative. This ambiguously doubled structure of the tale repeats the geographic relation between the doubled United States and Britain in "William Wilson", with the question of artistic independence standing in for questions of political independence.

Through the autodiegetic narrator Psyche Zenobia's struggle for literary autonomy, Poe establishes a poetical figure of authorship under the transatlantically inflected antebellum conditions of publication by combining elements of Gothic horror and satire with (more or less) practical advice on how to write a short story. In Blackwood's version of the culture of reprinting, for instance, he produces his political articles by "merely cut[ting] out and interspers[ing]" text parts from two newspapers and a slang dictionary (T&S 338).

While the satirical elements clearly dominate in the story, there is nevertheless a structure beneath Blackwood's improvised creative writing course that has rhetorical elements and that also corresponds to some of Poe's explicit critical demands. Zenobia complains of her literary society that "[t]here was no investigation of first causes, first principles" (T&S 338). This is met by Blackwood's "clear explanation of the whole process" of the "exact method of composition" (T&S 339, 338), an explanation in which nonsensical content jars with a sensible overall structure.

Satirically following the common sense approach of the Scottish rhetoricians, Blackwood describes model texts to be imitated, but also recommends relying on "experimental knowledge of the matter in hand" (T&S 340).[47] Zenobia is first to determine her subject, then "consider the tone, or manner," the basic distinction of which is into three tones, or indeed styles: "the tone didactic, the tone enthusiastic, the tone natural" (T&S 341), all of which are "commonplace enough" (T&S 341). The first term is apparently aimed at instruction, the second borders on the pathetic, while the third term marks a middle position, thus instantiating the division into three rhetorical levels of style.[48] Beyond the "commonplace" triad (T&S 341), Blackwood further distinguishes elevated, metaphysical, transcendental, and heterogeneous styles to lay the ground for the method of arriving at commonplaces that is to be used in writing: "little scraps of either learning or *bel-esprit-ism*" (T&S 343). These are distinguished according to *res* and *verba*: "*Piquant Facts for the Manufacture of Similes*" and "*Piquant Expressions to be introduced as occasion may require*" (T&S 343). Apparently at random, Blackwood selects a number of quotations from ancient and modern classics and, finally, comments on the importance of delivery in print, giving the example that "nothing makes so fine a show as your Greek," since the "very letters have an air of profundity about them": "Was there ever a smarter fellow than that Omicron?" (T&S 346). As this final question shows, Blackwood's writing advice 'consistently' mixes satirical content with a structure that is based on the appropriation of commonplaces in various styles in and beyond the basic triad.

This critical advice is then reflected back into the text,[49] adding a further, metapoetical level of doubling to its representation of authorship: "But then there is the tone laconic, or curt, which has lately come much into use. It consists in short sentences. Somehow thus: Can't be too brief. Can't be too snappish. Always a full stop. And never a paragraph." (T&S 341). Similarly, Zenobia's first tale, "A Predicament", which she writes and experiences after visiting Blackwood, is written in the style that seems congenial for a budding author, namely the "tone heterogeneous" (T&S 342).

"Every one has been to Edinburgh – the classic Edina," writes Zenobia in her tale, pointing out once again an instance of transatlantic movement, in this case

---

47 Bruce Weiner comments that "Mr. Blackwood's advice to Psyche Zenobia betrays the preference of Common Sense for the actual over the imaginative" (Weiner 1990: 51).
48 Cf. the discussion in chapter one.
49 I first observed this in Guttzeit (2014a: 129–130).

of people (T&S 352). In search of the proper sensation, Zenobia climbs the highest tower of a Gothic cathedral and, looking out from a hole on the top floor, realizes too late that she has placed her head directly beneath the huge arm of the cathedral clock, which has descended irreversibly upon her neck. Meeting the demands of the genre, she keeps her authorial composure despite dying a literal death of the author:

> I was not sorry to see the head which had occasioned me so much embarrassment at length make a final separation from my body. It first rolled down the side of the steeple, then lodged, for a few seconds, in the gutter, and then made its way, with a plunge, into the middle of the street.
> I will candidly confess that my feelings were now of the most singular – nay of the most mysterious, the most perplexing and incomprehensible character. My senses were here and there at one and the same moment. With my head I imagined, at one time, that I the head, was the real Signora Psyche Zenobia – at another I felt convinced that myself, the body, was the proper identity. (T&S 355–356)

What the two halves of "How to Write a Blackwood Article" dramatize is the relation between trying to become an author within the transatlantic print culture and, despite dying a death of the author, paradoxically succeeding in producing the desired product. In the transatlantic culture of printing and rhetoric, virtually "[e]very one has been to Edinburgh," reading *Blackwood's*, the *Edinburgh Review*, or Hugh Blair and George Campbell; authors like Zenobia need to be "here and there at one and the same moment" (T&S 355), torn between their theoretical heads and poetical bodies. While Poe had indeed travelled through Edinburgh as a child in the autumn of 1815 (PL 26), the tale of two halves is more about Poe's and America's relation to literary Edinburgh and Britain. In "How to Write a Blackwood Article," Poe satirically reflects upon the transatlantic relations that structured the force field between the rise of the author and the dispersal of rhetoric through which his own authorship became possible, real, and yet remained highly volatile, always on the brink of death.

* * *

Poe himself called his time "this age of so universal an authorship," and veered between describing the position of the author in antebellum America as "the most noble profession" (LTR II: 770 = LTR-304) and that of a "poor devil author" in "the magazine prison-house" (E&R 1036). Besides the economic turmoil and risk that the project of becoming and being an author posed, the conditions of American antebellum authorship in general and of Poe's authorship in particular were characterized by the inextricable interplay between print culture and contemporary rhetorical culture as well as a cultural force field tensed between the dispersal of rhetoric and the rise of the author and literature. The rhetorical theory codified in Blair, Campbell, Whately, and their American counterparts, continued to influence notions of poetry and literature up until 1850. The British debate about poetry between hearing and overhearing was followed closely in the United States and its results showed through in literary theories by William Cullen Bryant, in the university education of the time, and, more generally, in the many magazine publications of the age. As late as 1856, *Putnam's Monthly Magazine* still evoked "the monopoly of literary opinion, such as was held of old by Scotch reviewers" ("Editorial Notes" 1856: 655) and remarked that "the lecture system has not ceased to bloom" (654). While rhetoric had been brought under the empire of literature, its dispersal in the antebellum United States led to the continuing presence of a rhetorical culture.

Rhetorical knowledge was dispersed, partially suppressed, and modified to form the antebellum culture of rhetoric, in which many American 'literary' authors played an active and central role. While print culture was the key factor in the emergence of the modern concept of literature, which supplanted earlier notions of poetry, there was still a sense of this latter not as something overheard but as something to be heard, not as a quasi-natural event, but as the result of a conscious, goal-oriented poetical action. Most crucially, the aesthetic idea of the romantic genius was challenged by rhetorical theories of authorship that conceptualised literary writing together with other types of writing in terms of its effects on an audience. In the antebellum cultures of rhetoric and print, Poe's figures of authorship were shaped by this force field between literature, poetry, and rhetoric. How Poe's theoretical, poetical, and performative figures of the author emerged in and through it is the subject of the next part of this book.

Part II **The Figures of Edgar Allan Poe**

3 "Letters of Recommendation": The Transatlantic Poet-Critic between the Rules of Rhetoric and Romantic Aesthetics

> He who joins instruction with the agreeable, carries the votes of all *mankind*, by delighting, and at the same time admonishing the reader. This book gets money for the Sosii; this crosses the sea, and continues to its celebrated author a lasting duration.
>
> Horace, *The Art of Poetry*, Works, 1836: 413

The motto from Horace's *Ars Poetica* is here cited in a late eighteenth-century prose translation by Christopher Smart, which was still in circulation in Poe's times. While the first half of the quotation on the two rhetorical effects of instructing (*'monere'* = *docere*) and delighting (*'delectare'*) is well-known, the second half might be similarly enlightening for models and concepts of authorship: a successful book would be a profitable business for the Sosii, the major book-sellers of Augustan Rome, be sold internationally, and finally increase the reputation of its author. If Abrams and Harpham are right to argue that "Horace distinguishes between material and authorial, or intellectual, ownership, in that the author, even if he has no proprietary interest in a published book, retains the sole responsibility and credit for having accomplished the work that the text incorporates" (2009: 20), then the quotation from Horace shows that historically early, even ancient, texts could furnish critical concepts and models for later theoretical figures of the author – that is, her or his self-reflexive conceptions of what an author is and does. This is not to argue for an anti-historicist turn in authorship studies, which might be construed from Abrams and Harpham's insistence "that, in broad outline, the figure and functions of Horace's 'auctor' and of Jonson's 'author' were essentially what they are at the present time, in ordinary critical discourse" (2009: 21). Rather, it would be a plea to fully take into account different historical temporalities – including their transhistorical dimensions (Wess 1996: 14) – in the analysis and interpretation of authorship.

More specifically, the question of Poe's theoretical figures of the author is inherently connected to the question of how to periodise Poe's writings. In the words of Shawn Rosenheim and Stephen Rachman, Poe was "always both in and out of his time" (1995: xx). In similar fashion, two major views of Poe's theories either situate them in the romantic or transcendentalist aesthetics of his time or view them as a precursor of modernist or proto-modernist aestheticism. These two views are outlined, for instance, by Beverly Voloshin in a survey essay on Poe's literary theory: on the one hand, "Poe's doctrine of effect is usually expressed in transcendental terms, such as '*an elevating excitement of the Soul,*' and can thus be located within the field of Romantic literary theory."¹ On the other, "Poe's antididactic, antimimetic, and antiexpressive critical orientation; his doctrines of construction and of effect; his vision of the text as a system [...] are modernist" (Voloshin 1996: 278). Yet, Poe's being out of his own time also offers another possibility, namely that of the continuity with earlier theories, as, for example, René Wellek, Robert D. Jacobs, Leon Chai (1987: 7), and William E. Engel (2012) have pointed out.

Of these critics, Wellek and Jacobs point specifically to the relevance of late eighteenth-century and early nineteenth-century rhetorical traditions. While Wellek was generally dismissive of Poe, who in his view "remained an 18th-century rationalist with occult leanings" ([1965] 1966: 159), he also argued that "Poe's ideal of planning for effect is, basically, a rhetorical concept that places aesthetic value on the emotional excitement caused by the poem" ([1965] 1966: 161). Jacobs, the most diligent student of Poe's critical writings, goes even further when he asserts that "[i]n his practice of criticism Poe was a rhetorician" (1969: x) and details the influence of the "Scottish School" of criticism (1969: 19–33). While arguing in systematic rather than historical terms, Joseph Moldenhauer, in a seminal essay, also writes of "Poe's *rhetorical* theory of 'effect'" (Moldenhauer 1968: 297; my emphasis). When it comes to Poe's theoretical figures of the author, it is thus more than well warranted to keep in mind the potential continuity with earlier theories such as those developed by the New Rhetoric. One might hazard the guess that the difficulties of interpreting Poe remain a symptom of the problematic conceptualisation of the relation of literature to rhetoric in the romantic age and beyond even in today's criticism and theory, insofar as it is still adhering to what Jerome McGann succinctly characterised as the romantic ideology.²

This problem of Poe's timeliness with regard to the dispersal of rhetoric is compounded with a more systematic problem that can be addressed via the resources of the rhetoric of authorship as developed in chapter one. Poe's theoretical figures of the author are difficult to reconstruct in merely theoretical terms because of their strong figurativeness – a stark reminder that, even when one dimension is prominent (here, the theoretical), a figure of the author remains informed by the other two major aspects (the poetical and performative). Poe's

---

[1] Alan Shucard even suggests we view Poe as a "hyper romantic": "The demons that drove [Poe] caused him to speak in a voice so hyperromantic that he is on the far edge of American Romanticism and without the approval – or understanding – of many of his romantic peers" (1990: 109).

[2] Cf. McGann (1999 [1983]). Cf. also Justin Clemens' (2003) study on *The Romanticism of Contemporary Theory: Institutions, Aesthetics, Nihilism*.

central critical essays such as "The Philosophy of Composition" and "The Poetic Principle" also evince poetical and performative characteristics, so that the form and the rhetorical devices employed appear to problematize, satirize, or undermine the theoretical content of the texts. While they are primarily theoretical figurations, they are thus simultaneously poetical and performative figurations of the author.³ In accounts that foreground this latter aspect, Poe's theoretical texts are usually viewed as literary texts in disguise, in which the text's literariness devalues or even invalidates the theoretical arguments put forth. Poe is thus unmasked as an author who feigns autonomy but who is in fact dialectically overcome by the heteronomous forces he has unleashed (cf. Detering 2000). In what I argue is a more nuanced approach, the rhetorical-poetical theory of authorship I am developing here makes no absolute distinction between literariness and theory, since it inherits the attribution of cognitive value granted to poetical discourse in the rhetorical tradition – without devaluing the specific possibilities of theoretical and poetical discourse.

Poe's texts thus call for a reading that is attentive to the dual process of the author's figuring activity and his being figured by it; Poe actively figures conceptions of authorship but he does so by drawing on theoretical discourses and poetical forms that are available in the surrounding culture, and which therefore inform his figurations. In this and the following chapter, I shall combine these aspects into a double perspective that examines both the persuasive and the figurative aspects of Poe's critical discourses. The aim is thus two-fold: it is 1) to reconstruct the theoretical framework for authorship in terms of the tension between antebellum rhetorical and romantic positions and the ways in which Poe modifies it and 2) to analyse the poetical aspects of the texts which either subvert or reaffirm (or indeed both) the theoretical argument the texts make.

The first half of this chapter develops a reading of Poe's first major critical text, "The Letter to B—," which interprets its theoretical content in terms of its poetical figuration as a Horatian letter, in order to illustrate how Poe positions himself as a poet-critic within transatlantically informed American antebellum literature. More generally, the second half examines Poe's theoretical figures of the author in his mid- and late-career criticism, particularly the *Marginalia*, to recover a conceptual opposition of a rhetoric of the poet-critic against an aesthetics of genius, which is attested, for instance, by Poe's redefinition of the fancy and the imagination as both being combining. From the early figuration

---

3 This debate is most developed with regard to "The Philosophy of Composition" (cf. the discussion in chapter four). Examples of readings that stress the figurative, poetical and performative over the persuasive and theoretical aspects are Person (1990), Pahl (1996), Detering (2000). K. Burke (1961) and Jakobson (1981) are among the ones that take the opposite view.

of himself as a Horatian poet-critic to the rejection of the genius in what he called "the doggerel æsthetics of the time" (E&R 294), Poe's theoretical figures of the author are thoroughly rhetorical.

3.1 The Poet-Critic in the "Letter to B—"

Poe's characteristic combination of persuasive and figurative elements is already on full display in his first major critical text, "Letter to B—" (1831/1836). Many of the concepts Poe would only later fully develop were present here in a nascent state, and the text is also a case of Poe's seriocomic treatment of many of them. Most crucially, the text is representative of Poe's overall strategy of figuring himself as a poet-critic. This representativeness begins with the fact that "Letter to B—" was a reused and reprinted text. Originally written under the title "Letter to Mr—" as the preface to the revised edition of his *Poems* (1831), Poe reprinted this text during his first stint as editor at the *Southern Literary Messenger* in July 1836.[4] This is both an indication of the dominant features of the antebellum "culture of reprinting" as Meredith McGill has defined it and a sign of Poe's attitude towards his own already-written texts as a rhetorical storehouse, which worked like a collection of commonplaces to be reactualised in different contexts.

The "Letter to B–" stands at the beginning of Poe's career and is clearly his first attempt to constitute himself as a poet-critic, appropriating such romantic models as Wordsworth and Coleridge. The anticipatory character of the text is already mirrored in Poe's retitling thereof, one which makes sense only when read aloud: the change from "Letter to Mr.—" to "Letter to B—" makes the title homophonous with "letter-to-be,"[5] investing it with some of the anticipatory character that resounds throughout the whole text. Where the master-reader Auguste Dupin would later have to deal with a letter marked by the semiotic time of the past (in "The Purloined Letter"), the author Poe, in his first major critical piece, looks towards his own future as the man of letters he wants to become.

The Appropriation of High Romanticism

Most of the critical tenets of the text are influenced, as is characteristic of Poe's early writings, by key romantic writers, and, in many cases, simply culled from

---

[4] For critical reactions to the "Letter," cf. E. Phillips (1996: 79–80).
[5] This is also remarked by Hartmann (2008: 52).

their work – as if their texts were commonplace collections. Poe's text has significant similarities to Wordsworth's "Preface" to the *Lyrical Ballads* and the "Essay Supplementary to the Preface" (CT 14, 19); likewise, as discussed below, a part of Poe's definition of poetry is taken word for word from Coleridge's *Biographia Literaria* (II, 13). His strategy for dealing with the two eminent romantic poet-critics is two-fold: he condemns (Wordsworth) and elevates them (Coleridge), and then, accordingly, uses their own texts either against them and/or as his own. For example, Poe changes the poetical examples from Wordsworth's "The Idiot Boy" (1798) and "The Pet-Lamb: A Pastoral" (1800) and trivializes them to turn 'authentic' feelings into ridiculous ones, thus attacking Wordsworth for a ridiculousness that Poe himself has fabricated (CT 16–17, Hartmann 2008: 49–50).

Poe's attitude towards Wordsworth is rightly viewed by Jonathan Hartmann (2008: 39) as standing in the tradition inaugurated by Francis Jeffrey's (in)famous review of Wordsworth's "The Excursion" in the pages of the *Edinburgh Review* which opened with: "This will never do" (1814: 1).[6] Charles Astor Bristed, in a later article on "The Scotch School of Philosophy and Criticism" (1845) read and used by Poe, called Jeffrey "the legislator and executive of the critical code" of the Scottish New Rhetoric (392). Jeffrey's harsh review of Wordsworth is one of the key moments in the transition from the New Rhetoric to romantic aesthetics. By criticizing Wordsworth in a similar vein as Jeffrey, Poe either consciously or, and more likely, unconsciously inserts himself into a tradition that goes back to the Scottish New Rhetoricians. Writing in 1831 and revising in 1836, Poe was very likely to have soaked up such tenets from his classical education at school as well as the numerous articles from the British Isles, particularly from such journals as the *Edinburgh Review*, with which he came into contact as reader and editor.

Having attacked Wordsworth in a Jeffreyan vein, Poe positions himself differently to Coleridge. In taking the first sentence of Coleridge's "final definition" of a poem from the *Biographia*,[7] Poe – in something of a performative self-contradiction – virtually only adds "in my opinion." Only then does he depart from this framework by using the term "romance" and putting characteristic emphasis on music, giving 'his' first definition of a poem:

> A poem, in my opinion, is opposed to a work of science by having, for its *immediate* object, pleasure, not truth; to romance, by having for its object an *indefinite* instead of a *definite* pleasure, being a poem only so far as this object is attained; romance presenting percep-

---

6 For a general estimate of Jeffrey, cf. Wellek ([1955] 1970: 111–20).
7 It reads: "A poem is that species of composition, which is opposed to works of science, by proposing for its *immediate* object pleasure, not truth" (Coleridge [1817] 1983: II, 13).

> tible images with definite, poetry with *in*definite sensations, to which end music is an *essential*, since the comprehension of sweet sound is our most indefinite conception. Music, when combined with a pleasurable idea, is poetry; music without the idea is simply music; the idea without the music is prose from its very definitiveness. (CT 10–11)

As is obvious in Poe's well-known definition of "the Poetry of words as the *Rhythmical Creation of Beauty*" (E&R 688), Poe's modifications of the definition are crucial when it comes to his own poems (as discussed in chapter six), yet, in general terms, Poe is clearly appropriating the definition from Coleridge. As Jonathan Bate argues, "[i]n a sense, there could be no finer homage to Coleridge: 'in my opinion' and 'in Coleridge's opinion' have become one and the same": "The minds of the two poets have coalesced" (1990: 258). This view is reinforced in the 1836 version of the "Letter," in which Poe also cuts two references to Coleridge, which made clear in the initial version to what extent he was relying on Coleridge's reading.[8]

While the passage is remarkable for what and how Poe appropriates Coleridge's text, it is even more so for what he does *not* appropriate. As Moreland and Shaw comment, "Poe rejects what he considers to be the *metaphysicianism* of [...] Coleridge, while appropriating important aspects" of the latter's philosophy of art (2012: 51). My argument is that Poe's texts often turn out to have rhetorical sources at one remove,[9] and this is precisely the case in Poe's appropriation of Coleridge. In the *Biographia Literaria*, the definition of a *poem* comes before the definition of *poetry*; in Coleridge's own words: "But if this should be admitted as a satisfactory character of a poem, we have still to seek for a definition of poetry" (1983: II, 14). This definition is framed no longer in terms of the finished product, but of the process in the author. The passage itself is highly reliant on German romantic texts, which is why Jerome McGann calls it "Coleridge's famous *rifacimento* of certain important German documents" ([1983] 1999: 32). The passage is worth quoting at length for its identification of the heretofore separated questions of the definition of poetry and the definition of the poet:

> What is poetry? is so nearly the same question with, what is a poet? that the answer to the one is involved in the solution of the other. For it is a distinction resulting from the poetic genius itself, which sustains and modifies the images, thoughts, and emotions of the poet's own mind.
> The poet, described in *ideal* perfection, brings the whole soul of man into activity, with the subordination of its faculties to each other according to their relative worth and dignity.

---

8 Cf. Hartmann (2008: 51).
9 Cf. e. g. the discussion of the elocutionist background of "The Rationale of Verse" in chapter six.

> He diffuses a tone and spirit of unity, that blends, and (as it were) *fuses*, each into each, by that synthetic and magical power, to which I would exclusively appropriate the name of imagination. This power, first put in action by the will and understanding, and retained under their irremissive, though gentle and unnoticed, controul [...] reveals itself in the balance or reconcilement of opposite or discordant qualities. (Coleridge [1817] 1983: II, 15–16)

This is quite clearly a highpoint of the romantic notion of authorship as based on the imagination of the genius, and it is completely absent from Poe's extensive borrowing from Coleridge in "Letter to B—." Later, he will come to explicitly oppose Coleridge's concept of the imagination (as discussed below). The fact that Poe does not borrow Coleridge's answer to the question "what is a poet?" is crucial, since those parts that Poe appropriates, namely Coleridge's definition of the poem, were much more widespread. Indeed, M. H. Abrams argued that, in the passage in question, Coleridge "re-adapts to his purpose the time-tested distinctions of medium, subject matter, diction, and ends, which had constituted the main tools of criticism since the ancient rhetoricians" ([1953] 1971: 118).

The parts of Coleridge's text that Poe makes his own are thus those parts that remain rhetorical even in Coleridge. What Abrams defined as the "typical movement of Coleridge's criticism" from the product to the process, is thus not followed by Poe. For Abrams, this movement of "making the poet's mind and powers the focus of aesthetic reference" is an indication of the "consonance [of Coleridge's criticism] with the central tendency of his age" ([1953] 1971: 118). Yet what Abrams views affirmatively as the central tendency of Coleridge's age is the process of the emergence of romantic authorship and the devaluation of rhetorical poetics that is not adequately described in Abrams' account, since he, like many critics, in some respects, perpetuated the romantic terminology that is his object of study. As McGann has argued, "[n]ot every artistic production in the Romantic period is a Romantic one": "[t]he Romantic Age is so called not because all its works are Romantic, but rather because the ideologies of Romanticism exerted an increasingly dominant influence during that time" ([1983] 1999: 19).

While "Letter to B—" is indeed "set [...] as a response to Coleridge" (Hartmann 2008: 39), it is not – pace Hartmann and Bate – an exclusively affirmative one. Poe certainly positions himself with regard to romantic poet-critics, beginning with his rejection of Wordsworth and admiration of Coleridge. But he does not appropriate the decisively romantic aspect of Coleridge's definition; even when appropriating Coleridge's writings, Poe remains within what Abrams called the "time-tested" boundaries of rhetorical criticism based on the effects of poetical discourse. That he would take such rhetorical ideas from the high romantic Coleridge is a further indicator both of the continuities and of the tensions into which rhetorical thought about poetical discourse entered in the Age of Romanticism.

A Horatian Art of Poetry

How time-tested the rhetorical and pre-romantic foundations of Poe's position were becomes apparent when we examine his further definitions of poetry. My argument for reading "The Letter to B—" in terms of Horace's poetics, one of the foremost examples of a rhetorical poetics (Walker 2000: 168), is not to claim that Poe was reading a copy of Horace while writing the "Letter." What can be demonstrated, however, is the presence of Horatian ideas about poetry and its effects, with which Poe – who studied Horace as a school child (PL 47) – came into contact. Taking into account Horace's continuing presence in schools, universities, and magazines well into the nineteenth century as well as Poe's personal attachment, Horace's poetics – with its similarities in form and content – is worthy of consideration as a rhetorical pretext to Poe's "Letter."

The most apparent similarity between the two texts is that both are poetics couched in the form of a letter. Written in verse form as the last of his Epistles to the Pisos, Horace's *Ars Poetica* equals and in some respects eclipses Aristotle's *Poetics* in terms of its impact in the Western world, which was guaranteed especially by the eminent citability of its maxims. Horace's poems were "favorite reading during the Enlightenment;" his position in the school curriculum "helped him survive the advent of Romanticism longer than many other Latin authors, and through the 19th century he continued to fascinate classically trained and oriented poets and to provide a recognizable mark of gentlemanly breeding and taste" (Most 2010: 457). Considering the state of authorship in antebellum America as outlined in chapter two, the impression of gentlemanly breeding and taste is one of the attributes that the young author Poe had to aim for in his text. That he was familiar with Horace through his classical school education is evident from a comment by T. O. Mabbott on a no longer extant Latin letter written by the young Poe, probably in summer 1822, to his schoolmaster Joseph H. Clarke: "One regrets the loss of Poe's Latin verses, presumably (like the *Epistolae* of his favorite Horace) in dactylic hexameters" (PMS 4).[10] While the *Ars Po-*

---

10 More generally, Mabbott states that Poe's poetry "shows familiarity with Horace" (PMS xxvi). Poe's citation of the famous line about mountains giving birth to a mouse occurs as late as in the last version of "The Rationale of Verse" in 1848 (CT 117). Cp. "parturiunt montes; nascetur ridiculus mus" (Horace 1836: 394 = 139).

etica is a likely context of many poetological texts, Poe's "Letter to B—" thus lends itself particularly strongly to a reading in such terms.

Such a reading involves the second definition of poetry (rather than the poem) given by Poe only in the first version of the text, "The Letter to Mr—." When he transforms this into the 1836 article "Letter to B—," the following definition is the only full sentence that Poe cuts: "Poetry, above all things, is a beautiful painting whose tints, to minute inspection, are confusion worse confounded, but start boldly out to the cursory glance of the connoisseur" (CT 12).[11] The passage is dominated by the Horatian idea of the similarity of poetry and painting to the recipient. Here is Smart's eighteenth-century translation of the *Ars Poetica:* "As is painting, so is poetry: some pieces will strike you more, if you stand near; and some, if you are at a greater distance: one loves the dark; another, which is not afraid of the critic's subtile [sic] judgment, chooses to be seen in the light" (Horace 1836: 415).[12] The chief elements, namely poetry, painting, the critical observer, and a change in impression due to the position of the observer are identical in Horace and Poe. Poe's statement can be viewed as a modification of the commonplace that differs with regard to the emphasis on the distinction between the "minute inspection" of a layperson and "the connoisseur['s]" eye for the "big picture," i.e. the differences between being bogged down in the details of the poem and the appreciation of it as a whole.

One might surmise that Poe cut this definition from the 1836 version because he no longer agreed with it, yet the opposite seems more likely. He might have cut it because he had used the simile to give a more detailed description of poetry just five months prior (in February 1836) in a review of Slidell's *The American in England* in the *Southern Literary Messenger:*

> As the touches of a painting which, to minute inspection, are 'confusion worse confounded' will not fail to start boldly out to the cursory glance of a connoisseur – or as a star may be seen more distinctly in a sidelong survey than in any direct gaze however penetrating and intense – so there are, not unfrequently, times and methods, in which, and by means of which, a richer philosophy may be gathered on the surface of things than can be drawn up, even with great labor, *e profundis.* (MTC VIII: 215)

---

11 Here, Poe includes the popular Miltonian phrase "confusion worse confounded" from the dialogue between Satan and Chaos in book two of *Paradise Lost*, which he would reuse a few times (Milton 2007: 65 = 2.996).
12 Cp. also the Loeb edition (Horace [1926] 1945).

Poe's argument is clearly about literary representation and based on a comparison of painting and literature in terms of the effect on the recipient.[13] Neither art aims at a reflection of the real but at a representation of the apparent in order to give an artistic idea of the object: "*to give (speaking technically) the idea of any desired object, the toning down, or the utter neglect of certain portions of that object is absolutely necessary to the proper bringing out of other portions – portions by whose sole instrumentality the idea of the object is afforded*" (MTC VIII: 216; Poe's emphasis). In that regard, poetry is a beautiful painting whose tints start boldly out to the cursory glance of the connoisseur. Rather than dismissing this analogy, Poe would generalise it and use it both in his later critical writings and also as a key motif in his tales, for instance in "The Purloined Letter."[14] The Horatian motif of *ut pictura poesis* thus leads to the first in a long line of Poe's theorisations of the ends and effects of poetical discourse.

Horace's take on the aims of the poet has been such a perennial commonplace in the discussion of the ends of poetry that it seems virtually inevitable. What is perhaps the most-quoted poetological sentence from Horace was translated by Smart as: "The poets intend either to profit, or delight; or to deliver at once both the pleasures and necessaries of life" (Horace 1836: 413).[15] Utility or pleasure or their combination are the three possible effects for which the poet can strive, but the highest achievement, for Horace, lies in the combination of useful instruction with agreeable pleasure – as quoted in the motto to this chapter:

> He who joins instruction with the agreeable, carries the votes of all *mankind*, by delighting, and at the same time admonishing the reader. This book gets money for the Sosii [well-known Augustan booksellers]; this crosses the sea, and continues to its celebrated author a lasting duration (Horace 1836: 413).[16]

---

13 On Poe's "visual aesthetics" and his relation to the visual arts, cf. Cantalupo (2014: 2 and passim).
14 Cp. the review of Longfellow (*Graham's Magazine*, April 1842), in which Poe compares painting and poetry as mimetic arts (E&R 695). The rationale of Dupin's successful recovery of the purloined letter works on a similar analogy between seeing and interpreting: "the physical oversight is precisely analogous with the moral inapprehension by which the intellect suffers to pass unnoticed those considerations which are too obtrusively and too palpably self-evident. [The Prefect] never once thought it probable, or possible, that the Minister had deposited the letter immediately beneath the nose of the whole world, by way of best preventing any portion of that world from perceiving it" (T&S 990).
15 "Aut prodesse volunt, aut delectare poetae/aut simul et iucunda et idonea dicere vitae" (Horace [1926] 1945: 478; ll. 333–334).
16 Smart's "all *mankind*" is a humanistic exaggeration, yet he also explains that "Omne ... punctum" refers to getting every point in a Roman vote. This is the full passage: "Omne tulit

For our discussion, there are two major aspects to Horace's distinction: first, it is widely acknowledged as an application of the rhetorical triad of effects to poetical discourse.[17] While Horace's triad appears only to encompass *docere* and *delectare* and to omit *movere*, he also deals with the pathetic effects of poetry as in the demand that the author needs to feel grief first before he can make the recipient cry (Horace [1926] 1945: 459; ll. 102–3). The second aspect, which we have already touched upon, is that it is a distinction made in an environment some characteristics of which we would rather associate with antebellum America: Horace explicitly links the greatest success of the poet to the profit made by the booksellers and the success of the work is measured by its crossing the sea, not the Atlantic but the Mediterranean Sea to the more culturally advanced Greece. In other parts of the *Ars Poetica*, Horace mentions booksellers' advertisements,[18] and, in his advice to budding writers, literally speaks of the author of a poem: "carminis auctor" (Horace [1926] 1945: 454; l. 45).[19] While not produced under the conditions of print-capitalism (Anderson 2006: 37–46), Horace's rhetorical poetics addresses a situation that is, if by no means identical, then at least commensurable with the situation of antebellum writers like Poe. Hence, it might even have offered Poe a way to conceptualise his own situation. In any case, the similarities go to show Poe's attempt at turning himself into an author and a poet-critic.

The Horatian distinction informs the first articulation of what Poe would later call "the Heresy of *The Didactic*" (CT 182). The ubiquitous Horatian opposition between pleasure and instruction offered Poe a first opportunity to distinguish between the different kinds of effect produced by literary texts. While ex-

---

punctum, qui miscuit utile dulci,/Lectorem delectando, pariterque monendo./Hic meret aera liber Sosiis; hic et mare transit,/Et longum noto scriptori prorogat aevum." (Horace 1836: 412).
17 Under the entry "rhetorical criticism," Abrams and Harper's *Glossary of Literary Terms* has: "This view, by making poetry a calculated means to achieve effects on its audience, breaks down Aristotle's distinction between imitative poetry and persuasive rhetoric" (Abrams and Harpham 2009: 312).
18 As the Loeb editor Henry Rushton Fairclough comments: "Book-stalls were usually in arcades, the pillars of which were doubtless used for advertising the books within. One may compare the Parisian kiosques" (Horace [1926] 1945: 54–55).
19 Cp. the already cited entry on "author and authorship" in *A Glossary of Literary Terms:* "Horace distinguishes between material and authorial, or intellectual, ownership, in that the author, even if he has no proprietary interest in a published book, retains the sole responsibility and credit for having accomplished the work that the text incorporates. [...] It would seem that, in broad outline, the figure and functions of Horace's 'auctor' and of Jonson's 'author' were essentially what they are at the present time, in ordinary critical discourse" (Abrams and Harpham 2009: 20–21).

plicitly informed by Coleridge, Wordsworth, and Aristotle, Poe's discussion of the effects of poetry in "Letter" is thus also informed by Horatian thought about pleasure, instruction, and utility:

> Aristotle, with singular assurance, has declared poetry the most philosophical of all writing – but it required a Wordsworth to pronounce it the most metaphysical. He seems to think that the end of poetry is, or should be, instruction – yet it is a truism that the end of our existence is happiness; if so, the end of every separate part of our existence – every thing connected with our existence should be still happiness. Therefore the end of instruction should be happiness; and happiness is another name for pleasure; – therefore the end of instruction should be pleasure: yet we see the above mentioned opinion implies precisely the reverse.
>
> To proceed: ceteris paribus, he who pleases, is of more importance to his fellow men than he who instructs, since utility is happiness, and pleasure is the end already obtained which instruction is merely the means of obtaining. (CT 6–7)

Poe makes pleasure the measure of utility, turning it into a utility of a higher order. In arguing that pleasure is the final utility, Poe makes one of the Horatian effects of poetry central to his definition, yet also keeps the opposition in place. The passage is remarkable, since it appears to be the first of his few direct engagements with the nineteenth-century ideology of utilitarianism that was one of the major forces in the specialization and sacralization of literature, as we saw in chapter two. At the cost of philosophical exactness (whole schools of philosophy such as Epicureanism are partially based on the *opposition* of pleasure and happiness), Poe's argument reverses the key tenets of the ideology of utility, which Hayden White suggests as one of the key factors in the suppression of rhetoric in the nineteenth century.

This is not to argue that Poe was a faithful classicist adopter of Horace; rather, as in the case of his other connections to rhetorical poetics, it was in all likelihood mediated by Scottish magazine articles. The form of Poe's argument may well have been influenced by such articles as the one in the *Edinburgh Review* in January 1828 ("Review of *The Songs of Scotland*") which was reprinted as "On the Utility of Poetry" in 1835 – with each of the versions preceding each of the versions of Poe's "Letter." There, the unnamed author defended the usefulness of poetry "in an industrious community" by arguing that "[e]ven the rigorous definition of the proper object of all virtuous exertion, according to the utilitarians themselves, viz. the greatest happiness of the greatest number – obviously involves the consideration of pleasure and enjoyment; and makes this enjoyment, as indeed it truly is, the measure and test of utility" ("Review of *The Songs of Scotland*" 1828: 185). Like Poe's, this argument defends poetry against the demand of utility, using the term 'utility' itself against the early utilitarians in similar fashion. Significantly, the unnamed writer defends *poetry* by defining it in the exact same terms as Francis Bacon defined *rhetoric*. Poetry "is, in the words of the great philosopher, 'subservient to the Imagination, as Logique is to the Understanding;' and its *office* '(if a man well weigh the matter) *is no other than to apply and commend the dictates of Reason to the Imagination for the better moving of the Appetite and the Will*'" ("Review of The Songs of Scotland, Ancient and Modern, by Allan Cunningham" 1828: 187). The defence of poetry against utility in the *Edinburgh Review* thus ranged rhetoric amongst its ranks, yet dared not advocate it in the open – a move that seems characteristic of the early nineteenth century "under the ban of the empire of literature."

Poe's "Letter" can thus be viewed as a Horatian art of poetry that is mediated by contemporary discourses in magazines such as the *Edinburgh Review*. Adopting and modifying the idea that poetical discourse aims at the effects of pleasure (*delectare*) and instruction (*docere*), Poe attempts to define poetry by way of rejecting the utilitarian demand that the poet be useful and by reinterpreting the pleasure the author's text gives to the reader as the highest possible utility. According to this line of argument, the poet is theoretically figured, first and foremost, against the background of the possible effects of poetical discourse, as a producer of pleasure: as an entertainer rather than an instructor (and not even to speak of an agitator).

Letters of Recommendation

As Poe's appropriation of rhetorical theories from Coleridge and his adaptation of Horatian rhetorical poetics show, "Letter" is a complex response to the problems associated with distinguishing between rhetorical and poetical discourse in a time of aesthetics and utilitarianism. The key to the figurative and performative aspects of Poe's theoretical modelling of the author in the text lies in the epistolary genre that is both a hint towards Horatian poetics and an intervention into the literary market for Poe's own sake.

No matter who the addressee of the original "Letter to Mr.—" was (if there even was one),[20] if we look for model prefaces in which the writer of poetry addresses a specific person we are more likely to find it in texts produced under the neoclassical patronage system, in which the writer thanks his benefactor at the

---

20 The addressee cannot be conclusively determined. Possibilities include the publisher of Poe's 1831 *Poems*, Elam Bliss; Edward Bulwer-Lytton, whom a fellow-cadet at West Point reported as the person Poe had in mind; and William Cullen Bryant, who was also published by Bliss (CT 12).

outset. As Hayes rightly notes: "Poe's life bridged the manuscript culture of the gentlemanly virtuoso and the print culture of the literary professional" (Hayes 2000: 113). Effacing the specificity of the addressee but keeping alive the communicative situation of the letter enables Poe to make his text an echo chamber of the patronage system strongly associated with (aristocratic) poetical prestige.[21]

In one of the paragraphs that appears not to be cribbed from British sources, Poe himself gives a figurative clue as to another reason for the choice of the letter form. Here, he deals with transatlantic literary relations and the question of the conditions of an American author, focusing on how to establish one's own name as that of an author:

> You are aware of the great barrier in the path of an American writer. He is read, if at all, in preference to the combined and established wit of the world. I say established; for it is with literature as with law or empire – an established name is an estate in tenure, or a throne in possession. Besides, one might suppose that books, like their authors, improve by travel – their having crossed the sea is, with us, so great a distinction. Our antiquaries abandon time for distance; our very fops glance from the binding to the bottom of the title-page, where the mystic characters which spell London, Paris, or Genoa, are precisely so many letters of recommendation. (CT 5–6)

Poe thus explicitly foregrounds the transatlantic nature of the literary marketplace as the larger historical constellation in which he positions himself as an author. His response is, in his own words, a 'letter of recommendation.'

In the transatlantic culture of literary magazines, it is no surprise that even the importance of letters of recommendation was reflected in such articles as the anonymously published article "The Utility of Letters of Recommendation to Young Men Visiting Paris" (1825), printed in *The European Magazine in London* and reprinted by the Boston-based *Atheneum*. However, letters of recommendation underlie a dangerous dialectic in that their existence indicates the need for support such as a poet would hardly need in a strict aesthetics of genius. The fact that a poet was also not thought to be in need of such support in the Enlightenment republic of letters is corroborated by Jakob Friedrich von Bielfeld, a favourite eighteenth-century source for Poe's own critical and literary writings: "The bearers of so many letters of recommendation make me constantly suspect them: men of real merit are always known in the world" (1770: 219). Under the conditions of transatlantic antebellum literature, however, in "Letter to B—" or "letter-to-be," Poe figures himself as an author who is primarily a poet but who can attest to the quality of his own writings as a critic: the key aim is to

---

[21] It is worth noting the artist-heroes of Poe's tales, most prominently Dupin and Usher, are 'fallen aristocrats.' For a discussion of Dupin as a poetical figure of the author, cf. chapter five.

gain "an established name" for himself, a name which can work as "precisely so many letters of recommendation."

It is with precisely such an assertion of the authority of the poet-critic that "Letter to B—" opens: "It has been said that a good critique on a poem may be written by one who is no poet himself. This, according to *your* idea and *mine* of poetry I feel to be false – the less poetical the critic, the less just the critique, and the converse" (CT 5).[22] In writing "Letter to Mr—" and republishing it as "Letter to B—," Poe thus attempts figuratively to square the communicative circle by writing a recommendation letter for his own literary works through establishing himself as a critic. In so doing, Poe meticulously avoids mentioning any other American authors and focuses solely on discourses with a transatlantic appeal, texts that have "crossed the sea" (the phrase is the same in CT, 5–6 and Horace 1836: 413). Thus his expertise as a critic (gained by appropriating Coleridge and adapting Horatian poetics) combines with his insight into the transatlantic character of literary culture to offer an indication of his authority both as a critic and as a poet. The "Letter to B—" is thus ultimately an attempt to establish an author's name for himself via the theoretical figure of the poet-critic.

In "Letter," then, Poe's theoretical figures of the author range from the Horatian producer of pleasure to the powerful transatlantic figure of the poet-critic. Each of these figures constitutes Poe's active shaping of the literary and cultural discourses that were simultaneously shaping him. As we shall see in later chapters, especially chapter four, it is precisely Poe's attempt to combine what are in many ways uncombinable discourses that endows his criticism with the distinctly antic character for which it is either esteemed or condemned. It remains in this chapter to demonstrate philologically that Poe's explicit view of rhetorical craft was a positive one, while he strongly opposed the newly emerging discipline of romantic aesthetics with its emphatic notion of the genius. The resulting tensions between the rules of rhetoric and doggerel aesthetics would shape Poe's theoretical figures of the author like his engagement with the Romanticism of Wordsworth and Coleridge as well as Horatian poetics.

---

22 A later version of this insistence can be found, for instance, in his second review of Dickens' *Barnaby Rudge* (*Graham's Magazine*, February 1842), in which Poe criticized the idea that a proposition "may be good in theory, but will not answer in practice": "theory and practice are in so much *one*, that the former implies or includes the latter" (E&R 224–225). "A theory is only good as such," Poe argued, "in proportion to its reducibility to practice. If the practice fail, it is because the theory is imperfect" (E&R 225). In this insistence, Poe was not alone in the rhetorical tradition: a similar general rationale for the interdependency of theoretical science and poetical art can also be found in the opening statement of Campbell's *Philosophy of Rhetoric:* "All art is founded in science, and the science is of little value which does not serve as a foundation to some beneficial art." (Campbell [1776] 1988: lxix).

3.2 The Rules of Rhetoric and Doggerel Aesthetics

While Poe's connections to rhetorical theory were manifold, most of them were below the surface. This is quite typical of antebellum culture, in which the dispersal of rhetoric, the redefinition of poetry as something overheard, and the transformation of 'literature' were all in full swing, as we saw in chapter two. Nevertheless, there exist a number of explicit connections between Poe and rhetorical theory that are well worthy of discussion, particularly his explicit definition of rhetoric that appears not to have elicited any scholarly attention.[23] For Poe's explicit stance on rhetoric, we would be well-advised to follow Jerome McGann's advice (2014: 61) and look for Poe's explicit theoretical opinions in Poe's extensive *Marginalia*, his long-running series of critical comments (supposedly) first jotted down in the margins of books and the publication of which marks the later phase of his criticism from November 1844 onwards. In the *Marginalia* in particular, the opposition is developed between a figure of the author that stems from romantic aesthetics and one that is based on rhetorical craft. The same opposition can be employed to better understand Poe's opposition to Coleridge's concept of the imagination and Poe's concurrent privileging of the fancy, as I show in the middle section of this subchapter. It is crucial to bear in mind, however, that the explicit references to rhetoric constitute merely the tip of the iceberg of Poe's rhetorical theory, as we saw in the importance of rhetorical thought for Coleridge and Horatian poetics in the first section of this chapter. It is especially in chapter four that the totality of Poe's rhetorical infrastructure will emerge into view.

The Uses of "Rhetoric"

The *Marginalia* contain both evidence of the connections between Poe and the Scottish New Rhetoricians as well as Poe's only explicit definition of rhetoric. This is not to say that Poe himself overtly conceived of his own theories as rhetorical; in this regard he was a symptom of the increasing dispersal of rhetoric. Compared to his contemporaries, and in particular to the notions of aesthetic genius, however, he can be described as propounding a rhetorical rather than

---

[23] Jacobs (1958), Full (2007: 74–82) and Zimmerman (2005: 29–33) give useful overviews, yet none of them discusses Poe's explicit stance on rhetoric.

an aesthetic theory of literature. Poe's explicit view of rhetoric is generally positive and is also implicitly connected to poetical discourse.[24]

Poe's central definition of rhetoric appears towards the end of his life in 1849 in the context of a defence of rhetorical poetry. More specifically, Poe refutes the arguments of an unnamed reviewer of popular travel writer Bayard Taylor's poetry collection *Rhymes of Travel* (1848).[25] Poe quotes the anonymous reviewer's comments: "'Mr. Taylor's volume [...] is an advance upon his previous publication. We could have wished, indeed, something more of restraint in the rhetoric'" (E&R 1443). Poe quotes more than just this short passage, but what he singles out for his own response is the critique of Taylor's rhetoricity. The charge of being too rhetorical was one that would be repeated against Taylor, but Poe argues that "the 'rhetoric' of Mr. Taylor, in the sense intended by the critic, is Mr. Taylor's *distinguishing excellence*" (E&R 1443). Poe thus reverses the charge of the unknown critic, turning the weakness of rhetoric into a strength, repeating a classical rhetorical move since Protagoras and Gorgias.

Poe must have recognised certain similarities to his own poetry in the content and form of Taylor's and had come into contact with Taylor in the latter's capacity as editor of *Graham's*.[26] In the review, Poe quotes and lauds Taylor's historical-allegorical poem "The Continents," in which the continents are personified as goddesses. The beginning of that poem reads strikingly like Poe, as Taylor makes use of similar Gothic imagery to that found in Poe's late poems such as "Ulalume" (1847) and "The Bells" (1848).[27] Taylor's poem reads, for instance: "I had a vision in that solemn hour,/Last of the year sublime" and "when the bell of midnight, ghostly hands/Tolled for the dead year's doom" (Taylor 1849: 132, ll. 1–2; 9–10). Even more telling is Poe's rebuttal of the reviewer's arguments against the form of Taylor's poetry: Poe imagines "our anonymous friend's [the reviewer's] implied sneer at 'mere jingling of rhymes, brilliant and successful for the moment'" (E&R 1443). Called "*the jingle-man*" by Emerson (qtd. in Howells 1894: 450), Poe's defence of Taylor is of a poetry viewed in similar terms as his own.

Poe's definition of rhetoric, which forms the centre of his defence, does not, as one might expect, refer merely to a rhetorical style in poetry. The definition is

---

24 I first observed this in Guttzeit (2010: 121–123).
25 From Poe's comments it seems that he knew the reviewer: "In his whole life, the author of the criticism never published a poem, long or short, which could compare, either in the higher merits, or in the minor morals of the Muse, with the *worst* of Mr. Taylor's compositions" (E&R 1442).
26 Taylor appears to not have responded to Poe's letter (LTR II: 727 = LTR-287a).
27 Cf. the discussion in chapter six.

much broader: "By 'rhetoric' I intend the *mode generally* in which Thought is presented" (E&R 1443). "Rhetoric" here no longer refers simply to the form or style of Bayard's poetry, but applies both to poetical and non-poetical texts: "Thought" is an all-encompassing category that is opposed to presentation as content is to form. The definition raises the question as to which discipline "Thought" would fall into. If rhetoric is the discipline responsible for its presentation, then thought is very likely the subject-matter of the discipline of logic, yet we should not lose sight of the fact that Poe defends Taylor's poetry *as* rhetoric.

In most nineteenth-century treatises on rhetoric – for instance, in those by John Quincy Adams and Richard Whately, but also in John Stuart Mill's *A System of Logic* (1843) – rhetoric is opposed to logic. Adams argued that while their connection was "indissoluble," logic belongs "to the operations of the mind, within itself; rhetoric to the communication of their results to the minds of others" (Adams 1810: I, 40). Whately similarly distinguished between the logical process of investigation and the process of "*conveying truth* to others, by reasoning ([...] i.e. the *Rhetorical process*)" (Whately 1828: 23). This idea extended to Mill's *A System of Logic* (1843): "The sole object of Logic is the guidance of one's own thoughts: the communication of those thoughts to others falls under the consideration of Rhetoric, in the large sense in which that art was conceived by the ancients" ([1843] 1974: 6).

Poe's broad definition thus concurs with this tradition of viewing rhetoric as the opposite to logic, but Poe applies it to a poetical text: lauding Bayard's "sonorous, well-balanced rhythm," he states that the latter's "rhetoric in general is of the highest order" (E&R 1443). While Poe may have taken his definition from Mill, he employs it in a defence of poetry in a manner that is opposed to Mill's ideas about poetry as that which is overheard. While not consciously citing any authorities, he is clearly well aware of one of the most common definitions of rhetoric at that time and yet distinguishes himself from it by applying it directly to poetical discourse. Poe thus evinces what we might call, following Heinrich Lausberg (1998: 27 = § 49), a maximalist conception of rhetoric that applies rhetoric to poetry in the vein of George Campbell and other New Rhetoricians.

Such a maximalist conception of rhetoric can also be found in an earlier *Marginalia* item (January 1848), in which Poe refutes an anti-rhetorical commonplace from Samuel Butler's *Hudibras* (1663). Butler's mock heroic verse narrative features an attack on rhetoric that was rebuked in Campbell's *Philosophy of Rhetoric* (Campbell [1776] 1988: lxxv) and Adams' *Lectures* (Adams 1810: I, 56). Butler famously attacked rhetoric by alluding to overly long and pedantic lists of rhetorical figures supposedly of no use in actual discourse: "For all *a* rhetorician's rules/Teach nothing but to name *his* tools" (Butler 1846: 10, ll. 89–90; my emphasis).

While only very slightly, Poe's quotation differs from Butler's text in that it substitutes the definite article for the words I emphasized in the above quotation (once in place of the indefinite article "a" and once in place of the possessive pronoun "his"). This is a misquotation which exists, as far as I could trace it via various databases, in only one other author, namely the surgeon John Abernethy. Poe definitely knew the somewhat infamous Abernethy, since he also uses his name in an anecdote right before the dénouement in "The Purloined Letter" (T&S 982). Taken together, this makes it likely that Poe was responding to Abernethy's text. In the printed version of Abernethy's lecture it says:

> The new names which are used to denominate the affections of the skin, bother me; and I am in the habit of saying of them, as Hudibras says of rhetoricians;–
> 'For all *the* rhetorician's rules
> Teach nothing but to name *the* tools.'
> But they do not tell you how to cure the disease. (Abernethy 1828: I, 165, my emphasis)

Abernethy's use of the quotation shows that the lines were being used in a sense other than their original allusion to long pedantic lists of rhetorical figures. The passage opposes the use of new scientific nomenclature in favour of something along the lines of 'practical know-how.' Yet Poe ignores this scientific dimension of Abernethy's lecture to focus exclusively on the question of rhetoric. His argument is worth quoting at length:

> What these oft-quoted lines [from *Hudibras*] go to show is, that a falsity in verse will travel faster and endure longer than a falsity in prose. The man who would sneer or stare at a silly proposition nakedly put, will admit that 'there is a good deal in that' when '*that*' is the point of an epigram shot into the ear. The rhetorician's rules – if they *are* rules – teach him not only to name his tools, but to use his tools, the capacity of his tools – their extent – their limit; and from an examination of the nature of the tools – (an examination forced on him by their constant presence) – force him, also, into scrutiny and comprehension of the material on which the tools are employed, and thus, finally, suggest and give birth to new material for new tools. (E&R 1423–1424)

Two things are crucial about this passage: First, for Poe, the endurance of the false opinion from *Hudibras* proves the power of rhythmic and figurative language. Alluding to the perennial question of whether rhetoric is a means of persuasion regardless of the truth of a statement, Poe affirms the power of rhetoric by using the metaphorical ambiguity of "point" (meaning both the point of an arrow and the point of an argument), thus giving a figurative elucidation of the power of figuration. Secondly and more importantly, Poe argues that rhetoric is an art that is both critical and productive and is governed by rules and principles. Viewed in connection with Poe's defence of Taylor, a rhetorical mode of presentation becomes identical with an artful mode of presentation, one that echoes ancient ideas about τέχνη/*techne*. The rhetorical process he describes is both empirical and rule-based. Far from compiling a superfluous list of tools, the rules of rhetoric teach the student the uses to which a tool might be put and those which it cannot help to attain. Out of the interplay of method and material, new methods as well as new materials emerge. Poe's criticism of an anti-rhetorical commonplace thus shows him taking the affirmative in the contemporary discussion on the importance of rhetoric to poetry.

The importance of this description as an affirmation of rhetorical systems of art becomes apparent when we compare it to Richard Whately's use of the same quotation from *Hudibras*. In his discussion of popular objections to rhetoric, Whately also criticizes it,[28] and uses it to illustrate the falsity of the opinion that "natural genius and experience must do everything, and Systems of Art nothing" (Whately [1828] 1963: 18). This negation of the rationale behind the Hudibras argument amounts to no less than an affirmation of the possibility of systems of art over natural genius, and Poe's argument follows similar lines. The discussion of the Hudibras quotation in Whately and Poe illustrates the fundamental divide that Poe was facing between the artful rhetorical poet and the romantic natural genius.

Poe also offers a qualification of his view of rhetorical rules: The rules have to be helpful in order to be rules, i.e. it belongs to the concept of a rule that they are of use in the empirical process of writing; an empty commandment would not 'deserve' the title of a rule. Thus, Poe's notion of rule is one that is based on principles. What is more, it is also congruous with a third discussion of the same passage from *Hudibras*, this time by John Quincy Adams:

> what can be more necessary to the artist, than to know the names as well as the uses of his tools? Rhetoric alone can never constitute an orator. No human art can be acquired by the mere knowledge of the principles, upon which it is founded. But the artist, who understands its principles, will exercise his art in the highest perfection. (Adams 1810: I, 57)

Taken together and read in context, the defence of Baylor and the refutation of the *Hudibras* commonplace evince Poe's generally positive view of rhetoric. This is not to say that Poe did not use 'rhetoric' or its cognates to criticize an overly grandiloquent style; but even in such cases he coins neologisms such as "rhet-

---

28 He cites it yet slightly differently as "'[...] all a Rhetorician's rules,/But teach him how to name his tools'" (Whately [1828] 1963: 18).

oricianism" to denote such a style.²⁹ What emerges from Poe's explicit statements on rhetoric is a view of rhetoric as a system of (helpful) rules that are applicable to poetical discourse. How this theoretical assumption played out in performative terms is discussed in the example of "Ulalume" in chapter six. What remains certain is that Poe was not opposed to the rule(s) of rhetoric in the "empire of literature."

As Whately's discussion of the Hudibras topos shows, the possibility of such a rhetorical art was, in some ways, opposed to notions of genius, the dominant theoretical figure of the author in Poe's times. Keeping in view this opposition between a rhetorical art based on rules and the prevailing discourse of the genius, the following sections first reconstruct Poe's privileging of combinatory fancy over the creative imagination, and, secondly, Poe's explicit view of the genius and his dismissal of the discipline of aesthetics.

From the Imagination to the Fancy

Poe's openness to rhetoric and craft is concurrent with an opposition to certain aspects of romantic aesthetics. This is attested by his take on Coleridge's definition of the imagination, another of the central loci of high romantic thought that we met partially in Coleridge's answer to the question "what is a poet?" (Coleridge [1817] 1983: II, 15–16). In similar fashion as in "The Letter to B—," Poe takes over certain aspects of Coleridge's ideas, yet his relation to the romantic sage changes from initial enthusiasm to later rejection. Their relation has long been a topic in Poe studies, the development of which, intriguingly, suggests a similar trajectory from enthusiasm to rejection in critical thought *about* Poe and Coleridge. In one of the seminal essays, Floyd Stovall characterized "Poe's Debt to Coleridge," and concluded that "[o]n the whole, I agree with Professor [George Edward] Woodberry's original opinion that Coleridge was 'the guiding genius of Poe's entire intellectual life,' and regret that he [Woodberry] later substituted 'early' for 'entire'." (Stovall 1930: 127). Stovall's argument was thus, from early on, something of an attempt to 'salvage' Coleridge as Poe's "guiding genius." Though less encompassing, Jonathan Bate's argument about the coalescing minds of Coleridge and Poe (Bate 1990: 258) points in a similar direction, though,

---

29 "Rhetoricianism" occurs in a review of one of John Brainard's poems (*Graham's Magazine*, February 1842): "'Deep calleth unto deep' is a great improvement upon his [Brainard's] previous rhetoricianism" (E&R 410). On R. H. Horne's poem "Orion" (*Graham's Magazine*, March 1844) Poe comments "how insufficient has been all Mr Horne's poetical rhetoric in convincing even himself" (E&R 295).

as I argued earlier, it is mostly the rhetorical aspects that Poe appropriates. Alexander Schlutz goes even further by arguing that "Poe is in fact far from completing the philosophical structure that Coleridge had attempted to build, and if he inhabits it, he does so not as a headstone in its supporting arch, but rather as a threat to its desired foundations." (Schlutz 2008: 195). The development of Poe's relation to Coleridge becomes particularly apparent in the distinction between fancy and imagination. To assert the crucial nature of this distinction to Coleridge's philosophical and critical thought has long been a commonplace. As editors James Engell and Walter Jackson Bate point out, "[n]o aspect or subject of Coleridge's criticism is more famous than this distinction" (1984: xcvii). My interest here is not in a reading of that passage per se,[30] but rather in what the distinction meant for Poe who, partially appropriating it, also countered Coleridge's distinction by turning the imagination into a type of the fancy, thus inverting their priority.[31]

As we saw in the example of "The Letter to B—" Poe's view of Coleridge was enthusiastic with a bit of ambivalence at the beginning of Poe's career; it would develop into a complete dismissal in later publications. The Coleridge that Poe constructed initially was a champion of quasi-scientific principles.[32] In an 1836 review of Coleridge's *Letters*, Poe commended Coleridge as "the man to whose gigantic mind the proudest intellects of Europe found it impossible not to succumb," complaining of the lack of a republished edition of the *Biographia Literaria* (E&R 181, 188). Poe's expectation was that such a publication would "do away" with the American impression of Coleridge's "*mysticism*," expecting that Coleridge's work would render "an important service to the cause of psychological science in America" (E&R 188). As Poe's career went on, he would regard Coleridge considerably less as a contributor to psychological science, although the English sage remained an important source for his ideas. In 1840, Poe writes of the "dogmatism of Coleridge" (E&R 333) and views him as "erring at times" in 1844 (E&R 294). The development might be said to culminate in Poe's damnation of the Lake school in 1845 – no longer just echoing Jeffrey's damnation of Words-

---

[30] For a detailed reading of the passages in the context of the *Biographia Literaria*, cf. Jonathan Wordsworth's "'The Infinite I AM': Coleridge and the Ascent of Being" (1985).
[31] The most far-reaching claim on Poe's concept of the fancy was made by Patrick Full, who views Poe's oeuvre as the swan song of the imagination and the beginning of modern concepts of human creativity, as the German title has it: *Der Abgesang der Imagination: Edgar Allan Poes Neubestimmung der menschlichen Kreativität* (2007). "Fancy" is a contraction of "fantasy" via the forms 'fantsy' and 'phant'sy,' as the OED has it (OED s.v. *fancy* n.); the origin of these forms is located in the 15th century already (OED s.v. *fantasy* n.).
[32] The observations in this section have their origin in Guttzeit (2010: 82–86; 90–91).

worth but dismissing Coleridge as even worse – as a "school of all Lawlessness – of obscurity, quaintness, exaggeration" that consists, for Poe, in "the misplaced didacticism of Wordsworth, and the even more preposterously anomalous metaphysicianism of Coleridge." (E&R 140).

This growing opposition to Coleridge's position is mirrored in Poe's changing conception of the fancy. While Coleridge had strictly separated it from the imagination, Poe reasserted its poetical importance. In a way, Poe thus opposes a high romantic notion of the author as the creator and partaker in a divine order of being.[33] Coleridge's famous definition from the *Biographia Literaria* reads as follows:

> The IMAGINATION then I consider either as primary, or secondary. The primary IMAGINATION I hold to be the living Power and prime Agent of all human Perception, and as a repetition in the finite mind of the eternal act of creation in the infinite I AM. The secondary I consider as an echo of the former, co-existing with the conscious will, yet still as identical with the primary in the *kind* of its agency, and differing only in *degree*, and in the *mode* of its operation. It dissolves, diffuses, dissipates, in order to re-create; or where this process is rendered impossible, yet still at all events it struggles to idealize and to unify. It is essentially *vital*, even as all objects (*as* objects) are essentially fixed and dead." (Coleridge [1817] 1983: I, 304)

After these three elements – the divine "infinite I AM," the primary imagination, and the secondary imagination – Coleridge defines the fancy, which is, in some ways, another iteration of the same structure, yet as a mere mode of memory, invested only with the power of "choice," not of will. While the "infinite I AM" as well as the primary and secondary imagination are vital, organic, and have an ontological connection to a metaphysical level, the fancy is viewed as a merely empirical phenomenon governed by the laws of association:

> FANCY, on the contrary, has no other counters to play with, but fixities and definites. The Fancy is indeed no other than a mode of Memory emancipated from the order of time and space; and blended with, and modified by that empirical phenomenon of the will, which we express by the word CHOICE. But equally with the ordinary memory the fancy must receive all its materials ready made from the law of association. (Coleridge [1817] 1983: I, 305)

---

33 In her investigation into the origins of the romantic author, Martha Woodmansee discusses Karl Philipp Moritz' theory of the autonomy of art and classifies it as "clearly a displaced theology" (1984b: 33). In some ways, the same might be said of Coleridge, as will become clear particularly in the status of the "infinite I AM" for his concept of the imagination. According to Jonathan Wordsworth, "Coleridge is at all times a Christian thinker" and even came to reject the *Biographia Literaria* "as pantheist" within three years after its composition in 1815 (J. Wordsworth 1985: 31, 22).

In broad strokes, for Coleridge, every act of poetical creation is an act analogous to the creation of the world (or nature) by the 'infinite I AM,' while the fancy never creates. To imagine something is thus to partake in the divine realisation of the possible (Lobsien 2008: 117).[34] The divine realisation of the possible is part of a neoplatonic system in Coleridge where the diversity of nature is, in essence, a unity because of the unity of a – broadly conceived – Christian God that forms the basis or, rather, highest point of nature; the absolute will "manifests itself in the resulting many, namely nature, as structuration" based on proportion and mathematical relations (Lobsien 2008: 117).[35] The contrast between the two types of imagination and the fancy is marked. As Jonathan Wordsworth puts it, "[w]ith the primary imagination man unknowingly reenacts God's original and eternal creative moment; with the secondary he consciously vitalizes an object-world that would otherwise be dead; with the fancy he plays unvital games, dependent upon choice and the laws of association. There can be no doubt whatever that the least of the three powers is fancy" (J. Wordsworth 1985: 25). As the least of the powers, the fancy is limited to the empirical; according to Engell and Bate's gloss, it "can aggregate and combine only what it has received" and "it is limited, empirically, by what we can remember that we have perceived or experienced;" thus, "[f]ancy may produce unreal or impossible combinations, but their component parts will all be part of the experienced world" (Engell and Bate 1984: civ). Emphatic creation is thus reserved for the imagination only.

Poe takes up Coleridge's distinction between the fancy and the imagination several times, but his definitions change in line with his overall view of Coleridge. In April 1836, in the "Drake-Halleck Review" in the *Southern Literary Messenger*, Poe still maintains the opposition between the "*Fancy* or the powers of combination" and the "Poetic Sentiment, which is Ideality, Imagination, or the creative ability" (E&R 520). Yet, as early as the review of Thomas Moore's *Alciphron* (*Burton's Gentleman's Magazine*, January 1840), Poe criticizes the strict distinction, and maintains that it can be viewed at best as one of degree (E&R 334).

Later on, he flatly asserts its non-existence. In the first item of the *Literati* series, in a portrait of Nathaniel Parker Willis, Poe replaces Coleridge's differentiation by what we might perhaps best term, following early Poe scholar Pasquale Jannaccone and G. R. Thompson, the four "modes of the 'combining intelligence'" (Jannaccone [1895] 1974: 1), which still include the imagination but

---

34 My paraphrase of "Imaginieren heißt positiv: teilhaben an der göttlichen Realisierung des Potentiellen" (Lobsien 2008: 117).
35 My translation; absolute will "manifestiert sich in dem resultierenden Vielen, eben der Natur, als Strukturierung" (Lobsien 2008: 117; cf. also 78).

redefine it as a higher type of fancy rather than vice versa.³⁶ Coleridge's opposition of the creative imagination and the merely combining fancy is, Poe writes, "a distinction without a difference," and, departing from his own earlier stance, maintains: "without a difference even of degree" (E&R 1126). Real creation, Poe argues, is something which is only achieved by the thoughts of God: "The fancy as nearly creates as the imagination, and neither at all. Novel conceptions are merely unusual combinations. The mind of man can imagine nothing which does not really exist; if it could, it would create not only ideally but substantially, as do the thoughts of God." (E&R 1126). While for Coleridge, the poetic imagination offers a way 'upward' to the "infinite I AM," Poe views the creation of the world and poetic combination as homologous but gives primary emphasis to the poet. This goes so far that, as Jerome McGann has it, "we might say that Poe is an atheist, as Shelley declared himself. But he is only an atheist in a very special sense – a sense that is closer to the theist Blake than to the atheist Shelley. The God of philosophy and theology and the traditional churches is for him a multiply dispersed historical reality. Poe is interested in that God and his historical appearances as material for his poetic representations – strictly, as language." (McGann 2014b: 47–48).³⁷ In other words, Poe views the divine as an image of the poetic and not vice versa like Coleridge. Consequently, the products of the imagination are, for Poe, nothing substantially new but only new combinations or compositions. Just as the imagined (non-existent) griffin is the result of a combination of the existing lion and the existing eagle, so is every product of the imagination "no more than a collation of known limbs, features, qualities" (E&R 1126). For Poe, all the beautiful products of the imagination which claim to be absolutely new, are "re-soluble" into the old (E&R 1126); everything can be reduced to its component parts because no factual creation takes place. Hence, even when Poe speaks of the imagination, he understands it as what Coleridge named "fancy."

This can be seen clearly in the model with which Poe replaces Coleridge's distinction. The already-mentioned four "modes of the combining intelligence" are imagination, fancy, fantasy and humour. While Poe thus lists imagination and fancy as two different faculties, they would both fall under Coleridge's category of the fancy. All modes have in common, says Poe, the "elements combination and novelty" (E&R 1126). The three categories which structure the differ-

---

36 The first *Literati* item is from *Godey's Lady's Book*, June 1846 (E&R 1118–1153). The relevant passage is nearly identical with the one in the earlier review of Thomas Hood (*Broadway Journal*, Aug 9, 1845). Cf. E&R 277–279.
37 Cp. René Wellek's observation that "Poe, basically an agnostic, tried to base an aesthetics on remnants of religiosity" ([1965] 1966: 157).

entiation are the type of combination (in scope very similar to what Poe names elsewhere "tone" [CT 61]), the materials to be combined (in other words "incident" [CT 61]), and, of course, the effect of the combination.

The imagination as the "artist of the four" *combines* in a harmonious way both beautiful forms and deformed things to arrive at the effect of "*beauty itself;*" it selects the "most combinable things hitherto uncombined" (E&R 1126). In contrast, the novel combination made by the fancy gives the impression of a "*difficulty happily overcome,*" and being less harmonious, is only unexpected and does not have the revelatory quality of the product of the imagination. To the majority of the audience, the result which appertains to the fancy is "more grateful than the purely harmonious one" (E&R 1127) – another indication of Poe's privileging of the fancy over the imagination. If the harmony or proportion that is present in the products both of the fancy and the imagination is lost, fancy, "carrying its errors into excess" becomes fantasy, the result of which "to a healthy mind, affords less of pleasure through its novelty than of pain through its incoherence" (E&R 1127). Only if the incoherence is heightened and "not merely disproportionate, but incongruous or antagonistic elements" are combined, the effect is that of humour: "there is a merry effort of truth to shake from her that which is no property of hers, and we laugh outright in recognizing humour" (E&R 1127).

These four modes of combination are identified by Poe with faculties of the human mind. The artist can make use of them, but there is also the possibility that a writer lacks one or the other of the faculties.[38] The difference to Coleridge lies in Poe's insistence on the 'merely' combinatory character of *all* of these powers of the artist, including the imagination, and the denial of a connection to a divine or 'higher' level of reality which makes possible and, in a sense, author(ize)s the poet's creations.

Poe's distancing from Coleridge's valuation of the imagination and devaluation of the fancy is indicative of his opposition to characteristics of the poet as defined in high romantic aesthetics. Full (2007) interprets this distancing as an indication of Poe's being a forerunner of modernity and Schlutz (2008) argues in similar fashion about Poe's relation to Coleridge in general. While the principle of 'mere combination' that characterizes the fancy might be viewed – if taken to its extreme – as prefiguring modernist and postmodernist aleatory methods of text production such as cut-up and fold-in, it also points backwards to neoclass-

---

[38] Thomas Moore, for example, is characterized in his style as only fanciful (E&R 277), while Hawthorne is described by Poe as "truly imaginative" (E&R 571).

ical conceptions of the poet such as Dryden's or Pope's, in which the rhetorical presentation is central to poetic achievement.

One factor that speaks for this neoclassical hypothesis is that, in preferring fancy, Poe chooses a version of the term that used to be more prestigious until the eighteenth century, since it derived from the Greek φαντασία/*phantasia* rather than the Latin *imaginatio* (Engell and Bate 1984: xcvii). If we ask how the preference of the fancy is connected to earlier, particularly rhetorical models of the poet, then we need to look at the rhetorical concept most closely connected to combination, namely, arrangement (*dispositio*). Since the *dispositio* could function as a scheme for invention, it is systematically connected to bringing about new combinations of thoughts, and Poe's poetical emphasis would thus be mirrored in the rhetorical emphasis on disposition.

A historical moment that makes these rhetorical interconnections of poetic invention and arrangement particularly visible is John Dryden's translation of "dispositio" as "fancy."[39] In the prefatory letter to *Annus Mirabilis*, Dryden presented the poet's imagination as consisting of the first three *officia* of rhetoric:

> the first happiness of the Poet's imagination is properly Invention, or finding of the thought; the second is Fancy, or the variation, deriving or moulding of that thought, as the judgment represents it proper to the subject; the third is Elocution, or the art of clothing and adorning that thought so found and varied, in apt, significant, and sounding words: the quickness of the Imagination is seen in the Invention, the fertility in the Fancy, and the accuracy in the Expression. (Dryden [1667] 1956: 53)

Dryden's translation of *dispositio* as "fancy" places the term in the centre of an encompassing model of the rhetorical poet.[40] Poe's general interest in Early Modern poetics is well attested (Engel 2012), and, in Dryden's model, the emphasis is placed on "variation," a term that draws out the inventive implications of arrangement in a paradigmatic way. This is not to posit any direct line of influence but it exemplifies the crucial connection between the fancy as combination and rhetorical arrangement. Poe's "novel *arrangements* of old forms" (E&R 1126; my emphasis) have a rhetorical ring to them.

In similar fashion, Poe's preference – broadly speaking – of the empirical fancy over the Neoplatonic idealist imagination connects him to the philosophical background of the New Rhetoricians, who were steeped in British empiricism

---

39 Full (2007: 16) cites Dryden in his genealogy of the fancy, yet does not point out its rhetorical character.
40 Echoes of Dryden's emphasis on wit ([1667] 1956: 53) might also be heard in Poe's definition of humour as a mode of the combining intelligence.

rather than German idealism, as in Coleridge's case.[41] As Engell and Bate clarify, Coleridge's distinction was mostly based on German idealist philosophy: "It is the distinctions of these five writers [Platner, Tetens, Kant, Maass, and Schelling] that bear most similarity to Coleridge's. He had read them all and found a sophisticated series of distinctions showing only marginal differences. With the exception of Maass, the words used by these writers are *Phantasie* and *Einbildungskraft*." (Engell and Bate 1984: cii–ciii). While Coleridge also "wanted to stress that fancy is tied to sensory experience" (Engell and Bate 1984: ciii–civ), it is a view of fancy from the perspective of idealist rather than empiricist philosophy.

What the idealist philosophy of the time would view as creation, empiricist philosophy would view as (re)combination, and it was the latter that formed the context of the New Rhetoric. Elizabeth Larsen suggests that, in the eighteenth century, "*inventio* was less abandoned than transformed" (181) in an empiricist and associationist context defined by the Humean 'science of man' that also furnished the foundation of George Campbell's project of a philosophical rhetoric. In the Humean system, "simple ideas become complex through imagination. In this theory, nothing is made new; rather, all is readjusted. For Hume there is no such activity as invention in the sense of making from wholly new materials – all complex ideas come from recollected simple ones" (Larsen 1993: 188). Here, the imagination has a more mundane role – just like the fancy. Viewed in a Humean and New Rhetorical framework, Poe's insistence on mere combination is thus hardly remarkable but it becomes marked through its opposition to Coleridge's idealist thought.

Poe's tendency towards empiricist positions becomes especially visible in what might be viewed as a significant departure from Poe's insistence on the impossibility of human endeavour to create *sensu stricto*. Poe writes:

> The pure imagination chooses, *from either beauty or deformity*, only the most combinable things hitherto uncombined; the compound, as a general rule, partaking in character of sublimity or beauty in the ratio of the respective sublimity or beauty of the things combined, which are themselves still to be considered as atomic – that is to say, as previous combinations. But, as often analogously happens in physical chemistry, so not unfrequently does it occur in this chemistry of the intellect, that the admixture of two elements will result in a something that shall have nothing of the quality of one of them – or even nothing of the qualities of either. (E&R 1126)

---

[41] J. Wordsworth makes the case that British religious thinking rather than German idealist philosophy was formative for Coleridge (1985: 28). Nevertheless, this does not void the fact that Coleridge's extensive plagiarism in the so-called philosophical chapters of the *Biographia Literaria* was of German sources (cf. Coleridge [1817] 1984: II, 253–254).

There were contemporary ideas about 'chemical wit,' 'chemistry of mind,' and 'mental chemistry' (Engell and Bate 1984: ci), and the link to scientific conceptions of physical emergence, if not to Epicurean atomism, seems inevitable. Just like oxygen and hydrogen individually do not exhibit the quality of fluidity that they have when combined as water, Poe conceives of the emergence of originality in literature in analogy with the physical emergence of new qualities. Poe does not say that the individual elements gain a new quality;[42] instead there either appears a completely new quality in the new whole that results from the combinations or the new whole is of such a character that its qualities are completely different from the qualities that its elements used to have on their own, as is the case with the fluidity of water.

Despite the presence of a visionary vocabulary, for instance, in the early poetry or in "The Poetic Principle," Poe appears thoroughly moored in the author's craft and the empirical world.[43] While Poe speaks of "the creation of supernal Beauty" and "a wild effort to reach the Beauty above" (CT 184), his otherworldly imagery is used to figure the author rather than the other way around. McGann illuminates this in his reading of the metaphor of the "desire of the moth for the star" (CT 184), which Poe takes from Percy Shelley's "To –. [One word is too often profaned]" (1824). Poe effectively rewrites Shelley's metaphor and makes it a symptom of a "certain, petulant, impatient sorrow" (CT 184) which, according to McGann, "sink[s] Shelley's devotional gesture to a figure of ordinary, even infantile, frustration" (McGann 2014b: 41). In effect, "Poe disallows the Shelleyan premise of poetic 'inspiration'" so that "[t]he poet's limited capabilities are taken for granted." (McGann 2014b: 41). For McGann, this anticipates both Rimbaud and Nietzsche, but, as we saw with reference to Dryden, it also harks back to earlier rhetorical concepts of the fancy. Another parallel can be drawn with contemporary ideas of the orator who remains bound to earth. As John Quincy Adams phrases it in his *Lectures on Rhetoric and Oratory* (1810), the "poet may soar beyond the flaming bounds of space and time; but the orator must remember, that

---

42 This is how Full (2007: 127) reads the passage, which does not seem strong enough to me.
43 David S. Reynolds has pointed out the relevance of the secularisation of popular visionary imagery by Poe: "By Poe's time, many popular American writers had separated religion from the intellect and placed it in the realm of the creative imagination, bound to the celestial principally by the secular visionary mode. Poe took this secularizing process to its natural aesthetic ends. Having explored the celestial beauty of both beatific and horrific sensations in much of his poetry, he turned in his theoretical criticism to an equation of poetic effect with supernal beauty. Liberated from dogma by his extensive experimentation with the popular visionary mode, Poe came to the conclusion that beauty had nothing to do with Christian doctrine and was only tangentially related to reason or conscience." (Reynolds [1988] 2011: 46).

an audience is not so readily excursive, and is always under the power of gravitation" (Adams 1810: II, 327).

It seems that, as a theoretician of the fancy and as a poet, Poe – like an orator – chooses to feel the powers of gravitation. Judging from Poe's privileging of the combining fancy, the poet is, in effect, someone who arranges already existing combinations into new combinations; the posited theoretical figure of the author is thus connected to the autheme of *dispositio*; in other words, the author is figured as an arranger.

Countering the Aesthetics of Genius

Poe's positive view of rhetoric and his theoretical figure of the author as arranger are complemented by an explicit opposition to the still fairly new discipline of aesthetics.[44] The opposition of rhetoric and aesthetics as basic disciplines of 'literary' theory and thus of differing theoretical figures of the author becomes obvious in one of Poe's most explicit links to the Scottish school. In the same instalment of the *Marginalia* (January 1848) that also contains the Hudibras reference discussed above, Poe considers the aforementioned review article by Charles Astor Bristed on "The Scotch School of Philosophy and Criticism" (1845), which views Adam Smith and George Campbell as its main proponents.[45] Bristed concludes his presentation of the Scottish rhetoricians by claiming that "the best part of art is that which no analysis can seize, no method can subjugate." This formed the basis for his division of critics into two groups: "The least methodical are the best of our aesthetical critics," naming Hazlitt, Coleridge, and Carlyle as successful, "where Kaims [sic] and Campbell, with their canons and categories, would have failed" (Bristed 1845: 397). Bristed thus explicitly opposes aesthetical critics such as Hazlitt, Coleridge, and Carlyle to rhetorical critics such as Lord Kames and George Campbell.

Poe's reaction is to accuse Bristed of "the most singular admixture of error and truth" (E&R 1419). He does not take pains to rebut individual arguments but rather criticizes Bristed for his insufficient theory of versification whilst promoting his own forthcoming "Rationale of Verse."[46] But Poe had in fact already provided an answer to the question that is raised by the key tension between what Bristed describes as Scottish methodical rhetorical critics and non-methodical

---

[44] On the ideology of the aesthetic, cf. Eagleton (1990).
[45] In the article Bristed actually favourably quoted Poe's article on "The American Drama" (Bristed 1845: 387–88), yet this did not secure Poe's approval.
[46] Cf. the discussion in chapter six.

aesthetical critics, or what I outlined in chapter two as the opposition between rhetorical and romantic views of poetry and literature.

Poe's thesis on the relation between these two groups of critics encapsulates his own complex relationship to both traditions. In his far-reaching preface to the newly-conceived Critical Notices in *Graham's Magazine* in January 1842, Poe compared the earlier British Enlightenment critics with the German romantic critics. Crucially, Poe holds that the two do not substantially differ:[47]

> what need we say of the Germans? – what of Winkelmann [sic], of Novalis, of Schelling, of Göethe [sic], of Augustus William, and of Frederick Schlegel? – that their magnificent *critiques raisonnées* differ from those of Kaimes [sic], of Johnson, and of Blair, in principle not at all, (for the principles of these artists will not fail until Nature herself expires,) but solely in their more careful elaboration, their greater thoroughness, their more profound analysis and application of the principles themselves. That a criticism 'now' should be different in spirit [...] from a criticism at any previous period, is to insinuate a charge of variability in laws that cannot vary – the laws of man's heart and intellect – for these are the sole basis upon which the true critical art is established (E&R 1030–31)

By stating the invariability of critical principles and the laws of man's heart and intellect, Poe in effect defends a criticism based on the Enlightenment science of human nature of the eighteenth-century, which was the basis for the Scottish Common Sense rhetoricians. That he lumps together the quintessential German classicist Johann Joachim Winckelmann with the brothers Schlegel is not so much an indication of his ignorance of German criticism but of his attempt to unite all critics under his own version of criticism. Even more crucial, however, is the fact that he does not recognise the evident opposition between the two groups of critics and transforms the German romantics such as Novalis, Schelling, and the Schlegels into British neo-classicists and rhetoricians like Hugh Blair.

This is all the more relevant, since the text was intended as a foundation for the type of criticism that readers would be able to expect from *Graham's* under Poe's editorship. In it, Poe laid out his idea of "limit[ing] literary criticism to comment upon *Art*" in the sense of the principles of the artwork itself, and rejected extraneous concerns with "opinion," which he assigned to historians, metaphysicians, and other specialists (E&R 1032). While he does not refer to his type of criticism as rhetorical, the reference to eighteenth-century critics such as Blair and the reliance upon a view of the "art-product" as the object of criticism points towards just such a type of criticism. This ambivalence plays out especially in the

---

[47] Usually, the emphasis by critics has been put on Poe's apparent preference for the German critics (e.g. Thompson 1973: 26), yet what is more striking is his invention of a continuous tradition between the two groups.

first sentences of the piece, in which the rhetorical term for the opening of a speech is used and then almost immediately negated: "In commencing, with the New Year, a New Volume, we shall be permitted to say a very few words by way of *exordium* to our usual chapter of Reviews, or, as we should prefer calling them, of Critical Notices. Yet we speak not for the sake of the *exordium*, but because we have really something to say, and know not when or where better to say it" (E&R 1027). Poe invokes the technical term 'exordium' for the presentation of his thoughts, yet at the same time he distances himself from the rhetorical nomenclature in a quasi-romantic gesture of earnestness: not for the sake of the exordium, but because "we have really something to say."[48] As mentioned before, R. D. Jacobs concluded "[i]n his practice of criticism Poe was a rhetorician" (Jacobs 1969: x), yet the peculiar situation of antebellum American criticism makes it impossible for Poe to figure himself as a rhetorician.[49] Yet, while Poe's view of criticism remains implicitly rhetorical, there is explicit evidence that he did not conceive of it as aesthetical.

Compared to the wide-spread use of "aesthetics" nowadays, its contentious origins are far less often discussed: the term was often rejected throughout the first century of its history after Alexander Gottlieb Baumgarten coined the term in his *Aesthetica* in 1750. As the entry in the OED shows, "aesthetic" was regarded as not yet "an established English word" in 1832; by 1859, however, Sir William Hamilton thought it "now in general acceptation, not only in Germany, but throughout the other countries of Europe" (OED s.v. *aesthetic* n.). Even Coleridge discussed the shortcomings of the term in *Blackwood's* in 1821: "I wish I could find a more familiar word than æsthetic, for works of taste and criticism" (Coleridge 1821: 254). While this might be surprising, coming from an author very much working in that tradition, Coleridge, in the very next sentence, explicitly set it against and placed it above the belletristic rhetoric of Hugh Blair and his followers: "It [the word "æsthetic"] is, however, in all respects better, and of more reputable origin, than belletristic" (Coleridge 1821: 254). As a result of the transatlantic currents of texts, the situation in the United States is like-

---

48 This ambivalence continues to this day in the critical practice of naming the piece "Exordium," even though it appeared without a title when it was originally published in *Graham's*. As Jeffrey A. Savoye (2011) notes, most likely the first to give the piece the title of "Exordium" was James A. Harrison.

49 The general instability of the situation of antebellum criticism as a vocation is brought out by Aaron Gordon who interprets "The Philosophy of Composition" as "a sensitive reflection on the culture of criticism in antebellum America, a barometer of the hyper-critical zeitgeist, and a meditation on both the promises and pitfalls of literary criticism by one of the era's most prominent critics." (Gordon 2012: 28).

ly to be similar. The acceptance of the term 'aesthetics' thus falls into the period in which Poe was writing, yet – while Poe's genuine interest in the category of beauty might make us think of him as an aesthetical author – Poe rejected the term 'aesthetics' for a theory of the beautiful.[50] Neither did he have an aesthetic *sensu* Baumgarten for whom the term referred to a theory of inferior cognition[51] nor rely on Kant's notion in the *Critique of Pure Reason*, i.e. a theory of sensual perception.

Poe's explicitly positive attitude towards rhetoric in general is complemented by a no less explicit negative attitude towards aesthetics. Contrary to the assumption that Poe never uses the words "aesthetics" and "aesthetical,"[52] he employs them as derogatory terms. They occur in the long review of R. H. Horne's epic poem *Orion* in *Graham's Magazine* for March 1844 (E&R 289–310).[53] In the review Poe severely criticizes the quasi-religious tenets of British and American romantic and transcendalist critics, accusing Horne's critics in particular of "an ostrich affectation, which buries its head in balderdash" (E&R 290). "[R]hapsody and æsthetics" and "mere dogmas and doctrines, literary, æsthetical, or what not" are their characteristics (E&R 290). Poe associates "the doggerel æsthetics of the time" (E&R 294) with the position of the critic as a "seer" rather than "the man of Common Sense" (E&R 291).[54] The explicit reference to common sense is an indicator of the Scottish and rhetorical origin of Poe's stance, which he sets off vehemently from a figure of the critic as aesthetical "seer."

This theoretical figure of the *critic* as a seer has an obvious affinity to that of the inspired genius. Though nowhere near the exclusivity negativity of "aesthetics," Poe very rarely uses 'genius' in the sense of the romantic original genius,

---

50 Webster's dictionary defined 'esthetics' as "The science which treats of the beautiful, or of the theory of taste" (1848: 368).
51 On Baumgarten's relation to rhetoric, cf. Campe (2006). Poe's opposition against the romantics appears similar in some respects to Friedrich Gottlieb Klopstock's against Baumgarten in Germany, which Frauke Berndt has examined: Klopstock, a pivotal figure in the transformation of rhetoric into the aesthetics of genius in Germany, also focuses on effect and empirical studies of effects; Klopstock is interested in "what has caused effect" in order to produce a similar effect through his own texts (Berndt 2002: 27).
52 In the era before large databases such as Google Books and HathiTrust, Rachel Polonsky maintained, in her essay on "Poe's Aesthetic Theory," that the "word 'aesthetic' does not occur in Poe's literary, critical, or theoretical writings" (2002: 43).
53 I have not come across any other instances of cognates of 'aesthetic' in Poe.
54 The charge of 'Orphicism' was most likely directly aimed at the transcendentalist Amos Bronson Alcott's "Orphic Sayings," which appeared in "The Dial."

and is generally sceptical about its reality.⁵⁵ Thus he writes that "genius [...] invariably begins its career by imitation" (E&R 1400). Remarkably, genius is often linked to the realities of the antebellum literary marketplace, as a 'man of genius' can "write to suit himself – but in the same manner his publishers print": "[f]rom the nature of our Copy-Right laws, he has no individual powers" (E&R 1332). In some passages, 'genius' approaches the meaning of an extraordinary talent that has to be kept in check in order to avoid its "inequalities of mood [being] stamped upon its labors" (E&R 1417). While Poe was aware of the dimensions of "genius," he only rarely subscribed to it,⁵⁶ asserting, for instance, that "'works of genius' are few, while mere men of genius are [...] abundant" (E&R 1363).

Thus the relevance becomes clear of the opposition between rhetoric and aesthetics for the theoretical figures of the author as poet-critic. One of the basic distinctions for Poe's criticism is the opposition of a rhetoric of craft and an aesthetics of genius. This contrast comes out most clearly in Poe's posthumously published essay "About Critics and Criticism" (1850), in which he links rhetoric and genius in a single critic. Poe lauds Thomas Babington Macaulay for the "style and general conduct" of his critical papers, which could "scarcely be improved" (E&R 1040).⁵⁷ He goes on to make the following argument about Macaulay's rhetoric:

> For his short sentences, for his antitheses, for his modulations, for his climaxes – for every thing that he does – a very slight analysis suffices to show a distinct reason. His manner, thus, is simply the perfection of that justifiable rhetoric which has its basis in commonsense; and to say that such rhetoric is never called in to the aid of *genius*, is simply to disparage genius, and by no means to discredit the rhetoric. It is nonsense to assert that the highest genius would not be benefited by attention to its modes of manifestation – by availing itself of that Natural Art which it too frequently despises. Is it not evident that the more

---

55 Poe's theory of genius is thus often reminiscent of central tenets of eighteenth-century criticism, as, for example, in Alexander Gerard's *An Essay on Genius* (1774). As Elizabeth Larsen explains: "The result of Gerard's study of Hume, John Locke, and his fellow Scots is a general theory of creativity focusing on [rhetorical] invention – the result of his belief that genius is 'the faculty of invention' and invention, the 'infallible Criterion of Genius' [...] Not restricted to geniuses in art and science, what he describes is an act embedded within the normal human mental continuum and explained through the lens of associationism" (186).
56 One such exception is his characterisation of Shelley in the Review of Barrett Browning in the *Broadway Journal*, January 1845: "If ever poet sang (as a bird sings) – impulsively – earnestly – with utter abandonment – to himself solely – and for the mere joy of his own song – that poet was the author of the Sensitive Plant. Of Art – beyond that which is the inalienable instinct of Genius – he either had little or disdained all" (E&R 139).
57 With regard to Macaulay personally, this is a partial revision of Poe's earlier review (in *Graham's Magazine*, June 1841; E&R 321–324) of the latter's *Critical Writings*. The review is condensed in the "Chapter of Suggestions" (*The Opal*, 1845; E&R 1292–1296).

intrinsically valuable the rough diamond, the more gain accrues to it from polish? (E&R 1040–41)

Poe distinguishes a "justifiable rhetoric" from one that is not justifiable, namely the "quips, quirks, and curt oracularities of the Emersons, Alcots and Fullers" (E&R 1040). More importantly, rhetoric as a "Natural Art" with its basis in (Scottish) common sense is an aid, or a tool, for genius, a concept that Poe here applies to the author-as-critic. Hence, it is linked to Poe's aforementioned aim to "limit literary criticism to comment upon Art," upon a book "as an *art-product*" (E&R 1032). Thus, when it comes to his combined interest in the arts of criticism and composition, this would find its equivalent in what Whately called "the art of Composition": "'such rules as *every* good Composition must conform to,' whether the author of it had them in his mind or not" (Whately 1828: 20).

In all, we find in Poe a decidedly positive attitude towards a rhetorical rule-based craft of the author and a correspondingly negative attitude towards a romantic aesthetics with an emphatic or fundamentalist conception of genius. While this opposition can clearly be reconstructed, this does not mean that Poe viewed his own brand of criticism in consciously rhetorical terms. He certainly figures the poet-critic in general and himself in particular via such an opposition, and yet the peculiar situation of antebellum American criticism, torn between rhetoric and aesthetics, makes it impossible for him to fully figure himself as a rhetorician; in this regard he himself is a figure of the peculiar historical situation in which his theoretical texts emerge. In order to become a transatlantic poet-critic, Poe appropriates romantic and aesthetical ideas in his critical texts from "Letter to B " to the *Marginalia*, but in the end he will argue the case for the rule(s) of rhetoric.

4 The Genius Rhetorician: The Rhetoric of "The Philosophy of Composition"

> I mail you [...] a copy of my best specimen of analysis—"The Philosophy of Composition."
> Poe to Philip Pendleton Cooke, August 9, 1846 (LTR-240)

4.1 Poe, Dickens, Godwin and the Question of Writing Backwards

On March 6, 1842, a day after arriving in Philadelphia, Charles Dickens, who was touring the United States for the first time, wrote a short response to a letter from Poe. Poe had asked Dickens for an interview, enclosing books and articles, most likely the two volumes of his *Tales of the Grotesque and Arabesque* (1839) and his reviews of Dickens' novel *Barnaby Rudge* (1840–41). These had appeared in the *Saturday Evening Post* on May 1, 1841 and in *Graham's Magazine* in February 1842, the month before Dickens arrived in Philadelphia (PL 361–362).[1] Poe concluded the latter review with a comparison of Dickens and the English writer and philosopher, William Godwin, in which he subtly criticizes and provokes Dickens. Of Dickens' *Barnaby Rudge*, Poe wrote:

> We think that the whole book has been an effort to him – solely through the nature of its design. He has been smitten with an untimely desire for a novel path. The idiosyncrasy of his intellect would lead him, naturally, into the most fluent and simple style of narration. In tales of ordinary sequence he may and will long reign triumphant. He has a *talent* for all things, but no positive *genius* for *adaptation*, and still less for that metaphysical art in which the souls of all *mysteries* lie. (E&R 244)

Poe was in the position to make such claims because of his earlier review of the early parts of *Barnaby Rudge*, in which he surmised correctly, for the most part, the dénouement of Dickens' novel. He argued that what Godwin, the author of *Caleb Williams* (1794), lacked in imagination, Dickens, the author of *The Old Curiosity Shop* (1840–41), lacked in constructive power: "Mr. Dickens could no more have constructed the one than Mr. Godwin could have dreamed of the other" (E&R 244).

Dickens responded with a short note, in which he invited Poe to his hotel and mentioned the difficulties that the 'constructor' Godwin had had in compos-

---

[1] The timeliness of the second review has led Sidney Moss to argue that Poe may have timed it for Dickens' visit to the US (1978: 10).

ing *Caleb Williams*, difficulties, which, for Dickens, seem to spring from Godwin's procedure of "writing backwards":

> Apropos of the 'construction' of Caleb Williams. Do you know that Godwin wrote it <u>backwards</u> – the last volume first – and that when he had produced the hunting down of Caleb, and the catastrophe, he waited for months, casting about for a means of accounting for what he had done?[2]

Poe and Dickens most likely met on Monday, March 7, and talked about American poetry, and also, in all likelihood, about William Godwin's technique of "writing backwards." A few years later, Poe lightly edited Dickens' note of invitation and turned it into the beginning of "The Philosophy of Composition," which was first published in *Graham's Magazine* in April 1846:[3]

> CHARLES DICKENS, in a note now lying before me, alluding to an examination I once made of the mechanism of 'Barnaby Rudge,' says – 'By the way, are you aware that Godwin wrote his 'Caleb Williams' backwards? He first involved his hero in a web of difficulties, forming the second volume, and then, for the first, cast about him for some mode of accounting for what had been done.' (CT 60)

The situation in which Poe and Dickens discuss Godwin's writing is characterized by their attempts to persuade each other of the importance (Poe) and the difficulty (Dickens) of planning and constructing literary texts. Their debate, which Poe used and refashioned for the beginning of "The Philosophy of Composition," contains *in nuce* the crucial questions as to whether a rhetorical planning of effects is possible, and, if so, what kind of author is able to do so, two questions that merge in one: namely, the question of the possibility and advantages of "writing backwards."

This question forms part of the crucial prehistory of "The Philosophy of Composition," a text which, for its inherent contradictions and tempestuous reception history, is perhaps the most representative of the problem of Poe. It is

---

[2] This text is transcribed from Dickens' ALS to Poe in the Berg Collection at the New York Public Library (Call no. Berg Coll MSS Dickens). "Backwards" is underscored. "Volume" might be spelt with a capital "v" as might "catastrophe," but this does not change the meaning in any way.
[3] Poe first used Dickens' letter in his 1845 "A Chapter of Suggestions": "Godwin and Bulwer are the best constructors of plot in English literature. The former has left a preface to his 'Caleb Williams,' in which he says that the novel was *written backwards*; the author first completing the second volume, in which the hero is involved in a maze of difficulties, and then casting about him for sufficiently probable cause of these difficulties, out of which to concoct volume the first. This mode cannot surely be recommended, but evinces the idiosyncrasy of Godwin's mind" (E&R 1294).

certainly the most paradigmatic in terms of his theoretical figures of authorship. Written about his greatest success as a poet, "The Raven," which catapulted him to poetical fame on both sides of the Atlantic, "Philosophy" is one of Poe's most contested pieces of writing in the critical literature, cited at times as the epitome of method or of madness. While it sums up the central tenets of Poe's critical theory, it also has a decidedly literary quality about it. It appears to lie somewhere between serious persuasion and narcissistic boasting, between philosophical rationale and literary figuration, thus clearly inviting a rhetorical approach to its figures of authorship.

My approach to it is based on the crucial cultural opposition, outlined in chapter three, between authorship models based on rhetorical craft and the romantic aesthetics of genius. While some commentators have remarked upon the 'rhetorical' character of the article, no critic has attempted to reconstruct Poe's theory of effects, which appears in "The Philosophy of Composition" and in his other critical writings, as a specifically rhetorical poetics. As in the case of "The Letter to B—," the reconstruction of this persuasive aspect of the text will be combined with an analysis of its figurative dimensions. As one of the best-known and possibly even the first modern authorial autocommentary, Poe's text is informed by certain cultural expectations tied to authorship yet, at the same time, through its 'originality,' appears to found a new genre.[4] Its ambivalences are a crucial response to the shift from the rules of rhetoric to romantic aesthetics.

The Authority of the Author in the Autocommentary

Both "The Philosophy of Composition" and Godwin's text on his novel *Caleb Williams* (1794), to which Dickens indirectly refers, are examples of the genre of the so-called authorial autocommentary. The genre appears to have garnered more interest in German-speaking academia than in Anglophone scholarship,[5] but its standard treatment can be found in Gérard Genette's (1997) analysis of the genre as a kind of paratext.[6]

---

[4] The thoughts in this chapter were first sketched in Guttzeit (2010: 32–76) and further developed in an essay in German (Guttzeit 2014c).

[5] For a summary of the German debate on 'authorial poetics' ("Autorpoetik"), cf. Guttzeit (2014c, 379–82).

[6] Autocommentary does not have to be viewed as a genre in its own right but can also be a technique such as the one that played a role in the rhetorical evolution of the early modern essay of Montaigne out of the heterogeneous text forms of the letter, the dialogue, and collections of miscellanea: "Renaissance rhetoric ultimately constitutes the literary matrix of these heterogeneous

Genette classifies the autocommentary as an example of the public authorial epitext, defining it specifically as a "delayed autonomous epitext" (Genette 1997: 367), and notes that it is a socially problematic genre that was historically precluded or impeded by certain taboos.[7] Genette delineates three such taboos: in (neo)classicism, the autocommentary was viewed as improper; in Romanticism, it was feared it would destroy the impression of "quasi-miraculous spontaneity;" and in the modern period authors are viewed as incompetent of interpreting their own works (1997: 367). Of the three periods, the modern period is the most hospitable to autocommentaries, especially if they take the form of a "genetic commentary" (367) that explains how an author wrote her text rather than what it means.

Genette's discussion of the genre revolves around the single writer he perceives to be the founder of the modern genetic commentary: "The initiator of this approach was obviously Edgar Allan Poe, who, in his essay 'The Philosophy of Composition' appears very conscious of the revolutionary nature of his initiative" (1997: 368).[8] In a critical move that is familiar from the context of the French reception of Poe, Genette thus treats Poe as the founder of a distinctly modern tradition of what I call theoretical figures of the author. The genre in general is of particular interest because of its self-reflexive character: when writing his poetical text, the author works under the dialectic of autonomy and heteronomy, but, in an autocommentary, the author is almost forced to reflect upon his work with regard to such aspects and thus to produce explicit theorizations of the two aspects of autonomy and heteronomy. That the autocommentary usually takes the form of a genetic narrative, doubles the literariness of the poetical text such that the borders between 'original' poetical production and 'secondary' critical reflection easily become blurred. Thus, authorial autocommentaries can present a whole range of authorship models from strong notions of autonomy to strong notions of heteronomy, while, at the same time, the texts themselves oscillate between factual representation and theatrical performance.

Besides figuring Poe as the 'revolutionary initiator' of the authorial autocommentary, Genette also analyses the peculiar advantage of the textual and writerly

---

texts and [...] they eventually acquire an autonomous status through the addition of autocommentary: the *locus communis* becomes the medium of writers who [...] meditate as well on the material they collect and imprint it with their own [...] interpretation" (Gray 1999: 272).

7 These taboos appear to apply, to a certain extent, specifically to the Western world. In the commentarial tradition of Hindu theology and philosophy, "[a]n author might also compose an auto-commentary on verses which he himself has composed" (Flood 1996: 231), and in traditional Chinese fiction of the sixteenth and seventeenth centuries, autocommentary is a common phenomenon, sometimes even to the point of interlinear comments (Rolston 2010: 946–947).
8 Genette is not alone in suggesting this; cf. e.g. Bickenbach (2008: 45).

autonomy of the genre, i.e. the way in which the stand-alone format of the autocommentary offers the writer a certain freedom to reflect upon her text as she sees fit. Compared to other modern forms of mediated authorial commentary such as the Q&A session after a public reading, "these autonomous epitexts [...] have the obvious advantage of autonomy, which shields them from the constraints and hazards of dialogue: here the author firmly takes the initiative and retains control of his commentary" (Genette 1997: 369). Its disadvantage, however, "is the absence of the dialogic excuse" to break the taboos of autocommentary; nonetheless, "the public request (an invitation to deliver a lecture, a commission from a publisher) often stands in for it to exempt the author from the reproach of indiscretion" (369).

According to Genette's criteria, Poe appears to have been very conscious of his autocommentarial enterprise. While Poe makes full use of the autonomous potential of the authorial autocommentary, he also avoids the disadvantage of its being too monological by making use of the dialogical situation with Dickens that I outlined at the outset. Poe himself creates the public request for his autocommentary by invoking, and partially constructing, his debate with Dickens about Godwin.

The authority of the author in commenting upon *his* own work is thus tenuous in all literary periods but it is so for different reasons, as Genette's differentiation of taboos shows. Since Poe's autocommentary lies at the threshold between Romanticism and Modernism, "The Philosophy of Composition" must thus counteract two taboos regarding authorial autocommentary: it has to overcome both the romantic taboo of quasi-miraculous spontaneity and the modern taboo of incompetence.

However, the supposedly revolutionary nature of the text becomes problematic when we reconstruct the source of the debate between Poe and Dickens, namely William Godwin's autocommentary on his novel *Caleb Williams* (1794), which he published as part of a preface to a later novel, *Fleetwood*, in 1832, fourteen years before Poe's "Philosophy." The intertextual connection between the two thus necessitates a comparison of these texts in terms of how they figure their own authorship as a process of what Dickens called "writing backwards."

Such a comparison illuminates not only the similarities between the two texts in terms of their generic characteristics as autocommentaries. It also allows us to discern strong similarities in their persuasive content: in their authors' views of the effect of their works on the audience, both texts evince a rhetorical poetics. That these rhetorical poetics appear in the Age of Romanticism makes them responses to all of the tensions between rhetorical craft and the aesthetics of genius outlined in the previous chapter. Poe and Godwin thus not only figure their own authorship as situated between constructing and dreaming, but are themselves figured by the taboos and commandments of their historical situation. Ultimately, the comparison of the two will enable us to question whether or not Poe's autocommentary really was revolutionary and, if so, to what extent.

4.2 From "The Philosophy of Composition" to *The Philosophy of Rhetoric*

The success of Poe's "genèse d'un poème," as Baudelaire translated it, has often been called into question. As early as 1939, Roman Jakobson noted that critics had called "The Philosophy of Composition" a "misleading mystification, a premeditated farce, unparalleled effrontery, and one of [Poe's] mischievous caprices to catch the critics." It had also been referred to as "a juggling trick or grand hoax upon its readers" (Jakobson 1981: 12, 13). In their 2009 edition of Poe's *Critical Theory*, Stuart and Susan Levine maintain that "no critic, no literary historian, no poet has ever believed that Poe literally produced 'The Raven' as systematically and cold-bloodedly as he says" (CT 57–58). On the contrary, Jakobson found that "[i]t is indeed difficult to understand [...] the continuous repudiations of Poe's piece of self-analysis" (Jakobson 1981: 12).

Other than that it simply cannot be true, the most common points of criticism in those readings of Poe's text which do not take it seriously are: 1) that Poe's seeming demystification of the poetic process is nothing but a further mystification of it,[9] 2) that his interpretation is nothing but a rationalization of his own idiosyncratic predilections,[10] or 3) that he is hoaxing the reader as he did, for instance, in what was later called "The Balloon Hoax" (1844).[11]

The historical facts offer little clarification of the genesis of "The Raven." While an exact reconstruction of a genesis of any text is virtually impossible, there is hardly anything to go on in the case of "The Raven." There are no foul papers extant and all evidence that the so-called Whittaker manuscript, the J. Lorimer Graham copy of *The Raven and Other Poems*, and other proof sheets contain is minor corrections. Source studies also cannot answer the question of the genesis. It is likely that Dickens' pet raven Grip or the raven in *Barnaby Rudge* inspired Poe's ominous bird. An obvious model is Elizabeth Barrett

---

9 Take Leland S. Person's argument that "[h]aving demystified the compositional process, Poe proceeds to remystify it" (Person 1990: 6).
10 This comes out most clearly in Joseph Wood Krutch's early psychoanalytic argument that he had "traced Poe's art to an abnormal condition of the nerves and his critical ideas to a rationalized defense of the limitations of his own taste" (Krutch 1965: 234).
11 Poe's one-time editor, George R. Graham, thought as much (CT 58). Cf. also Hoffmann (1978): 80–96).

Browning's "The Lady Geraldine's Courtship" (1844), a poem with similar rhyme scheme and the same trochaic octameter. Poe is supposed to have said that the line "With a rushing stir uncertain, in the air, the purple curtain" inspired "The Raven" (Kopley and Hayes 2002: 193), yet he does not mention it in "Philosophy."[12] Indeed, there has been so much speculation about the origin of "The Raven" in "accusations of plagiarism, stories of collaboration, eyewitness accounts of the poem's creation, posthumous versions delivered by spirit mediums, hoax prototype poems, parodies, and translations" that Eliza Richards argues that the key reason for the poem's popularity is its "ability to encourage readers to search for its origins" (E. Richards 2005: 206). Nor can this search for origins be resolved on the basis of biographical statements about the text, since they evince the same division. The poet Susan Archer Talley Weiss maintained that Poe had confided in her that he had not been serious (CT 58), yet Poe wrote in a letter to Philip Pendleton Cooke: "I mail you [...] a copy of my best specimen of analysis – 'The Philosophy of Composition'" (LTR I: 596 = LTR-240), which lacks any reference to any ludic nature.

Regardless of the factual genesis of "The Raven," Poe's autocommentary on it illustrates many of his central assumptions about literature and poetry in particular. As we saw in chapter three, the model that Poe aspired to was that of the poet-critic and it is as a poet-critic that he treats his own text. A central aspect of the peculiar tension that characterizes the text lies in the fact that Poe, in writing an autocommentary on "The Raven," is also, and in some ways primarily, writing a philosophy of composition, an explanation of the principles of poetical writing. If we bracket the dominantly figurative aspects of Poe's text and, for the time being, take it seriously, then we have to ask: What is the form of poetical production that Poe outlines? What is, and to what end does he undertake, a process of 'writing backwards'?

After situating his text in the debate with Dickens, Poe states his central thesis, the elements of which appear in many of his critical writings. For Poe, this thesis has the status of a self-evident principle of Aristotelian dimensions:

> Nothing is more clear than that every plot, worth the name, must be elaborated to its *dénouement* before any thing be attempted with the pen. It is only with the *dénouement* constantly in view that we can give a plot its indispensable air of consequence, or causation, by making the incidents, and especially the tone at all points, tend to the development of the intention. (CT 60)

---

[12] Poe's dedication of *The Raven and other Poems* to her seems an attempt to partially make up for this.

The dénouement, a technical term originally applied to the drama that is equivalent to Aristotle's idea of the solution (λύσις/lysis),[13] is that from which the writer, in Poe's scheme, is 'writing backwards.' The authorial, or as Poe often spells it, "autorial" (CT 60, 61), intention (CT 60, 62) is thus located at the beginning of the poetical process. The origin of this intention Poe dismisses as "irrelevant to the poem *per se*" (62), thus excluding the biographical dimension of his own writing and demonstrating that he is focusing on the technical and teachable aspect of writing. Poe's notion of intention is thus not to be understood as psychological, but rather as logical, a technical intention in the sense of a teachable τέχνη/*techne*.

In addition to his evocation of the debate with Dickens, this constitutes his second strategy for evading the taboos of authorial self-commentary: he states that his interest is not really in his own text, but in the poetical process as such, for which "The Raven" as "the most generally known" offers a good example: "since the interest of an analysis, or reconstruction, such as I have considered a *desideratum*, is quite independent of any real or fancied interest in the thing analyzed, it will not be regarded as a breach of decorum on my part to show the *modus operandi* by which some one of my own works was put together" (CT 61).

The author's intention is, for Poe, co-extensive with the choice of an effect: Rather than committing the "radical error" in constructing a story "from page to page," Poe writes, "I prefer commencing with the consideration of an *effect*" (CT 60). The effect is an anticipated one that the text is supposed to have on the intended recipient, and this notion informs virtually all of Poe's critical writings, especially his theory of the tale.[14] The major end that the poet aims at is the "immensely important effect derivable from unity of impression" (CT 62).

Poe's concept of effect has long been known as being influenced by August Wilhelm Schlegel's *Lectures on Dramatic Art* – ever since Margaret Alterton's seminal 1925 book on the *Origins of Poe's Critical Theory*[15] – but this story of influence needs to be revisited from a rhetorical-poetical perspective. Poe certainly adapted

---

[13] "Every tragedy is in part complication and in part dénouement" (Aristotle 1995b, 2329 = 1455b).

[14] In one of his reviews of Nathaniel Hawthorne's *Twice-told Tales*, Poe writes: "A skillful artist has constructed a tale. He has not fashioned his thoughts to accommodate his incidents, but having deliberately conceived a certain *single effect* to be wrought, he then invents such incidents, he then combines such events, and discusses them in such tone as may best serve him in establishing this preconceived effect. If his very first sentence tend not to the outbringing of this effect, then in his very first step has he committed a blunder. In the whole composition there should be no word written of which the tendency, direct or indirect, is not to the one preestablished design" (E&R 586).

[15] G. R. Thompson notes that the "evidence that Poe read A. W. Schlegel's *Lectures* carefully is conclusive" (1973: 30).

the term "unity or totality of *interest*" (my emphasis) from the German romantic August Wilhelm Schlegel. In one of his rare acknowledgements of his critical sources, Poe writes in his review of Lydia Sigourney's *Zinzendorff and other Poems* (in the *Southern Literary Messenger* for January 1836): "in [poems] of less extent [...] the understanding is employed, without difficulty, in the contemplation of the picture *as a whole*; and thus its effect will depend, in great measure, upon the perfection of its finish, upon the nice adaptation of its constituent parts, and especially, upon what is rightly termed by Schlegel *the unity or totality of interest*" (E&R 877).[16] Yet, at the end of this passage, Poe already speaks of "the *totality* of **effect**" (E&R 877; bold emphasis added), thus changing the emphasis of the concept, in a manner typical throughout his career.

In contrast to Schlegel, who had effectively replaced the neoclassical unities of time, place, and action internal to the drama with the external "unity of impression" (326) that the play attains in the *spectator*,[17] Poe views the unity of effect as the unity of the work as viewed from the perspective of the *author's* intention and purpose: the unity of impression on the recipient's part is simply the unity of effect from the producer's vantage point. This is a process that is mediated by the critics in *Blackwood's*, who, as Alterton demonstrates, take "Schlegel's principle of effect [and] begin to take into account not only the idea of an effect or impression that a reader or spectator will feel from the printed page or the acted drama; they appear also to recognize a conscious method on the part of a writer to produce that impression" ([1925] 1965: 32). Both Poe and the Scottish *Blackwood's* critics thus enlarge Schlegel's concept, which evinces a primarily critical interest in the experience of the audience, to a rhetorical interest in the writer's art of producing an effect on an audience.

Similar to Poe's appropriation of Coleridge's writings outlined in chapter three, this is not simply a matter of romantic versus rhetorical but rather of the rhetorical *within* the romantic. In fact, Schlegel's own conceptualisation is based on the same opposition between rhetoric and poetry that we encountered in chapter two between the rhetorical tradition and Mill. Representative of the notion of effect that would become a hallmark of *Blackwood's* criticism, Alterton

---

16 Poe reuses this whole passage in his review of Longfellow's *Ballads and Other Poems*, *Graham's Magazine*, April 1842 (E&R 691).
17 Schlegel had defined the term, taken from the French early eighteenth-century dramatist Antoine Houdart de la Motte, thus: "*De la Motte*, a French author, who wrote against the whole of the unities, wishes, in the place of unity of action, to substitute the words, *unity of interest*. If the expression is not confined to the interest in the fate of a single person, but is used to signify in general the direction of the mind during the aspect of an event, I should then consider it, so understood, as the most satisfactory and the nearest to the truth" (Schlegel 1833: 189).

quotes Schlegel's definition: "The object proposed is to produce an impression on an assembled multitude, to rivet attention and to excite their interest and sympathy" (Alterton [1925] 1965: 32).[18] The very next sentence in Schlegel then mentions the familiar analogy between poet and orator on which he relies for the remainder of the chapter: "This part of his business is common to the poet with the orator. How does the latter attain his end?" (1833: 19).

What Schlegel views as the theatrical end of the dramatic poet, the impression on the audience, turns out to be an aim in common with that of the orator; thus, even the romantic context from which Poe gains his understanding of effect turns out to be a rhetorical one. Neither "unity of effect" nor "totality of effect" are used in the American edition of Schlegel's lectures, but Poe, absorbing the development in *Blackwood's*, unfolds the implicit aspects of the concept as it relates to the audience (unity of impression) and to the writer (unity of effect), placing an emphasis upon the producer's viewpoint. While both Poe's reinterpretation and the original context of Schlegel's own term point towards the presence of rhetorical theories of poetical production, the connection goes even deeper.

The general rhetorical rationale behind Poe's philosophy of composition becomes apparent when we compare it to George Campbell's philosophy of rhetoric, the basic principle of which I discussed in chapter two: "In speaking there is always some end proposed, or some effect which the speaker intends to produce on the hearer. The word *eloquence* in its greatest latitude denotes, 'That art or talent by which the discourse is adapted to its end.'" ([1776] 1988: 1).[19] Viewed in terms of its theoretical content, Poe's project in "Philosophy" conforms precisely to the third of the stages delineated by Campbell in the overall development of rhetoric: in this stage, "the rules of composition are discovered, or the method of combining and disposing the several materials, so that they may be perfectly adapted to the end in view" ([1776] 1988: lxxv).[20] The "end in view," for Poe as for Campbell, is the effect of the discourse on the recipient.

---

18 Alterton quotes Black's translation, first published in 1815, yet apparently in a version revised by A. J. W. Morrison in 1846. The 1833 edition has this wording: "The object proposed is to produce an impression on an assembled crowd, to gain their attention, and to excite in them an interest and participation" (Schlegel 1833: 19).
19 Patrick Full rightly suggests the importance of Campbell's *Philosophy* as an intertextual reference for Poe's "Philosophy," though he interprets the text primarily in terms of Coleridge's 'morphosis' (Full 2007: 76–79, 63–65).
20 Campbell argues that rhetoric develops from 1) the simple, quasi-natural observation of speech in oneself and others to 2) the beginnings of rhetoric as a classificatory science to 3) the establishment of systems of effects achieved in particular situations and, finally, to 4) a proj-

Where Campbell aims to provide the scientific fundamentals of rhetoric, Poe inquires into the principles of composition. Both Poe's "Philosophy of Composition" and Campbell's *Philosophy of Rhetoric* follow a common practice of the time in titling texts: as the *Revised Edition of Webster's Dictionary* (1848) explains, "philosophy" "denotes the collection of general laws or principles under which all the subordinate phenomena of facts relating to that subject are comprehended" (1848: 739).[21] The term *composition* has a long rhetorical pedigree and was assimilated to a variety of other arts, most prominently perhaps music and painting. As Brian Vickers has demonstrated for musical terminology, "music has usually been the debtor to rhetoric" (Vickers 1984: 23), and this is the case for "composition," too (Vickers 1984: 17). In classical theories, 'compositio' is the prose equivalent to versification in poetry: the syntactic and phonetic construction of the sentence and its adjacent larger and smaller units (the period, the colon, and the comma; cf. Quintilian [2001d: 229–233=9.4.121–129]). Quintilian, the prime rhetorical authority for Campbell, defined composition in terms of its functions in oratory and its sensory effect:

> Composition plays the same part in oratory as Versification in poetry. The best judge of Composition is the ear, which senses completeness, feels the lack when something is incomplete, is offended by unevenness, soothed by smoothness, and excited by speed; it approves stability, detects lameness, and is bored by redundancy and excess. The learned therefore know the principles of Composition, but even the unlearned know its pleasures. (Quintilian 2001d: 225=9.4.116)

By the nineteenth century, the term "composition" had already been generalised, and Poe's own use of "species of composition" (E&R 126, 153) for 'genres of writing' echoes the use in Blair, Campbell, and many contemporaries. Blair, for instance, maintains that the "most general division of the different kinds of Composition is, into those written in Prose, and those written in Verse." (Blair [1785] 2005: 396). While no longer primarily understood as classical *compositio*, even this generalised sense takes on a distinctly rhetorical sense. How deeply nineteenth-century ideas of composition were informed by rhetorical thinking is evident from Webster's dictionary definition of composition:

---

ect such as his own to build a philosophical-epistemological foundation for rhetoric that explains why rhetorical principles work. Cf. Campbell ([1776] 1988: lxxiv–lxxv).

21 Poe's other uses of the term indicate that his understanding was very much in line with what Webster codified, as shows, for instance, in his projected, but never executed magazine paper on "The Philosophy of Point" (E&R 1425) and his use of the "philosophy of verse" in "The Rationale of Verse," meaning similarly the principles of versification (E&R 54, 70).

> 1. In a general sense [...] the act of forming a whole or integral, by placing together and uniting different things, parts, or ingredients [...] --2. In literature, the act of inventing or combining ideas, clothing them with words, arranging them in order, and, in general, committing them to paper, or otherwise writing them. (Webster 1848: 203)

Webster's definition is a striking testament to the continuing influence of rhetorical ideas about the writing process. The definition of literary composition offered here is nearly identical with the rhetorical authemes: "inventing or combining" is *inventio*, "clothing them with words" is *elocutio*, "arranging them in order" is *dispositio*, and "committing them to paper" is *actio*.[22] That Webster offers such a definition of composition shows the continuing influence of rhetorical schemata in antebellum America. In light of Webster's definitions, the claim inherent in Poe's title is that he presents the principles of how to shape a literary text with a certain effect, with particular attention to its syntactic and phonetic shape (*compositio*).

Specifying the general principle that texts work as means to achieve effects, Poe offers the following distinction of three fundamental kinds of effect:

> I designate Beauty as the province of the poem, merely because it is an obvious rule of Art that effects should be made to spring from direct causes – that objects should be attained through means best adapted for their attainment – no one as yet having been weak enough to deny that the peculiar elevation alluded to, is *most readily* attained in the poem. Now the object, Truth, or the satisfaction of the intellect, and the object Passion, or the excitement of the heart, are, although attainable, to a certain extent, in poetry, far more readily attainable in prose. Truth, in fact, demands a precision, and Passion, a *homeliness* (the truly passionate will comprehend me) which are absolutely antagonistic to that Beauty which, I maintain, is the excitement, or pleasurable elevation, of the soul. (CT 63)

The passage foregrounds beauty as the legitimate province of the poem, yet the perennially neglected tripartite distinction which hovers in the background is even more worthy of attention. When it comes to dividing the most general kinds of effect that an author can achieve, Poe offers a version of the familiar rhetorical triad of *docere*, *delectare*, and *movere*, which I previously reconstruct-

---

22 In Webster, *style* comes before *arrangement*. This deviation from the standard order (i.e. the one in which the *officia* are enumerated in Quintilian) is also not without authoritative precedent, since Aristotle had analysed style (λέξις/*lexis*) in the *Rhetoric* in book 3, chapters 2–12, and thus before arrangement (τάξις/*taxis*) in book 3, chapters 13–19. The absence of memory is also conclusive; in the Baconian tradition of rhetoric, one might easily view the final act of 'committing the ideas to paper' as the equivalent of these two. Vickers explains that Bacon's "'Art of Custody or Memory' [...] deals with writing (including the keeping of commonplace books), and the art of memory as found in classical rhetoric." (Vickers 1996: 210).

ed from George Campbell to William Cullen Bryant: Truth, Beauty, and Passion are not metaphysical entities, but three types of effect, defined as "the satisfaction of the intellect," "the excitement, or pleasurable elevation of the soul," and "the excitement of the heart." Far from essentialising truth, beauty, and passion as qualities of objects or even as objects themselves, Poe views them as effects of symbolic and, in particular, poetical processes.[23] Poe's fundamental division of the central term of his literary theory conforms to that of a rhetorical poetics:

Types of effect	Docere	Delectare	Movere
Campbell	Enlighten the understanding	Please the imagination	Move the passions
Bryant	Gratify the understanding	Excite the imagination	Touch the heart
Poe	Satisfaction of the intellect (Truth)	Excitement/pleasurable elevation of the soul (Beauty)	Excitement of the heart (Passion)

As this adjusted version of the table from chapter two illustrates,[24] there are some small differences between the three versions of the triad of effects: Campbell has "enlightening" the understanding rather than "gratifying" (Bryant) or "satisfying" it (Poe), and Poe uses "intellect" and "soul" in place of "understanding" and "imagination."

Overall, however, the correspondences are striking and warrant the thesis that it is fundamentally the same rhetorical distinction at work in all three writers. They all distinguish three corresponding effects which fall into the same cognitive and affective categories. This is not, however, to construct a direct line of influence between the three texts; Bryant and Poe would have come into regular contact with the rhetorical distinction in classical and modern sources in the antebellum culture of rhetoric. What the correspondences demonstrate is the pervasiveness of rhetorical theory in "The Philosophy of Composition" and Poe's other writings.

There are a number of further similarities that attest to the common rhetorical grounding of Campbell's *Philosophy of Rhetoric* and Poe's "Philosophy of Composition," of which the triad of faculties and the idea of a system of predominant and subservient effects are two major examples. Just as in Campbell and

---

[23] Poe makes this explicit: "When, indeed, men speak of Beauty, they mean, precisely, not a quality, as is supposed, but an effect" (CT 63). Full rightly stresses this (2007: 74).
[24] I here leave out the general rhetorical end of persuasion named separately by Campbell.

Bryant, Poe's tripartite distinction of effects is based on and, in turn, informs a threefold partition of the mind: in Poe, the effects of truth, beauty, and passion correspond to the faculties of the intellect, the soul, and the heart.[25] While foregrounding beauty as the province of the poem, Poe's theory of effect also includes the basic idea that every text is a means of producing a system of effects in which one is predominant and the others are subservient to the main end.[26] Poe's understanding of the effects of poetical discourse is thus thoroughly rhetorical and has to be viewed in the tradition of the eighteenth-century New Rhetoric.

The poet can achieve these effects, in particular beauty, via the process Dickens named writing backwards. This process involves a series of technical decisions, which have the logical form of "conclusions" (CT 61). These conclusions are the result of inferences. The premises of these inferences are general rules or principles from which individual texts are derived. In a too-little-discussed essay on "The Principle of Composition," Kenneth Burke (1961) offers a clarification of the principles involved in Poe's procedure. Burke has in mind a model of the literary text as an action, the result of a series of decisions, regardless of whether these decisions were made consciously by the author or not:

> regardless of whether the author of the work explicitly asked himself why he formed the work as he did, the work embodies a series of decisions which *imply* answers to such questions. For instance, if the work is a play with a blood-and-thunder-ending, implicit in its sheer nature there is, first of all, a principle that amounts to saying: 'Resolved: That this kind of work should be a play with a blood and thunder ending' [...] [I]nsofar as a work is developed in accordance with the author's sense of propriety (insofar as he constructs it in ways that 'feel right' to him), then no matter how spontaneous and purely 'intuitive'

---

[25] In Campbell, they are understanding, imagination, passions (and will) (Campbell [1776] 1988: 1); in Bryant: understanding, imagination, heart (Bryant 1884: 8). It is not superfluous to stress that these faculties have to be shared by producers and recipients.

[26] Poe writes: "It by no means follows from any thing here said, that passion, or even truth, may not be introduced, and even profitably introduced, into a poem – for they may serve in elucidation, or aid the general effect, as do discords in music, by contrast – but the true artist will always contrive, first, to tone them into proper subservience to the predominant aim, and, secondly, to enveil them, as far as possible, in that Beauty which is the atmosphere and the essence of the poem." (CT 63)

Campbell writes: "Any one discourse admits only one of these ends as the principal. Nevertheless, in discoursing on a subject, many things may be introduced, which are more immediately and apparently directed to some of the other ends of speaking, and not to that which is the chief intent of the whole. But then these other and immediate ends are in effect but means, and must be rendered conducive to that which is the primary intention" (Campbell [1776] 1988: 1).

his approach to his material may be, implied in all his choices there is a corresponding set of 'principles'. (1961: 49)[27]

Following Burke, we can view Poe's theses as (re)constructions of the principles and operations that the author of the "Raven" must have followed and completed – consciously or unconsciously – even if the author had not been Poe. The hyperbole of Poe's autocommentary lies in his claim that he was fully conscious of all the operations involved. This is unlikely, yet, as the examination of the situation of the genesis of the "Raven" demonstrated, there is no way of answering whether this was the case or not; more important is that, strictly speaking, this neither voids nor validates the principles *sensu* Burke.

For Burke, this procedure of inferring the principles of a text occurs *post factum*. The assumption of nineteenth-century rhetoric, however, is that once such rules are inferred for discourses that have had the intended effect, they can be applied to similar discourses that are yet to be produced. Thus the definition of "the art of Composition" in Whately, which was already discussed in chapter three, is identical with Burke's critical procedure: the art consists of "'such rules as *every* good Composition must conform to,' whether the author of it had them in his mind or not" (Whately 1828: 20).

This productive perspective is what explains the concept of writing backwards. Poe argues – paradoxically – that "The Raven" "may be said to have its beginning – at the end, where all works of art should begin" (CT 66). The beginning of the text lies in its end, which is not necessarily the ending of the text. The final part of the text *differs* from the text's end, i.e. its intended totality of effect. Dickens' metaphorical expression of writing backwards is interpreted by Poe as the rational relation of means-to-ends of poetical writing, thus transforming it into a figure of rhetorical authorship.

That it is the inventor of the narrative form of the detective story who propounds such theories is hardly surprising, since it is precisely such tales of ratiocination that demand this kind of planning. While it is possible to "write from pillar to post" in some genres, Burke comments, it is "almost inconceivable" that a story such as "The Gold-Bug" could be written in such a way (K. Burke 1961: 47). The tale of ratiocination is the paradigm of writing backwards.[28] Poe's criticism of Dickens' lack of "that metaphysical art in which the souls of all *mysteries*

---

[27] Burke develops this thought and its relation to poetics in particular and symbolicity in general in K. Burke (1973a).
[28] It is analysed as such on the basis of Poe and Dickens' debate as "backward construction" by D. Porter (1981: 24–52).

lie" is thus not a demand for mysticism but rather an affirmation of the quasilogical art of writing tales of ratiocination (E&R 244).

A reconstruction of the theoretical statement of "The Philosophy of Composition" thus shows it to be an example of Poe's overall rhetorical poetics. As a rhetorical model of poetical writing which sees literary texts as organized systems of means geared towards achieving an effect on the audience, this is an affirmation of weak autonomy: the poet's success is one that is mediated through the rules of rhetoric which apply, as Whately defined it, to the art of "*every* good composition" (1828: 20).

4.3 The Poetical Madness of Composition

Yet this is by no means the whole story of "The Philosophy of Composition," since this reconstruction of its theoretical content has so far neglected the peculiarly figurative aspects of Poe's inauguration of the autocommentary. Poe is not content with affirming a weak autonomous model of the author in line with a rhetorical poetics. Rather, by pitting his model against romantic notions of "fine frenzy" and "ecstatic intuition" (CT 61), Poe bids farewell to heteronomous notions of authorship, both weak and strong. This provocation is most strongly phrased in the statement "that the work proceeded, step by step, to its completion with the precision and consequence of a mathematical problem" (CT 61–62). Indeed, in "Philosophy of Composition," Poe appears – consciously or unconsciously – to undermine the general validity of the rules of rhetoric, with its stress on weak autonomy, through the theatrical and figurative moments of its own performance.

The figurative, narrative, or literary character of Poe's critical text has been remarked upon by a number of critics, among them Leland Person, Dennis Pahl, and Heinrich Detering. In the most pertinent take on "The Philosophy of Composition" in terms of authorial autonomy and heteronomy, Detering argues: : "The heteronomy that the text aimed to do away with [...] is carried to such an extreme that the madness, which was supposed to be exorcised, ultimately triumphs" (2000: 304, my translation).[29] The narrative elements in the text, such as the division between an experiencing and a narrating I, the use of the simple past after the theoretical introduction (from paragraph 12; CT 62), an increase of grammatical constructions in the passive voice, and the inner dialogue that Poe drama-

---

[29] "Die Heteronomie, die zu erledigen der Text unternahm, wird [...] so auf die Spitze getrieben, daß der Wahnsinn, der ausgetrieben werden sollte, am Ende triumphiert" (2000: 304).

tises lead Detering to conclude that there appears in the text a second voice that is not the author's:

> What presents itself here as evident, crystal-clear, and as bright as day is merely reason oriented by an aesthetic of effect, calculating, totally earthly, rhetorically staged, and nothing more. Except that, in this scenario, it speaks exactly like Homer's muse, as something different and strange that whispers words to an I – a speaking instance completely emancipated from the writing subject, and who talks to him autonomously. (2000: 309, my translation)[30]

For Detering, the repression of the heteronomous aspects of authorship leads to a return of the repressed that manifests itself in a second textual voice. Invoking Horkheimer and Adorno's concept of the dialectic of enlightenment, Detering interprets Poe's text as representing the "spectral primal scene of a modern enlightened poetics," in which reason dialectically collapses to reveal all aspects of madness (309, my translation).[31] Hence, it is no surprise that Detering, rather than viewing Poe's theory in terms of his tales of ratiocination, compares the speaker in "Philosophy" to the mad narrator that Poe perfected in such tales as "The Tell-Tale Heart" (311).

In terms of the difference between rhetoric and aesthetics, two aspects of Detering's argument are representative of the critical response to Poe's text. For Detering, the theory of effects is a question of "Wirkungsästhetik," which – if we view it in terms of its decisive definition in Wolfgang Iser's seminal works[32] – is primarily a question of the relation between text and reader, not of the poetical dimension between author and text. Thus, secondly, rhetoric for Detering is only

---

30 "Offenkundig, sonnenklar und taghell zeigt sich hier bloß die wirkungsästhetisch kalkulierende, ganz diesseitige Vernunft, rhetorisch inszeniert, nichts weiter. Nur daß sie eben in dieser Inszenierung genau so wie Homers Muse redet, als ein Anderes und Fremdes, das einem Ich die Worte eingibt – als eine vom Schreibsubjekt emanzipierte, autonom zu ihm redende Instanz." (Detering 2000: 309).
31 Detering's phrase is "gespenstische Urszene einer aufgeklärt-modernen Poetik" (309).
32 Iser defines it thus: "Effects and responses are properties neither of the text nor of the reader; the text represents a potential effect that is realized in the reading process" (1980: ix). Iser explicitly distinguishes "two poles" of the "literary work," "which we might call the artistic and the aesthetic: the artistic pole is the author's text and the aesthetic is the realization accomplished by the reader" (1980: 21). Iser's term for the specifically poetical dimension, which he analyses in its epistemological and ontological relation to the real and the imaginary, is the Latin translation of ποιεῖν/poiein, namely *fingere:* "For the fictionalizing act is a guided act. It aims at something that in turn endows the imaginary with an articulate gestalt – a gestalt that differs from the fantasies, projections, daydreams, and other reveries that ordinarily give the imaginary expression in our day-to-day experience" (1993: 3).

a trivial matter of the theatrical dimension of the text ("rhetorically staged, and nothing more") rather than a possible foundation for a theory of literature. This understanding of 'rhetoric' as the mere theatrics of "The Philosophy of Composition" finds its equivalent in statements such as that of Dennis Pahl, who views a 'rhetoric,' which is not further defined, as a characteristic element of "The Raven": "While seeming to offer from afar, in its own self-contained manner, a detailed history of the poem's composition, 'The Philosophy' nevertheless ends up reproducing many of the poem's features – becoming as it were seduced by the very rhetoric it is supposed to analyze" (1996: 10). As argued in chapter two, such understandings of rhetoric do not correspond to the actual historical meaning of the term (nor to an exactly defined systematic use today); rather, they project an understanding of rhetoric that is ultimately a result of the dispersal of rhetoric, of the replacement of rhetorical poetics by an aesthetics of genius in the nineteenth century.

Nevertheless, what Detering and Pahl are right to insist on is that Poe's critical text evinces characteristics of "another kind of narrative, just as highly wrought and complex as other of Poe's works – fictive as well as poetic" (Pahl 1996: 2). Yet rather than viewing these elements as 'mere rhetoric' that does nothing but undermine Poe's theoretical figure of the author as a rhetorical poet-critic, the task is to account for these narrative elements in terms of the genre that Poe's text partially inaugurated: that is, it is an autocommentary, and its characteristics thus necessarily include the narrative form of the story it tells to explain the genesis of the text. Just how Poe figures and is figured by this autocommentarial structure emerges clearly if we compare his version to Godwin's earlier autocommentary on which the debate between Dickens and Poe was based.

4.4 Godwin's Autocommentary

Published as part of the preface to the Standard Novels edition of *Fleetwood* in 1832, Godwin's short text narrates and theorizes the composition of *Things As They Are; or, The Adventures of Caleb Williams* (1794).[33] Reputedly the first thriller, Godwin's *Caleb Williams* makes a similar combined appeal to the "popular and the critical taste" as Poe did in "The Raven" (CT 62). The novel tells of the servant Caleb who discovers that his ostensibly virtuous master Ferdinando Falk-

---

[33] Following Pamela Clemit, the editor of the Oxford World's Classics edition of *Caleb Williams*, who names the text "Godwin's 1832 Account of the Composition of *Caleb Williams*" (Godwin 2009: 347–52) I refer to it as Godwin's "Account."

land is in fact a murderer; as a result, Caleb has to flee Falkland and his henchmen. In Godwin's autocommentary, we find a similar problem and terminology to that in Poe, aspects of which 1) are only inadequately summarised in Dickens' notion of writing backwards and 2) show that the peculiar form of the authorial commentary is generically prone to problems of credibility.

Long before the autocommentary of 1832, Godwin had intended to supply the book with a preface on its original publication in 1794, yet his publisher argued against it because of ongoing arrests for high treason.[34] This earlier paratext presented *Caleb Williams* as a companion to Godwin's treatise *Enquiry Concerning Political Justice* (1793). Godwin wrote the following in the 1794 preface: "It is now known to philosophers that the spirit and character of the government intrudes itself into every rank of society," calling the novel a "vehicle" for "a general review of the modes of domestic and unrecorded despotism, by which man becomes the destroyer of man" (Godwin 2009: 312). This call to read the novel politically is omitted from the 1832 Account, which deals exclusively with the poetological question of how *Caleb Williams* was composed: any hint of a political or didactic purpose has disappeared.

In the Account, Godwin explains his motivation and three phases of production: 1) the process of *planning* the novel, 2) the process of imagining the scenes, and 3) the process of *writing* from the beginning. He also describes problems arising in all three phases. Godwin justifies his autocommentary by saying that the proprietor of the Standard Novels edition (Richard Bentley) had asked him to write an account for the interest of the public. At no point does Godwin use the phrase "writing backwards" but his description of the text's genesis makes Dickens' appellation plausible.

The most important distinction that Godwin makes is between the first phase of the invention of the action of the individual volumes of the novel and the last phase of the actual writing of it. While Godwin asserts that he *invented* the volumes in a reverse order, starting with the last one and ending with the first, he nevertheless carried out the actual *writing* by starting on page one of the first book and ending on the last page of the third book (he does not mention revisions). The middle phase is devoted to "imagining and putting down hints" for the story (Godwin 2009: 349).

This is how Godwin describes the technical beginning of the inventive process: "I formed a conception of a book of fictitious adventure, that should in some way be distinguished by a very powerful interest," stating what would be described by Dickens as "writing backwards": "Pursuing this idea, I invented first the

---

[34] Clemit explains this in detail (Godwin 2009: 360).

third volume of my tale, then the second, and last of all the first" (Godwin 2009: 348). Accordingly, Godwin goes on to give quick summaries of the content of the third, the second, and the first volume (Godwin 2009: 348–49). He then takes stock and evaluates his method of design in a description that sounds strikingly like Poe:

> I felt that I had a great advantage in thus carrying back my invention from the ultimate conclusion to the first commencement of the train of adventures upon which I purposed to employ my pen. An entire unity of plot would be the infallible result; and the unity of spirit and interest in a tale truly considered, gives it a powerful hold on the reader, which can scarcely be generated with equal success in any other way. (Godwin 2009: 349)

"Unity of plot" and "unity of spirit" sound very much like Poe's dual terms. "Unity of interest" is, of course, precisely the term that Poe adopted from Schlegel as the unity of effect. Godwin's "powerful hold on the reader" echoes Poe's description of the soul of the reader "at the writer's control" in the Hawthorne reviews (E&R 572, 586).[35] Godwin also relates that his friend Joseph Gerrald "had received my book late one evening, and had read through the three volumes before he closed his eyes" (Godwin 2009: 352), thus claiming that his novel could be read, in Poe's words, "at one sitting" (CT 62). Calling the unity of plot an "infallible result" and asserting that equal success can scarcely be "generated" "in any other way" also belong to the same register as Poe's assertions of principles in art (Godwin 2009: 349). All these similarities point towards the fact that the elements and moments of Godwin's and Poe's poetics are guided by the same fundamental categories: a technical intention, a rule-based and purposive writing process, and an anticipated effect on the reader.

This is obvious from Godwin's further description which might well have been the origin of Dickens' phrase of writing backwards: he speaks of "carrying back my intention from the ultimate conclusion to the first commencement of the train of adventures" (Godwin 2009: 349). When it comes to an exact description of Godwin's approach, however, Dickens' phrase is somewhat infelicitous. Dickens criticized Godwin's method by arguing that "when [Godwin] had produced the hunting down of Caleb, and the catastrophe, he waited for months, casting about for a means of accounting for what he had done."[36] The causal attribution Dickens infers is difficult to defend. Godwin simply writes that he found himself "completely at a stand" in the period from January to April 1794 when he is al-

---

35 Poe's phrase echoes one of Campbell's definitions of rhetoric as the "art, whose object it is, by the use of language, to operate on the soul of the hearer" (Campbell [1776] 1988: lxvii).
36 ALS Charles Dickens to Edgar A. Poe, March 6, 1842. New York Public Library. Berg Coll MSS Dickens.

ready beginning work on the third volume (Godwin 2009: 351), explaining that he experiences such writer's block in all of his longer projects. The process of writing or composition, as Godwin describes it, is from the first to the last page and is thus 'normal' in the sense that it follows the same linearity as the basic Western reading convention. Dickens' misrepresentation of Godwin's account stems from the fact that he does not distinguish the planning phase and the phase of composition. While Godwin writes forwards, he is planning backwards *sensu* Poe: The end of the text, its intended effect on the reader, determines the choice of literary means.

At first glance, Godwin's account is level-headed and down-to-earth, yet there is a similar dialectic of autonomy and heteronomy at work to that found in Poe. Any author's poetics based on the assumption of the purpose of the text needs explanation, if the purpose of the whole text *shifts* during the process of composition. Godwin does not mention such a shift in his Account, yet the extant manuscripts tell this story well. As D. Gilbert Dumas (1966) first demonstrated, Godwin did not publish the manuscript ending of the novel but a revised ending that differs largely from the 'original' version. In the published version, Caleb Williams defends himself in court with such a genuine and authentic speech that Falkland confesses his murders, effectively freeing Caleb: "Williams, said he, you have conquered! [...] the artless and manly story you have told, has carried conviction to every hearer" (Godwin 2009: 301). Three days later, Falkland dies and the novel ends with Caleb blaming himself for Falkland's death.

The manuscript ending is very different: Caleb's lawsuit is defeated, whereby he comments upon it in a way that it makes him sound like a mouthpiece for Godwin's original political purpose: "Alas! alas! it too plainly appears in my history that persecution and tyranny can never die" (Godwin 2009: 309). Caleb descends into madness and instead of an epideictic obituary for Falkland, the ending consists of Poe-esque fragmentary and melancholy thoughts: "True happiness lies in being like a stone – Nobody can complain of me – all day long I do nothing – am a stone – a GRAVE-STONE! – an obelisk to tell you, HERE LIES WHAT WAS ONCE A MAN!" (Godwin 2009: 311).

While the original ending depicts the legal and social conditions as so relentless as to drive the protagonist to madness, all it takes in the published version to give the story a 'happy' turn is an honest and preromantically 'authentic' speech. What is thus crucial in discerning the theoretical validity of autocommentaries such as Godwin's and Poe's – ones that are based on a notion of writing backwards – is the question: Can a text whose ending is rewritten (and which is revised for later editions), to quote Poe again, "have its beginning – at the end" (CT 66)? If not invalid, a different ending makes Godwin's account at the very least problematic, a fact which recurs in the secondary literature from early on. As Dumas writes, "[o]ne inescapably suspects that he is hiding something" (1966: 596).

However, to conclude that the later ending makes the autocommentary obsolete would be going too far. Of course, the difference between the two endings shows that Godwin's account is a curtailed idealisation of the writerly process. Yet it does not prove that Godwin's writing process did not take the form he describes, and it in no way invalidates the relation of means to ends which Godwin and Poe describe. In their model, the new ending is simply a part of the novel like all the other parts: all of them are means to produce the effect on the reader. If the ending changes, the effect changes and so does the purpose. What made Godwin change his mind is a difficult question to answer, since it would require a careful political and psychological analysis of the exact circumstances of his decision, one that cannot be pursued here. However, it seems quite obvious that Godwin tempered his revolutionary purpose rather than reinforcing it.

4.5 Figuring the Rhetorical Poet-Critic in Times of Romanticism

Whether literary 'writing backwards' is possible and sensible thus becomes the central question in a dispute about the nature of literature and the fundamental theoretical figures of the literary author. In theoretical terms, this debate is a question of the autonomy or heteronomy of the author. What the transatlantic comparison of Poe's to Godwin's autocommentary shows is a fundamental similarity in terms of theoretical content. Like Poe, Godwin describes the logical form of the poetic process in terms of a rhetorical poetics that is valid in principle because it describes a general form of goal-oriented and purposive human action.[37] In retrospect, both Godwin and Poe, as Kenneth Burke argues, etch into relief and abstract the logical form of the poetical process which they understand as a fundamentally rhetorical process.

The first major difference between the two autocommentaries, however, lies in the extent of their narrative aspect. Godwin, writing almost forty years after the initial publication of his novel, idealises the process; he fulfils the demands

---

[37] In Niklas Luhmann's terms, the rhetorical poetics in Poe and Godwin are a form of the scheme of means and ends ("Zweck-Mittel-Schema") that differentiates ends and means as two variable aspects of action, a scheme that makes it possible to decide on how to act in causal terms (Luhmann 2009: 73). Höss (2003) interprets the presence of such a model as an indication of Poe's role in the process of modern rationalisation *sensu* Max Weber, disregarding, however, the tradition of rhetorical poetics.

of the autocommentary in a manner that includes giving an account of the origin of his motivation and the personal situation which gave rise to the novel.[38] Poe, however, isolates the theory and "dismiss[es], as irrelevant to the poem per se, the circumstance – or say the necessity – which, in the first place gave rise to the intention" (CT 62).

The second major difference lies in the epitextual autonomy of the two texts: while Poe published "The Philosophy" as a stand-alone text, Godwin's only became so through the antebellum culture of reprinting. The American magazine *Museum of Foreign Literature, Science and Art* excerpted Godwin's remarks from the preface to *Fleetwood* and reprinted them, turning them into a proper "delayed autonomous epitext" (Genette 1997: 367). Poe's is thus certainly not the first authorial autocommentary, yet neither is Godwin's, as the editor's prefatory comment in the *Museum of Foreign Literature* makes clear: "[a]n author's own history of his production is always interesting; we shall therefore give Mr. Godwin's account of the 'concoction' of *Caleb Williams* nearly entire." ("Godwin's Caleb Williams" 1833: 403). Far from being an entirely new phenomenon, "an author's own history of his production" is something in demand in antebellum culture; that it is a history of "production" rather than, as Genette and most moderns would have it, a "genetic commentary" (Genette 1997: 367) may be viewed as an echo of understanding poetical processes as *poiesis* in a classical sense.

The third major difference furnishes a reason for why Poe's autocommentary might still, and in some ways has to, be regarded as revolutionary. Godwin is also aware of the demands of originality upon him: "The world, I believed, would accept nothing from me with distinguishing favour that did not bear upon the face of it the undoubted stamp of originality" (Godwin 2009: 348). Yet he – unlike Poe – does not seek to disprove the romantic concept of genius. This is not to say that Godwin's "Account" does not imply an opposition to romantic figures of the author that are based on inspiration, yet it certainly is to claim that he does not conceive of his text primarily as an attack on a false conception of authorship. Poe, however, is absolutely adamant in his intention to dismantle the myth of the romantic inspired genius by overcoming the romantic taboo against the autocommentary, as is clear right from the beginning of "The Philosophy of Composition": "Most writers – poets in especial – prefer having it understood that they compose by a species of fine frenzy – an ecstatic intuition –

---

[38] Godwin writes: "I had always felt in myself some vocation towards the composition of a narrative of fictitious adventure" (Godwin 2009: 347) and "Very often I was disposed to quit the enterprise in despair. But still I felt ever and anon compelled to repeat my effort" (Godwin 2009: 348).

and would positively shudder at letting the public take a peep behind the scenes, at the elaborate and vacillating crudities of thought" (CT 61).

Not only is the figure of the author that Poe presents in "The Philosophy of Composition" one of a rhetorical craftsman in times of late-romantic inspiration, but it is explicitly foregrounded as a counter-model in theoretical terms. In "The Philosophy of Composition," his self-proclaimed "best specimen of analysis" (LTR I: 596 = LTR-240), Poe uses the debate with Dickens and the rhetorical triad of effects to establish his own position, via a rhetoric of composition, as both a critic and a writer: he figures himself as a rhetorical poet-critic, thus attempting to disprove the romantic aesthetics of genius.

The result of this attempt, however, is a contradictory text which becomes explicable only if we view it in terms of the larger historical situation to which Poe was responding. Indeed, viewed historically, Poe is figured by the overall cultural situation and the larger struggles between rhetorical and poetical discourse, out of which the modern sense of literature emerged. Faced with the question of what an author of a poem in the Age of Romanticism actually is, Poe effectively transposes rhetorical authemes from the rules of rhetorical art into the psyche of the individual writer. The function of his own text is to interiorise the rhetorical rules that are normally external to the author and which are based on an analysis of empirical situations. The weak autonomy that can be attained through study of the rules of rhetoric is hyperbolized, as he transposes it onto, or, to be more exact, *into* the poet. In other words, Poe is trying to rhetoricize the romantic individual author by negating genius and replacing it with art. Yet as a result of this attempt, the internalised rules of rhetoric are invested with the certainty of the divine inspiration of the strongly heteronomous genius.

Poe is thus singularly representative of the emerging divide between rhetorical and poetical discourse in the nineteenth century. His theoretical figure of the author in "The Philosophy of Composition" can only come into being at a time when a rhetoric of craft is in the process of being displaced by an aesthetics of genius. In response to the rise of the author and the dispersal of rhetoric, Poe combines the individualist autocommentary with an explication of a general rhetorical poetics. The result is a paradoxical and oxymoronic figure of the author: the genius rhetorician.

5 "The Ingenuity of Unravelling": Abductive Powers and Rhetorical Inventors in the Tales of Ratiocination

> You are right about the hair-splitting of my French friend: – that is all done for effect. These tales of ratiocination owe most of their popularity to being something in a new key. I do not mean to say that they are not ingenious – but people think them more ingenious than they are – on account of their method and *air* of method. In the "Murders in the Rue Morgue", for instance, where is the ingenuity of unravelling a web which you yourself (the author) have woven for the express purpose of unravelling? The reader is made to confound the ingenuity of the supposititious Dupin with that of the writer of the story.
>
> Poe to Philip Pendleton Cooke, August 9, 1846[1]

Poe's quote about the hair-splitting of his French friend, his most famous literary character, Chevalier C. Auguste Dupin, is often interpreted as an admission of what is more generally regarded as a kind of empty and ersatz intellectuality of the classic detective story that supplants real cognitive activity by a mere puzzle. As David Van Leer argues, the "hyper-rational language of these tales is, as Poe well knows, a pose." Van Leer correspondingly introduces the above quotation with the words "[a]s Poe *admits* to a friend" (1990: 312; my emphasis). A similar line of thought is that Poe does not dismiss the genre so much as his readership: "even as he relished the praise he received for the ingenuity of his ratiocinative tales, he dismissed such reactions as a sign of the audience's misunderstanding," James L. Machor maintains: "Seeking to define himself as once again a step ahead of his readership led Poe to identify his Dupin stories as virtual aesthetic hoaxes" (2011: 132). Among critical reactions to Poe's statement on the Dupin tales, there are then similar debunking arguments as in the case of "The Philosophy of Composition," this time geared towards the genre as well as the readership. Given Poe's rhetorical approach to composition, however, such phrases as "that is all done for effect" should make us wary of the thesis that he is here dismissing any part of his literary art. Detecting a distancing tone in the passage, T. O. Mabbott viewed it as "humorous" (T&S 521), but no matter whether we view it as comic or serious, the most prominent element in Poe's comment – rather than the genre or the reader – is actually "the writer of the story": "you yourself (the author)" (LTR I: 595 = LTR-240). Whether the

---

[1] LTR I: 595 = LTR-240. This is the same letter in which Poe also calls "The Philosophy of Composition" "my best specimen of analysis" (596). As the editors rightly comment, the letter is "a long, able restatement of many themes enunciated by Poe in various writings, and of considerable importance in interpreting his ideas" (597).

"supposititious" Dupin is a fraudulent offspring or a hypothetical figment, his actual role is that of a stand-in for the author and his ingenuity.

Rather than viewing this relation biographically as an expression of Poe's personality – however conceived – the following arguments will draw out the implications of Poe's analogies between the figure of the detective and the figure of the author in his tales of ratiocination: Poe's ratiocinative detectives are thus viewed as poetical figures of the author. In so doing, my suggestion is that we view Poe's creation of the detective and his story in terms of rhetorical-poetical invention, the first of the authemes or stages of production discussed in chapter one. These similarities become most apparent in the reliance of both processes upon what Charles Sanders Peirce – in connection to his notion of speculative rhetoric (Peirce 1998a: 19) – defined as abductive inferences, but also in rhetorical writings contemporary with Poe such as John Quincy Adams' *Lectures on Rhetoric*. Abductive inferences *sensu* Peirce evince the same duality that we found in the definitions of the rhetorical autheme of invention: both processes oscillate between invention *stricto sensu* and discovery, combining that "which brings into existence something new" and that "which finds what is already there" (Watson 2001: 389). The autheme of invention manifests itself on a personal level as the analytical and creative capabilities of the author – powers that, in turn, characterize the detective. The latter's investigation and the former's poetical invention thus come to represent each other in Poe's tales of ratiocination.

In order to make clear the import of the rhetorical duality of invention and discovery for Poe, the first section of the chapter reconstructs the relation of what he calls creative and resolvent powers in "The Murders in the Rue Morgue" and other writings, and the second then interprets them in terms of specifically poetical invention. The fundamental assumption of the rhetoric of authorship – namely, that the theoretical, poetical, and performative aspects of figures of the author are always co-present, even where one is dominant – will become particularly apparent in the case of the tales of ratiocination: since these tales evince a narrative form that is defined by logical inferences, primarily poetical figures of the author become invested with strong theoretical elements.

5.1 The Author's and Detective's Creative and Resolvent Powers

What makes the detective so interesting as a poetical figure of the author is that she or he can figure as a representation of both the analytical and the creative aspects of authorship, which tend so often to be separated and isolated: the detective is a figure of the author both as reader and as writer. The most famous of Poe's descriptions of Dupin encapsulates this defining duality: "I often dwelt meditatively upon the old philosophy of the Bi-Part Soul, and amused myself with the fancy of a double Dupin – the creative and the resolvent" (T&S 533). In "The Purloined Letter," Dupin comments on his own double, the Minister D–, that, as "poet *and* mathematician, he would reason well" (T&S 986). In unifying creative and analytical (i.e. poetical and theoretical) aspects of authorship, Poe's detective figure attains mythic dimensions, as Robert Daniel (1971) argued in his essay on "Poe's Detective God." The most detailed investigation of the similarities between Dupin and mythic "heroes of consciousness" has been completed by John T. Irwin (1994), who interprets the double Dupin as an innovation based on Roderick Usher and William Wilson and points out his similarities to the classical "heroes of consciousness" (1994: 207) such as Oedipus or Theseus who are characterized by two things:

> First, their myths tend to emphasize the hero's mental rather than physical abilities. This is not to suggest that they lack physical prowess but rather that their distinctive character as heroes is more a function of intelligence or cleverness than brute strength. Second, their myths tend in part to be parabolic expressions of the development and stabilization of individual self-consciousness. That is, a prominent theme in these stories is the relationship between self-recognition on the one hand and self-mastery on the other, a relationship that has in these cases not only personal but communal significance. (Irwin 1994: 207–208)

Heroes of consciousness such as Odysseus, Oedipus, Theseus, or Dupin are thus figures of the specifically cognitive relations between autonomous and heteronomous aspects of the subject. The thesis that Poe's foremost mythical figure Dupin is representative of these traits when transposed into the realm of authorship has been argued and illustrated by several studies. Edward Davidson, for instance, argues that "Dupin is the supreme artistic ego: everything external to himself can be made to fit the theoretical, the ideal logic" (Davidson 1973: 221). Besides this mathematical or theoretical aspect, Davidson also stresses the creative aspect: "The man who solves a crime is a poet: he is a re-creator of things as they truly are, not as they seem" (Davidson 1973: 218). As Bruce Weiner puts it, Dupin is often viewed as "Poe's ideal projection of himself as artist, the poet-mathematician who combines imagination and reason to achieve transcendental vision" (1986: 32). As Weiner's argument shows, it is often a biographical connection that is drawn from Dupin to Poe when it comes to questions and myths of authorship.

Advancing a more nuanced claim, my approach in what follows will not be based on the notion that the figure of the detective is representative of aspects of Poe as a biographical author but rather that it is representative of Poe's poetical figures of the author. In order to reconstruct the interdependence of the analytical and creative powers as Poe figures them, I shall first reconstruct Poe's notion of the "constructive power" of the author and then argue that Peirce's "abductive inference" or "abduction" is the term which connects it to the complementary analytical, or "reconstructive," power.

The Constructive or Combining Power

As could be seen in Poe's taunting of Dickens for his lack of the ability to construct (E&R 244; cf. chapter four), Poe's works abound with critical, literary, and mythological conceptions of the constructive power of the author, but its interconnections with the corresponding analytic powers come out particularly clearly in "The Murders in the Rue Morgue." Both constructive and analytical power are conceived by Poe as general traits of the subject but also as specifically authorial powers. Poe's comment that "[t]he mental features discoursed of as the analytical are, in themselves, but little susceptible of analysis" (T&S 527) have fuelled one of the most famous exchanges on Poe from Lacan and Derrida to Barbara Johnson and beyond.[2] Compared to the scrutiny devoted to the analytical and deconstructive powers, the corresponding constructive or creative powers in Poe have attracted considerably less attention, an imbalance that is currently in the process of being redressed, especially through Paul Hurh's work (2012; 2015: 119–160), who has emphasized the importance of "composition" for Poe's understanding of analysis. Hurh argues that, for Poe, "resolution and composition are two stages of the same analytical method" (Hurh 2015: 125). Hurh traces their origins to "the sixteenth-century revision of Aristotelian science in the Padua medical school," noting in passing that they are the result of the "application of Galen's rhetorical terms to the doubled form of Aristotelian method" (Hurh 2015: 126). My goal here is no genealogy but to foreground the rhetorical interrelations between analytical and creative powers, particularly insofar as they inform the features of the detective that come to shape a poetical figure of the author, invested with inventive powers that are a combination of constructive and analytical powers. The "slippage between 'composition' as a literary term and 'composition' as an analytical one" (Hurh 2015: 127), I argue, is a result of their rhetorical interrelations.

Like the whole introduction of "The Murders in the Rue Morgue," Poe's "constructive power" originally inhabits a phrenological context but goes on

---

[2] The major contributions to this debate are collected in Muller and Richardson (1988).

to transcend it.³ This is especially so in those versions of the story originating later than 1845 in which Poe deletes the first paragraph, which clearly frames the question of analysis in phrenological terms.⁴ The phrenologists had spoken of "constructiveness" as one of the 'organs' of the brain situated next to ideality, but nevertheless as a basic faculty, 'a primitive organ.' In one of his "Lectures on Phrenology and Its Application,"⁵ George Combe stated that: "To construct, means to put detached materials together so as to make a single object" (Combe 1839: 172). The faculty was supposed to be "a tendency to *fashion* in general, which may be done by putting materials together, or by chipping off fragments, or by moulding, or by drawing lines and laying on colours" (Combe 1839: 172). While it "does not *invent*" in an emphatic sense of creation, it "fashions or configurates" (Combe 1839: 172). As such, constructiveness is supposed to be at work primarily in engineering but also painting, and, somewhat comically, it characterizes animals such as beavers. To Poe, the theorist of the fancy rather than the imagination, the emphasis of 'constructiveness' on combination rather than creation was appealing. In "The Murders in the Rue Morgue," Poe strips the concept of most of its phrenological connotations by criticizing the phrenologists yet also making use of some of their arguments. In the last paragraph of the introductory part, Poe writes:

> The analytical power should not be confounded with simple ingenuity; for while the analyst is necessarily ingenious, the ingenious man is often remarkably incapable of analysis. The constructive or combining power, by which ingenuity is usually manifested, and to which the phrenologists (I believe erroneously) have assigned a separate organ, supposing it a primitive faculty, has been so frequently seen in those whose intellect bordered otherwise upon idiocy, as to have attracted general observation among writers on morals (T&S 530–31)

The argument evinces a movement typical of Poe's *critical* texts, which we saw at work in his treatment of high romantic authors in "Letter to B—," and which shows the continuity between his poetical and theoretical figurations of authorship: the use of others' examples to argue against their own positions. Distanc-

---

3 On Poe and phrenology, cf. Hungerford ([1930] 1993). On Poe's notion of "constructiveness" specifically, cf. Peeples (2002).
4 For an overview of Poe's different revisions of the text, cf. Savoye (2014). Versions earlier than 1845 begin: "It is not improbable that a few farther steps in phrenological science will lead to a belief in the existence, if not to the actual discovery and location of an organ of *analysis*" (T&S 527).
5 The lecture in question was also published in the *Southern Literary Messenger*, vol. 5, November 1839, 766–770.

ing himself from the erroneous assumptions of the phrenologists, the narrator's example used against the phrenologists is drawn straight from the pages of phrenologist George Combe: "This organ Constructiveness is sometimes large when Intellect is deficient. Thus, some of the cretins of Switzerland are employed in making watches" (1839: 174).[6]

Once the term "constructiveness" has been thus defined as 'fashioning' or 'configuring,' Poe explicitly links it (through ingenuity) to the faculties of the author: "Between ingenuity and the analytic ability there exists a difference far greater, indeed, than that between the fancy and the imagination, but of a character very strictly analogous. It will be found, in fact, that the ingenious are always fanciful, and the truly imaginative never otherwise than analytic" (T&S 531). The larger argument of the passage thus leads to Coleridge's already-discussed opposition of the creative and "vital" imagination and the fancy as a mere "mode of Memory," which was so decisive in the history of the romantic author ([1817] 1984: I, 304–305).

Poe's reference to the definition is all the more significant since he had at this point already heavily criticized the distinction between the mechanical, combinatory fancy and the vital, creative imagination. As discussed in chapter three, Poe argued that there was no difference between the two, "even of degree," since the "fancy as nearly creates as the imagination, and neither at all. Novel conceptions are merely unusual combinations" (E&R 1126). The reason for this difference in opinion, between denying the distinction in 1840 and reaffirming it in 1841, is not to be sought in the fictional character of "The Murders in the Rue Morgue." Rather, analysis is such a powerful faculty to the narrator and Poe that it also becomes, in its perfection, a constructive faculty, as is epitomized in the image of the "double Dupin – the creative and the resolvent" (T&S 533). The theoretically informed introduction to "The Murders in the Rue Morgue" frames the constructive or creative power as one that is necessarily connected to the analytical or resolvent power, thus positing an insoluble connection between poet and detective.

---

[6] What the terms "idiocy" and "cretins" misjudge in a manner typical of their time is the so-called savant syndrome in persons with serious mental disabilities; the derogatory term first used to describe the syndrome in the later nineteenth century, 'idiot savants,' shows the link quite clearly. Cf. Treffert (2009). While appearing at times like a precursor of today's neuroscientific attempts to map the brain, phrenology overall was a pseudoscientific project of entrenching ruling class privileges, particularly in racist terms.

Constructive and Analytical Powers as Abductive Powers

In "Murders" Dupin's analytic powers appear most strikingly in the 'mind-reading' episode at the beginning of the story, in which he follows the narrator's inner train of thought despite the fact that "neither of us had spoken a syllable for fifteen minutes at least" (T&S 533).[7] They are also visible in his solution to the mystery of the *"unequal* voice" (T&S 555) that no witness is able to identify as speech. Nancy Harrowitz (1983), Ilkka Niiniluoto (1999) and Paul Grimstad (2005; 2013: 42–64) have conclusively established that Dupin's inferences are neither deductive nor inductive, but 'abductive' – a term they take from Charles Sanders Peirce. My argument in what follows is based on two implications of Peirce's definition of abduction: it is the type of inference that leads to the advent of a *new* idea and it is *rhetorical* to the core.

To recapitulate, Peirce argued that "there are but three essentially different modes of reasoning: Deduction, Induction, and Abduction" (1998c: 234). He referred to the third type of logical inference under various terms throughout his work such as "retroduction," "hypothesis," and "presumption," among others.[8] The name that has stuck is 'abduction.' Here is what might be considered the most canonical of its many definitions:

> Abduction is the process of forming an explanatory hypothesis. It is the only logical operation which introduces a new idea; for induction does nothing but determine a value, and deduction merely evolves the necessary consequences of a pure hypothesis.
>
> Deduction proves that something *must* be; Induction shows that something *actually is* operative; Abduction merely suggests that something *may be*. (1998f: 216)

Peirce's classic example of this is a bag with beans in it (1992: 187–188). The absolute logical certainty of deduction tells us that if there are only white beans in the bag, then every single one we take out will be white. Induction would ultimately mean taking out all of the beans in order to establish whether or not they are all white, something which we cannot tell for sure until we have taken all of the beans out of the bag and seen that every single one of them is indeed white. However, it would be abduction when we already know (as a result of induction) that all the beans in the bag are white and find a few white beans on the table in front of it: we can abductively infer that the beans are from the bag; this is probable, but not certain, since the beans may have come from another bag or from somewhere else

---

[7] Cf. Lee (2010: 372) for a reading of the episode in terms of associationism, which was crucial for the philosophical foundations of the New Rhetoric and also an element of Coleridge's definition of the fancy (Coleridge [1817] 1983: I, 305), as discussed in chapter three.
[8] Good overviews are Fann (1970) and Wirth (2008).

entirely.⁹ Abduction would also come into play when one is confronted with even more complicated questions such as when you want to know what is in a bag and there is a faded script which only says ...ITE B...NS (which could also be 'white buns'). Put briefly, an abduction is an inference to the best explanation of a surprising observation that leads to a new idea.¹⁰

Take the example of the orang-utan's "unequal voice" in Poe's "Murders," which is interpreted by several witnesses in the story as speaking *a* different human language. None of the witnesses – from the gendarme, Isidore Musêt, to the confectioner, Alberto Montani – can identify the language that is actually spoken. Their mistake lies in their misperception of the sounds as speech, rather than in their deductive reasoning: If 1) every human language I understand is a particular language and 2) I cannot understand the language I am hearing, then 3) the language I am hearing is a particular language other than one I understand. Nor can the problem be solved by inductively amassing more and more witness statements. Dupin, by contrast, arrives at the solution by inferring from the testimonies of the peculiar quality of the voice and the similarities of the witnesses' statements that the rule governing this particular case is that a voice that is identified by all witnesses as speaking a language that they do not understand is one which, while highly similar to the human voice, does not speak a language. While Dupin himself calls this a "deduction[...]" (T&S

---

9 Peirce's more formal representation looks as follows (1992: 188):
Deduction
Rule. – All the beans from this bag are white.
Case. – These beans are from this bag.
∴ *Result.* – These beans are white.
Induction
Case. – These beans are from this bag.
Result. – These beans are white.
∴ *Rule.* – All the beans from this bag are white.
[Abduction]
Rule. – All the beans from this bag are white.
Result. – These beans are white.
∴ *Case.* – These beans are from this bag.

10 'Inference to the best explanation' is widely used as a term for Peirce's abductive inference. It is important to stress that, in any investigation, all of these inferences are combined in order to arrive at facts or truths: "The whole operation of reasoning begins with *Abduction* [...] Deduction produces from the conclusion of Abduction predictions as to what would be found true in experience in case that conclusion were realized. Now comes the work of Induction, which is not to be done while lolling in an easy chair, since it consists in actually going to work and making the experiments, thence going on to settle a general conclusion as to how far the hypothesis holds good" (Peirce 1998d, 287–288).

550),[11] its character as a guess well-founded in observations makes it a prime example of the abductive inference.

What is more, the abductive inference is connected in Poe to the author's analytical power. "The Murders in the Rue Morgue" would seem to affirm that abductive reasoning is indeed a characteristic trait of the truly imaginative author who necessarily also excels in analysis. While Poe mainly used "deduction" and "induction," or the more neutral "conclusion," to describe the detective's inferences in the tales of ratiocination, Poe's own later criticism of deduction and induction in *Eureka* offers the alternative "intuition," which is strikingly similar to what Peirce described as "abduction."

One of the central epistemological arguments in *Eureka* consists in Poe's criticism of Aries Tottle (Aristotle) and Hogg (Francis Bacon) as representatives of deductivism and inductivism, respectively: "both are snail processes" (ERK 11) and "narrow and crooked paths" (ERK 14). Sole reliance on deduction is impossible, Poe argues, because of the historically mutable nature of axioms outside of logic (ERK 50–51). Sole reliance on induction makes it impossible to account for the multiplicity of causal relations, i.e. that several causes can lead to one and the same result (ERK 66). In its place Poe offers what can best be conceptualised as abductive inference and which he calls "intuition." The following passages from Eureka come very close to defining abduction avant-la-lettre since they reaffirm the connection between the constructive power of the imagination and the analytical power of intuition:

> these vital laws Kepler *guessed* – that is to say, he *imagined* them. Had he been asked to point out either the *de*ductive or *in*ductive route by which he attained them, his reply might have been – 'I know nothing about *routes* – but I *do* know the machinery of the Universe. Here it is. I grasped it with *my soul* – I reached it through mere dint of *intuition*.['] (ERK 15)
> We have attained a point where only *Intuition* can aid us [...] It is but *the conviction arising from those inductions or deductions of which the processes are so shadowy as to escape our consciousness, elude our reason, or defy our capacity of expression.* (ERK 22)

This comes very close to Peirce's argument that the logical form of guessing is abductive (1998b: 107).[12] While Poe seems to regard intuition as either induction or deduction without consciousness, he is aware of the possibility of a third type of inference and begins to sketch it out. His scathing criticism of deduction and

---

[11] For a bibliographical overview on Poe's uses of "induction" and "deduction," cf. Nygaard (1994: 230).
[12] It is tempting to look for a line of direct influence. Peirce certainly read Poe, even trying his hand at calligraphy by writing the beginning of Poe's *Raven*, but, to my knowledge, there is no indication (thus far) that he had also read *Eureka*.

induction makes Poe's thought even more pertinent as a definition of abduction avant la lettre. Even though intuition is assigned to scientists like Kepler, its connection to the imagination quite obviously makes it a poetical quality. Within the broader realm of scientific observation and analysis, it is abductive inferences which lead to original insight and shifts in paradigms. This context also highlights the creative or constructive quality in abductive reasoning which is the only type of reasoning to lead to qualitatively new ideas. In order to demonstrate the interdependence of constructive and analytical powers, the description of abduction as a primarily analytical inference in the context of the detective's investigation can be connected to Poe's description of constructive power as a power of adaptation.

The Constructive or Adapting Power

Poe's critical thoughts on the constructive power as an adapting power appeared in various of his critical and poetical writings.[13] In "The American Drama," Poe declares one of the playwright's necessary faculties to be "the adapting or constructive power which the drama so imperatively demands" (E&R 385). As he characterizes it there, constructive power with regard to the drama includes the selection or invention of incidents (*inventio*) as well as their arrangement (*dispositio*); the element of a play in which constructive power shows most clearly is its plot.

Poe's discussion of plot quickly widens into a context of mythological and religious figures of authorship. The topos of the poet as another god, *poeta alter deus*, that was used in the Renaissance to legitimize poetical writing (Dyck 1991: 116), was reinterpreted in the course of the romantic rise of the author as an emphatic ability to create. Poe's discussion of the dramatist's subjectivity stands in this context. His argument leads him to the question of the relation between the poet-as-maker and plot and hence to the relation between the poet-as-author, the Christian God-as-author, and the universe-as-plot.

In an interesting movement of authorial self-affirmation, Poe quotes himself, from a piece first published as a *Marginalia* item in 1844, which would also become part of *Eureka*. In this item, Poe criticized a series of treatises in Natural

---

13 Poe discussed adaptation in at least three texts: first in a *Marginalia* item in the *Democratic Review* in November 1844 (E&R 1315–1316), in "The American Drama" in the *American Whig Review* in August 1845 (E&R 364–368) and in *Eureka* in 1848 (ERK 88–89).

Theology, named after their commissioner, the 8th Earl of Bridgewater.[14] Against the Bridgewater treatises, Poe argues that the difference between human and divine constructiveness lies in the latter's "complete mutuality of adaptation":

> in human constructions, a particular cause has a particular effect – a particular purpose brings about a particular object; but we see no reciprocity. The effect does not re-act upon the cause – the object does not change relations with the purpose. In Divine constructions, the object is either object or purpose, as we choose to regard it, while the purpose is either purpose or object; so that we can never (abstractly – without concretion – without reference to facts of the moment) decide which is which. (E&R 1315/366)

Poe combines a plethora of philosophical distinctions in this short passage, but the focal point of them all is the types of causality which characterize productive operations performed by the subject. Two fundamentally different types of causality are here distinguished: one is linear, the other circular. Be it with regard to the act of changing or creating physical things or with regard to other types of goal-oriented action, linear causality is human, while circular causality is primarily divine. Since Poe does not think of circular causality in the twentieth-century sense of cybernetic feedback loops, this is a highly problematic notion in ontological terms. Yet, Poe's focus seems to be not so much the types of causality *existent* in the world (which might even be recognized as linear once we refer to the facts); rather, the distinction between linearity and circularity in the causality of constructions is seen as a question of perception: of epistemology rather than ontology. The perfect circularity of divine constructions brings about an epistemological uncertainty for the observer to the extent that the observer is free to choose how to regard such constructions.

Poe then reapplies these cosmologico-theological speculations about the perception of causality to literature. What we would normally expect from theories of the unity of drama and plot in particular is a clear structure of cause and effect, even though this may only unfold over the course of the play, as for instance in Aristotle's prime example of μῦθος/mythos in the drama, *King Oedipus*.[15] Yet Poe's point is different, since he links the uncertainty about cause and effect to the recipients' response:

---

14 Cp. Terence Whalen's work on the treatises: Whalen argues that Charles Babbage's *Ninth Bridgewater Treatise* was the inspiration for Poe's angelic dialogues such as "The Power of Words" (1845): "Poe's dream of a material language, most fully realized in 'The Power of Words,' derives from the work of a scientist and economist rather than from the ruminations of an impractical romantic visionary" (1999: 250).
15 For my take on the relevance of *King Oedipus* to the detective story, cf. Guttzeit (2015b).

> The pleasure which we derive from any exertion of human ingenuity, is in the direct ratio of the *approach* to this species of reciprocity between cause and effect. In the construction of *plot*, for example, in fictitious literature, we should aim at so arranging the points, or incidents, that we cannot distinctly see, in respect to any one of them, whether that one depends from any one other or upholds it. In this sense, of course, perfection of plot is unattainable *in fact*, – because Man is the constructor. The plots of God are perfect. The Universe is a plot of God. (E&R 1316/366–367)

While careful to stress that authorial ingenuity only aspires to the absolute reciprocity of cause and effect and can never actually achieve it, in comparing the two types of constructive power Poe implicitly reaffirms the topos of the *poeta alter deus*. The constructive power of authors is god-like in the sense that they fashion plots in which the elements appear to be as interdependent as possible. The pleasure of the reception of artworks thus has its ground in the circular causality of the artwork in which every element of the story depends on every other element, or at least makes that impression on us. In other words, the artwork constantly keeps us guessing about the relation of cause and effect.

Poe's concept of adapting or constructive power is thus inherently connected to the analytical power of the recipient. To say, as Poe does in his letter to Philip Pendleton Cooke, that "the reader is made to confound the ingenuity of the suppositious Dupin with that of the writer of the story" (LTR I: 595 = LTR-240) is thus an affirmation of the adapting power of the writer: the impression in the reader is, ideally, a result of the adaptedness of the parts of the detective story which evinces – as a whole – the same structural integrity as a dramatic or cosmological plot.

"[A]bduction is," to quote Peirce again, "after all, nothing but guessing" (1998b: 107). What Poe is describing on the side of the recipient is abductive reasoning without arriving at a definite result: the perceived reciprocity between cause and effect keeps the recipient engaged in constant guess-work. What the constructive or poetical power of the writer thus consists in is the ability to establish the conditions for the reader's guesswork. This guesswork entails the excitement of discovering the new, yet without arriving at something definite.

This is precisely the point at which it first becomes evident that Dupin is not only like the reader, to whom he is often compared,[16] but also like the author, as for instance, Peter Thoms has argued: "a detective like Dupin also becomes an author, who figuratively writes the hidden story of the crime" (Thoms 2002: 133). Dupin is not kept in a constant state of guessing by the case that presents

---

16 Cf. e.g. Richard Kopley: "His [Dupin's] detection may be taken as an allegory of our own potential reading" (2008: 2).

itself to him; rather, he is the one who follows his abductions through to the end. Like the author is conscious of all literary characters' inferences, Dupin is conscious of the witnesses', the police's, and his narrator-friend's inferences. His genre-defining taciturnity (D. Porter 1981: 33), which keeps him silent about the progress of his investigation, is a construct of Poe's, yet it mirrors the latter's silence on the story of the crime (D. Porter 1981: 25; Todorov 1977). Dupin is like the author in his own guessing and in keeping others guessing.[17]

What makes Dupin a figure of the author in the tales of ratiocination, then, is the inventive aspect of the abductive inference *per se*. Umberto Eco's work offers a crucial building block for such an argument, because he maintains that many abductive inferences in detective fiction are "creative" or what I would call "inventive." Analyzing the thought process of Arthur Conan Doyle's famous detective, Eco points out that:

> Many of the so-called 'deductions' of Sherlock Holmes are instances of creative abduction. Holmes, in ["The Cardboard Box"], detects what Watson was mumbling to himself, reading his train of thought through his features, and especially through his eyes. The fact that the train of thought Holmes imagined coincided perfectly with Watson's actual one is the proof that Holmes invented 'well' (or in accordance with a certain 'natural' course). Notwithstanding this, he did *invent*. (1983: 215)

The scene Eco describes is a deliberate intertextual answer by Doyle (2009: 31) to the already-mentioned mind-reading episode at the beginning of "Murders" (T&S 533–537). Here, too, Dupin invents well, pointing out that the actor Chantilly "is a very little fellow, that's true, and would do better for the Théâtre des Variétés" which "was precisely what had formed the subject of my [the narrator's] reflections" (T&S 534). Dupin speaks to the narrator-friend as if the latter had voiced his thoughts, yet he has not. "'The larger links of the chain run thus'," Dupin explains and enumerates the links in the perceptive and associative chain of the narrator in inverse chronology: "'Chantilly, Orion, Dr. Nichol, Epicurus, Stereotomy, the street stones, the fruiterer'" (T&S 535).[18] Dupin's abductive power enables him to infer, or reconstruct, another person's interior speech. This abductive power has constructive and analytical aspects, and its success can only be guaranteed by the author. As Eco points out in the case of Golden Age writer Rex Stout's detective Nero Wolfe: the detective "invents elegant solutions for inextricable situations, then gathers all the suspects in his

---

[17] As we will see in the second half of this chapter, this involves Dupin literally becoming a writer of texts.
[18] For a detailed analysis of all the links in the chain, cf. Irwin (1992).

room and spells his story out *as if* it were the case. [The author] is so kind to him as to make the 'real' culprit to react, thus confessing his own guilt and acknowledging [the detective's] mental superiority." (1983: 220). The detective's powers thus present a figuration of the author's powers. In "Murders," Dupin becomes a representative of the author's figuration of the narrator-friend's and characters' thoughts, since only the author can guarantee the coincidence or correspondence of the detective's invented train of thought with such 'factual' trains of thought as in the narrator-friend's musings about the actor Chantilly.

More generally, Dupin becomes a poetical figure of the author because the author's ability to construct a plot and characters' thoughts, his poetical figuration, is like Dupin's ability to *re*construct the plot and the characters' thoughts within the storyworld. Both are only able to do one of these things because they can also do the other: not only is there "a double Dupin – the creative and the resolvent" (T&S 533) but there is also a double Poe, one who is creative through presenting the resolving activity of the detective. Hence, there emerges out of the story a double figure of the author that is both creative and resolvent, constructive and analytical, an author that has adapting power to make the readers keep guessing about the relations within the text.

In many ways, the decisive element of Poe's figuration of authorship in the tales of ratiocination lies in the fact that the detective's abductive inferences structure the narrative form – the generic features of the detective story. This is especially pertinent, since Poe is nearly unanimously regarded as the inventor of the genre of the detective story. As Maurice Lee puts it, "no set of tales has had more impact on literature and culture in the English-speaking world and beyond" (2010: 370).

My approach to Poe's 'invention' of the genre is to examine how the two sides of rhetorical *inventio* outlined in the first chapter – constructive 'invention' on the one hand and analytical 'discovery' on the other – structure this new poetical form of the tale of ratiocination. Hence, going beyond Poe's own terminology of constructive and adapting powers, the subject of the second half of this chapter is the question of the ways in which the narrative form of the tale of ratiocination is defined by the essential of abductive inferences. That is, it argues that both the author's production of a text, i.e. *inventio* in the sense of 'invention,' and the detective's reconstruction of the crime, i.e. *inventio* in the sense of 'discovery,' come together in the quintessentially rhetorical inference of abduction.

162 — 5 "The Ingenuity of Unravelling"

5.2 Author and Detective as Rhetorical Inventors of Truth

There is no other literary genre that centres on abductive inference as detective fiction does. As Nancy Harrowitz puts it, "[d]etective fiction has been and still is today the literary form which is devoted to the expression of abduction" (1983: 197). The reason for this lies in its narrative form, as becomes particularly clear when it is opposed to its direct generic relative, crime fiction. As Peirce explained, abduction is "reasoning [...] from effect to cause" (1992: 194), which is exactly what happens in a detective story when the dead body of the victim is discovered as an effect of as-yet unknown causes. One and the same story can be presented as either a crime narrative or a detective narrative, depending on whether we go along with the criminal as the crime originates or we follow the detective figure as the crime is being investigated.[19] Taking as an example one of the oldest extant crime narratives, the story of Cain and Abel, Richard Alewyn argues that this exact story could also be told in the different narrative form of the detective story:[20]

> A corpse is found. Who is it? Answer: Abel. – How did he die? – Through violence. – By an accident? No. – Then murder! Who is the culprit? Well, the human family was very small back then. There are only three who could have done it: Adam, Eve, Cain. They are questioned one after the other. Who could have been at the crime scene at the time of the murder? Who had a motive? Result: Cain alone has no alibi. He alone has a motive. Only Cain can be the culprit. (1998: 53; my translation)[21]

This version does not differ from the one in Genesis 4 with regard to its content – both render the murder of Abel by Cain – but it differs very much in its form. This, for Alewyn, marks the distinction between a 'crime novel' such as Dostoyevsky's *Crime and Punishment* and a 'detective novel' (Alewyn 1998: 53) such as *The Hound of the Baskervilles*. Despite its simplicity, Alewyn's story evinces the characteristics of the uniquely clear-cut narrative form of detective fiction;

---

19 This is often explained by reference to the distinction between story and discourse (Chatman 1978: 9). The criminal's and the detective's story lines might also be viewed as two separate stories connected by the narrative discourse, as seminally suggested by Todorov (1977).
20 The reconstruction of Alewyn's argument is taken from an article of mine on figurations of the Oedipus myth in detective fiction (Guttzeit 2015b: 148–49).
21 "Eine Leiche wird gefunden. Wer ist es? Antwort: Abel. – Wie ist er umgekommen? – Durch Gewalt. – Ein Unglücksfall? Nein. – Also Mord! Wer ist der Täter? Nun, die Menschheitsfamilie war damals noch klein. Es kommen nur drei in Frage: Adam, Eva, Kain. Sie werden nacheinander befragt. Wer konnte zur Tatzeit am Tatort gewesen sein? Wer hatte ein Motiv zur Tat? Ergebnis: Kain allein hat kein Alibi. Er allein hat ein Motiv. Kain allein kann der Täter gewesen sein." (Alewyn 1998: 53).

it consists, firstly, of the discovery of the criminal deed – most often a murder though sometimes the disappearance of a person; secondly, the investigation into *whodunnit*, *howdunnit*, and *whydunnit*; and finally, the dénouement in which the results of the investigation are revealed. While for Alewyn the detective story depends on the anatomy of question and answer, its logical form is more precisely described as abductive: as the fictional representation of the investigative process of reasoning from effect to cause.

Rhetorical and Poetical Invention as Abductive Processes

We have already seen how abductive powers characterize Dupin and, through him, Poe's poetical figure of the author in the tales of ratiocination. In this regard, the further relevance of abductive inference is two-fold: 1) Peirce, in keeping with the rhetorical tradition, defines abduction as a rhetorical inference that characterizes the autheme of *inventio* and 2) abduction is accompanied by a verificatory test of the relation between effects and causes that is also at the heart of the philosophical method of pragmatism. I shall first outline these two aspects of abduction, before applying the insights to the narrative form of Poe's tales of ratiocination specifically.

Since Peirce's reception in literary and cultural studies, fostered by critics such as Eco and Uwe Wirth,[22] has been dominated by semiotic interests, the case for the importance of Peirce's rhetoric has been less forcefully made, if at all. In philosophy, however, there is a large number of studies of Peirce's work that have reconstructed the centrality of rhetoric for his philosophy and semiotics.[23] The most relevant of these for our purposes is James Jakob Liszka's study of "Peirce's New Rhetoric" (2000), in which he demonstrates that central ideas of Peirce's understanding of rhetoric stem from the British New Rhetoric, in particular from Campbell and Whately. The list of Peirce's suggestions for the understanding of rhetoric is enormous, since he uses "at least seven different names for his rhetoric and something like 30 different definitions" (Liszka 2000: 440), but our focus here is on the relation between rhetoric and abduction specifically.

Abductive inference and rhetoric meet in (rhetorical) invention. As Liszka clarifies: "The obvious counterpart to invention in Peirce is abduction" (2000: 465). In what is the strongest formulation in his writings, Peirce identifies the

---

[22] Cf. e.g. Eco and Sebeok (1983) and Wirth (1995, 2008).
[23] Recent studies include Liszka (1996, 2000), Bergman (2007, 2010), and Colapietro (2007).

discipline of speculative rhetoric with abduction, writing that it "concerns abduction alone."²⁴ The abductive inference can hence be viewed as the key to what is usually termed the "logic of discovery," so named after Karl Popper's seminal work in the theory of science, *The Logic of Scientific Discovery* (1934); yet, if we actually follow through Peirce's argument to its logical conclusion, this discipline is better described as a '*rhetoric* of discovery.'

While I have heretofore focussed upon the formulation of this insight in Peirce's work specifically, it is by no means alien to the rhetorical tradition. A 'rhetoric of discovery' is a rhetoric that, phrased in classical terms, is based on *inventio*. As we saw in chapter one, the first autheme or stage of production of *inventio* is translated into English as either "invention" or "discovery," and denotes that process in the production of discourse that is both analytical and creative. In the antebellum culture of rhetoric, a contemporary version of the distinction was elaborated by John Quincy Adams. Adams' explication of invention is particularly relevant since he views rhetorical invention and poetical invention as part of the same continuum. The systematic argument based on Peirce's definition of the abductive inference is thus also supported by the view of rhetorical invention in Poe's time.

The continuum of invention is divided by Adams into three areas. The most fundamental is that of rhetorical invention: "invenire, to find, implied not the coming of the thought into the mind, but the going of the mind in search of the thought. This is the sense, in which rhetorical invention is understood" (Adams 1810: I, 165). The second meaning of invention, embodied in the colloquial meaning of mechanical invention, means "a higher degree of ingenuity; a more powerful exertion of intellect" (Adams 1810: I, 165). The third meaning of invention is poetical invention: "the language of poetry [...] lays claim not merely to the praise of finding, but to the glory of creating." Thus "[p]oetical invention disdains the boundaries of space and time" and "ranges over worlds of her own making" (Adams 1810: I, 165–166).²⁵ Adams' emphasis on the continuity of rhetorical and poetical invention is important, but his specification of their difference is even more relevant for the question of authorial invention in the tales of ratiocination.

The difference between the rhetorical and poetical types of invention, according to Adams, is that the poet's mind "must be released from all the restraints of truth and reason, and his imagination emancipated from all the

---

24 This is in MSL75 DraftD, 329, quoted in Liszka (2000: 465).
25 As illustration, Adams (1810: I, 166) quotes the same passage on the poet's frenzy from Shakespeare's *Midsummer Night's Dream* (Shakespeare 2005: 419 = 5.1.12–18) that Poe cites in "The Philosophy of Composition" (CT 61).

5.2 Author and Detective as Rhetorical Inventors of Truth — 165

laws of real and even of probable nature" (1810: I, 166). Rhetorical invention, on the other hand, has as its "indispensable feature" "[t]ruth, or at least the resemblance of truth" (1810: I, 166–167). It is "the discovery by thought of those things, the truth, or verisimilitude of which renders the cause probable" (1810: I, 163). This distinction is key to Poe's opposition of the effect of beauty that is to be achieved in poetry and the defining effect of the tale, in particularly the tale of ratiocination, namely truth.

As we saw in chapter four, the effect of beauty is what Poe views as "the sole legitimate province of the poem" (CT 63). The tale, however, is able to achieve a variety of effects such as "terror, or passion, or horror, or a multitude of such other points," the most important being "Truth": "Truth is often, and in very great degree, the aim of the tale" (E&R 573). Poe's gloss that "[s]ome of the finest tales are tales of ratiocination" makes clear that it is particularly in the tale of ratiocination that the effect of truth can be achieved (E&R 573). His metaphor of the "obstinate oils and waters of Poetry and Truth" (E&R 685) thus echoes Adams' emphasis that the poet's mind "must be released from all the restraints of truth and reason" (Adams 1810: I, 166). If we are looking for a model of both the author's poetical invention and the detective's investigation, then there is hardly a better one available than rhetorical invention: "the discovery by thought of those things, the truth, or verisimilitude of which renders the cause probable" (Adams 1810: I, 163). In addition, these similarities between rhetorical and poetical authorship were already clearly stated by Adams:

> Rhetorical invention however has this in common with the invention of poetry, that it is the most powerful test, both of the speaker's genius and of his learning. Though confined within the regions of truth or of verisimilitude, the range of invention is yet coextensive with the orator's powers. It consists in the faculty of finding whatsoever is [...] adapted to the purpose of his discourse; [...] of gathering from the whole domain of real or apparent truth their inexhaustible subsidies, to secure the triumph of persuasion. (Adams 1810: I, 167–168)

Invention, both in poetical and rhetorical discourse, is thus the test of the author's talent and craft: the "range of invention" is also "coextensive" (Adams 1810: I, 168) with the author's powers. Both in rhetorical invention, as conceived by Adams and Peirce, and in poetical invention, as Poe defines it for the tale of ratiocination, the aim is the effect of real or apparent truth. In order to effect this impression of real or apparent truth on the audience and to give proof of his discursive powers, Poe structures his tales of ratiocination according to the rhetorico-logical form of the abductive inference.

The Verification of Abductive Inferences in the Tales of Ratiocination

While the value of an abductive inference lies in the fact that it can discover something new, it is precisely this novelty that is the reason for why an abductive inference shows only what *may* be true. A deductive inference that is based on true premises *always* yields a true conclusion and an inductive inference yields a conclusion that is *actually* true. But an abductive inference always has to be complemented with further inferences of a deductive and inductive kind in order to test its validity. The general test that Peirce proposed for any concept and that constitutes the core of his pragmaticist philosophy, the so-called pragmatic maxim, suggests what such a test might look like. Its earliest and to some extent most canonical formulation is this: "Consider what effects that might conceivably have practical bearings we conceive the object of our conception to have: then, our conception of those effects is the whole of our conception of the object" (Peirce 1998e, 135). Any thought process (such as the detective's) is thus one that has ultimately to be tested with regard to its "practical bearings." Peirce's understanding of thought processes is broad, and, like Poe's concept of 'intuition' in *Eureka*, includes the imagination:

> if pragmatism is the doctrine that every conception is a conception of conceivable practical effects, it makes conception reach far beyond the practical. It allows any flight of imagination, provided this imagination ultimately alights upon a possible practical effect, and thus many hypotheses may seem at first glance to be excluded by the pragmatical maxim that are not really so excluded. (1998c: 235)

Hence, if the tales of ratiocination are structured according to the rhetorico-poetical logic of abduction, Peirce's pragmatic maxim suggests that we have to look for tests of the "practical bearings" of the detective's hypotheses, because no matter how wild a flight of imagination gave rise to the hypotheses, they still have to be evaluated according to their practical effect.[26] Poe's tales of ratiocination incorporate such elements of verification, and the different ways in which they are poetically fashioned in each individual tale is indicative of the poetical figures of the author that emerge from the stories.

Already in the first tale of ratiocination, "Murders," we encounter just such a verificatory test, one which would become one of the typical forms of the dénouement scene in the later history of detective fiction, especially in the so-

---

[26] Peirce's phrase is reminiscent of Adams' distinction between poet and orator: "The poet may soar beyond the flaming bounds of space and time; but the orator must remember, that an audience is not so readily excursive, and is always under the power of gravitation" (1810: II, 327).

called Golden Age – John G. Cawelti calls it an "immortal" example of the generic feature of the "announcement of the solution" (1976: 87, 86). Immediately after investigating the scene of the crime, Dupin places an advertisement in *Le Monde*, an event that is clearly underreported by the narrator: "On our way home my companion stepped in for a moment at the office of one of the daily papers" (T&S 547). After what is almost exactly one half of the discourse of "Murders" (and thus at a time in the reading experience where popular fiction usually offers a turning point),[27] Dupin informs the narrator of the impending test of his inference, without having informed him of these inferences themselves:

> "I am now awaiting," continued he, looking toward the door of our apartment – "I am now awaiting a person who, although perhaps not the perpetrator of these butcheries, must have been in some measure implicated in their perpetration. Of the worst portion of the crimes committed, it is probable that he is innocent. I hope that I am right in this supposition; for upon it I build my expectation of reading the entire riddle. I look for the man here – in this room – every moment. It is true that he *may* not arrive; but the probability is that he will." (T&S 548; my emphasis)

The man Dupin is waiting for is the French sailor who had trapped the orang-utan on Borneo and brought it to Paris, where it escapes, and, driven into a corner, kills the two women in the Rue Morgue.[28] Dupin's "expectation of reading the entire riddle" comes down to a yes-or-no-question that is governed by the modality of possibility: will the person come or not? Poe makes explicit the abductive character of Dupin's inferences leading to this question, when – after Dupin has explained his train of thought to the narrator – he mentions the French sailor once more:[29]

> I will not pursue these guesses – for I have no right to call them more – since the shades of reflection upon which they are based are scarcely of sufficient depth to be appreciable by my own intellect, and since I could not pretend to make them intelligible to the understanding of another. We will call them guesses then, and speak of them as such. (T&S 560)

---

27 I am using "discourse" here in its basic narratological sense of the opposition of story and discourse. Cf. Chatman (1978: 9, 26) In Mabbott's edition "Murders" is 41 pages long (T&S 527–568), and the passage in question is 21 pages in, in the middle of page 548.
28 The Gothic horror of the orang-utan that is to be contained by Dupin's ratiocination should also be viewed in historical terms as "illustrating Southern white fears concerning slave insurrection" (A. Smith 2013: 64).
29 Like the first statement about the orang-utan's 'owner,' this marks a division in the discourse of "Murders," occurring after roughly four fifths.

Dupin's train of abductive reasoning, "guesses" based on "shades of reflection," is ultimately validated by the sailor's appearance, which, in the storyworld, turns what *may* be true into what is *actually* true. In the later history of the genre, such correct predictions would open up a space for satire but, as it is, Dupin is granted authority in the way that Eco described it for Rex Stout and Nero Wolfe: Poe "is so kind" to Dupin "as to make the 'real' culprit to react" (Eco 1983: 220). As we learn right before Dupin and the narrator hear the sailor's step on the stairs, the success of Dupin's investigation is not only a question of his abductive reasoning about the case[30] but also of his rhetorical-*poetical* abductions about the sailor as the intended audience of his advertisement in *Le Monde*. This is the text Dupin composes for the advertisement:

> CAUGHT — In the Bois de Boulogne, early in the morning of the —— - inst., (the morning of the murder,) a very large, tawny Ourang-Outang of the Bornese species. The owner, (who is ascertained to be a sailor, belonging to a Maltese vessel,) may have the animal again, upon identifying it satisfactorily, and paying a few charges arising from its capture and keeping. Call at No. ——, Rue ——,' Faubourg St. Germain - au troisième. (T&S 560–561)

Peter Thoms argues that the sequence "illustrates [Dupin's] skill with words as he pens the advertisement, a tactic that, in luring the sailor to Dupin's home, suggests his narrative control over the characters in his case" (2002: 134),[31] a thought I would like to reframe in two regards: 1) strictly speaking, Dupin does not have "narrative" control over the sailor, i.e. can define the latter's story, but rather rhetorical control; as Poe would put it in his Hawthorne reviews, "the soul of the reader is at the writer's control" (E&R 586). 2) This power is primarily a result of Dupin's ability abductively to infer the effect his advertisement would have upon the sailor. As an illustration of these two decisive points the passage in which Dupin explains his abductive reasoning about the audience of his text is worth quoting at length:

---

[30] In an abductive train of reasoning that is typical of the genre, Dupin interprets a ribbon with a knot found at the crime scene as the trace of a sailor on a Maltese ship (T&S 561).

[31] Dupin's development can also be framed as a movement from analytic to compositional thinking, as Paul Hurh has pointed out: "Given their conspicuous redoubled narrative structure, Poe's detective tales may be considered dramatizations of the regress [i.e. the doubled methodological process of analysis and composition] itself. 'Murders in the Rue Morgue,' for instance, begins with effects, two dead bodies and a locked room, which Dupin traces back to their causes, an escaped orang-outang, by the processes of resolution. The tale isn't over until this process of resolution is reversed in the process of composition, in which Dupin reconstructs the meaning of the effects, the solution of the crime, by retelling the story of the murders as an effect with a determinate cause." (Hurh 2015: 127)

5.2 Author and Detective as Rhetorical Inventors of Truth — 169

Now if, after all, I am wrong in my induction from this ribbon, that the Frenchman was a sailor belonging to a Maltese vessel, still I can have done no harm in saying what I did in the advertisement. If I am in error, he will merely suppose that I have been misled by some circumstance into which he will not take the trouble to inquire. But if I am right, a great point is gained. Cognizant although innocent of the murder, the Frenchman will naturally hesitate about replying to the advertisement – about demanding the Ourang-Outang. He will reason thus: – 'I am innocent; I am poor; my Ourang-Outang is of great value – to one in my circumstances a fortune of itself – why should I lose it through idle apprehensions of danger? Here it is, within my grasp. It was found in the Bois de Boulogne – at a vast distance from the scene of that butchery. How can it ever be suspected that a brute beast should have done the deed? The police are at fault – they have failed to procure the slightest clew. Should they even trace the animal, it would be impossible to prove me cognizant of the murder, or to implicate me in guilt on account of that cognizance. Above all, *I am known*. The advertiser designates me as the possessor of the beast. I am not sure to what limit his knowledge may extend. Should I avoid claiming a property of so great value, which it is known that I possess, I will render the animal at least, liable to suspicion. It is not my policy to attract attention either to myself or to the beast. I will answer the advertisement, get the Ourang-Outang, and keep it close until this matter has blown over'. (T&S 561–562)

Like the mind-reading sequence at the very beginning of "Murders" and the interpretation of the "unequal voice" of the orang-utan, Dupin's train of thought is a prime example of abductive reasoning. The difference between the earlier episodes and the advertisement, which sets up the verificatory test of Dupin's main train of abductive reasoning (about the overall case), is that it involves an author's reasoning about the effect of his text on his audience. This chain of reasoning and writing is rhetorical at heart since it epitomizes the two sides of rhetorical *inventio:* discovery and invention. The figure of Dupin is thus a combination of analytical and constructive powers unified through the process of abductive reasoning. Above and beyond the general similarities in the descriptions of the individual powers, this is what makes Dupin one of Poe's foremost poetical figures of the author.

Though it is nowhere else as clear as in "The Murders in the Rue Morgue," we find similar examples of this verificatory test in Poe's other tales of ratiocination, where they are either poetically or theatrically inflected. In "The Purloined Letter," for instance, Dupin is able to replace the original letter with a facsimile after hiring a man to act maniacally and fire an unloaded musket in the street (T&S 992). In Poe's less well-known "Thou Art the Man," "the first comic detective story" (Mabbott's headnote in T&S 1042), the figure of the narrator-detective is infused with decidedly theatrical or performative elements: he makes the murderer confess by faking a letter with a wine delivery, propping the victim's corpse into the fake wine box so that it jumps out – like a jack-in-the-box – when the murderer opens it and appears to utter the words "Thou art the man." As the narrator explains at the end: "For the words which I intended the corpse to speak, I confidently depended upon my ventriloquial abilities; for their effect, I counted upon the conscience of the murderous wretch" (T&S 1059). Poe's detective characters thus make regular use of both poetical and performative means in their verifications of their abductive reasonings: their rhetorical trains of thought are followed by an anticipation of the rhetorical impact of their discourses and confirmed via the pragmatic test on the audience.

The figuration of the detectives in poetical, theoretical and performative terms of authorship also figures the author in terms of the masterly analytic ability of the detective. As we saw in the success of Dupin's advertisement in "The Murders in the Rue Morgue," the detective's planning for effect is as exact as any author in the antebellum culture of rhetoric could ever dream of. Yet, while the detective has all the time in the (story)world to set up traps for suspects and to prepare dazzling dénouements, the author can only verify whether his intended effect has become an impression on the audience after the text has been published. The analogy, however, remains: just as Dupin's text sets up the verificatory test for his abductive hypotheses about the case and a proof of his ingenuity, so the texts written by the author set up the verificatory test of her or his abductive reasoning regarding the potential audience and, as Poe argued, constitute a proof of the author's ingenuity. In this regard, both detective and author act like rhetoricians. Hence, it might be no mere accident that, as Buford Jones and Kent Ljungquist (1976) have argued, the real life model for the Chevalier Auguste Dupin was André Marie Jean Jacques Dupin (1783–1865), known as Dupin the Elder, a French advocate and politician. When Poe referred to the real life model of his fictional detective in the second-but-last Marginalia of July 1849, he referred to him neither as the advocate nor as the politician, but as the "orator" (E&R 1466).[32]

The Ingenuity of Unravelling a Web Woven for Unravelling

"[W]here is the ingenuity of unravelling a web which you yourself (the author) have woven for the express purpose of unravelling?" Poe's question deserves an answer, one that can be grasped abductively. The defining characteristic of the detective story lies in its particular form, one whose relevance for poetical figurations of the author is encapsulated in the duality of the rhetorical concept of invention: in detective fiction, the author's poetical invention is the detective's

---

32 I first observed this in Guttzeit (2010: 124).

rhetorical invention. In other words: what the author fashions is the detective's process of investigation. In the structural similarity between the two types of invention, a similarity that can be grasped by applying the notions of rhetorical *inventio* and Peircean abductive inference, lies the appeal of the detective as a poetical figure of authorship.

Dupin's ability to reconstruct the plot within the storyworld is like the author's ability to construct a plot in the real world, yet both are only able to do one of these things because they can also do the other. Like the double Dupin that is "creative and [...] resolvent" (T&S 533), there also emerges out of the story a double figure of the author that is both constructive and analytical. As characters with analytical and constructive powers that are unified through the power of abductive reasoning, Poe's detectives represent the autonomous aspect of authorship.

The ingenuity of unravelling a web woven for the purpose of unravelling thus lies in the construction of a figure that can weave and unravel textual webs at will. Despite its connections to mythical heroes of consciousness, no modern literary figure that united analytical and constructive powers in the manner of Dupin was available to Poe as a model. Hence, by inventing and discovering the literary genre of detective fiction, Poe produced a new poetical figure of the author. That is, the new, abductively gained figure of the author as both creative and resolvent was inseparable from the invention of detective fiction itself.

6 The Jingle-Man and the Damned Rhetorician: Poetry, Elocution, and the Political Rationale of Verse

> *Elocution*, is reading, and speaking, with *science*, and *effect*.
> Cotesworth P. Bronson: *Elocution*, 1845: 28

This motto from the elocutionist Cotesworth P. Bronson's 1845 book on *Elocution, or Mental and Vocal Philosophy* offers a one-line definition of elocution. Its elements evince the performative character of elocution, both with regard to the printed and the spoken word. This performativity is even demonstrated in formal terms, since the definition stages its own performance – its own being read aloud, marking emphasis by italicization, and showing speech pauses for emphasis through the use of commas, even where they would be ungrammatical according to today's standards. What is more, it maintains the scientific character of elocution, and that it is, in the last instance, governed by the rationale of rhetorical effect.[1] All of the rhetorical elements of elocution are also present in Poe's criticism and tales – where they affect his theoretical and poetical figures of the author. What role they play for his performative figures of the author, is the subject of the final two chapters.

As explained earlier, the performative dimension of the figures of the author refers to the rhetorical operations of memory and performance and, more generally, to stagings of the authorial self, not only in such settings as public readings, but also in theatrical contexts in other media. As I will show with regard to Poe's poetry, his theory of verse, his own lectures, and the depiction of the interplay between print and speech in his tales, his connections to the culture of rhetoric, and to elocution in particular, must be seen as essential to rhetoricizing Poe and to what J. Gerald Kennedy and Jerome McGann have characterized as the overall project of "remapping" antebellum print culture through Poe.

In this chapter, I examine some of the most representative interrelations between antebellum eloquence and Poe's poetry, to lay bare the heart of what one might call Poe's elocutionary rationale of verse. Rather than focusing on the French and European modernist afterlife of Poe,[2] I argue that – at this time of the romantic opposition to rhetorical poetry – Poe was responding specifically to elocutionary theories, discourses, and practices – partially affirming and par-

---

[1] On the history of elocution, and the elocutionary movement in particular, cf. Brown (1996).
[2] Cf. Eliot (1949), Quinn ([1957] 1971), Vines (1999).

tially subverting them. This historical reframing concurs with the recent systematic argument put forth by Jerome McGann that Poe's compositions "require actual performance" by the reader (McGann 2013b: 871). My argument is mainly based on a reconstruction of Poe's connections to elocutionism and close readings of the poem "Ulalume" and Poe's theoretical essay "The Rationale of Verse." After considering some influential commonplaces in the reception of Poe's poetry, I focus on the ways in which poetical performance was viewed as elocutionary in Poe's times and on how Poe figures the poet as elocutionist performer and thus establishes a performative figure of the author between 'jingle-man' and 'damned rhetorician.'

6.1 Poe and the Failure to Distinguish Between Poetry and Rhetoric: A Short Reception History

It was one of antebellum America's foremost public lecturers who furnished the most (in)famous epithet to characterize Poe as a poet: in a conversation with William Dean Howells, Emerson called Poe "*the jingle-man*" (Howells 1894: 450). The epithet is often quoted and worth discussing on its own but the rhetorical situation in which it was uttered is particularly instructive. According to Howells' recollection in 1894, Emerson had asked whether Howells "knew the poems of William Henry Channing" (449), and Howells had to confess and "answered then truly that I knew them only from Poe's criticisms: cruel and spiteful things which I should be ashamed of enjoying as I once did" (449–450). Poe is thus at the same time invoked as well as rejected as a critic with authority; rather his criticism is something morally dubious, something the enjoyment of which is followed by shame. The conversation continues:

> "Whose criticisms?" asked Emerson.
> "Poe's," I said again.
> "Oh," he cried out, after a moment, as if he had returned from a far search for my meaning,
> "*you mean the jingle-man!*" (Howells 1894: 450)

The passage is arranged like a dramatic dialogue that leads to a punchline. Lost "in a far search for [...] meaning" when it comes to remembering Poe as a critic, Emerson remembers Poe by what we can presume was, for him, the central feature of Poe as a poet: the jingling sound of his poems. Presumably doubly ashamed for not only invoking a dubious authority but also a poet whose poetry consisted of mere tinkling melodies, Howells reacts confusedly and guiltily: "I do not know why this should have put me to such confusion, but if I had written the criticisms myself I do not think I could have been more abashed. Perhaps I felt an edge of reproof, of admonition, in a characterization of Poe which the world will hardly agree with; though I do not agree with the world about him, myself, in its admiration" (1894: 450).

In the dialogue between Howells and Emerson, we thus meet a variation of the familiar trope of the problem of Poe, reframed in moral terms of shameful admiration. Howells' implied conclusion is that the world should be as ashamed for its admiration as he has learned to be. What is striking though, is that, to the best of my knowledge, Poe never even wrote a critique of William *Henry* Channing, the poet about whom Emerson and Howells are presumably speaking, but only of the latter's cousin William *Ellery* Channing (the younger) (E&R 459–472).[3] The recollection of the conversation thus contains a memory slip, a very understandable one, yet one that – in combination with the pervading sense of shameful admiration – seems paradigmatic of the reception history of Poe's poetry. In similar fashion, Emerson's figure of the jingle-man was joined by another epithet for Poe that gives a clue that a major role in this history is played by the rhetorical dimension of Poe's poetry.

In two letters to Harriet Monroe in 1915, Ezra Pound diagnosed the dangers of Poe as lying in an odd mixture of pleasurable readability and a rhetorical classicism not to be imitated. Pound compared Poe to one of the most obviously rhetorical of poets: "I don't think Pindar any safer than Poe. 'Theban Eagle' be blowed. A dam'd rhetorician half the time. The infinite gulph between what you read and enjoy and what you set up as a model" (Pound 1971: 55).[4] Pound does not make it explicit, but besides their rhetoricity, the Theban eagle, Pindar's representation of himself as a poet (Stoneman 1976: 188), appears to connect him to Poe and his raven, too. According to Pound's (strikingly sophistic) argument, Poe deserves poetic licence for his rhetoricity but he is not to be imitated or emulated: "[o]ne condemns a fault in Poe," Pound argues, "not because it is in Poe. It is all right for Poe if you like, but it is damn bad for the person who is trying uncritically to write like Poe." (Pound 1971: 55). Like Howells', Pound's view is thus also a mixture of reservation and admiration.

---

[3] This is corrected in the republished version in Howells (1911: 63) but there can only be speculation which of the two Channings Emerson mentioned originally. In any case, at least one memory slip remains.

[4] The rhetorical tradition indeed values Pindar highly, as Quintilian's statement makes clear: "Of the nine lyric poets, Pindar is far the greatest, for inspiration, magnificence, *sententiae*, Figures, a rich stock of ideas and words, and a real flood of eloquence" (Quintilian 2001d: 283=10.1.61).

Yet Pound's view came to be rewritten in the course of the critical history of the original letter. At the end of it, Poe (and not Pindar) has become not simply a "dam'd rhetorician" but – with the striking addition of "bad" – a "dam'd *bad* rhetorician" (Hubbell 1972: 20; Meyers 2000: 274; Zimmerman 2005: 28; my emphasis). Regardless of when and where the "bad" crept in, this textual slip occurs after a similarly ambiguous reaction as Howells'. What is more, the problematic ambiguity of Poe's poetry is explicitly connected to a figure of the author that stems from the rhetorical tradition. Pound's attitude is certainly ambivalent, since he calls Poe "a good enough poet, and after Whitman the best America has produced", yet adding in brackets "(probably?)" (1971: 50). But Pound really only indirectly opposes Poe's rhetoricity and connects it to classical Greek models. If there is an impetus we can take from Pound's comments on the poet Poe, it would rather be to look at Poe as a damned *good* rhetorician.

Such a sense of shameful admiration and ambivalence as we find in the conversations between Howells and Emerson as well as between Pound and Monroe has been characterized by Jonathan Elmer as "a curious tic in the criticism on Poe" in that "[t]he very people who will dismiss Poe's artistic excesses will often attest to a past pleasure in those same excesses" (1996: 203), mentioning Daniel Hoffman's *Poe Poe Poe Poe Poe Poe Poe* (1978) as an additional case in point. Elmer locates the reason for this tendency in Poe's resistance to certain aesthetic or poetical standards: "What always returns us to Poe, and Poe to us, is a pleasure under interdiction, a pleasure resistant to the dominant norms of aesthetic value that, by reason of this very resistance, are reasserted with an ever-greater force." (1996: 204). If we take "aesthetic" not as a technical but as an historical term, the "dominant norms" Elmer posits can be linked to the opposition between poetry and rhetoric as we met it in chapter two in the discussion of Mill's opposition of hearing and overhearing. What matters when it comes to the "pleasure under interdiction," to the "admiration" or condemnation of the "jingle-man" is the rhetorical characteristics of his poetry.

A third critical response can lead us on to the foremost rhetorical context of Poe's poetry and its performative figures of the author. In what is surely the harshest critique of Poe as a poet, the American Leavisite poet-critic Yvor Winters argued in 1937 that Poe, "although he achieved, as his admirers have claimed, a remarkable agreement between his theory and his practice, is exceptionally bad in both" (Winters [1937] 1993: 55). Winters' critique is mainly directed against Poe's idea that the poem should not inculcate a moral (the idea of the "poem written solely for the poem's sake"; E&R 76, 295) and against the hypnotic style of the poetry. Thus, according to Winters, on the one hand, Poe is oblivious to "the function of intellectual content in poetry" (Winters [1937] 1993: 59) and guilty of a "willful dislocation of feeling from understanding [...] growing out of the uncertainty regarding the nature of moral truth in general and its identity in particular situations" ([1937] 1993: 65). On the other, Poe's work represents "an effort to establish the rules for a species of incantation, of witchcraft; rules whereby, through the manipulation of certain substances in certain arbitrary ways, it may be possible to invoke, more or less accidentally, something that appears more or less to be a divine emanation" ([1937] 1993: 67). To a certain extent, Winters' critique might be refuted by pointing out the sexist and classist assumptions that parts of his argument are based on (cf. Peeples 2004: 66). He argues, for instance, that Poe's "is an art to delight the soul of a servant girl; it is a matter for astonishment that mature men can take this kind of thing seriously." (Winters [1937] 1993: 76).

Yet, perhaps even because of the severity of his critique of Poe's "aesthetic of obscurantism" (65), Winters captures a central aspect of Poe's poetry and theory in an epithet he uses to characterizes their chief exponent, "The Raven": Winters calls the poem "that attenuated exercise for elocutionists" (Winters [1937] 1993: 71). Winters thus points out the connection of Poe's poetry to rhetoric, and specifically elocution, but, in doing so, negates it as inferior.

What Winters did not know in all likelihood, is the place of the first book publication of "The Raven" that was noted by T. O. Mabbott in 1943, six years after the publication of Winters' article. Less than three months after its first appearance in the papers *The American Review* and *The New York Evening Mirror* in late January 1845, "The Raven" was published in the second edition of George Vandenhoff's *A Plain System of Elocution. Or, Logical and Musical Reading and Declamation With Exercises in Prose and Verse* (1845).[5] The immediate reception thus shows the same elocutionary character that Winters recognises yet dismisses out of hand.

This three-stage reception history of Poe's characteristics as a poet shows him transforming in the critical glance from jingle-man to damned rhetorician to bewitching elocutionist. At every stage, moral ambiguity and ethical dubiousness arise out of the sheer power of "a species of incantation, of witchcraft" as Winters puts it. While this mirrors central late-nineteenth and early-twentieth century debates about poetry,[6] it also revisits one of the oldest and most constant assumptions about the powers and dangers of rhetoric: Gorgias' idea of rhetoric as "witchcraft" (2001: 32 = §10) that can radically alter ethical certainties. "Sacred incantations with words," argues Gorgias, "inject pleasure and reject

---

[5] Poe had reviewed the first edition of the volume in the *Broadway Journal* in April 1845: Poe, Edgar A. 1845. "Review Notice of a Plain System of Elocution, by G. Vandenhoff." *Broadway Journal*, April 12.
[6] Cf. particularly Quinn ([1957] 1971).

pain, for in associating with the opinion of the mind, the power of an incantation enchants, persuades, and alters it through bewitchment" (2001: 32 = §10). Gorgias' assumption of the power of rhetoric (understood as all language arts including poetry) was turned against him by opponents of the tradition, and Winters' critique in particular is an instantiation of this opposition against the morally dubious witchcraft of rhetorical poetry.

There are other ways of explaining the divide between rhetorical and poetical discourse, as we saw in chapter two. While F. O. Matthiessen's seminal monograph on the *American Renaissance* is famous in Poe studies for its relegation of Poe – in the age of Emerson and Whitman – to a footnote, it is also instructive with regard to the reception history of Poe's poetry sketched above. One of the reasons of Matthiessen's disregard might well lie in what he perceived as "the age's general failure to distinguish between the nature of the two arts" of poetry and rhetoric (Matthiessen [1941] 1968: 23).

While Matthiessen was pointing primarily to factual uses of rhetoric,[7] this is also true of the interconnections between elocutionism and poetry. As Shira Wolosky argues in her revisionist account of nineteenth-century poetry, "the problem is not poetry's integrity as against rhetoric [...] Poetry, far from being the pure, self-enclosed language demanded by formalist aesthetics, inevitably constructs its forms and its language out of the discourses of the cultural worlds it inhabits." (Wolosky 2010: 65). Wrestling in his poems with Gothic and Orientalist tropes, romantic imagery, and visionary figures, Poe, in his later work as a poet, arrives at a kind of sound poetry that anticipates modernist developments from Baudelaire's symbolism to Edward Lear's nonsense poetry, yet one that also responds to central aspects of the rhetorical culture of antebellum America, particularly elocution and elocutionism.

6.2 The Elocutionary Production of Beauty: Style and Performance in "Ulalume"

If the problem of Poe's poetry is a symptom of the romantic dispersal of rhetoric in an age which fails "to distinguish between the nature" of rhetoric and poetry, as Matthiessen put it, it is also the result of the reinterpretation of one of its central terms, *elocutio*, as 'elocution.' As outlined in chapter one, the term is usually

---

[7] However, like many other critics of antebellum literature, Matthiessen also argues that rhetorical modes of writing affected other discourses: "To a degree that we have lost sight of, oratory was then the basis for other forms of writing, and its modes of expression left a mark on theirs." (Matthiessen [1941] 1968: 22)

translated as 'style,' yet the term is affected by two central processes around 1800: on the one hand, the category of style is reinterpreted as an ever closer and finally insoluble unity between the *what* and the *how* of discourse, as we can trace in the increasing rejection of the ancient metaphor of style as the dress of thought. On the other, as a result of the rise of the elocutionary movement, the Anglicised term 'elocution' comes to denote the process of rhetorical performance, or *actio/pronuntiatio*, thus no longer signifying the style of a text but its enunciation. Thus, *elocutio* loses its integrity in the rhetorical system and, at the same time, comes to enjoy unprecedented attention. Both processes are crucial to understanding Poe's poetry and the performative figure of the author that they contain.

In the process of the interiorisation of inspiration and originality that ultimately led to the romantic author, the traditional idea of style as an apt dress of thought came to be rejected.[8] Significantly, this process originates in the belletristic – or indeed stylistic – branch of the New Rhetoric: Hugh Blair criticized the "very erroneous idea, which many have of the ornaments of Style, as if they were things detached from the subject, and that could be stuck to it, like lace upon a coat" (Blair 2005: 195–196). George Campbell suggested to rather view language and thought as interrelated "like body and soul" (Campbell 1988: 215). While "the qualities of the one [are] exactly to co-operate with those of the other," however, the ultimate rationale remained effect: "It is not ultimately the justness either of the thought or of the expression, which is the aim of the orator; but it is a certain effect to be produced in the hearers." (Campbell 1988: 215). More generally, eighteenth-century and nineteenth-century New Rhetoricians adapted classical features of the rhetorical theory of style. They often distinguished – like Whately in his *Elements of Rhetoric* (1828: xiv) – three major categories of it: perspicuity; energy or vivacity; and elegance or beauty, thus retaining a functional perspective on style.[9]

The "dissociation of the concept of style from rhetoric" (Müller 2001: 745) culminated in High Romanticism. Even in Wordsworth, the most rhetorical of ro-

---

[8] Purcell and Snowball (1996) and Müller (2001) give an overview of the history of style in its relation to rhetoric on which I draw in this and the next paragraph.

[9] After its initial publication in 1828, Whately's version of the triad "was widely adopted as a framework for the general qualities of style" (Johnson 1991: 59–60). For an earlier version of the triad and the use of "music" to denote a quality of style, cf. also Campbell ([1776] 1988: 215–216). The last of these categories, elegance or beauty, corresponds to the earlier category of ornament. Cf. Johnson (1991: 49). Whately mentions grammatical correctness but dismisses it as not specific for rhetoric: "It is requisite for an Orator, e. g. to observe the rules of Grammar; but the same may be said of the Poet and the Historian, &c." (Whately 1828: 173).

mantic poets,[10] the idea of "proper ornaments" (Blair 2005: 196) was replaced with an idea of incarnation, and his criticism of the clothing metaphor became much more pronounced, to the extent of assigning it deranging power: "If words be not [...] an incarnation of the thought but only a clothing for it, then surely will they prove an ill gift; such a one as those poisoned vestments, read of in the stories of superstitious times, which had power to consume and to alienate from his right mind the victim who put them on" (W. Wordsworth 1974: 84). Wordsworth's description is reminiscent of the poisoned garment that mentally deranged and killed Hercules, given to him by his credulous wife Dejanira.[11] Wordsworth thus negated the ancient idea of style by referring to ancient myths: here, the idea of the dress of thought has become lethal. Beginning in Blair and culminating in Wordsworth, *elocutio* thus turns into *style:* it ceases being a technical variable that can be rhetorically manipulated and becomes an incarnated quality of solitary writing and romantic authorship.

This aspect of style is one of the two central changes to the meaning of *elocutio*; the second concerns the rise of the elocutionary movement and their definition of elocution as performance.[12] This change in the critical vocabulary is observable from Campbell to Whately, and it was also noted by John Quincy Adams. When Campbell wrote of the canon of *elocutio*, he used "elocution" (Campbell [1776] 1988: vi), whereas Whately used "style" (Whately 1828: xiv). Whately also used "elocution," yet he employed it for the final phase of delivery (*actio, pronuntiatio*) (Whately 1828: xiv). "Elocution" could thus be understood in two senses, which Adams – in his neoclassicist account that still retained the metaphor of style as the dress of thought – was careful to distinguish: "The elocution, of which I shall speak to you, belongs not to the delivery, but to the composition of the discourse. It is the act, not of the voice, but of the pen. It is the clothing of the thoughts with language; and applies to all written compositions." In the latter sense, "[e]llocution [...] is the act of committing your discourse to writing." (Adams 1810: I, 170 – 71). Despite Adams' meticulous definitions, the result of this semantic process, which mirrors central developments in oratorical culture,[13] is a merging of aspects of the canons of style and delivery in light of elocution.

---

10 Cf. Bialostosky and Needham (1995).
11 The centaur Nessus had tricked Dejanira into believing it would secure Hercules' love for her. For a contemporary retelling, cf. Lemprière (1839: 129).
12 Cf. e.g. Sheridan 1762; Walker 1781; Austin 1806; Russell 1844.
13 The implications of the rise of elocutionary rhetoric for antebellum rhetorical culture and Poe's speeches and texts in particular are also discussed in the final chapter.

What emerges out of the momentous changes to the idea of *elocutio* is a tension between rhetorical and romantic meanings that can be used to reframe Poe's lyrical poetry. Rather than incarnating ideas in the style, Poe's poems functionalise style for effect to such an extreme extent that it appears cut loose from the content – which also showed as a reproach in the reception history outlined above. At the same time, Poe's privileging of sound effects over meaning mirrors developments of the elocutionary movement, turning his poems into ever more performative texts. What happens in Poe's poems, particularly the later ones, is quasi a literalisation of the merging of style and delivery in poems that demand to be performed. Poe himself had defined "the Poetry of words as the *Rhythmical Creation of Beauty*" (E&R 688), yet in light of the contemporary double meaning of elocution as style and delivery, we can also look at it as the elocutionary production of beauty. In contrast to Mill's demand for poetry that is overheard, Poe's poems seem to shout: listen to me!

Mine is far from the first attempt to analyse and interpret Poe's poems as inextricably bound up with performance. In a number of publications, Jerome McGann has argued that Poe's compositions "require actual performance" by the reader (McGann 2013b: 871) and that "[a]ll of Poe's significant poetry is a performative demonstration of his theoretical ideas." (McGann 2014b: 6). For McGann, what lies "[a]t the heart of these problems is the modernism of Poe's severe aesthetic formalism," encapsulated in his stance against "the heresy of *The Didactic*" (CT 182). Thus the significance of Poe as a poet originates in his pre-modernist view that poetry "should not be approached as a repository of ideas or an expression of feelings but as an event of language" (McGann 2014b: 2–3). Rather than an emphasis on the incipient modernity of Poe's poetry, my attempt here is to historically reframe this dynamic of theory and performance in terms of contemporary rhetorical culture and elocution to show how elocutionism could turn a poem into an event of rhetoric.

This is particularly visible – and audible – in "Ulalume," written in 1847 and published in 1848 (PMS 409–423). The poem is about a man's repressed memory of the death of his beloved, and invokes visionary and Gothic imagery of the bereaved lover, a desolate landscape, and ghostly beings familiar from many other of Poe's poems such as "Dream-Land."[14] Hand-in-hand with his soul Psyche, the lyrical speaker walks through a dream-like nightly landscape on Hallowe'en to finally discover – with horror – that he has reached the tomb of his dead beloved Ulalume, whom he had buried a year ago to the day.

---

[14] For a detailed discussion of Gothic elements in "Dream-Land," cf. Guttzeit (2015a: 81–86).

Without a doubt, the poem is one of best examples of the interconnections between Poe's poetry and antebellum elocutionism. From its title to its last line, the poem is full of rhythmic and phonic effects, overflowing with alliteration, assonance, and rhyme. As T. O. Mabbott rightly commented, "Ulalume" "must be read aloud or sounded to the 'inner ear'." (PMS 409).

To begin with, the poem had an elocutionist pedigree. Poe wrote "Ulalume. A Ballad" at the request of one of the most famous elocutionists of the day – cited in the motto of this chapter –, namely Cotesworth P. Bronson, who had published an *Abstract of Elocution and Music* (first edition in 1842) and the already-mentioned encyclopedic treatise *Elocution, or, Mental and Vocal Philosophy* (in 1845). Most likely in June 1847, Poe and Maria Clemm were visited by Bronson and his daughter Mary Elizabeth for the first time in their cottage in Fordham (PL 700). In September, Bronson asked Poe to compose a poem that he could recite in his lectures on elocution (PL 704). In October 1847, Poe wrote to Bronson that he wished "to ascertain if the poem which, at your suggestion, I have written, is of the len[g]th, the character &c you desire" (LTR II: 634 – 635 = LTR-256a). As far as I am aware, there is no evidence that Bronson used the poem in his lectures, yet elocutionism had certainly left its mark in more than the historical genesis of the work.

Rather than leaving it at this context reference, we should look at what characterized elocutionist writings such as Bronson's and earlier British proponents of the elocutionary movement in order to throw into stark relief the elocutionist character of "Ulalume." The full title of Bronson's manual is typical of many similar publications and gives an indication of the hopes and selling-points such manuals would fuse: *Elocution; or, Mental and Vocal Philosophy, Involving the Principles of Reading and Speaking; and Designed for the Development and Cultivation of both Body and Mind, in Accordance with the Nature, Uses, and Destiny of Man, Illustrated by Two or Three Hundred Choice Anecdotes; Three Thousand Oratorical and Poetical Readings; Five Thousand Proverbs, Maxims and Laconics, and Several Hundred Elegant Engravings.* While some phrases read like a panacea for the emerging middle classes, the book falls into two major sections on the "Principles of Elocution" that are illustrated by "Readings and Recitations." The part on "Principles of Elocution" is organized as a mixture between graphemes and phonemes: a typical section takes a letter and then explains its different sounds, beginning with the vowels and moving on to the consonants. In case of the letter "G," for instance, the sound /g/ is presented as in 'gem,' 'game,' and 'protege' (44 – 46). This is interspersed with paragraphs on irregular sounds as well as anecdotes and proverbs but also general comments that show the continuity between elocutionism and earlier rhetorical theories: "*Read*, and *speak*, in such a *just* and *impressive* manner, as will **instruct**, **interest** and **affect** your hearers, and *reproduce* in them all those *ideas* and *emotions*, which you wish to convey." (Bronson 1845: 49; bold emphasis added). The most striking passages, however, are those that attempt to convey a sense of oral performance in the medium of print such as this example of the letter (and sound) L:

> *Lem*-u-el *Ly*-ell loves the *lass*-lorn *lul*-la-by of the *land*-lord's *love*-ly *la*-dy, and, with blissful *dal*-li-ance, gen-*teel*-ly *lis*-tens to the *low*-ly *lol*-lard's lively song (Bronson 1845: 48).

While George Vandenhoff, the elocutionist who anthologized "The Raven," argued that "sense cannot be sacrificed to sound" (1845: 107), this and many more examples from Bronson's treatise clearly privilege sound over meaning. Stripped of their context and presented in isolation, they sound like nonsense poetry. This is, of course, a result of the function of the passage: to demonstrate the sound qualities of the letter L, piling up instances of the sound so as to make it practicable. In many ways, the elocutionists were early phonologists. Even more so, they were teachers of linguistic performance, be it on the stage, in the Lyceum or at a soirée. Incorporating elements of criticism and interpretation, they held that the smallest difference in sound could make the greatest difference in meaning, and, in the process, often privileged sound over meaning.

A prime example of the effects of the prevalence of sound over meaning in "Ulalume" is the eponymous Ulalume. As T. O. Mabbott, the most meticulous of Poe scholars, points out, "no completely satisfactory explanation of the etymology as a whole has been found" (PMS 419). Apparently invented by Poe, the word "Ulalume" is unstable in its pronunciation, as early misspellings as "Ullalume" show (419); similarly, we might ask the question: is the final 'e' silent or not? But the debate is mostly about whether the initial syllable is pronounced as /ju/ or /u/; in other words, is "Ulalume" assonant with 'you' or with 'ooh' as in 'to ooh and ah.' Mabbott apparently solves this question by referring to oral tradition, namely that Susan Ingram had heard Poe pronounce the initial syllable /ju/. While this still leaves open numerous other possibilities for its phonetic interpretation in later performances by other elocutionists, the only key to the intended sound shape of the word is thus the actual performance by Poe.

While its intended sound shape might thus be reconstructed, the meaning of "Ulalume" remains as puzzling as ominous but, above all, ambiguous. Etymologically, there is no way of tracing any kind of original intention on Poe's part, yet this does not in any way hinder speculations about it. Mabbott lists no fewer than eight different etymologies based on words from Latin, Gaelic, and Turkish; they range from Latin "ululare" ('to wail') and "lumen" ('light') to an "eccentric" suggestion of "*Ulema*, a Turkish term for ecclesiastical hierarchy" (PMS 419–420). Mabbott's motley list of suggestions by various scholars is thus reminiscent of the witnesses' reports on the "unequal voice" in Poe's "The Murders in the Rue Morgue," discussed in the previous chapter: like the witnesses, the scholars attempt to gauge the original meaning of the sounds but it remains a mystery. "Ulalume" thus keeps its sophisticated readers guessing, making the word an instance of its author's adapting power: like the parts of a perfect plot, the individual phonetic parts of the word are so arranged that "we cannot distinctly see, in respect to any one of them, whether that one depends from any one other or upholds it" (E&R 366).

This does certainly not mean that the word and the poem lose any of their power: rather, it suggests a variable "under-current, however indefinite of meaning" (CT 70) that depends on individual utterances of the word. "Ulalume" might not be pinned down etymologically but it still sounds like a direct address ('you'), a Romanic article ('le'/'la'), and the verb and noun 'loom'. The latter even appears to encapsulate the dynamics at play in the whole poem as it mixes imagery of weaving and thus of textuality with the idea of an indistinct appearance that looms large over or in the text. All of these semantic shades, however, are ultimately subjected to the elocutionist application of Poe's explicit principle of varied repetition (CT 64): the potential meanings occur in various acts of speaking a word that is in itself already the product of the varied repetition of two syllables based on the central consonant /l/. Like that "most producible" of consonants, /r/, that furnished Poe's rationale for "The Raven's" "nevermore" (CT 64), /l/ becomes the phonetic turning point of the title and text of the poem "Ulalume."[15]

Repetition with variation also forms the foundation of Poe's employment of other devices such as refrain-like structures.[16] The cumulation of such devices made it easy for Aldous Huxley to lambast his style as vulgarity in literature (Huxley [1930] 1969), since the semantic impression borders on the pleonastic, and, in some places, the repetition becomes so overwhelming that the eye, in reading off the printed page, is easily confused. This is the (in)famous first stanza:

> The skies they were ashen and sober;
> The leaves they were crispéd and sere —
> The leaves they were withering and sere;
> It was night in the lonesome October

---

15 More generally, the importance of /l/ for the titles and main characters of Poe's texts has struck scholars and poets alike: "The name of the lost love [Ulalume], like so many of Poe's female characters – Annabel Lee, Eulalie, Helen, Lenore, Ligeia, Morella – favors the letter "L," an aspect of Poe's use of sound that poets from Konstantin Balmont to Thomas Hardy have appreciated" (Kopley and Hayes 2002: 200).

16 On the philosophical significance of Poe's uses of refrains, cf. Moreland and Shaw (2012).

Of my most immemorial year:
It was hard by the dim lake of Auber,
In the misty mid region of Weir —
It was down by the dank tarn of Auber,
In the ghoul-haunted woodland of Weir. (PMS 415–416, ll. 1–9)

Semantically speaking, the stanza sets the scene in late autumn and its topographic description suggests a thoroughly Gothic mood. Non-contemporary readers are often struck by the names "Auber" and "Weir," thinking they were invented for reasons of sound only, possibly turning the whole poem into a piece of nonsense poetry like Bronson's lullaby. Yet this was disproved by philologists' uncovering (PMS 420–421) of the references to the French composer of operas, Daniel-Francois-Esprit Auber (1782–1871), and the painter of the Hudson River School, Robert Walter Weir (1803–1889). Their importance for the poem is two-fold: on the one hand, their names sound Gothic and 'weird'[17]– to the extent that it does not matter who they were (McGann 2014b: 131); and on the other, as historical references, they foreground the artistic character of the poem through contexts of opera and painting (Kopley and Hayes 2002: 199).

Phonetically speaking, some of the most striking features of "Ulalume" are the repetitions of entire lines with only minimal variation; thus, lines 2 and 3 unify both anaphora and epiphora, forming an example of symploce (Zimmerman 2005: 312). The repetitions in "Ulalume" might be explained as a feature of the ballad form, yet many of the lines are invested in something untypical even of euphonious ballads. This is evident from the first symploce in the first stanza, lines 2 and 3: "The leaves they were crispéd and sere —/The leaves they were withering and sere;" (ll. 2–3). While we should not discount the semantic movement from crispéd leaves to withering ones, illustrating types of decay which set the scene, the literal meaning is secondary here. What the lines do, however, is to make the reader attentive to what are very small phonic differences, almost akin to structuralist minimal pairs or, indeed, elocutionist explications: there is only a one-word difference between the first and the second part of the symploce. The metre gives us "with'ring": two syllables which correspond to the two syllables of "crispéd," thus forming an assonant cluster. In turn, this forces us to pay extraordinary attention to the sound of the words which is rewarded by the new meaning in the second word "withering" that becomes apparent only when it is performed: marked by assonance and metre, "withering" shifts between 'with ring' or 'with a ring.' The poem thus contains

---

[17] Auber sounds like Emily St. Aubert in Ann Radcliffe's Gothic classic *The Mysteries of Udolpho* (1794) and "Weir" like the weird sisters in Shakespeare's *Macbeth*.

6.2 The Elocutionary Production of Beauty: Style and Performance in "Ulalume" — 185

a phonetic self-description that makes readers doubly aware of its sound qualities, not so much of its 'jingling' but of its 'ringing.' Line three thus describes leaves – of paper, as we can now fill in – that ring out to us as readers, but they do so only when pronounced: 'the leaves they were with a ring.' Poe's elocutionist minimal pair thus self-reflexively foregrounds its phonetic qualities, working like a meaningful exercise in elocutionism and instantiating poetry as performance.

In accordance with his definition of poetry as the rhythmical creation of beauty, Poe himself often framed these phonetic qualities as musical, and scholars have followed suit, remarking on the "insistent musicality" of Poe's poetry (Thorpe 1996: 90). This does not invalidate the links to the elocutionists, however, since the connection of music and recitation was a similarly prominent part of the elocutionist tradition. Bronson, for instance, claimed that "Elocution and Music [are] inseparable in their nature" (Bronson 1845: 34), and argued that: "*Reading* and *Speaking* are inseparably connected with *music*; [...] for *Music* is but an *elegant* and refined *species* of Elocution" (Bronson 1845: 33). The elocutionists' primary intention was to teach the power of spoken (and even sung) words: the rhetorical effects of words which are performed. Just like the elocutionists, Poe seems to say to us in "Ulalume": "repeat after me." When we actually perform his lines, his poems ring out to us.

This impression is further strengthened by other elocutionist characteristics such as homophony and persuasion. "And star-dials pointed to morn" (l. 31), for instance, plays on the homophony between "morning" and "mourning." The overall rhetorical character of the poem is strenghtened by the debate between the lyrical speaker and Psyche that occurs in stanzas five to seven. As Kopley and Hayes point out, they argue "over whether or not they should approach Astarte, he taking the affirmative and she the negative." As a "cross between a political debate and a lover's quarrel" (Kopley and Hayes 2002: 201) the section also points to the persuasive contexts of elocutionism: speaking in such manner, as will "*reproduce* in [your hearers] all those *ideas* and *emotions*, which you wish to convey" (Bronson 1845: 49).

The phonetic and semantic characteristics of "Ulalume" come together in a way that suggests the ubiquity of performance. The varied repetition of /l/, the symploces, and homophonies are joined by the rhetorical debate and also by a thoroughly dramatic situation. The dramatic qualities come out particularly clearly in the climax. Another dialogue with his soul makes the speaker recognize that he has come to the vault of his lost Ulalume and reverses his fortune after his earlier (ignorant) desire to press on, making the climax a classic combination of ἀναγνώρισις/*anagnorisis* and περιπέτεια/*peripeteia*. Such dramatic elements become metapoetical when viewed in combination to the references to painting and opera through which "Poe figuratively set the stage and then opened the curtain onto the picture." (Kopley and Hayes 2002: 199). In similar fashion, "the action of the poem occurs largely in dialogue, and, with a subtle invocation of phantasmagoria, the last stanza closes the curtain." (Kopley and Hayes 2002: 202). Beginning, middle, and end of the poem are thus informed by dramatic and metadramatic elements.

This ubiquitous performativity on the levels of both form and content turns the speaker into a figure of the poet as performer. Thus the lyrical speaker takes on the role of the poet-as-rhapsodist at the beginning of line 10: "Here" is homophonous with the imperative 'hear,' thus asking us to listen closely and recite so as to hear new meanings and to become aware to the sound of the power of words.

In this endeavour, the speaker operates out of a narrative or lyrical, perhaps even rhapsodist, present tense, evoking a dream-land through the use of re-sounding words; yet since he does not realize this, he is subjected to its effects. As McGann argues: "While we are reading 'Ulalume,' its speaker is still caught up in the poetic narrative he is himself delivering. We hear the echoes [...], but the speaker, though he utters the echoing words, is unaware of the memory they represent." (McGann 2014b: 143). For McGann, this makes us as readers realise that the speaker "cannot remember what he cannot forget" (McGann 2014b: 143), which "measures the depth of his immemorial sorrow" and represents "an objectified condition [of poetic fear] intended to affect the reader" (McGann 2014b: 143).

If we reframe McGann's observations with regard to the elocutionist and metadramatic elements – the 'metaperformative' elements, if you like – what we as readers are witnessing is a performative failure of the speaker: his performance is hampered by a weakness with regard to the penultimate of rhetorical stages, that of memory. While the reason for failing is made plausible in terms of the Gothic biography of the speaker, his failure can be viewed metapoetically as an artistic shortcoming that would be of momentous consequences for any performance: after all, "Memory [...] hands on to Elocution what it receives from Invention" (Quintilian 2001e: 61 = 11.2.3), and all the other four arts are "futile," unless held together "by this animating principle" (Quintilian 2001e: 59 = 11.2.1). This is not to suggest we read "Ulalume" as an allegorical dramatisation and poeticization of stage fright but to insist on the multi-layered foregrounding of the poet as elocutionary performer in the poem.

"Ulalume" does not stand alone on the elocutionary stage of Poe's poetry. Symploces form part of "Eulalie," the counterpart in a major key to "Ulalume." Internal rhymes abound in "The Raven," and refrains structure "Dream-Land." Rather than aiming for style as an incarnation of the idea, Poe makes his poems don the most pompous of dresses.[18] This was not lost on his detractor Aldous Huxley who found it hard to forgive Poe "the wearing of a diamond ring on every finger" (Huxley [1930] 1969: 161). Poe's fascination lies in "the tintinabulation that so musically wells/From the bells, bells, bells, bells,/Bells, bells, bells" (ll. 11–13: PMS 435).[19] While such lines are almost unreadable in print where the individual instances begin to run into each other, they can be performed as an onomatopoetic fashioning of the sound of bells. Poems such as "The Bells" and "Ulalume" insist on being performed and thus figure their poet as a performer.

What is explicitly dismissed by Mill's concept of poetry as overhearing is also implicitly dismissed by the romantic negation of rhetorical style, or better, *elocutio:* the performative character of poetry. As we saw in the example of "Ulalume," Poe's later poetry is best termed performative, or, taking into consideration the term's contemporary double meaning, elocutionary: Poe's poetry focuses on elocution, i.e. style and delivery unified in the act of poetry being spoken aloud rather than being read silently. While Emerson criticized Poe's model of the poet as the "jingle-man," it is more aptly described as that of a "damned rhetorician" who composed for elocutionists: in other words, as an elocutionary figure of the poet.

6.3 "A Well Understood Poetical License": The Politics of Performance in "The Rationale of Verse"

Poe's elocutionary figure of the poet is closely related to his figure of the author as a rhetorical poet-critic discussed in chapters three and four. The reasons for this lie in the importance of his critical tenets for his poetry and vice versa, as we saw in the first half of this chapter as well as in the discussion of "The Philosophy of Composition." Because of this relation, the performative dimension of the author as it is evident in Poe's poems such as "Ulalume" also plays an important role in his theory. The remainder of this chapter is devoted to an examination of the performative figure of the author as it emerges from Poe's most important treatment of English-language verse in "The Rationale of Verse." Rather than focusing exclusively on its (potential) theoretical validity, what follows will deal with the specific political and cultural value of poetical performance both to

---

[18] Cf. the discussion in chapter three of Poe's defence of Bayard Taylor's poetry, in which Poe criticizes "our anonymous friend's [the reviewer's] *implied* sneer at 'mere jingling of rhymes, brilliant and successful for the moment'" (E&R 1443).

[19] Cf. Mc Gann's reading of "The Bells," which demonstrates that the "poem is a challenge to meaning because it is a challenge to recitation" (McGann 2014b: 180).

Poe personally and to American and Southern poetry in general. While the figure of the author that emerges from the text is ostensibly primarily theoretical, a reading of its performative dimension uncovers a political aspect of elocution and its meanings in Poe.

First published as "Notes Upon English Verse" (1843), "The Rationale of Verse" (1848) is Poe's longest critical essay, and, as a theoretical statement, it has not fared well with the critics. To a certain extent, it is easy to see why. Poe bases his definition of verse in the English language on length rather than accent which leads to such notions as "bastard" feet (CT 108–109). He also introduces an idiosyncratic notation system that uses mathematical fractions for relative syllable length, defining his concept of length on the basis of the claim that there is no such thing as a short syllable except in relation to a long one (CT 109–111). As Stuart and Susan Levine state in their edition: "Viewed in the terms in which we customarily think of English verse, 'The Rationale of Verse' seems perverse and not very sensible" (CT 77).

The article, however, is highly relevant for Poe's rhetorical figuration of the poet in terms of performance. While he invokes a typical phrase for the description of the differences between print and speech, writing about "this oil and water of the eye and ear" (CT 106), he constantly insists that "[t]he rhythmical must agree, *thoroughly*, with the reading, [sic] flow" (CT 107), thus framing printed poetry in terms of oral performance. What makes the text further relevant are three things: the first concerns the theoretical background of elocutionism against which Poe's speculations should be viewed; the second entails a reconsideration of Poe's tenets on verse quantity in light of recent linguistic research on actual linguistic performance *sensu* Chomsky; and the third pertains to the larger significance of Poe's seemingly idiosyncratic position on the importance of quantity, which can be read as attempting to establish a political and cultural position for the performance of poets from the American South and the US in general.

Poe's manner of dealing with his sources begins with a familiar critical gesture: he makes it appear as if he were battling an array of enemies who composed "our ordinary grammars and [...] our works on rhetoric or prosody in general," when in fact he cites only one author. At the same time this author is not, as the Levines phrase it, merely "one unoffending compiler of a grammar book" (CT 80). Poe's target is Goold Brown, the writer of the nineteenth-century "acme" of English nativist, i.e. non-Latinate, grammars (Algeo 2009: 497), published in final form as the apparently aptly titled *The Grammar of English Grammars* (1851). Brown can thus be regarded as a representative grammarian, particularly since the definition of versification from Brown's earlier *Institutes of English Grammar* (rev. ed. 1833), which Poe uses, was copied widely in other grammars of the time. One of the main reference points for Brown's work, as becomes particularly clear in *The Grammar of English*

Grammars, was George Campbell's *Philosophy of Rhetoric*, which Brown cites throughout the book and quotes at the conclusion to the preface: "The rudiments of every art and science exhibit at first, to the learner, the appearance of littleness and insignificancy. And it is by attending to such reflections, as to a superficial observer would appear minute and hypercritical, that language must be improved, and eloquence perfected" (Brown 1851: vi).[20] In Brown's Campbellian model, the grammatical improvement of language and the rhetorical perfection of eloquence thus go hand in hand.

This connection of Poe's text through Brown's grammars to Campbell's rhetorical treatise is representative of the sources for Poe's text: they generally draw on the epistemological, belletristic, neo-classicist, and elocutionist traditions of rhetoric, yet they are all mediated through grammar. In sweeping fashion, Poe mentions a number of grammarians who are not identified as rhetoricians or elocutionists by the Levines: "Bacon, Miller, Fisk, Greenleaf, Ingersoll, Kirkland, Cooper, Flint, Pue, Comly, and many others" (CT 82–83; 128–29). However, even in those grammars which have ostensibly nothing to do with the rhetorical tradition, one still finds opening statements that address precisely the indebtedness of grammar to rhetorical thinking. For instance, Hugh A. Pue's *A Grammar of the English Language: In a Series of Letters, Addressed to Every American Youth*, which Poe had reviewed in Graham's Magazine in July 1841, begins with the following disclaimer: "In the following Letters you will find very little of what is called eloquence" (Pue 1841: 11). Other grammarians on Poe's list expressly mention elocutionism as the basis of their prosodies in the titles of their books, as is the case, for example, with Abel Flint's *Murray's English Grammar Abridged; to Which is Added, under the Head of Prosody, an Abridgment of Sheridan's Lectures on Elocution* (1807).

Like Abel Flint, the grammarians Poe mentions are all ultimately influenced by Lindley Murray's grammar, which sold an enormous sixteen million copies in the United States and four million in Great Britain (M. Martin 2012: 39). Poe makes this influence explicit, not without attacking the grammarians' reliance on authority: "These gentlemen, it is presumed, adopted [this phraseology] without examination from Murray" (CT 83). Murray, whose grammar Poe himself had studied as a school boy,[21] is indeed the crucial link between rhetoric and elocutionism on the

---

20 In keeping with the spirit of the quotation, I should point out that Campbell has "a learner" instead of "the learner" ([1776] 1988: 222). For connections to Campbell in Brown's earlier *Institutes*, cf. Brown (1833: xi, 12, 57).
21 Before leaving the United States for England in 1815, John Allan purchased textbooks by Lindley Murray for young Edgar (cf. Hayes 2000: 1–4). Murray was strongly influenced not only by the elocutionist Sheridan but also by the belletrist Hugh Blair.

one hand and grammar on the other, when it comes to Poe's theoretical assumptions underpinning his view that English versification is based on syllable length.

As Meredith Martin demonstrates in her study on the interrelation of metre and national culture in England, Lindley Murray reopened the possibility for the redefinition of poetry in terms of quantity that had essentially been foreclosed by Sheridan and his contemporaries (M. Martin 2012: 39–42). Martin argues convincingly that for British elocutionists such as Sheridan, William Enfield or John Walker, "providing rules for quantity in English would mean securing, standardizing, and fixing pronunciation in a concrete way that neither [Enfield] nor Walker was yet able to imagine" (18). The reason for positing accentuation or emphasis as the only determinant of English verse would be that differences in vowel duration as they existed between the Scots and the English, for instance, would no longer be decisive for inclusion among speakers of 'proper' English. Martin explains:

> [The elocutionists] are invested in speech accent as the only ruling constituent of the English verse line. By erasing questions of English quantity, Enfield and Walker effaced the very differentiation of speakers from different regions of the country. If accent is the only measure of English meter (rather than the time it would take to pronounce the words, or the different ways the vowels might sound), then all Englishmen (irrespective of their Scottish origin) can access it. An idealized and yet-still-unestablished 'English' accent, when properly learned and performed, would not, according to these rules, differentiate speakers; rather it would blend them into the 'one mass' of the English nation. (2012: 18)

A central aspect of the politics of linguistic performance was thus determined by the elocutionist tradition – through making accentuation the basis of English linguistic identity. Significantly, however, this strategy was not taken up by Lindley Murray. Beginning with the fourth edition of his *English Grammar* (1798), Murray cribbed the definition of English versification from Sheridan's *The Art of Reading* (1775), leaving out Sheridan's position that "the whole modern theory of quantity will be found a mere chimera" (Sheridan 1775: 27). What was left in Murray and his followers was a definition that did not exclude quantity as a determinant of English-language verse but rather gestured "to the Roman genealogy of English verse as if to give it a high-cultural precedent" (M. Martin 2012: 41).[22]

Against this background Poe's apparently peculiar position on quantity in "The Rationale of Verse" becomes meaningful. He gives the example of the an-

---

[22] The full definition in Murray's various editions thus reads: "In English, syllables are divided into accented and unaccented; and the accented syllables being as strongly distinguished from the unaccented, by the peculiar stress of the voice upon them, are equally capable of marking the movement, and pointing out the regular paces of the voice, as the long syllables were by their quantity, among the Romans" (1808: 351).

cient Greeks when highlighting quantity as a universalising factor rather than stress: "The fact is that *Quantity* is a point in whose investigation the lumber of mere learning may be dispensed with, if ever in any. Its appreciation is universal. It appertains to no region, nor race, nor æra in especial" (CT 86). Poe thus inverses the logic of the British elocutionists such as Sheridan, Enfield, and Walker – who had excluded quantity definitions from standards of speaking so as to universalise the received pronunciation of English –, and makes quantity the universally appreciable factor in prosody.[23]

This elocutionist and grammatical prehistory makes clear the political import and theoretical conditions of Poe's position, yet the question remains: why did Poe emphasize quantity rather than stress? The attempt to compose poetry in the English language according to quantitative metres built on Greek models was a failed early attempt to invest English with the "grandeur" of ancient poetry. This could be viewed in the way that Murray had suggested as an attempt to make English partake in the high cultural value of ancient prosody. However, this is hardly what Poe attempted in "The Rationale of Verse," since he criticizes similar attempts and explicitly faults others' "irrational deference to antiquity" (CT 81).

Another explanation claims that cross-cultural and transhistorical linguistic evidence validates his central assumption of length as being a central determinant of rhythm. The theoretical purpose of Poe's essay, according to Christopher Aruffo, is "to explain the controlling principles of poetry – including all traditions, across all language throughout all history" (2011: 69), and this explanation is to be based on "a natural principle" (72). Poe writes: "Verse originates in the human enjoyment of equality, fitness. [...] [The] idea [of equality] embraces those of similarity, proportion, identity, repetition, and adaptation or fitness" (CT 87). Uncovering the core of Poe's argument from its questionable presentation, Aruffo states: "1. The rationale of verse is equality. 2. Equality is realized through equal lengths of time. 3. When feet are equal, relative syllabic lengths may be accurately measured" (2011: 76). Aruffo's successful attempt to salvage Poe's theory adopts the opposite position of the detractors, yet, in a way, the argument thus remains on the same level as the essay's opponents.

I would like to suggest a third explanation that takes both factors – cultural value and potential universalism – into account and interprets them in terms of Poe's cultural situatedness. If we regard the essay as attempting to establish a

---

23 In the *Broadway Journal*, Poe explicitly criticized Walker and Sheridan: "Walker's Sheridan has been long objectionable, of course; for during the last fifty years the advance of literature, and more especially of science, has introduced into the language a vast number of words which had no existence at the period of the work" (CW 3, 148).

performative figure of the author, the question as to whether Poe was right or wrong is irrelevant. The point, then, is no longer to examine the truth conditions of Poe's theory but to seek out what speech act theory and linguistic pragmatics term the felicity conditions of linguistic utterances. Rather than taking Poe at his word and viewing quantity as a timeless criterion, we can interpret his ostensibly theoretical move as the establishment of a performative figure of the author within the political and cultural situation of the antebellum United States – a situation characterized by political tension between North and South as well as by multiple dialects.

That Poe was aware of differences in dialect is evinced by his biography and his literary attempts to mimic (what are perceived to be) comical dialects in his tales. He himself is likely to have spoken "with a slight Southern drawl," as Mabbott argues (PMS xxv). There are other influences, too: Poe's foster father John Allan was a Scot and Poe himself spent time at a school in England. Growing up in Richmond and living in the major publishing centres of the Southern and Eastern United States exposed Poe to a variety of different dialects. His conscious engagement with some of them is evident in the comical use of dialects and sociolects in the tale, often of people who belong to minorities such as African Americans, the Dutch, or the French.[24] No matter how these are interpreted in the case of individual characters, Poe's interest in dialectal differences as a marker of social belonging is evident.

Pinpointing factual dialectal differences in the antebellum United States is made difficult by the impossibility of collecting reliable data for the period. Nonetheless, a recent phonological study has found that, in our time, spoken Southern American English correlates with a significantly longer vowel duration (Jacewicz, Fox, and Salmons 2007).[25] That this probably also holds true for the nineteenth century becomes obvious when we consider the longevity of the popular understanding of the "Southern drawl" as a markedly slower way of speaking. As early as 1845 George Palmer Putnam speaks of the opposition of the "New England nasal twang" and "the Southern drawl."[26] Since vowel duration

---

[24] Cf. e.g. the African-American slave Jupiter in "The Gold-Bug" (T&S 799–847) or the town of Vondervotteimittiss in "The Devil in the Belfry" (T&S 362–375). On Poe's "average racism," cf. Whalen (1999: 113–121).

[25] For an overview of the phonological characteristics of contemporary Southern American English, cf. Labov, Ash, and Boberg (2006: 240–63).

[26] Putnam writes: "I think that in spite of the New England nasal twang, and the Southern drawl, among 'the million,' the English language is more generally spoken by all classes in the United States, than it is in England" (14).

is the essential determinant of syllable length, Poe's insistence on quantity in his theory of prosody has an implicit political and cultural valence.

Syllable length can be assumed to have been a marker of dialectal and hence cultural and political differences between North and South in the United States. Poe's investment in furthering Southern letters and opposing New England "Frogpondians" (E&R 1097–99) is generally acknowledged and was a factor in such events as his appearance at the Boston Lyceum (discussed in the next chapter). By arguing that the appreciation of quantity "is universal" and stressing that "[i]t appertains to no region" (CT 86), Poe, in terms of performance, made a distinctive feature of Southern pronunciation, its length, the basic and defining characteristic of verse, of "rhythm, rhyme, metre, and versification" (CT 80). Thus length becomes crucial for poetry in general, according to his already-cited definition of "*The Rhythmical Creation of Beauty*" (CT 73; E&R 78, 688). Viewed in performative terms, the political rationale behind Poe's theory of verse was thus an assertion of Southern pronunciation and especially of such authors as himself who would perform poetry in Southern ways of speaking. The author as elocutionist could thus represent a poet even if his performance was potentially marred by a Southern drawl.

Such an account offers a possibility to rethink the relationship between Poe's insistence on rhetorical effect with his idea of the "poem written solely for the poem's sake" (E&R 76, 295), since an analogy can be drawn between his autonomous ideal of the poem and his political and cultural isolation as a Southerner. For instance, Kenneth Alan Hovey argued that, towards the end of his life, "Poe attempted to free the South from Northern thought at the same time that he attempted to free poetry from truth. Both attempts were really one." (Hovey 1987: 349).[27] At the same time, the subtlety of these political aspects of Poe's writing shows his distance to propagandistic projects, and is indicative of Poe's explicit political interests that lie in establishing a medial space for (Southern and American) authorship, for instance through realising his lifelong project of a magazine or arguing for an international copyright agreement. This would tie in with the assumption that "Poe's great subject is poetic representation itself, and the deeper truth is that he takes this to be an imperative social and political subject" (McGann 2014b: 150).

That Poe's argument in "The Rationale of Verse" is indeed neither a merely personal nor regional affair, is also evident from his attempt at an American uni-

---

[27] Hovey's argument is partially based on the unsigned review of Longfellow published in the April 1845 *Aristidean* that was, in all likelihood, co-authored by Thomas Dunn English and Poe. On the status and interpretation of this text, cf. Whalen (1999: 136).

versalism that takes up the transatlantic gauntlet of Britain's political and cultural domination. When we go beyond vowel length as a marker of distinctive linguistic features, Poe's "Rationale of Verse" also implicitly takes a stand on transatlantic dialectal differences, thus universalising a performative figure of the poet who is American rather than British.

In his establishing of a performative figure of the poet in "The Rationale of Verse," Poe also opposes one of the defining linguistic features of English Received Pronunciation and even defines poetic language according to this opposition. Received Pronunciation (RP) "developed at the end of the eighteenth century, during the period of the American Revolution," and the term was coined by the already-mentioned elocutionist John Walker to designate the 'approved' standard of the London elite that explicitly excluded the lower classes (J. Fisher 2001: 71, 73). One of its features that still exists today is the "suppression of secondary accents" in such words as *secretary*, *satisfactory*, or *temperament*: "Until the end of the seventeenth century, textbooks indicate that the approved pronunciation continued to preserve fairly even stress on all syllables, with secondary and tertiary stress on the unaccented syllables of words with three or more syllables, [...] which is still the characteristic American pattern" (J. Fisher 2001: 74). Again, the origins of this can be seen in an elocutionary text, namely the third edition of Sheridan's *Dictionary* (1780), which indicates that the "plosive accentuation and suppression of secondary accents had already begun to appear in elite London pronunciation" (J. Fisher 2001: 74).

Discussing a trochaic tetrameter that has a dactyl in place of the second trochee, Poe applies his theory of the "bastard trochee": a trochee that has a long syllable and two syllables that are so shortened that they correspond to the normal short second syllable of the trochee. The line is:

"Sēe thĕ | **dĕlĭcătĕ** | fōotĕd | rēin-deĕr. |" (CT 97; bold emphasis added)

Some prosodies, Poe maintains, would "insist upon a Procrustean adjustment thus (del'cate) – an adjustment recommended to all such words as *silvery*, *murmuring*, etc., which, it is said, should be not only pronounced, but written *silv'ry*, *murm'ring*, and so on, whenever they find themselves in trochaic predicament" (CT 97). What Poe's ordinary grammars would insist on is thus a clear case of the suppression of secondary accents "on the unaccented syllables of words with three or more syllables," a key feature of English RP.

Poe's prosody is completely opposed to this suppression: "all words, at all events, should be written and pronounced *in full*, and as nearly as possible as nature intended them" (CT 97). Indeed, Poe calls for the universalization of his alternative approach and attempts to claim it as a natural principle. He thus advocates a position that was characteristic of those American grammarians who opposed English 'rule' in grammar and argued that words should be spoken as they were written, the most prominent amongst them being Noah Webster.[28] That Poe had retitled his essay from "Notes Upon English Verse" to "The Rationale of Verse" might thus be an additional indication of his attempt to deemphasize English RP influence on American English poetry.

Poe thus attempted to carve out an elocutionist stage for the poet through arguments about linguistic performance in verse. While affirming the different vowel length of spoken Southern English and denying British RP influences, Poe was not far away from ridiculing his own continuous insistence on "reconciling this oil and water of the eye and the ear" (CT 106), on reconciling print and performance in poetry: "The chief thing in the way of [a complex] species of rhythm, is the necessity which it imposes upon the poet of travelling in constant company with his compositions, so as to be ready at a moment's notice, to avail himself of a well understood poetical license – that of reading aloud one's own doggerel." (CT 101–2). Even in jest, though, Poe's insistence remains on the performative nature of poetry and a performative figure of the poet.

If "elocution theorizes a way to reintroduce the persuasive power of authorial 'presence' into a cultural context in which written texts had become the predominant site of public discourse" (Mahon 2001: 69), then these elocutionist contexts offered Poe a stage on which to establish a figure of the poet that is informed by oral performativity. As we saw in "Ulalume" and "The Rationale of Verse," in both practice and theory, Poe's poetry established an elocutionary figure of the poet, which made him more of a damned rhetorician than a jingleman.

---

28 Cf. J. Fisher (2001: 75).

7 "The Only Proper Stage for the Literary Histrio": Delivery and its Dangers in the Antebellum Cultures of Rhetoric and Print

> Time was when we imported our critical decisions from the mother country. For many years we enacted a perfect farce of subserviency to the *dicta* of Great Britain. At last a revulsion of feeling, with self-disgust, necessarily ensued. Urged by these, we plunged into the opposite extreme. In throwing *totally* off that "authority," whose voice had so long been so sacred, we even surpassed, and by much, our original folly. But the watchword now was, "a national literature!" – as if any true literature *could* be "national" – as if the world at large were not the only proper stage for the literary *histrio*.
> Poe, [Exordium to] Critical Notices, *Graham's Magazine*, January 1842 (E&R 1027)

Poe's emphatic statement is a paradigmatic example of his stance against a narrow literary nationalism and his conception of the place of the author within and beyond American literature. His argument that Americans are throwing out the proverbial baby of American literature with the bathwater of British (and particularly Scottish) criticism calls for a middle position with regard to the transatlantic import of critical and literary works from overseas. Alluding to Shakespeare's dictum that all the world's a stage, Poe, the biological son of two actors, positions the author on the largest stage imaginable. Taken as a self-description, the statement enables us to view Poe as both a literary histrio attempting to fill as large a (transatlantic) stage as possible and a critic attempting to achieve the authority of the "sacred" voice of Great Britain.[1] Poe's performative figure of the author as literary histrio also enters the stage in "The Philosophy of Composition" (CT 61) and, to a certain extent, in "Ulalume" and "The Rationale of Verse," as discussed in previous chapters. As we shall see in this final chapter, the figure of the literary histrio encompasses the roles of orator, reciter, and actor, all of which correspond to the dimensions of oral delivery – the fifth rhetorical autheme.[2] These performative figures of the author as orator, reciter, and actor are framed in terms of the inextricable intersections between the cultures of rhetoric and print.

The antebellum literary marketplace was clearly dominated by the medium of print, offering printed products in historically large quantities, yet the development of authorship was also substantially informed by a corresponding market for spo-

---

[1] The same topos of also appears in Poe's manuscript for his projected *The Living Writers of America*, in which he constructs the American country as an ethnically white continuation of Britain but also claims that "there should be *no* nationality – the world the proper stage" (Pollin 1991: 166).

[2] Cf. the discussion in chapter one.

DOI 10.1515/9783110520156-008

ken performances that was one major aspect of the culture of rhetoric. As an article in the magazine *Scientific Tracts and Family Lyceum* put it in 1834, "[i]f this is rightly denominated the mechanical age, it is no less a lecturing era" ("Public Lectures" 1834: 33). An article in the *Edinburgh Review* spoke of the contemporary "market of eloquence" ("Earls Grey and Spencer" 1846: 257) – a term that I adopt here for the antebellum situation. This market of eloquence often reinforced the existing commercial relations of the print market, yet it could also be at odds with it. As becomes apparent in the case of Poe, such tensions strongly informed the cultural figure of the author, particularly its performative aspects. As defined in the first chapter, performative figures of the author refer not only to the rhetorical operations of memory and performance but also to all stagings of the authorial self – in such settings as public readings, but also in theatrical contexts in other media. The intersecting antebellum cultures of rhetoric and print presented numerous opportunities for the rhetorical art of delivery, promising authorial success on a new scale but also leading to new types of risks.

This chapter explores the instantiation and representation of delivery in various media and genres employed by Poe in order to elucidate representative intersections between the cultures of print and rhetoric: this concerns speeches, tales, poems, and essays, and their respective performative figurations of authorship. The first section of the chapter takes its cue from Gavin Jones' (2014) suggestion to examine literary culture through the phenomenon and language of failure. It discusses Poe's figurations of the author as they are connected to failing performances and the anxiety of the loss of inspiration. This includes the most infamous of Poe's own performances as an orator, his appearance at the Boston Lyceum in 1845, where he 'failed' to recite an original poem. The performative aspects of the drama and, with it, the figure of the actor, appear to offer a way out of these performative quandaries, yet they are also inherently connected to authorial anxieties, as my analysis of the satiric tale "Loss of Breath" in the middle section demonstrates. The last section turns to Poe's final tale "X-ing a Paragrab" to uncover Poe's strategies of preempting the potential failure of technologically inflected performative figurations of the author. Delivery striated the antebellum cultures of rhetoric and print, indicating their insoluble interplay. It will be seen that Poe's performative figures of the author emerge out of this interplay and are just as much a result of the existing conventions of his time as of his attempts to persuasively and figuratively gain control of them.

* * *

In 1881, a childhood friend of Poe's, Thomas H. Ellis, recalled an event that must have taken place sixty years earlier, in 1821, when Poe was twelve years old: "Talent for declamation was one of his [Poe's] gifts. I well remember a public exhibition at the close of a course of instruction in elocution which he had attended [...] and my delight when he bore off the prize in competition with [...] others who were regarded as amongst the most promising of the Richmond boys" (qtd. in PL 50). Ellis' reminiscence gives a brief glimpse of the immersion of Southern culture in rhetoric, declamation, and elocution, and of how, even before adolescence, Poe was incorporated into it. In 1843, long after these humble beginnings, Poe would reprise the role of declaimer as a lecturer on such topics as "The Poets and Poetry of America" and "The Universe," the latter better known under its published title *Eureka*. As late as September 24, 1849, two weeks before his death, Poe gave a lecture on "The Poetic Principle" in Richmond, the city he had grown up in along with Thomas Ellis. Poe's literary career is thus bookended by oratorical performances.

As the example of such performances as Poe's infamous Boston Lyceum reading makes clear, in which a variety of societal expectations and personal overdeterminations were at play, an examination of the aspects of vocal delivery in isolation is difficult; rather, it has to be embedded in an interpretation both of the typical and the individual situation in which it appears. A good example of this is the gendering of delivery. As Lindal Buchanan shows in her work on the nineteenth century, the exclusive focus on vocal and bodily delivery is "too narrow to do justice to the complexities of women's delivery" (2005: 156). Such a focus does not take into account the intricate social arrangements, for instance with childcarers and chaperons, that were necessary for a woman to be able to stand on the rostrum in the first place, where she would then have to present her arrangements to assure the audience of her agreement with the relevant social norms. Hence, Buchanan suggests expanding delivery "to include both the social context surrounding the speaker and the network of collaborative relationships that makes her rhetorical performance possible in the first place." (Buchanan 2005: 156). The difficulties of women speakers testify to the problems connected to public speaking, and hardships also awaited African-American orators such as Frederick Douglass and Sojourner Truth, and speakers of other social minorities. While Poe had to make different arrangements and represent other social norms, Buchanan's emphasis on the relevance of the situation is a necessary reminder of the complexity of delivery in antebellum America.

The figures of the orator presented on the wider oratorical scene of antebellum rhetorical culture were by no means morally uniform, ranging from itinerant peddlers intent on selling bits of knowledge to highly esteemed Lyceum lecturers such as Ralph Waldo Emerson.[3] A parodical piece in Mordecai Noah's *New York*

---

[3] The emerging difference between public and itinerant lecturer has been reconstructed by Don-

Enquirer, which Kent Ljungquist (1997a) unearthed, shows the connection between lecturing and swindling. The piece is likely to have furnished Poe with the logic of his essay on "diddling."[4] The idea of diddling, or petty swindling, appears linked, as Ljungquist shows, to the pseudonymous Jeremy Diddler's article on lecturing, which states: "Full surely, man may be defined as a lecturing animal. Of all the modern ways devised to raise the wind and keep the starving fiend away, there is nothing now like lecturing" (Diddler 1829: 2). Not only did models of the lecturer include the swindler as early as 1829 but it is also likely that Poe was very much aware of them. It does not seem too far to suggest that, besides the role of the respectable lecturer, reciter, and poet, the fashion for lecturing also produced models for Poe's famous tricks and hoaxes.

When it comes to delivery, specifically, the particularity of a literary author's performance might be most marked in the recitation of poetry, but it also shows in the reading of fiction or the presentation of critical remarks. In his work on paratexts, Gérard Genette sketches a possible study of "authors' public readings of their works" and their importance for the interpretation of literary texts. The sketch sums up the problems and possibilities of such a study and the terms employed in the English translation clearly point towards the dimensions of delivery:

> I am referring to the reading (or recitation from memory) itself, which in its delivery, its stresses, its intonations, in the gestures and facial expressions used for emphasis, is already quite obviously an 'interpretation.' We necessarily lack all traces of such performances earlier than the late nineteenth century, but we do have some indirect pieces of evidence that it would perhaps be useful to collect and compare (Genette 1997: 370).

The most-cited examples from the nineteenth century are Charles Dickens' public readings of his fiction.[5] While not the first author to give paid readings of her or his works, Dickens might well be said to have created a blueprint for authorial reading performances with a characteristic combination of literary and histrionic skills. Dickens gave about 472 performances in total, with his career as a paid lecturer both in Britain and the United States beginning in 1858 and lasting until 1870, the year of his death. While Dickens began reading for money in

---

ald Scott for the 1840s (Scott 1983). Kent Ljungquist points out that Scott's categories apply to the 1830s already (Ljungquist 1997a: 70).

4 Poe's piece on "Diddling Considered as one of the Exact Sciences," (1843) also published with the main title "Raising the Wind," concerns petty swindling, and, echoing Poe's satire on "The Business-Man," defines: "Man is an animal that diddles, and there is *no* animal that diddles *but* man" (T&S 869).

5 For information on Dickens' lecturing, I rely on Philip Collins' introduction to his edition of Dickens' *Public Readings* (Collins 1975).

1858, his first private and public performances fall into the 1840s, as we saw in his face-to-face discussion with Poe about writing backwards. Dickens' performances are remarkable for the fact that he prepared versions of his texts especially for performance, complete with stage-directions in the margins such as "'Low', 'Action', 'Cheerful narrative'" (Collins 1975: lxviii). Dickens' readings were theatrical insofar as he differentiated in voice and gesture between up to twenty characters in an individual piece. He also refrained from any critical commentary or explanation of the context (Collins 1975: lxii). There is also a large number of exact comments by audience members on how Dickens performed individual parts of his texts, down to single words on specific nights.

The lecture tour would go on to become a crucial aspect of transatlantic literary culture, as Amanda Adams (2014) has detailed in her study of authorial performances between 1834 and 1904. Frederick Douglass, Harriet Beecher Stowe, and Mark Twain went on British lecture tours, and Charles Dickens, Harriet Martineau, Oscar Wilde, and Matthew Arnold made the journey in the other direction.[6] While the transatlantic cultural relationship was, in many ways, characterized by feelings of American inferiority and European superiority, the interest of audiences on both sides of the Atlantic was mostly "in the issues on the American side of the Atlantic" (Adams 2014: 21). With the exception of Dickens' readings, "[t]he content of the lectures, whether they were delivered by American authors to British audiences or by British authors to American audiences, covered *American* subjects." (Adams 2014: 21). In a historical phase characterized by the attempt to follow political independence with cultural independence, the transatlantic lecture tour was thus of double importance for the United States.

When it comes to the indirect pieces of evidence of spoken performances that Genette evokes, there is a variety of possible sources. Some of them are enumerated by David Perkins in his work on the recitation of poetry by English romantic writers, a list that can be easily applied to the situation in the antebellum United States: "In addition to whatever inferences concerning delivery we can draw from the poetry itself and from [...] critical theory, sources of information are rhetorics and elocution manuals, writings on prosody, examples of scansion, and descriptions of poets reciting" (Perkins 1991: 656). It is obvious that

---

6 As Adams points out, "American lecturers went for an expanded audience, but especially earlier on in the century, with a sense that to gain the British audience would mean more than simply increased revenue," for instance, gaining support for abolitionism (A. Adams 2014: 19). At the same time, "a list of British authors who lectured in America during the period includes a who's who of prominent British writers of the day: Thackeray, Trollope, Arnold, Wilde, Stevenson, Stoker, and, of course, [Henry] James himself, after he had happily accepted Britain as his home." (A. Adams 2014: 20).

only the descriptions of poets reciting can be a source for individual performances, while all the others can only give a general impression of performances in a specific period. Each type of source has to be treated with a caveat in mind: "though the rhetorics usually give instructions for reading aloud, it is not always clear whether they teach what was generally done or correct it. The descriptions of Romantic poets reciting are, in most cases, themselves Romantic; in other words, they are impressionistic, enthusiastic, and bardolatrous. One doesn't know how much to trust them" (Perkins 1991: 656). True in any time, be it romantic or not, the beauty or ugliness of the performance was certainly in the eyes – and ears – of the beholders.

7.1 "Stand and Deliver": Poe's Boston Lyceum Appearance and its Aftermath

Poe entered the lecturing market in order to earn a living and to gain funding for his long-planned magazine (J. G. Kennedy 2001: 49). Not counting his cancelled lectures and his informal recitals of (his) poetry, Poe lectured on at least twelve separate occasions. This might not seem a large number, yet some of his lectures had crucial importance for his career as an author in general and a wide reception beyond the audiences present. In a review of one of Poe's performances, George Lippard commented that "Mr. Poe is rapidly adding to his towering fame as Poet, Author, Critic, in his new capacity of lecturer," which shows that Poe's public persona was influenced by his role as lecturer (qtd. in PL 448). In his performances he attempted – with varying success – to fulfil and subvert the roles of the author as orator on the Lyceum lecture circuit.

Right from his first appearance at the William Wirt Institute in Philadelphia on November 21, 1843, Poe used the lecture platform to further establish himself as a leading critic of American poetical discourse and its authors, criticizing anthologies such as Rufus Griswold's *The Poets and Poetry of America* (1842), the many editions of which were beginning to form an American poetical canon. That the initial phase of Poe's lecturing is characterized by an emphasis on the role of the critic becomes clear in a long report on the lecture at Newark Academy, Delaware, which was published pseudonymously by Academicus in the *Delaware State Journal*.[7] Steeped in rhetorical terminology, Academicus

---

[7] The original publication was in the *Delaware State Journal*, 2 January 1844: 2. I am citing Benjamin F. Fisher's edition: Academicus ([1844] 2010). The pseudonym "Academicus" might point to a representative of the academy, possibly principal Willliam S. Graham, but the identity remains uncertain.

does not mention any recitation of Poe's own poems but is full of praise for his critical acumen, saying that the "lecture was an eloquent production eloquently delivered by Edgar A. Poe" (Academicus [1844] 2010: 43).[8] Poe's lecture on the same topic – "The Poets and Poetry of America" – in the New York Society Library on February 28, 1845 was instrumental in gaining him access to the literary clique of Young America that centred around Evert Augustus Duyckinck, yet it also made him an instrument of Young America's nationalist agenda (McGill 2003: 197–204). There certainly were ups and downs in Poe's career as a lecturer: while presenting the original Eureka manuscript to an audience of no more than sixty people in New York on February 3, 1848 (PL 720), Poe also gave his lecture on "The Poetic Principle" on December 20, 1848 in Providence – in a series that included as speakers Boston Brahmin Oliver Wendell Holmes and one of antebellum America's most famous orators, two-time Secretary of State Daniel Webster – to an auditorium of about 1,800 people (PL 764, 778).

In some of the reports on Poe's performances, there are specific comments about his delivery. For instance, Poe was said to have that "strength of voice which enables a speaker to give full expression to whatever he may desire to say" (PL 442). His recitation was "judicious" (PL 442) and his sentences "vigorous, energetic and impassioned" (PL 443). Robert Morris of the *Pennsylvania Inquirer*, who had himself been the object of Poe's lauding, returned the favour, saying that: Poe's "style of delivery is finished and effective" (PL 448). From John S. Du Solle's comment in the *Spirit of the Times* that Poe's lecture was "beautifully written" (PL 447), we learn that Poe read rather than spoke freely.[9] Du Solle also commented that "Mr. Poe is a correct and graceful reader" (PL 447). While "graceful" is certainly not intended as a technical term in the sense of, say, George Vandenhoff's distinction of the graces of elocution,[10] Du Solle

---

[8] It is difficult to say whether Academicus' comments only frame Poe's speech in classicist terminology or whether Poe himself also made these dimensions explicit; at the very least Academicus' report, which is full of rhetorical concepts ("exordium," "body of his theme;" 43), features rhetorical figures such as the litotes, and cites Alexander Pope's *Essay on Criticism*, shows how imbued audiences were in rhetorical terminology.

[9] One wonders whether Poe had Griswold's anthology with him to show it to his listeners. The exactness with which Academicus refers to "the *five* steel plate faces of Mr. Griswold's frontispiece, in their order – Dana, Bryant, Halleck, Sprague and Longfellow" speaks at least for the use of the image as an ordering device for the discourse (Academicus [1844] 2010: 45). It is certain that Poe's remarks on Longfellow would have made a good finale for a section on those whom he viewed as overrated poets.

[10] Vandenhoff, in whose elocutionary handbook Poe's "Raven" was first published in book form (discussed in chapter six), distinguishes three graces of elocution: "the highest triumph of Elocu-

sees Poe reaching beyond a basic to an artistic level of delivery. Since these reviews are generally matter-of-fact rather than romanticized, there is good evidence that Poe was an able reader, though, to really gauge its meaning, Poe's delivery needs to be placed in a detailed context.

What is widely regarded as the decisive episode in Poe's career as a lecturer and one that had immense implications for his career as a professional author is his appearance at the Boston Lyceum on October 16, 1845, and its aftermath. At James Russell Lowell's recommendation Poe had been invited to deliver an original poem never before published.[11] Boston, or Frogpondium, as Poe liked to call it after the pond in Boston Common, had always been the object of Poe's fiercest critical attacks, as, for example, in his accusations of plagiarism against the quintessential Boston Brahmin writer, Henry Wadsworth Longfellow, which had been met with similarly vitriolic responses from some Boston coteries.[12]

On the evening in question, Poe's entrance was preceded by a two-and-a-half-hour speech by the politician Caleb Cushing. Poe then introduced himself with a lengthy preamble which was apparently based on his lecture on "The Poets and Poetry of America," with the result that some members of the audience already left. Then, instead of the original poem he was expected to recite, Poe read the audience his highly complex poem "Al Aaraaf," first published in Poe's second collection of poetry in 1829, announcing it under the title "The Messenger Star." At the demand of the audience, Poe finally also recited "The Raven."

The recitations were certainly not as successful as Poe's earlier lectures in Philadelphia and New York, but the real scandal began at the reception afterwards when Poe revealed to Caleb Cushing and others present that his poem was not an original composition, and (falsely) asserted that it was "what is occasionally called a 'juvenile poem'": "we wrote it, printed it, and published it, in book form, before we had fairly completed our tenth year" (CW 3: 299).[13] In the aftermath of the event, Poe then claimed to have hoaxed the Bostonians,

---

tion;—*the truthful utterance of intense and passionate feeling* [...] is to be attained by the power of Intonation, Expression, Energy; the crowning Graces of Elocution" (Vandenhoff 1845: 94).
11 The most detailed account is S. Moss (1963: 192–207). Cf. also Ljungquist (1997b), McGill (2003: 214–217), P. Phillips (2013).
12 For the documents in the so-called Little Longfellow War, cf. E&R 696–777. Cf. Carlson (2002). For the pre-history of the Boston Lyceum event, cf. Prown (1993).
13 This is Poe's own version, from the "Editorial Miscellany" in the *Broadway Journal*, November 1, 1845.

but – rather than as a hoax – most of the Boston papers viewed the event as a "failure."[14]

Later critics mostly agreed, calling it at the very least a "regrettable" affair (Mabbott in PMS 559) or a "fiasco" (S. Moss 1963: 207). It is certain that "Poe's debacle was instrumental in undermining his credibility in northeastern literary circles" (B. Fisher 2010: 52). In order to explain the event, critics have pointed to the Poesque motif of perversity as a biographical motivation (Casale 1973: 428) and claimed that "Poe ended up hoaxing himself" (Carlson 2002: 44). Philip Edward Phillips points to the fact that the place where Poe delivered his poem to the Boston Lyceum, the Odeon, used to be the Boston Theatre where his mother had successfully performed as an actress (2013: 46–47): That Poe "could not expect the same degree of affection or adoration from his Bostonian audience would have been a profound source of anxiety for one who openly despised but inwardly desired Boston's approval." (P. Phillips 2013: 49). Poe's earlier involvement with the Young America movement that had presented Poe as an authorial figure of "instant maturity" (McGill 2003: 204) leads Meredith McGill to argue that by presenting a juvenile poem Poe attempted to subvert the expectations towards his authorial performance, "insisting on placing his poem within a developmental narrative" and trying "to shatter his status as an exemplary subject by aggressively reasserting the contingent facts of his biography" (2003: 216). Biographically speaking, then, Boston – as his birthplace and associated with many of his mother's theatrical performances – was overdetermined for Poe personally but it was also the place of a 'showdown' between Poe and part of the literary establishment.

This biographical, social, and cultural prehistory is evinced in the few aspects we can reconstruct about Poe's oratorical performance per se, and, in particular, the delivery of his poems. Thomas Wentworth Higginson's recollection of Poe's introduction is an indication of the demands Poe was experiencing then: "I remember that when introduced he [Poe] stood with a sort of shrinking before the audience, and then began in a thin, tremulous, hardly musical voice, an apology for his poem, and a deprecation of the expected criticism of the Boston public; reiterating this in a sort of persistent, querulous way, which did not seem like satire, but impressed me at the time as nauseous flattery." (Higginson 1888: 13). Since Higginson, then an undergraduate at Harvard, is overall very approving of Poe's performance, the tension between satire and flattery appears to have been strong indeed – so strong that it seems to have affected Poe's "thin, tremulous, hardly musical voice" in particular.

---

[14] This is Cornelia Wells Walter's comment in the *Boston Evening Transcript*, 17 October 1845: 2. Qtd. in B. Fisher (2010: 52).

However, some members of the audience were also much affected by Poe's performance, as was Higginson himself. After Poe's reading of "Al Aaraaf" and "The Raven," Higginson writes, "I remember nothing more, except that in walking back to Cambridge my comrades and I felt that we had been under the spell of some wizard." (Higginson 1888: 15). The reason for this lies in what Higginson describes as the successful delivery of a melodious poem: "his voice seemed attenuated to the finest golden thread; the audience became hushed, and, as it were, breathless; there seemed no life in the hall but his; and every syllable was accentuated with such delicacy, and sustained with such sweetness, as I never heard equalled by other lips." (Higginson 1888: 14). The mutability of Poe's voice in Higginson's account is remarkable but it indicates the dependence of the impression of the voice on the overall impression of the orator. Poe's voice and, concurrently, his ethos as a speaker depend on the overall effect of his performance and vice versa.

The ambivalence of Poe's performance that Higginson caught shows the nexus of autonomy and heteronomy that structures speaking on the antebellum market of eloquence. Poe's attempt to sell the poem as a juvenile production that would guarantee him the status of a prodigy author and also deny Bostonian standards is countered by the Boston papers insisting on his drunkenness or even madness. Meredith McGill felicitously speaks of the shift from "the total surrender of authorial control" to "the pole of absolute self-possession" (215) when she discusses Poe's *post factum* narrative in the pages of the *Broadway Journal*.

Poe's heteronomy was specifically connected to the generic rhetorical situation of occasional poetry that was a part of the antebellum market of eloquence. Poe never composed an original occasional poem, denying or avoiding invitations such as the one from the Philomathean and Eucleian Societies of New York University on July 1, 1845 (PL 540–547).[15] While this might be interpreted in terms of what Louis Renza calls Poe's "poetics of privacy" (Renza 2002: xiii), the generic demands of delivering occasional poetry were not lost on Poe's contemporary supporters and detractors. William Gilmore Simms commented on Poe's Lyceum appearance: "it was a blunder with Mr. Poe [...] to *deliver himself* in poetry before the Boston Lyceum [...] The sort of poetry called for on such occasions, is the very reverse of the spiritual, the fanciful or the metaphysical. To win the ears of a mixed audience, nothing more is required than moral or patriotic commonplaces in rhyming heroics." (qtd. in PL 588; my emphasis; cp. E&R 1094 for Poe's reprinting of the passage in the *Broadway Journal*

---

15 Poe even "asked Fanny [Osgood], as well as T. D. English, to compose the new poem he felt incapable of writing for his October appearance at the Lyceum. Aware of her 'astonishing facility,' he reasoned she could easily and quickly give him 'a poem that shall be equal to my reputation'" (Silverman 1991: 286).

on November 22, 1845). Simms, as a Southern apologist of slavery, was more than inclined to attack the centre of abolitionism, Boston, and the word choice of Poe "delivering himself" might be said to invoke discourses of expropriation and enslavement. Yet even Poe's foremost detractor Cornelia Wells Walter also argued based on genre. She maintained that Poe's apology for not presenting a "didactic poem" was self-defeating, as the "audience listened in amazement to a singularly didactic exordium, and finally commenced the noisy expedient of removing from the hall, and this long before they had discovered the style of the measure, or whether it was rhythm or blank verse" (PL 579). There certainly was a disjunction between the expectation for a particular type of poetry and Poe's performance at the Lyceum – both the absent Simms and the present Walter attest to this. But this should not blind us to the crucial requirement of the type of occasional poetry that is demanded when "Poe finds himself unable to write an original poem to read before the Boston Lyceum, as required by the rules of that institution" (PL 573): the poem was to be original in the sense of never before *published*. While the interest in original contributions also played a large role in the culture of reprinting, it appears that originality, in this case, plays a role in affirming the specificity of the market of eloquence: if the contribution *must* be original, then this differs substantially from reprinting an already existing text, or indeed reciting an already existing text.

To counter these demands of occasional poetry on the antebellum market of eloquence, Poe defended himself through figuratively reinterpreting "delivery." Retrospectively speaking about the generic demands of the situation, Poe initially emphasises the meaning of "delivery": "We occupied some fifteen minutes with an apology for not 'delivering,' as is usual in such cases, a didactic poem, in our opinion, being precisely no poem at all" (CW 3: 298). Foregrounding the various meanings of "delivering," he draws an analogy between rhetorical delivery and commercial "delivery," first in its criminal, then in its legal form: "We *were* invited to 'deliver' (stand and deliver) a poem before the Boston Lyceum" (CW 3: 298). The double entendre of 'taking a stand and giving a speech' and 'standing still and surrendering one's money' thus introduces the idea of an asymmetrical power relation between the audience and the poet. Poe reduces the severity of the image in what follows, but establishes an even closer link between commercial and rhetorical delivery.[16] He calls his previous speaker's discourse a "very capital" one and writes: "We delivered 'The Raven' forthwith – (without taking a receipt)" (CW 3: 298). Poe's statement of the

---

[16] Cp. also the emphasis in the phrase "[i]t is the first – the original edition – the *delivered* edition" (E&R 1098).

"facts of the case" thus subtly identifies and rejects the Boston Lyceum audience's notion of the poetical domain as commercialised and the poetical recitation as commodified. One of Poe's strategies to cope with the aftermath of the event is thus to identify oratorical with commercial delivery, an identification that he claims he has resisted by his actions at the Lyceum.

This is not to say that this strategy was or can be successful in the particular situation; Poe's identification was *post factum* and far too subtle to fundamentally change the meaning ascribed to the performance by the Bostonian papers. Yet the equation of oratorical and commercial delivery also points to the larger implications of the relation of the Lyceum to the antebellum print marketplace. Like the magazines, the Lyceums fulfilled a decisive function in the emerging literary market, placing particular demands of originality on the author. They served both as places of criticism and of poetry, as Poe's very own example of touring the antebellum publishing centres of Philadelphia, New York, and Boston shows.

In a biographically overdetermined, culturally charged, and generically unfavourable situation, Poe thus attempted to escape his own shortcomings by subverting the logic of the market that governed his performance. Rather than fulfilling the demands on the author as a performer of his own occasional poetry, Poe retrospectively ironizes these demands, which he was not able to do in the performative situation itself. Earlier in the same year, he had written an incisive analysis of the predicament of the "poor devil author" in the "Magazine Prison-House" (E&R 1036–1038). Thus he should perhaps have known better than to try and escape the Lyceum Prison-House in Boston – the historical irony being that it was the antebellum prison-houses of the magazine and the Lyceum that allowed him to write and speak as an author in the first place.

Poe's failure is one that illuminates the demands placed upon antebellum writers to meet certain criteria of what we might rhetorically describe as the authorial ethos, one of the central means of the orator to persuade an audience. It is this failure that would make him emblematic of the wider relationships between the literature of failure and economic poverty, which Gavin Jones has reconstructed,[17] not least because Poe's initial motivation to enter the lecturing market was economic. Regardless of whether we ascribe Poe's failure to the history of critical animosity between him and the Bostonians, the demands of the market of eloquence or a personal shortcoming or even perversity on Poe's part, the fact remains that it was an or-

---

17 This applies despite the fact that Jones himself dismisses the Boston Lyceum performance rather cursorily, saying Poe "showed up drunk and read before an expectant and educated audience his juvenile poetry. Perhaps this was part of Poe's effort to elevate his own literary status, either in contrast to the works of the aesthetically challenged or by gulling New England's intelligentsia" (2014: 33).

atorical performance that marked a central turning-point in Poe's career as an author. In similar fashion, the debate that followed concerned the definition of the relation between orator and audience as well as the generic demands of occasional poetry. The various aspects of the success and failure of delivery as they congeal in the event itself and the magazine aftermath evince a central intersection between the American antebellum cultures of print and rhetoric. In order to be fully successful as an author, one had to deliver a particular authorial self, a public persona, to a large audience, which represented a demand on the authorial *histrio* that Poe either could or did not want to fulfil.

7.2 "The Characteristics of a Popular Performer": Acting Against "Loss of Breath"

If Poe's appearance at the Boston Lyceum was an indication of the dangers of the potential lack of inspiration under the conditions of the market of eloquence, then the authorial anxiety of the loss of inspiration applied no less to the print market. The way in which Poe viewed one in terms of the other forms the subject of one of his most reworked tales, "Loss of Breath: A Tale Neither In Nor Out of 'Blackwood'," first published as "A Decided Loss" in 1832 and substantially reworked in four successive versions, ultimately leading to its final form published in the *Broadway Journal* in January 1846, roughly two months after his Boston Lyceum appearance. Based on a punning literalisation of the metaphorical phrase, the male narrator of the sensational and burlesque tale, Mr Lackobreath, loses his breath, goes through various stages of bodily mutilation, and – perceived dead – ends up in a crypt, where he finally regains his breath and voice through a devilish contract with his neighbour, rival, and doppelganger, Mr Windenough.

The story's primary subtext, so to say, is a thinly-veiled play on the loss of male sexual potency, as Marie Bonaparte, David Ketterer, and Michael J. S. Williams have argued.[18] Some of the more obvious clues include the fact that the narrator loses his breath in a one-sided violent altercation with his newly-wed wife after their wedding night (T&S 62) and that he finds signs of her involvement with the neighbour, Mr Windenough; it is linguistically mirrored in such blunt phrases as the play on the subjective and objective genitive in "I returned to my *boudoir* – there to ponder upon some method of eluding my wife's penetration" (T&S 64).

---

18 Cf. the concise summary in Williams (1988: 51).

However, this implied type of sexual failure can also be connected to anxieties of authorship, as Williams and Sherlyn Abdoo have argued. In such a reading, "breathlessness, like writer's block, indicates a temporary failure (or fear of failure) to write." (Abdoo 1990: 586). In similar fashion, Robert Tally suggests that "[a]bove all, perhaps, 'Loss of Breath' is a satire of literature and the literary marketplace" (2014: 15). If the loss of breath stands for a lack of inspiration, the evocation of the performative arts of drama, acting, and elocution in the tale serves to elucidate Poe's performative strategies of evading failure on the literary market, thus adding a central dimension to his figure of the literary histrio.

The link between breath and (divine) inspiration is ancient, and, as is universally acknowledged, it was "a favorite figure of the romantics" (M. Williams 1988: 50; cf. Dayan (1987: 205–209)). M. H. Abrams termed it the "correspondent breeze," and argued that it is embodied in such metaphors as Coleridge's Eolian harp: "The wind-harp has become a persistent Romantic analogue of the poetic mind, the figurative mediator between outer motion and inner emotion" (Abrams 1984: 26). As the mediator between outer motion and inner emotion, the harp as trope of the poetic mind invites comparison with Quintilian's dialectics of self-affection (outlined in chapter one), the major difference being that the origin of emotion in the self in Quintilian is governed by artistic rules, rather than external inspiration. To illustrate such a dynamic of emotion and art, Poe utilised the metaphor, for instance, in his 1831 poem "Israfel," in which Israfel's "heart-strings are a lute" (PMS 173), and "The Fall of the House of Usher," in which Usher's heart is framed as a "hanging lute" – "un luth suspendu" – by the motto (T&S 397, 417). Satirising the romantic figure, Poe's depiction of Mr Lackobreath's predicament represents "a dig at the possibility of inspired original composition" (M. Williams 1988: 50). What Poe develops in "Loss of Breath" is the fear of the predicament that befalls authors if they lose inspiration in the antebellum print culture, and he develops it by pitting against this fear of failure the performative art of the actor.

In the tale, the actor's rhetorical delivery is central to Poe's farcical portrayal of the woes of the author. Initially, after his loss, Lackobreath starts looking for his breath in the drawers and closets of the room where he lost it. Having realised that he cannot retrieve his breath as if it were a lost thing, the narrator returns to his boudoir to ponder solutions to his misery, all of which focus on the conditions and problems of delivery. The narrator seeks to escape his predicament by becoming a reciter and actor who diligently performs the final two rhetorical stages as described in chapter one: memory and delivery (*memoria, actio/pronuntiatio*).

Discovering that he can still make "deep guttural sounds," the narrator memorizes a play: "I committed to memory the entire tragedy of 'Metamora.' I had the good fortune that in the accentuation of this drama, or at least of such a portion of it as it is allotted to the hero, the tones of voice in which I found myself deficient were altogether unnecessary, and that the deep guttural was expected to reign monotonously throughout" (T&S 65). This link between memory and delivery is present in all of the versions of the tale. In the earlier version, "A Decided Loss," the narrator memorizes two tragedies (T&S 55) and reads a poem in order to sharpen his "invention."[19] In similar fashion, in versions up to 1840, Lackobreath's power of memory is "quadrupled" when he performs the part of a hanged man (sic) so that he can "repeat to myself entire lines, passages, chapters, books, from the studies of my earlier days" (T&S 78). While this characterisation of memory appears hyperbolized, it had a basis in Poe's serious take on mnemonic methods, the significance of which William Engel has demonstrated.[20] In a review of Francis Fauvel-Gouraud's *Phreno-Mnemotechny; or the Art of Memory* for the *Southern Literary Messenger*, Poe vigorously defended the concept of artifical memory and "the Art, generally, to which the wise Simonides devoted a life, and which has occupied the serious attention of such intellects as those of [...] Cicero [and] Quintilian" (CW 5: 371). He concludes that the "powers of memory, as aided by [Gouraud's] system, are *absolutely illimitable*" (CW 5: 371). Artificial memory is thus a key to understanding the hyperbolized attempts on Lackobreath's part to regain his powers of speech.

What comes out particularly clearly in the 1846 version is the staging of the interrelation of the rhetorical aspects of memory and delivery: the possibility of memorizing the play so quickly is premised upon the particularity of the "accentuation" of the hero's part in the drama. The scene thus dramatises the attempt to regain inspiration through techniques of memory and delivery. In order to regain the possibility of acting through speech, the narrator takes recourse to a poetic product (the tragedy), since he is no longer able to compose lines for himself. He learns them by heart like an actor and uses them like a reciter or elocutionist.

Acting, elocution, and the fear of the loss of inspiration then coagulate in a comparison with the most famous of ancient 'elocutionists,' Demosthenes – a comparison that stresses Lackobreath's originality: "I practised for some time by the borders of a well frequented marsh; – here, however, having no reference to a similar proceeding of Demosthenes, but from a design *peculiarly and conscientiously my own*" (T&S 65; my emphasis). The politician and speech-writer Demosthenes has been regarded as the foremost among orators since the time of Cicero, primarily be-

---

19 The full passage runs: "To sharpen my invention, I took down a prize poem on——, and reading half an hour, found myself fuddled. Jumping up in despair, I hit upon an expedient, and immediately set about carrying it into execution" (T&S 55).
20 Cf. Engel's detailed account of the importance for Poe of memory conceptions from early modern poetics and rhetoric and, in particular, his discussion of Fauvel-Gouraud (Engel 2012: 107–109).

cause of his uncompromising stance, his grand style, and his relentless training methods that helped him overcome speaking deficiencies such as his stammer.²¹ While none of the ancient anecdotes about Demosthenes' self-training can be verified as historical fact,²² one popular image in particular, to which Poe is alluding in the passage, has him standing on a shore and speaking over the sound of the breaking waves.²³ The most familiar of these images is probably Jean Jules Antoine Lecomte du Nouÿ's orientalist painting *Demosthenes Practising Oratory* (*Démosthène s'exerçant à la parole*, 1870), but in Poe's times many illustrative etchings could be found. Authors, and especially elocutionists, could assume the audience's familiarity with the motif to such an extent that Andrew Comstock used it as the frontispiece for one of his handbooks without giving Demosthenes' name. The title of the handbook is *A System of Elocution with Special Reference to Gesture, to the Treatment of Stammering, and Defective Articulation* (1841):

Figure 2: Frontispiece of Andrew Comstock: A System of Elocution with Special Reference to Gesture, to the Treatment of Stammering, and Defective Articulation (1841)

---

21 For Demosthenes' reception as an orator I rely on Harding (2000: 248–257). Demosthenes later became a role model for politicians particularly in England and the United States (Huss 2013: 355).
22 Douglas M. MacDowell estimates the credibility of anecdotes about Demosthenes' self-training: "Perhaps most worthy of credence are those which Demetrios of Phaleron recorded that he was told by Demosthenes himself in his old age: to cure a lack of clarity in his articulation he practised delivering speeches with pebbles in his mouth; he exercised his voice by speaking while running uphill; he rehearsed his speeches standing in front of a large mirror. [...] It is clear that in later centuries Demosthenes' self-training became the stuff of legend" (MacDowell 2009: 21).
23 Mabbott mentions the motif, but wrongly attributes it to Quintilian (T&S 75, footnote 10). The citation from Quintilian only contains the motifs of running uphill and speaking with pebbles in the mouth (Quintilian 2001e, 113 = 11.3.54).

In his version of a competition with Demosthenes, Poe ironically transforms the shore with its loud waves into a marsh. Rather than addressing sublime natural scenery, then, Poe has his narrator implicitly compete with a few toads.[24] As ridiculous as this is, it remains the most original idea the narrator can come up with in his situation: "a design peculiarly and conscientiously my own" (T&S 65). Emulating the greatest Greek orator's delivery thus becomes part of a satirical figuration of the loss of authorial inspiration.

For Poe, as for many others at the time, elocutionary delivery and acting were inextricably linked. His engagement with acting stands in the context of his larger interest for the drama, which was first examined thoroughly by N. Bryllion Fagin in *The Histrionic Mr. Poe* (1949). While Poe published only individual scenes from *Politian*, his early unfinished attempt at a verse drama, he worked as a serious theatre critic, particularly in his time at the *Broadway Journal*, and he also defined hallmarks of "The American Drama" (E&R 357–388). Poe's interest in and positive view of acting are well attested. Of successful actress and dramatist Anna Cora Mowatt, he wrote that "all her movements evince the practised elocutionist" (MTC 12: 187), comparing her gestures to "the poet deeply imbued with the truest sentiment of the beauty of motion" (MTC 12: 188). Besides her movements, he also commented on her voice, the other major aspect of elocution, yet interestingly, the focus in his use of the term is on bodily movements – just like the focus in "Loss of Breath" is on bodily movements. More generally, Poe's statements show that he understands elocution as central to the art of acting.

The oratorical figure of Demosthenes, the actor as elocutionist and the dramatic poet come together to give a hyperbolized and yet complete description of the author as a contemporary "popular performer" (T&S 65):

> Thus armed at all points, I determined to make my wife believe that I was suddenly smitten with a passion for the stage. In this, I succeeded to a miracle; and to every question or suggestion found myself at liberty to reply in my most frog-like and sepulchral tones with some passage from the tragedy – any portion of which, as I soon took great pleasure in observing, would apply equally well to any particular subject. It is not to be supposed, however, that in the delivery of such passages I was found at all deficient in the looking asquint – the showing my teeth – the working my knees – the shuffling my feet – or in any of those unmentionable graces which are now justly considered the characteristics of a popular performer. To be sure they spoke of confining me in a straight-jacket – but, good God! they never suspected me of having lost my breath. (T&S 65)

---

[24] While the image is present in versions of the story from 1835 onwards, it is tempting to imagine a connection between the marsh and Poe's idea of Boston, or better, Frogpondium. On the connection between the frog-like voice of the narrator and the Grimm's fairy tale "The Frog-King," cf. Abdoo (1990: 589).

Using the parts of the tragedy as material *topoi* for his own speech, the narrator continues speaking in the one monotonous mode of pronunciation that is still available to him. The style employed in the description of the individual gestures – particularly the quadruple parallelism – imbues the passage with a rhythmical flow that suggests the mimicry of a performer's moves. The narrator reaches his goal – both in the inner terms of the story and in terms of authorial self-representation, as there is deliberation about putting him in a straight-jacket but no one suspects him of having lost his breath: while he has the appearance of a madman, he still looks like an inspired poet. As a popular performer – a histrio – he thus acts and elocutionises his way out of his initial dilemma.

However, in accordance with the sensational Blackwood formula that Poe utilises, his problems do not end there. Just like Psyche Zenobia reports her literal death of the author in "How to Write a Blackwood Article," Lackobreath's transgressive status of being "dead, with the propensities of the living" (T&S 63) sends him on several theatrically inflected episodes of bodily movements and mutilations that are out of his control. As in a *Stationendrama*, Lackobreath's body is first squashed by a fellow traveller, then thrown off the stage coach, eviscerated by a physician, mistaken for a mail robber, hanged, and finally stowed away in a crypt. There, after "tumbling over a carcass," he begins to "soliloquize[...]" (T&S 70) and ponder "the blessings of mortality" (T&S 71), holding a head like Hamlet holds Yorick's skull in the popular imagination.[25] In each of the episodes, Lackobreath acts as if he were on a stage and "stage-struck" (T&S 72). At the execution, his major interest is in the effect on the audience: "For good reasons [...] I did my best to give the crowd the worth of their trouble. My convulsions were said to be extraordinary. My spasms it would have been difficult to beat. The populace *encored*. Several gentlemen swooned; and a multitude of ladies were carried home in hysterics" (T&S 69–70). As a result of Lackobreath's view of the shouts of the onlookers as a demand for an encore performance, the contrast between the finality of an execution and the repeatability of theatrical play is satirically hyperbolized.

Like an actor playing several roles, Mr Lackobreath is inserted into a mirror system of doubles, in which he himself, Mr Windenough and the mail-robber W play aspects of the author-as-performer caught in a series of stagings. The three characters are connected on the levels of sound and text. William E. Engel points to the phonetic connections between *W*indenough and *W*: "as with William Wilson (a name also beginning with the letter 'W,' which by a phonetic slip connotes 'double you'), Poe exploits the confusion and doubling of identities and texts"

---

25 In an echo of Shakespeare's *Julius Caesar*, Lackobreath also pauses "[l]ike Brutus" (T&S 74).

(Engel 2012: 111). Mr Windenough is even referred to at one point as "Mr. W" (T&S 64), thus rendering him virtually identical to the mail-robber for whom Lackobreath is mistaken. Their bodies are also related through texts-within-the-text such as the billets de doux from Mr Windenough to Mrs Lackobreath and the mail that W steals, thus turning them into figurative texts themselves: Lackobreath's "body, like the body of a text, undergoes many transformations and even changes its shape," and "the portions of his body that are cut off and cut out are expendable, just as portions of text that add nothing of value to meaning are deleted." (Abdoo 1990: 587). It is, among other things, this self-reflexive textuality – human bodies as bodies of text – that has made Poe such a favourite in deconstructionist interpretations,[26] yet in terms of the interplay between the culture of rhetoric and the culture of print, the body can also be viewed in terms of elocutionist performance.

The crucial aspect of rhetorical culture in this context is the elocutionary movement's attempts to standardise body language in performances by speakers, reciters and actors. In his *American Elocutionist* (1844), Russell maintained that public address consisted "of two parts, – elocution, or the regulated functions of the voice, – and gesture, or the proper management of the body" (Russell 1844: 199). We saw the regulated functions of the voice at work in "Ulalume" in the previous chapter, yet the body of the elocutionist was the other of the two major subjects in the writings of the elocutionary movement, and would thus also be referred to under the heading of elocution. The idea of a "proper management of the body" that would parallel the linguistic standardisations of pronunciation led to intricate notation systems for gestures such as Gilbert Austin's *Chironomia; Or, A Treatise on Rhetorical Delivery*, which codifies individual gestures such as the "colloquial elevations of the arm" (1806: 313; cf. also 269–290; plates 1–12). An example of what Austin calls a complex significant gesture evinces how certain elocutionists attempted to codify the movements of the performer's body: the performer is represented in a sphere, in which the centre of the breast of the performer corresponds to the centre of the sphere; several lines and circles then map body positions and movements can be noted by using the alphabetical letters assigned to the positions (Austin 1806: 309–317; see figure 3).

As the use of alphabetical letters indicates, it is essential not to view Austin's intricate system as isolated from print culture; on the contrary, Austin's and other elocutionists' work effectively incorporated the logic of print "into the realm of embodied performance" (McCorkle 2012: 109): the regularity that standardised writing attained in and through print was thought viable in gesture, too.

---

26 Cf. Hurh (2015: 28, 75–160).

7.2 "The Characteristics of a Popular Performer": Acting Against "Loss of Breath" — 215

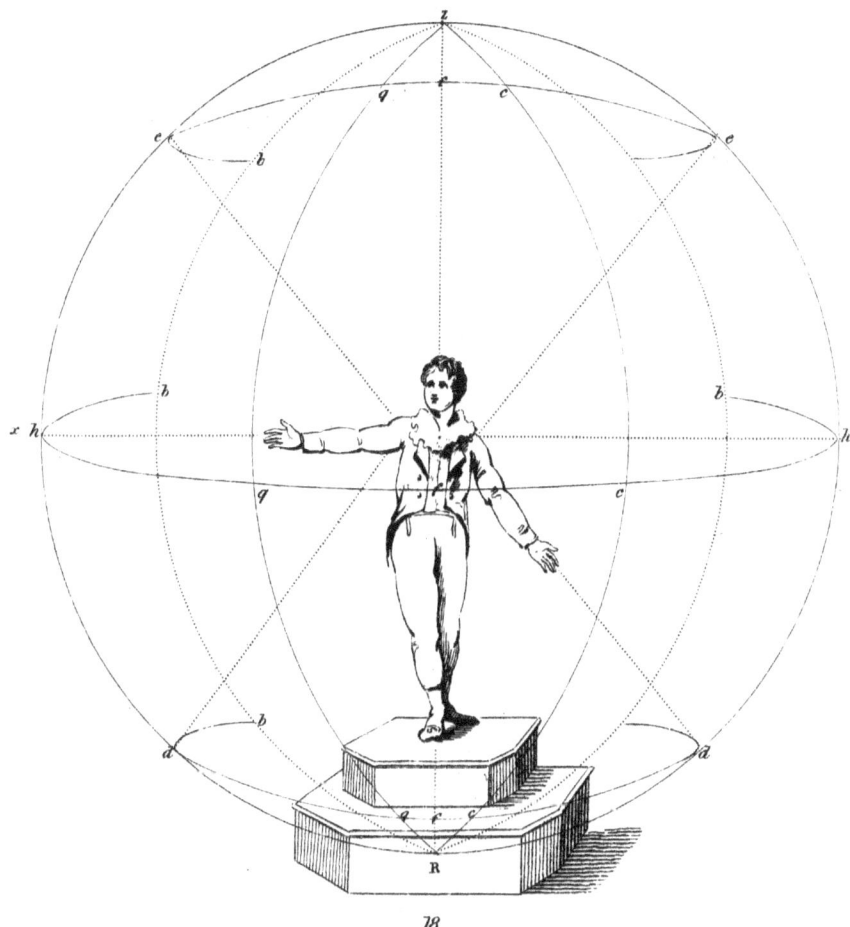

Figure 3: The sphere from Gilbert Austin, *Chironomia: Or, a Treatise on Rhetorical Delivery. Comprehending Many Precepts, Both Ancient and Modern, for the Proper Regulation of the Voice, the Countenance, and Gesture* (1806: 308).

In hindsight, this seems an absurd project, yet the standardisation of the other aspect of elocution, 'pronunciation,' whose workings we saw in the background of Poe's "Rationale of Verse," might have seemed similarly bizarre. Public performance thus became an object of a technology that bridged print and gesture. As Philippa Spoel argues, in Austin's "*Chironomia*'s case the non-verbal language of the body is the object and target of power," "representing [the] body as both intelligible and manipulable" (Spoel 1998: 24). The non-verbal language of the body, its movements and gestures, is what is at the heart of Poe's "popular performer" and the isolated manipulation of his body without a voice. In a sense, the popular performer embodies the isolation and abstraction of gesture in the elocutionary tradition as it was developed most extremely by Gilbert Austin.

What happens to the body of the "popular performer" is thus not only similar to the sufferings of texts in the culture of reprinting – that they would be disassembled, reassembled, and repeated in different contexts – but also to the literal body of the elocutionist if elocutionist advice was followed. Then, distortions such as "all my limbs were dislocated and my head twisted on one side" (T&S 66) graphically hyperbolize and satirize what could be a description of one of Austin's complex significant gestures.

Such an overwrought acting style – or elocutionary style – is at the heart of Lackobreath's display at the gallows: "My convulsions were said to be extraordinary. My spasms it would have been difficult to beat. The populace *encored*." In similar fashion, when he tries to "confute" – yet another rhetorical term – the apothecary's idea that he is dead, he "kick[s] and plung[es] with all [his] might, and mak[es] the most furious contortions" (T&S 67). Like an isolated gesturing elocutionist on the page, however, he can still not speak: "It was a source of mortification to me nevertheless that although I made several attempts at conversation, my powers of speech were so entirely in abeyance, that I could not even open my mouth" (T&S 67). This obsession with the types of violence connected to bodily movement also informs Lackobreath's view of others. Thus he contemplates the corpse in the vault as "an unfortunate man" because it "has been his terrible lot not to walk, but to waddle [...] His attempts at getting on have been mere abortions, and his circumgyratory proceedings a palpable failure" (T&S 70).

This criticism of the overacting popular performer is particularly apparent against the background of Poe's advocacy of a type of natural(istic) acting. Poe's ideal of "naturalness" in acting is also formulated in a discussion of Anna Cora Mowatt, who "moves, looks, and speaks with a well-controlled impulsiveness as different as can be conceived from the customary rant and cant – the hack conventionality of the stage" (MTC 12, 188). The phrase "well-controlled impulsiveness" epitomizes a relationship of heteronomous and autonomous aspects in an artist so succinctly as we rarely find it in Poe, and it contrasts sharply with the picture of Mr Lackobreath, the satirical stand-in for the uninspired author as actor/elocutionist.

Towards the end, Lackobreath meets his double, Windenough, in a crypt, and the two distribute breath equally amongst themselves. In similar fashion to his defence after the Boston Lyceum performance, Poe frames the resolution of the lack of inspiration through a wordplay on rhetorical and economic delivery: "Preliminaries being at length arranged, my acquaintance delivered me the

7.2 "The Characteristics of a Popular Performer": Acting Against "Loss of Breath" — 217

respiration; for which (having carefully examined it) I gave him afterwards a receipt" (T&S 74).[27] While the exchange can be said to be framed in terms of economics, homosociality, and black magic, the dead Lackobreath is revivified through (a) delivery. The tale thus plays on another aspect of eloquence, elocution, and delivery which were all said to make (ancient) texts alive again. For instance, Cotesworth Bronson invokes Demosthenes and states that *"[m]ost of the effects of ancient, as well as of modern eloquence, may be attributed to the manner of delivery:* we read their *words,* but their *spirit* is gone; the body remains, *beautiful* indeed, but *motionless* – and *dead,* TRUE eloquence – revivifies it." (Bronson 1845: 49). The dead body of the text and, in the case of "Loss of Breath," the author himself is thus brought back to life through delivery, the final and, according to Demosthenes, most important stage of rhetoric.

Acting against his "Loss of Breath," Poe's figure of the author in the tale has to become a "popular performer" in a variety of ways. In other words, the figures of the actor and the elocutionist informed Poe's overall idea of the author as *histrio*. As the comparison with Demosthenes, the theatrical elements, the investment in questions of memory and delivery, and the implied criticism of the elocutionary school of gesture show, Poe viewed the histrionic dimension of the author as a way to preempt failure on the antebellum literary market. At the same time, Poe knew its constrictions well enough to satirise this very concept, almost from the beginning of his career to his most crucial performance at the Boston Lyceum, as the many revisions of "Loss of Breath" attest.

"Loss of Breath" is not untypical in this regard, since Poe's conceptualisation of the author as literary histrio also informed his theory of the tale per se, just like it informed his theory of the poem (in "The Philosophy of Composition") and his view of criticism (as in the motto cited at the beginning of this chapter). This is one of the most-cited phrases from the Hawthorne reviews in context:

> Worldly interests intervening during the pauses of perusal, modify, annul, or counteract, in a greater or lesser degree, the impressions of the book. But simple cessation in reading would, of itself, be sufficient to destroy the true unity. In the brief tale, however, the author is enabled to carry out the fulness of his intention, be it what it may. During the hour of perusal, the soul of the reader is at the writer's control. (E&R 572)

Poe's doctrine of the single sitting essentially transforms the private reading act of the individual into a decidedly performative scene with the author in charge. It is as

---

[27] As discussed above, Poe also makes use of such a pun on delivery in his comments on the Boston Lyceum appearance. Poe's use of it is even older, first in Mabbott's text A (T&S 52), which was published in the *Southern Literary Messenger,* vol. 1, no. 13, September 1835: 735–740).

if the reader and author are in the same room, the latter hypnotising the former. Poe envisions a reader who becomes completely absorbed in the tale, which is – strikingly actively – told by the author. This kind of performance may surely be compared to one on the stage or the rostrum, performative situations that fit both Poe's theoretical indebtedness to rhetorical positions and the performative aspects of authorship as encapsulated in the figure of the literary *histrio*.

7.3 "X-ing a Paragrab": Technological Delivery, Anastatic Printing and Crossing Out the Author

As we have seen in the previous and this chapter, antebellum America was characterized by the insoluble interplay of the culture of rhetoric with the culture of print – neither being monolithic but characterized by a multitude of intersections. Rhetoric covered both oral and written discourse, and the development of print influenced aspects of bodily performance. Cross-medial analogies that linked oral performance, handwriting, and typesetting can be found in rhetorical handbooks such as Ebenezer Porter's *Analysis of the Principles of Rhetorical Delivery as Applied in Reading and Speaking*: "It has been well said, that a good articulation is to the ear, what a fair hand-writing, or a fair type is to the eye" (1827: 22). One way of explaining the persistence of earlier media such as oral delivery, their transformation by newer media such as industrialised print, and the influence of older media on newer media is the concept of remediation, as proposed by Jay Bolter and Richard Grusin. Adopting the logic of Hegelian sublation to contemporary new media, they argue that "*all* mediation is remediation," and that there are two interconnected processes at work when new media emerge: on the one hand, there is "something like a historical progression, of newer media remediating older ones," and on the other, if viewed from the perspective of "a genealogy of affiliations [...], older media can also remediate newer ones" (Bolter and Grusin 1999: 55).

The development of the elocutionary movement's ideas, which furnished points of comparison for "Ulalume," "The Rationale of Verse," and "Loss of Breath," can be seen as paradigmatic for the remediating processes operating between the inextricably linked cultures of print and rhetoric in Poe's times. First, in situations characterized by 'primary orality' (Ong 2013: 133–134), there existed a certain continuity between the roles of orator, reciter, and actor from antiquity to the nineteenth century – and thus in the conception of delivery. At the same time, the development of the medium of print had a major impact on any understanding of delivery with regard to the elocutionary movement that "achieved its prominence thanks in part to the increased reach of print" (McCorkle 2012: 109). A third process affected the meaning of 'delivery,' which expanded its field of application and came "to focus on presentation, typeface, [and] ways of reading" (Welch 2001: 218). The differing models of performance thus become fully explicable only when we take into account the remediating interrelations of oral performance and print. Hence, in this final section, the subject is Poe's figurations of the literary histrio when it comes to technological delivery in print.

That Poe and other authors were plagued by the quite literal problems of delivery in print is evidenced by their daily interactions with the means of production and distribution of texts. Poe's remarks on the quality of print and paper in his reviews are numerous, and, in particular, his remarks on anastatic printing in an article for the *Broadway Journal* in 1845 (CW 3: 83–86) show him hoping for an improvement in print technology that would also have positive remediating effects on handwriting and thus on writing styles and, ultimately, literary invention and arrangement.

Anastatic printing was a short-lived invention similar to lithography by means of which an exact duplicate of a text was supposed to be producible, yet the acid involved tended to destroy the original.[28] Poe, however, was full of hope: "By means of this discovery anything written, drawn, or printed, can be made to stereotype itself, with absolute accuracy, in five minutes" (CW 3: 84), the idea being that it would make 'print on demand' possible (CW 3: 85). Envisaging the combination of the advances of print publication with the values of manuscript culture, Poe held that if the author could directly print his own texts by duplicating his manuscript, it would free the author from the publisher. Imagining books anastatically printed directly from authors' manuscripts, Poe predicts the return of "the cultivation of a neat and distinct style of handwriting – for authors will perceive the immense advantage of giving their own MSS. directly to the public without the expensive interference of the type-setter, and the often ruinous intervention of the publisher" (CW 3: 85).

Making use of the etymological link between style and the Roman writing instrument *stilus*, Poe had initially planned to call his own magazine, based in Philadelphia, Pennsylvania, "The Penn Magazine."[29] The actualisation of this link between the classical writing instrument and printed text, made possible by anastatic technology, is interpreted by Poe in terms of its influence on the rhetorical phases of invention ("thought"),[30] arrangement, and style:

---

28 Copies of William Blake's *Songs of Innocence and Experience* had been made using the procedure. Cf. Benesch (2002: 104). Cf. also Guttzeit (2010: 107–108).
29 Cf. Poe's own draft of the frontispiece, reproduced and discussed by Jackson (2010: 140).
30 Poe defined rhetoric as the "the *mode generally* in which Thought is presented" (E&R 1443). Cf. the discussion in chapter three.

> The cultivation of accuracy in MS., thus enforced, will tend with an irresistible impetus to every species of improvement in *style* – more especially in the points of concision and distinctness – and this again, in a degree even more noticeable, to precision of thought, and luminous arrangement of matter. There is a very peculiar and easily intelligible reciprocal influence between the thing written and the manner of writing – but the latter has the predominant influence of the two. The more remote effect on philosophy at large, which will inevitably result from improvement of style and thought in the points of concision, distinctness, and accuracy, need only be suggested to be conceived. (CW 3: 86)

The movement of clarity from the handwriting to the writer's style to his arrangement and thoughts right through to philosophical thought depends on the extreme emphasis that Poe puts on the manner of writing: while "the thing written and the manner of writing" influence each other reciprocally, "the latter" – also understood as the medium of writing – "has the predominant influence." As Klaus Benesch frames it, Poe "managed to turn technology itself into an essential palliative for the writer's estrangement from his privately written, soon-to-be published text" (Benesch 2002: 107). The remediation of print by anastatic technology would thus transform the basic authemes of literary and philosophical writing, as delivery in print can effectively be replaced by the older medium of manuscript delivery. Poe's ideas about anastatic printing can thus be read as an attempt to escape the "Magazine Prison-House" (E&R 1036): to reject being figured by the conditions of antebellum publishing by actively refiguring the texts produced through the performance of handwriting.

The reasons for his vision of handwriting-as-publication are particularly apparent in his last published tale "X-ing a Paragrab" (May 1849), which satirises the quandaries, of the antebellum author with regard to delivery in print.[31] Zooming in on the topic of editorial rivalry familiar from "Thingum Bob," the tale depicts the feud in the city of Nopolis between a newly arrived editor from Frogpondium (Boston), Mr. Touch-and-go Bullet-head, and the editor of the local Gazette, John Smith. In his first invective against the local editor, through which he hopes to establish his magazine as the dominant publication in Nopolis, Bullet-head reveals a penchant for the use of "Oh" as interjection and vocative. Smith comments wryly, in a paronomasia that works only when the

---

[31] Michael J. S. Williams points to this link, arguing that "Poe's anxieties about such vagaries" "that intervene[...] between the act of writing a manuscript and its final printed version and threaten[...] to deflate by X-ing an author's sense of 'conscious power' in composition" "lie behind his celebration in 1845 of 'the invention of Anastatic Printing'" (Williams 1988: 46). Cp. also Perkins and Dupras' thesis that "[a]ll texts – not just the Tea-Pot's 'paragrab' – are X'd: subject to the uncertainty principle, which conclusive meaning supposedly supplements." (Perkins 1990: 492).

printed text is read aloud: "he came away from Down-East in a great hurry. Wonder if he *O*'s as much there as he does here?" (T&S 1370). Bullet-head takes up the gauntlet and, "consuming the midnight oil" (T&S 1371), attempts to compose an o-less paragraph, arriving at the exact opposite. "Firmly, composedly, yet with an air of conscious power," Bullet-head gives the manuscript "to the devil in waiting," the printer's boy, Bob (T&S 1372).[32] Yet Bob finds himself in a predicament: all the O's have been stolen from the case by someone from John Smith's party, and after consulting the foreman, who tells him to "just stick in some other letter for *o*; nobody's going to read the fellow's trash, any how," he replaces all O's with X's (T&S 1373). The next morning the town is mystified by the "mystical and cabalistical article" that begins with "Sx hx, Jxhn! hxw nxw? Txld yxu sx, yxu knxw. Dxn't crxw, anxther time, befxre yxu're xut xf the wxxds!" (T&S 1374). The townspeople's reactions to the text are divided, but Poe soon unifies them in medial terms when he begins to substitute X's for O's in the narrator's discourse: "One gentleman thought the whole an X-ellent joke" and the fifth responder thinks it was "to set an X-ample to posterity" (T&S 1374–75).

As we saw in the example of "O's"/'owes,' the text abounds in paronomasias which depend on double entendres produced by the difference between print and speech. Moreover, many of them also mimic speech patterns. For instance, the place of the action is actually called "Alexander-the-Great-o-nopolis, or some place of a similar title, out West," which the narrator, when he has to write/pronounce it for the fifth time, simply abbreviates, thereby quasi negating its existence (no polis): "Mr. Bullet-head found himself in Alex – suppose we call it Nopolis" (T&S 1369).

In this paronomasiac world of remediation, it is not only Bullet-head's meaning that is lost in the process of the delivery of print. After the publication, the author himself vanishes from the face of the earth, "and not even the ghost of him has ever been seen since" (T&S 1374). This "poor devil author," who is obsessed with that "most sonorous" of vowels, as Poe called /o/ in "The Philosophy of Composition" (CT 64), is ultimately at the mercy of the printer's devil. The disappearance of Touch-and-go Bullet-head is a result of having bet the printer's devil his head, as every author needs to do under the conditions of antebellum publishing.[33] The authorial control over delivery in print, if there ever was one, is lost and, in the end, the indecipherable text can only be read by the printer's boy. Rather than being able to inhabit the performative figure of

---

[32] "Printer's devil" was the common name for the boy in the printing office.
[33] Poe's "Never Bet the Devil Your Head" (1841) tells the tale of one Toby Dammit, who does not take the title's proverbial advice and loses his bet (T&S 619–634). Cf. Dern (2013).

the author embodied in such practices as handwriting, the author is ultimately erased by the conditions of print publication.

*   *   *

From Poe's attempts to redefine the spoken and written elocution of poetry, which led to his epithets of the jingle-man and the damned rhetorician, to his own performances as an orator and his depiction of the literary histrio, Poe's performative figures of the author emerge out of the inextricable interplay between the cultures of print and rhetoric. While Poe's hopes of attaining autonomy on the literary market were not to come true in many regards, the final figure of speech in which he stylizes this utopian dream could not be more fitting, given the rhetorical strategies with which he attempted to achieve it. Imagining the antebellum literary culture of print in terms of the culture of rhetoric, he speaks of the only proper stage for literary *histrios*, the world at large, as one eloquent dialogue that figures authors as equal speakers (CW 3: 86):

> At present the literary world is a species of anomalous Congress, in which the majority of the members are constrained to listen in silence while all the eloquence proceeds from a privileged few. In the new *régime*, the humblest will speak as often and as freely as the most exalted, and will be sure of receiving just that amount of attention which the intrinsic merit of their speeches may deserve.

Concluding Remarks

The problem of Poe cannot be fully understood, let alone solved, without rhetoric. As his theoretical, poetical, and performative figures of the author show, Poe's discourses were the products of a time that was fundamentally characterized by the rise of the author, the emergence of literature, and the dispersal of transatlantic rhetorical traditions in the antebellum culture of rhetoric. The theoretical figures of the transatlantic poet-critic in "The Letter to B—" and the paradoxical genius rhetorician in "The Philosophy of Composition" only become visible against the background of the romantic rupture of the relation between poetical and rhetorical discourse. Poe actively shaped the consequences of this rupture and at the same time was shaped by them. Similarly, Poe's poetical figure of the ratiocinative detective is a strategic and stylized answer to the question of how an author's constructive and analytical powers were to be related; his poetical figuration of the two aspects, shaped by an understanding of abductive inferences *avant la lettre*, not only reconnected rhetorical and poetical invention, but, via this process, led to the establishment of one of modernity's most influential popular genres: detective fiction. Finally, amid the political and medial tensions of the antebellum markets and cultures of rhetoric and print, Poe established performative figures of the author in his poems, lectures, and satires. As a damned rhetorician rather than a jingle-man, Poe elaborated and criticized elocutionist performance and staged the author as a transatlantic literary histrio. After all, an adequate understanding of Poe's authorship in theory, poetics, and performance is impossible if we do not reckon with the manifold traditions of the New Rhetoric – epistemological, neo-classical, belletristic, and elocutionary – that shaped the transatlantic culture of his time.

Naturally, a case study of one author can only constitute a first step towards developing the possibilities of rhetorical approaches to authorship more generally. However, both the theoretical rhetoric of authorship delineated in chapter one and the historical reconstruction, in chapter two, of the interrelations between author, poetry, and literature in the context of the transatlantic dispersal of rhetoric, invite applications beyond their use in this book.

The peculiar dialectic, so visible (and audible) in Poe's discourses, between the author as she or he who figures autonomously and she or he who is heteronomously figured, is captured by the concept of 'figures of the author.' This concept should be seen as central to a theoretical rhetoric of authorship. Its grounding in the rhetorical notions of figuration, persuasion, and situation offers a route for navigating between the Scylla and Charybdis of the contextualist dissolution and textualist reification of the author. Its integration of autonomous and heteronomous aspects is thus a crucial step along "the middle way of situated authorship" (S. Burke [1992] 2008: 194). Similarly, the differentiation of theoretical, poetical, and performative figures of the author is pertinent not only to Poe's work in antebellum America but to authorship in other epochs. The rhetorical triad of effects, whose history reaches from antiquity to the present, can still be used to define relations between the producers and the recipients of any discourse. The interpretation of the rhetorical arts as 'authemes' (*sensu* Love) offers a way of conceptualising the different stages of production in both rhetorical and poetical discourse. The strength of such an approach lies in its dual focus on persuasion and figuration, thus enabling the investigation of poetical texts as rhetorical actions rather than as aesthetically autonomous works, yet in a manner which sacrifices none of their literary specificity. The rhetorical approach thus encompasses at once the *persuasive strategies* and *figurative stylizations* that define literary and non-literary texts alike.

The age of Poe (J. G. Kennedy 2016) was a crucial period for the birth of literature. While, in some ways, this occurred at the cost of the dispersal of rhetoric, there were many transatlantic rhetorical connections between the United States and Great Britain, as evidenced by the antebellum culture of rhetoric. One aspect which has been little investigated is the importance of the transatlantic strands of belletristic and elocutionary rhetorics, which mirrored the larger cultural opposition between print and speech. As became apparent in the examples of Poe's medially variable performative figures of the author discussed in the final chapters, these traditions played a vital part in the (re)definition of American discourse in terms of performance. Begun by scholars whose work I discussed in chapter six, further research in this direction would enable us to rethink the question of Poe's singular representativeness for antebellum literary culture and to broaden the scope to other authors involved in the antebellum culture of rhetoric. Our understanding of poetry in particular would benefit from a literary history that contrasts J. S. Mill's definition with that of William Cullen Bryant, who defines poetry as "the eloquence of verse" (1884: 13). While there exists scholarship on individual authors and related issues (discussed in the final section of chapter two), it is high time for a synoptic study of the different ways in which antebellum authors negotiated the shift from 'rhetoric' to 'literature' in a transatlantic context.

The transatlantic situation of Poe's complex figurations of the relation of rhetorical and poetical discourse also raises the question of the cross-cultural history of rhetoric. Even within the rhetorical tradition, the opposition of figuration and persuasion is premised upon a dimension of cultural history which, while remarked upon, has not yet been thoroughly investigated. George A. Kennedy speaks of "the gap that widened in the eighteenth century between rhetoric as the study of tropes and figures and rhetoric as speech communication, between Europe and the English-speaking world" (2005: 364). In many ways, the antebellum culture of rhetoric was an earlier stage of today's rhetorical culture in the United States, where virtually every university has a rhetoric department. This vast American academic field still dwarfs European programmes. The historical reasons for this disparity are well worth investigating in more detail, especially at a time when the institutional basis of rhetoric in Europe is changing for the better, as evidenced by such events as the founding of the Rhetoric Society of Europe in 2013. Our changing institutional and political contexts make even more urgent the need for an awareness of the historical reasons for the cultural differences between American and European conceptions and practices of rhetoric.

If "those problems that at first blush appear utterly insoluble receive, in that very circumstance, as Edgar Poe remarked in his *The Murders in the Rue Morgue*, their smoothly fitting keys" (Peirce 1991: 264), then one such smoothly fitting key to the problem of Edgar Allan Poe is the theory and history of rhetoric: Poe is a figure of the momentous changes in the relation between rhetoric and literature in the antebellum era. At a time in which the two were being torn asunder, he was both a symptom of the rupture and a producer of it. Poe thus represents, in all meanings of the phrase, a rhetorical figure of the author, and as such he will continue to haunt us.

Works Cited

Abbott, Don P. 2006. "Splendor and Misery: Semiotic and the End of Rhetoric." *Rhetorica: A Journal of the History of Rhetoric* 24 (3): 303–323.

Abdoo, Sherlyn. 1990. "Poe's "Loss of Breath" and the Problem of Writing." In *The Elemental Passions of the Soul Poetics of the Elements in the Human Condition: Part 3*, edited by Anna-Teresa Tymieniecka, 581–594. Dordrecht: Springer Netherlands.

Abernethy, John. 1828. *Lectures on Anatomy, Surgery, and Pathology.* 2 vols. Boston: Benjamin Perkins.

Abrams, M. H. (1953) 1971. *The Mirror and the Lamp: Romantic Theory and the Critical Tradition.* London: Oxford University Press.

Abrams, M. H. 1984. "The Correspondent Breeze: A Romantic Metaphor." In *The Correspondent Breeze*, 25–43. New York: Norton.

Abrams, M. H., and Geoffrey G. Harpham, eds. 2009. *A Glossary of Literary Terms.* 9th ed. Boston: Wadsworth Cengage Learning.

Academicus. (1844) 2010. "For the Delaware State Journal." In *Poe in His Own Time: A Biographical Chronicle of His Life, Drawn from Recollections, Interviews, and Memoirs by Family, Friends, and Associates*, edited by Benjamin F. Fisher, 43–45. Iowa City: University of Iowa Press.

Adams, Amanda. 2014. *Performing Authorship in the Nineteenth-Century Transatlantic Lecture Tour.* Ashgate Series in Nineteenth-Century Transatlantic Studies. Burlington, VT: Ashgate.

Adams, John Quincy. 1810. *Lectures on Rhetoric and Oratory.* 2 vols. Cambridge, MA: Hilliard and Metcalf.

Alewyn, Richard. 1998. "Anatomie des Detektivromans." In *Der Kriminalroman: Poetik – Theorie – Geschichte*. Edited by Jochen Vogt, 52–72. München: Fink.

Algeo, John. 2009. "Grammar Wars: The United States." In *The Handbook of World Englishes*. Edited by Braj B. Kachru, Yamuna Kachru, and Cecil L. Nelson, 496–508. Malden, MA, Oxford: Blackwell.

Allen, Michael L. 1969. *Poe and the British Magazine Tradition.* New York: Oxford University Press.

Alterton, Margaret. (1925) 1965. *Origins of Poe's Critical Theory.* New York: Russell and Russell.

Anderson, Benedict. 2006. *Imagined Communities: Reflections on the Origin and Spread of Nationalism.* Rev. ed. London, New York: Verso.

Aristotle. 1995a. "Metaphysics." In *The Complete Works of Aristotle: The Revised Oxford Translation*. Edited by Jonathan Barnes, 1552–1728. Bollingen series 71:2. Princeton, NJ: Princeton University Press.

Aristotle. 1995b. "Poetics." In *The Complete Works of Aristotle: The Revised Oxford Translation*. Edited by Jonathan Barnes, 2316–2340. Bollingen series 71:2. Princeton, NJ: Princeton University Press.

Aristotle. 1995c. *Poetics.* Edited by Stephen Halliwell. The Loeb Classical Library 199. Cambridge, MA: Harvard University Press.

Aristotle. 1995d. "Rhetoric." In *The Complete Works of Aristotle: The Revised Oxford Translation*. Edited by Jonathan Barnes, 2152–2269. Bollingen series 71:2. Princeton, NJ: Princeton University Press.

Aristotle. 2007. *On Rhetoric: A Theory of Civic Discourse*. 2nd ed. Edited by George A. Kennedy. New York: Oxford University Press.
Aruffo, Christopher. 2011. "Reconsidering Poe's 'Rationale of Verse.'" *Poe Studies* 44: 69–86.
Assmann, Jan. (1992) 2007. *Das kulturelle Gedächtnis: Schrift, Erinnerung und politische Identität in frühen Hochkulturen*. 6th ed. München: Beck.
Assmann, Jan. 2008. "Communicative and Cultural Memory." In *Cultural Memory Studies: An International and Interdisciplinary Handbook*, edited by Astrid Erll and Ansgar Nünning, 109–118. Berlin, New York: de Gruyter.
Auerbach, Erich. 1984. "'Figura'." In *Scenes from the Drama of European Literature*, 11–78. Minneapolis, MN: University of Minnesota Press.
Austin, Gilbert. 1806. *Chironomia: Or, a Treatise on Rhetorical Delivery. Comprehending Many Precepts, Both Ancient and Modern, for the Proper Regulation of the Voice, the Countenance, and Gesture*. London: T. Cadell and W. Davies.
Austin, J. L. 1973. *How to do Things with Words*. New York: Oxford University Press.
Barthes, Roland. (1968) 1994. "La mort de l'auteur." In *Œuvres complètes: Tome II 1966 – 1973*, 491–95. Paris: Éditions du Seuil.
Barthes, Roland. (1968) 1977. "The Death of the Author." In *Image, Music, Text*. Edited by Stephen Heath, 142–48. London: Fontana.
Barthes, Roland. 1970. "L'ancienne rhétorique: Aide-mémoire." *Communications* 16: 172–223.
Barthes, Roland. (1970) 1988. "The Old Rhetoric: an Aide-Memoire." In *The Semiotic Challenge*, 11–94. New York: Hill and Wang.
Bate, Jonathan. 1990. "Edgar Allan Poe: A Debt Repaid." In *The Coleridge Connection: Essays for Thomas McFarland*. Edited by Richard Gravil and Molly Lefebure, 254–270. Basingstoke: Macmillan.
Bate, Walter Jackson. 1945. "The Sympathetic Imagination in Eighteenth-Century English Criticism." *ELH* 12 (2): 144–164.
Baudelaire, Charles. (1857) 1969. "New Notes on Edgar Poe." In *The Recognition of Edgar Allan Poe: Selected Criticism since 1829*. Edited by Eric W. Carlson, 43–60. Ann Arbor, MI: University of Michigan Press.
Baumgarten, Alexander Gottlieb. 2007. *Ästhetik: Lateinisch-deutsch*. Edited by Dagmar Mirbach. Hamburg: Meiner.
Baumlin, James S. 2001. "Êthos." In *Encyclopedia of Rhetoric*. Edited by Thomas O. Sloane, 263–277. Oxford, New York: Oxford University Press.
Bender, John B., and David E. Wellbery. 1990. *The Ends of Rhetoric: History, Theory, Practice*. Stanford: Stanford University Press.
Benesch, Klaus. 2002. *Romantic Cyborgs: Authorship and Technology in the American Renaissance*. Amherst: University of Massachusetts Press.
Bennett, Andrew. 2005. *The Author*. The New Critical Idiom. London: Routledge.
Berensmeyer, Ingo, Gert Buelens, and Marysa Demoor. 2012a. "Authorship as Cultural Performance: New Perspectives in Authorship Studies." In "Authorship as Cultural Performance." Edited by Ingo Berensmeyer, Gert Buelens, and Marysa Demoor. Special issue, *Zeitschrift für Anglistik und Amerikanistik* 60 (1): 5–29.
Berensmeyer, Ingo, Gert Buelens, and Marysa Demoor, eds. 2012b. "Authorship as Cultural Performance." Special issue, *Zeitschrift für Anglistik und Amerikanistik* 60, no. 1.
Bergman, Mats. 2007. "The Secret of Rendering Signs Effective: The Import of C. S. Peirce's Semiotic Rhetoric." *The Public Journal of Semiotics* 2 (1): 2–11.

Bergman, Mats. 2010. "Productive Signs: Improving the Prospects of Peirce's Rhetoric." *Signs* 3: 54–68.
Berlin, James A. 1984. *Writing Instruction in Nineteenth-Century American Colleges*. Carbondale: Southern Illinois University Press.
Berlin, James A. 1996. *Rhetorics, Poetics, and Cultures: Refiguring College English Studies*. Urbana: National Council of Teachers of English.
Berndt, Frauke. 2002. "Die Erfindung des Genies: F. G. Klopstocks rhetorische Konstruktion des Au(c)tors im Vorfeld der Autonomieästhetik." In *Autorschaft: Positionen und Revisionen*, edited by Heinrich Detering, 24–43. Germanistische Symposien-Berichtsbände 24. Stuttgart: Metzler.
Berndt, Frauke. 2005. "Topik-Forschung." In *Gedächtniskonzepte der Literaturwissenschaft: Theoretische Grundlegung und Anwendungsperspektiven*. Edited by Astrid Erll and Ansgar Nünning, 31–52. Berlin, New York: de Gruyter.
Bernstein, Richard J. (1971) 1999. *Praxis and Action: Contemporary Philosophies of Human Activity*. Philadelphia: University of Pennsylvania Press.
Bevilacqua, Vincent M. 1968. "Philosophical Influences in the Development of English Rhetorical Theory: 1748 to 1783." *Proceedings of the Leeds Philosophical and Literary Society* 12: 191–215.
Biagioli, Mario, Peter Jaszi, and Martha Woodmansee. 2011. *Making and Unmaking Intellectual Property: Creative Production in Legal and Cultural Perspective*. Chicago: University of Chicago Press.
Bialostosky, Don H. 1992. *Wordsworth, Dialogics, and the Practice of Criticism*. Cambridge: Cambridge University Press.
Bialostosky, Don H., and Lawrence D. Needham, eds. 1995. *Rhetorical Traditions and British Romantic Literature*. Bloomington: Indiana University Press.
Bickenbach, Matthias. 2008. "Autorpoetik." In *Metzler-Lexikon Literatur- und Kulturtheorie*. Edited by Ansgar Nünning. 4., aktualisierte und erw. Aufl., 44–45. Stuttgart: Metzler.
Bielfeld, Jakob F., Freiherr von. 1770. *Letters*. Edited by William Hooper. 3. London: Robinson and Roberts.
Bitzer, Lloyd F. 1968. "The Rhetorical Situation." *Philosophy and Rhetoric* 1 (1): 1–15.
Blight, David W. 1998. "Editor's Introduction: The Peculiar Dialogue Between Caleb Bingham and Frederick Douglass." In *The Columbian Orator*. Edited by David W. Blight, xiii–xxvii: New York University Press.
Bloom, Harold. (1973) 1997. *The Anxiety of Influence: A Theory of Poetry*. 2nd ed. New York: Oxford University Press.
Bloomer, Martin W. 2001. "Topics." In *Encyclopedia of Rhetoric*. Edited by Thomas O. Sloane, 780–782. Oxford, New York: Oxford University Press.
Bogel, Fredric V. 2013. *New Formalist Criticism: Theory and Practice*. Basingstoke: Palgrave Macmillan.
Bolter, J. D., and Richard Grusin. 1999. *Remediation: Understanding New Media*. Cambridge, Mass: MIT Press.
Bonaparte, Marie. [1933] 1971. *The Life and Works of Edgar Allan Poe: A Psycho-Analytic Interpretation*. New York: Humanities Press.
Booth, Wayne C. 1963. "The Rhetorical Stance." *College Composition and Communication* 14 (3): 139–145.
Booth, Wayne C. 1983. *The Rhetoric of Fiction*. 2nd ed. Chicago: University of Chicago Press.

Booth, Wayne C. 2004. *The Rhetoric of RHETORIC: The Quest for Effective Communication.* Blackwell manifestos. Malden, MA: Blackwell.
Bristed, Charles Astor. 1845. "The Scotch School of Philosophy and Criticism." In *The American Review: A Whig Journal of Politics, Literature, Art, and Science,* 2: 386–397.
Bronson, Cotesworth P. 1845. *Elocution, or Mental and Vocal Philosophy.* Louisville: Morton and Griswold.
Brown, Brenda G. 1996. "Elocution." In *Encyclopedia of Rhetoric and Composition: Communication from Ancient Times to the Information Age,* edited by Theresa Enos, 211–214. New York: Garland.
Brown, Goold. 1833. *Institutes of English Grammar.* Revised. New York: Samuel Wood and Sons.
Brown, Goold. 1851. *The Grammar of English Grammars.* London: Delf and Trübner.
Bryant, William Cullen. 1884. "Lectures on Poetry." In *Prose Writings of William Cullen Bryant.* Edited by Parke Godwin, 3–44 1. New York: Appleton.
Bühler, Karl. 2011. *Theory of Language: The Representational Function of Language.* Edited by Achim Eschbach and Donald F. Goodwin. Amsterdam: John Benjamins.
Buchanan, Lindal. 2005. *Regendering Delivery: The Fifth Canon and Antebellum Women Rhetors.* Carbondale: Southern Illinois University Press.
Burke, Kenneth. 1961. "The Principle of Composition." *Poetry* XCIX: 46–53.
Burke, Kenneth. 1968. "Lexicon Rhetoricae." In *Counter-Statement,* 123–183. Berkeley: University of California Press.
Burke, Kenneth. 1969a. *A Grammar of Motives.* Berkeley: University of California Press.
Burke, Kenneth. 1969b. *A Rhetoric of Motives.* Berkeley: University of California Press.
Burke, Kenneth. 1973a. "Poetics in Particular, Language in General." In *Language as Symbolic Action: Essays on Life, Literature, and Method,* 25–43. Berkeley: University of California Press.
Burke, Kenneth. 1973b. "Terministic Screens." In *Language as Symbolic Action: Essays on Life, Literature, and Method,* 44–62. Berkeley: University of California Press.
Burke, Kenneth. 1973c. "The Philosophy of Literary Form." In *The Philosophy of Literary Form,* 1–137. New York: University of California Press.
Burke, Kenneth. 1978. "Methodological Repression And/or Strategies of Containment." *Critical Inquiry* 5 (2): 401–416.
Burke, Seán, ed. 1995. *Authorship from Plato to the Postmodern.* Edinburgh: Edinburgh University Press.
Burke, Seán. (1992) 2008. *The Death and Return of the Author: Criticism and Subjectivity in Barthes, Foucault and Derrida.* 3rd ed. Edinburgh: Edinburgh University Press.
Burwick, Frederick. 1996. *Poetic Madness and the Romantic Imagination.* University Park, PA: Pennsylvania State University Press.
Butler, Samuel. 1846. *Hudibras: In Three Parts.* Hartford: S. Andrus and Son.
Campbell, George. (1776) 1988. *The Philosophy of Rhetoric.* Edited by Lloyd F. Bitzer. Delmar, NY: Scholars' Facsimiles and Reprints.
Campe, Rüdiger. 2006. "Der Effekt der Form: Baumgartens Ästhetik am Rande der Metaphysik." In *Literatur als Philosophie, Philosophie als Literatur,* edited by Eva Horn, Bettine Menke, and Christoph Menke, 17–34. München: Wilhelm Fink.
Cantalupo, Barbara. 2014. *Poe and the Visual Arts.* University Park, PA: Pennsylvania State University Press.
Carlson, Eric W., ed. 1996. *A Companion to Poe Studies.* Westport, CT: Greenwood Press.

Carlson, Eric W. 2002. "Poe's Ten-Year Frogpondian War." *Edgar Allan Poe Review* 3 (2): 37–51.
Carton, Evan. 1985. *The Rhetoric of American Romance: Dialectic and Identity in Emerson, and Dickinson, Poe, and Hawthorne.* Baltimore: Johns Hopkins University Press.
Chai, Leon. 1987. *The Romantic Foundations of the American Renaissance.* Ithaca, NY: Cornell University Press.
Chartier, Roger. 1994. *The Order of Books: Readers, Authors, and Libraries in Europe between the Fourteenth and Eighteenth Centuries.* Stanford: Stanford University Press.
Charvat, William. 1936. *The Origins of American Critical Thought, 1810–1835.* Philadelphia, PA: University of Pennsylvania Press.
Charvat, William. 1968. *The Profession of Authorship in America 1800–1870: The Papers of William Charvat.* Edited by Matthew J. Bruccoli. Ohio State University Press.
Chatman, Seymour. 1978. *Story and Discourse: Narrative Structure in Fiction and Film.* Ithaca, NY: Cornell University Press.
Cawelti, John G. 1976. *Adventure, Mystery, and Romance: Formula Stories as Art and Popular Culture.* Chicago: University of Chicago Press.
Cicero, Marcus Tullius. 1942. *De oratore.* Edited by E. W. Sutton and H. Rackham. The Loeb Classical Library 348. Cambridge, MA: Harvard University Press.
Clark, Gregory, and S. M. Halloran. 1993. *Oratorical Culture in Nineteenth-Century America: Transformations in the Theory and Practice of Rhetoric.* Carbondale, IL: Southern Illinois University Press.
Clemens, Justin. 2003. *The Romanticism of Contemporary Theory: Institutions, Aesthetics, Nihilism.* Aldershot: Ashgate.
Cohen, Lara L. 2012. *The Fabrication of American Literature: Fraudulent and Antebellum Print Culture.* Philadelphia, PA: University of Pennsylvania Press.
Colapietro, Vincent. 2007. "Charles S. Peirce's Rhetorical Turn." *Transactions of the Charles S. Peirce Society* 43 (1): 16–52.
Coleridge, Samuel Taylor. (1817) 1983. *Biographia literaria, or, Biographical sketches of my literary life and opinions.* Edited by James Engell and Walter J. Bate. The Collected Works of Samuel Taylor Coleridge 7. Princeton, NJ: Princeton University Press.
Coleridge, Samuel Taylor. 1821. "Selection from Mr Coleridge's Literary Correspondence, No. I." *Blackwood's Edinburgh Magazine* 10 (56): 243–262.
Collins, Philip. 1975. "Introduction." In Charles Dickens, *The Public Readings*, edited by Philip Collins, xvii–lxix. Oxford: Clarendon Press.
Combe, George. 1839. *Lectures on Phrenology.* London: Simpkin, Marshall and Co.
Comstock, Andrew. 1841. *A System of Elocution.* Philadelphia.
Corbett, Edward P. J., and Robert J. Connors. 1999. *Classical Rhetoric for the Modern Student.* 4th ed. New York: Oxford University Press.
Court, Franklin E. 2001. *The Scottish Connection: The Rise of English Literary Study in Early America.* Syracuse, NY: Syracuse University Press.
Crawford, Robert, ed. (1996) 2008. *The Scottish Invention of English Literature.* Cambridge: Cambridge University Press.
Culler, Jonathan D. 1978. "On Trope and Persuasion." *New Literary History* 9 (3): 607–618.
Curtius, Ernst R. (1953) 2013. *European Literature and the Latin Middle Ages.* Princeton, NJ: Princeton University Press.

Daalder, Saskia, and Andreas Musolff. 2011. "Foundations of Pragmatics in Functional Linguistics." In *Foundations of Pragmatics*. Edited by Wolfram Bublitz and Neal R. Norrick, 229–260. Handbook of Pragmatics 1. Berlin, Boston: De Gruyter Mouton.

Daniel, Robert. 1971. "Poe's Detective God." In *Twentieth-Century Interpretations of Poe's Tales*. Edited by William L. Howarth. Englewood Cliffs, NJ: Prentice-Hall: 45–54.

Davidson, Edward H. 1973. *Poe: A Critical Study*. Cambridge, MA: Belknap Press of Harvard University Press.

Dayan, Colin (Joan). 1987. *Fables of Mind: An Inquiry into Poe's Fiction*. New York: Oxford University Press.

Dayan, Colin (Joan). 1991. "Poe's Women: A Feminist Poe." *Poe Studies* 24 (1–2): 1–12.

de Man, Paul. 1979. *Allegories of Reading: Figural Language in Rousseau, Nietzsche, Rilke and Proust*. New Haven, London: Yale University Press.

De Quincey, Thomas. 1828. "Review of Elements of Rhetoric, by Richard Whately." *Blackwood's Edinburgh Magazine* XXIV: 885–908.

De Quincey, Thomas. 1862. "Rhetoric." In *Style and Rhetoric and Other Papers*, 21–78. Edinburgh: Adam and Charles Black.

Den Boer, Pim. 2008. "Loci memoriae—Lieux de mémoire." In *Cultural Memory Studies: An International and Interdisciplinary Handboo*k, edited by Astrid Erll and Ansgar Nünning, 19–25. Berlin, New York: de Gruyter.

Dern, John A. 2001. "Poe's Public Speakers: Rhetorical Strategies in 'The Tell-Tale Heart' and 'The Cask of Amontillado'." *Edgar Allan Poe Review* 2 (2): 53–70.

Dern, John A. 2013. "A Sense of Stile: Rhetoric in Edgar Allan Poe's 'Never Bet the Devil Your Head'." *Edgar Allan Poe Review* 14 (2): 163–177.

Detering, Heinrich. 2000. "Wahnsinn und Methode: Poe, Benn und die Dialektik der aufgeklärten Poetik." *Merkur. Deutsche Zeitschrift für europäisches Denken* 54: 300–311.

Detering, Heinrich, ed. 2002. *Autorschaft: Positionen und Revisionen*. Stuttgart: Metzler.

Dickens, Charles. 1975. *The Public Readings*. Edited by Philip Collins. Oxford: Clarendon Press.

Diddler, Jeremy. 1829. "A Lecture on Lecturing." *New York Enquirer*, March 11, 2.

Dockhorn, Klaus. 1995. "Wordsworth and the Rhetorical Tradition in England." In *Rhetorical Traditions and British Romantic Literature*. Edited by Don H. Bialostosky and Lawrence D. Needham, 265–280. Bloomington: Indiana University Press.

Donovan, Stephen, Danuta Fjellestad, and Rolf Lundén, eds. 2008. *Authority Matters: Rethinking the Theory and Practice of Authorship*. Amsterdam, New York: Rodopi.

Dowling, David O. 2009. *Capital Letters: Authorship in the Antebellum Literary Market*. Iowa City, IA: University of Iowa Press.

Doyle, Arthur Conan. 2009. "The Cardboard Box." In *The Memoirs of Sherlock Holmes*, edited by Owen D. Edwards and Christopher Roden, 30–52. Oxford, New York: Oxford University Press.

Dryden, John. (1667) 1956. "Annus Mirabilis." In *The Works of John Dryden*, edited by Edward N. Hooker and H. T. Swedenberg, 48–105. Berkeley: University of California Press.

Dubois, Jacques, and et al. 1981. *A General Rhetoric*. Baltimore: Johns Hopkins University Press.

Dumas, D. G. 1966. "Things as They Were: The Original Ending of Caleb Williams." *Studies in English Literature 1500–1900* 6: 575–597.

Dyck, Joachim. 1991. *Ticht-Kunst: Deutsche Barockpoetik und rhetorische Tradition*. 3rd ed. Tübingen: Niemeyer.

Eagleton, Terry. 1981. "A Small History of Rhetoric." In *Walter Benjamin, or, Towards a revolutionary criticism*. London: Verso.
Eagleton, Terry. 1990. *The Ideology of the Aesthetic*. Oxford: Blackwell.
Eagleton, Terry. 2008. *Literary Theory: An Introduction*. Anniversary edition. Minneapolis: University of Minnesota Press.
Eagleton, Terry. 2008. *How to Read a Poem*. 5th ed. Malden, MA: Blackwell.
"Earls Grey and Spencer." 1846. *Edinburgh Review* 83 (168): 240–273.
Eco, Umberto, and Thomas A. Sebeok, eds. 1983. *The Sign of Three: Dupin, Holmes, Peirce*. Bloomington: Indiana University Press.
Eco, Umberto. 1983. "Horns, Hooves, Insteps: Some Hypotheses on Three Types of Abduction." In *The Sign of Three: Dupin, Holmes, Peirce*, edited by Umberto Eco and Thomas A. Sebeok, 198–220. Bloomington: Indiana University Press.
"Editorial Notes: American Literature and Reprints." 1856. *Putnam's Monthly Magazine* 8: 654–659.
Eliot, T. S. 1949. "From Poe to Valéry." *Hudson Review* 2 (3): 327–342.
Elmer, Jonathan. 1996. *Reading at the Social Limit: Affect, Mass Culture, and Edgar Allan Poe*. Stanford: Stanford University Press.
Elmer, Jonathan. 2003. "Review of Poe and the Printed Word, by Kevin J. Hayes." *Modern Philology* 101 (1): 129–132.
Emerson, Ralph Waldo. 2001. "New England: Genius, Manners, and Customs." In *The Later Lectures of Ralph Waldo Emerson, 1843–1871*, edited by Ronald A. Bosco and Joel Myerson. 2 vols, 39–56 1. Athens: University of Georgia Press.
Engel, William E. 2012. *Early Modern Poetics in Melville and Poe: Memory, Melancholy, and the Emblematic Tradition*. Aldershot: Ashgate.
Engell, James. 1989. *Forming the Critical Mind: Dryden to Coleridge*. Cambridge, MA: Harvard University Press.
Engell, James. 1995. "The New Rhetoric and Romantic Poetics." In *Rhetorical Traditions and British Romantic Literature*. Edited by Don H. Bialostosky and Lawrence D. Needham, 217–232. Bloomington: Indiana University Press.
Engell, James, and Walter Jackson Bate. 1984. "Introduction." In *Biographia Literaria, Or, Biographical Sketches of My Literary Life and Opinions*, edited by James Engell and Walter Jackson Bate. 2 vols, xli–cxxvi. The Collected Works of Samuel Taylor Coleridge 7. Princeton, NJ: Princeton University Press.
Enos, Richard L., and Jeanne Fahnestock. 2001. "Arrangement." In *Encyclopedia of Rhetoric*. Edited by Thomas O. Sloane, 40–50. Oxford, New York: Oxford University Press.
Eschbach, Achim. 2011. "Karl Bühler: Sematologist." In *Theory of Language: The Representational Function of Language*. Edited by Achim Eschbach and Donald F. Goodwin, xlix–lxxx. Amsterdam: John Benjamins.
Esplin, Emron. 2016. *Borges's Poe: The Influence and Reinvention of Edgar Allan Poe in Spanish America*. Athens: University of Georgia Press.
Esplin, Emron, and Margarida Vale de Gato. 2014. *Translated Poe*. Bethlehem, PA: Lehigh University Press.
Fagin, Nathan Bryllion. 1949. *The Histrionic Mr. Poe*. Baltimore: Johns Hopkins University Press.
Fahnestock, Jeanne. 1996. "Arrangement." In *Encyclopedia of Rhetoric and Composition: Communication From Ancient Times to the Information Age*. Edited by Theresa Enos, 32–36. New York: Garland.

Fann, K. T. 1970. *Peirce's Theory of Abduction*. The Hague: Martinus Nijhoff.
Farrar, Julie M. 1996. "Proof." In *Encyclopedia of Rhetoric and Composition: Communication From Ancient Times to the Information Age*. Edited by Theresa Enos, 564–565. New York: Garland.
Fauvel-Gouraud, Francis. 1845. *Phreno-Mnemotechny: Or, The Art of Memory*. New York: Wiley and Putnam.
Felman, Shoshana. 1988. "On Reading Poetry: Reflections on the Limits and Possibilities of Psychoanalytical Approaches." In *The Purloined Poe: Lacan, Derrida and Psychoanalytic Reading*. Edited by John P. Muller and William J. Richardson, 133–156. Baltimore: Johns Hopkins University Press.
Filippakopoulou, Maria. 2015. *Transatlantic Poe: Eliot, Williams and Huxley, Readers of the French Poe*. Frankfurt am Main: Peter Lang.
Fisher, Benjamin F., ed. 2010. *Poe in His Own Time: A Biographical Chronicle of his Life, Drawn from Recollections, Interviews, and Memoirs by Family, Friends, and Associates*. Iowa City: University of Iowa Press.
Fisher, John H. 2001. "British and American, Continuity and Divergence." In *The Cambridge History of the English Language: English in North America*. Edited by John Algeo, 59–85 6. Cambridge: Cambridge University Press.
Fliegelman, Jay. 1993. *Declaring Independence: Jefferson, Natural Language and the Culture of Performance*. Stanford: Stanford University Press.
Flood, Gavin D. 1996. *An Introduction to Hinduism*. New York: Cambridge University Press.
Foucault, Michel. 1984. "What Is an Author?" In *The Foucault Reader*. Edited by Paul Rabinow, 101–120. New York: Pantheon.
"Fragment of an Essay on Eloquence." 1820. *Blackwood's Edinburgh Magazine* 7: 644–647.
Frye, Northrop. (1957) 2000. *Anatomy of Criticism: Four Essays*. Princeton, NJ: Princeton University Press.
Full, Patrick. 2007. *Der Abgesang der Imagination: Edgar Allan Poes Neubestimmung der menschlichen Kreativität*. Trier: Wissenschaftlicher Verlag Trier.
Gadamer, Hans-Georg. 1993. "Rhetorik, Hermeneutik und Ideologiekritik: Metakritische Erörterungen zu Wahrheit und Methode." In *Hermeneutik: Wahrheit und Methode. Ergänzungen. Register*. 2nd ed, 232–250. Gesammelte Werke 2. Tübingen: Mohr.
Gaillet, Lynee L., and Winifred B. Horner, eds. 2010. *The Present State of Scholarship in the History of Rhetoric: A Twenty-First Century Guide*. 3rd ed. Columbia: University of Missouri Press.
Genette, Gérard. 1982. "Rhetoric Restrained." In *Figures of Literary Discourse*, 103–126. New York: Columbia University Press.
Genette, Gérard. 1992. *The Architext: An Introduction*. Berkeley: University of California Press.
Genette, Gérard. 1997. *Paratexts: Thresholds of Interpretation*. Edited by Jane E. Lewin. Cambridge: Cambridge University Press.
Gerard, Alexander. 1774. *An Essay on Genius*. London: Strahan, Cadell, and Creech.
Glindemann, Barbara. 2001. *Creative Writing in England, den USA und Deutschland*. Frankfurt am Main: Peter Lang.
Godwin, William. 2009. *Caleb Williams*. Edited by Pamela Clemit. Oxford: Oxford University Press.
"Godwin's Caleb Williams: From the London Literary Gazette." 1833. *Museum of Foreign Literature, Science and Art* 22: 403–405.

Gordon, Adam. 2012. "'A Condition to Be Criticized': Edgar Allan Poe and the Vocation of Antebellum Criticism." *Arizona Quarterly* 68 (2): 1–31.
Gorgias of Leontinoi. 2001. "Encomium of Helen." In *The Norton Anthology of Theory and Criticism*, edited by Vincent B. Leitch, 29–33. New York: Norton.
Graff, Gerald. 2007. *Professing Literature: An Institutional History*. 20th ed. Chicago: University of Chicago Press.
Gray, Floyd. 1999. "The Essay as Criticism." In *The Renaissance*. Edited by George A. Kennedy and Glyn P. Norton, 271–277. The Cambridge History of Literary Criticism 3. Cambridge: Cambridge University Press.
Greenblatt, Stephen. 1980. *Renaissance Self-Fashioning: From More to Shakespeare*. Chicago: University of Chicago Press.
Grimstad, Paul. 2005. "C. Auguste Dupin and Charles S. Peirce: An Abductive Affinity." *Edgar Allan Poe Review* 6 (2): 22–30.
Grimstad, Paul. 2013. *Experience and Experimental Writing: Literary Pragmatism from Emerson to the Jameses*. Oxford: Oxford University Press.
Gross, Daniel M. 2006. *The Secret History of Emotion: From Aristotle's Rhetoric to Modern Brain Science*. Chicago: University of Chicago Press.
Guttzeit, Gero. 2010. "'Both In and Out of his Time': Edgar Allan Poe's Model of Authorship." Unpubl. M. A. Thesis, Justus Liebig University Gießen.
Guttzeit, Gero. 2012. "Cultures of Conviction: Review of *The Rhetorical Emergence of Culture*, edited by Felix Girke and Christian Meyer" *KULT_online* (33). <http://kult-online.uni-giessen.de/archiv/2012/ausgabe33/rezensionen/cultures-of-conviction> [last accessed 27 November 2016].
Guttzeit, Gero. 2014a. "Authorship in Literary Theory and Fiction: Writing on Writers." In *Key Concepts and New Topics in English and American Studies: Schlüsselkonzepte und neue Themen in der Anglistik und Amerikanistik*. Edited by Ansgar Nünning and Elizabeth Kovach, 115–134. Trier: Wissenschaftlicher Verlag Trier.
Guttzeit, Gero. 2014b. "From Hearing to Overhearing? Eloquence and Poetry, 1776–1833." *Anglistentag 2013 Konstanz. Proceedings of the Conference of the German Association of University Teachers of English* 35, 261–270. Trier: Wissenschaftlicher Verlag Trier.
Guttzeit, Gero. 2014c. "Writing Backwards? Autorpoetik bei Poe und Godwin." In *Theorien und Praktiken der Autorschaft*. Edited by Marcus Willand and Matthias Schaffrick, 377–402. Berlin: de Gruyter.
Guttzeit, Gero. 2015a. "American Romanticisms: Edgar Allan Poe and Herman Melville." In *A History of American Poetry: Contexts – Developments – Readings*, edited by Oliver Scheiding, René Dietrich, and Clemens Spahr, 79–94. Trier: Wissenschaftlicher Verlag Trier.
Guttzeit, Gero. 2015b. "Fearful Fantasy: Figurations of the Oedipus Myth in Scorsese's *Shutter Island* (2010)." In *Fear and Fantasy in a Global World*, edited by Susana Araújo, Marta P. Pinto, and Sandra Bettencourt, 143–62. Amsterdam: Brill.
Guttzeit, Gero. 2016. "Figur oder Kommunikation? Überlegungen zu Kulturen der Rhetorik zwischen Kontinentaleuropa und der englischsprachigen Welt." In *Rhetorik und Kulturen*, edited by Michel Lefèvre, Katharina Mucha-Tummuseit, and Rainer Hünecke, 55–70. Frankfurt am Main: Peter Lang.
Habermas, Jürgen. 1998. "Toward a Critique of the Theory of Meaning." In *On the Pragmatics of Communication*, 277–306. Cambridge, MA: MIT Press.
Halliwell, Stephen. 1998. *Aristotle's Poetics*. Chicago: University of Chicago Press.

Hammerschmidt, Sören, Gero Guttzeit, and Gert Buelens, eds. 2015. "Between Geniuses and Brain-Suckers: Problematic Professionalism in Eighteenth-Century Authorship." Special issue, Authorship 4.1. <http://www.authorship.ugent.be/issue/view/248>. [last accessed 27 November 2016].
Harding, Phillip. 2000. "Demosthenes in the Underworld: A Chapter in the *Nachleben* of a *rhētōr*." In *Demosthenes: Statesman and Orator*. Edited by Ian Worthington, 246–271. London: Routledge.
Harrowitz, Nancy. 1983. "The Body of the Dectective Model: Charles S. Peirce and Edgar Allan Poe." In *The Sign of Three: Dupin, Holmes, Peirce*. Edited by Umberto Eco and Thomas A. Sebeok. Bloomington: Indiana University Press.
Hartley, Daniel. 2016. *The Politics of Style: Towards a Marxist Poetics*. Amsterdam: Brill.
Hartmann, Jonathan H. 2008. *The Marketing of Edgar Allan Poe*. New York: Routledge.
Hayes, Kevin J. 2000. *Poe and the Printed Word*. Cambridge: Cambridge University Press.
Hayes, Kevin J. 2012. "Preface." In *Edgar Allan Poe in Context*. Edited by Kevin J. Hayes, xv–xvii. Cambridge: Cambridge University Press.
Higginson, Thomas W. 1888. *Short Studies of American Authors*. Enlarged ed. Boston: Lee and Shepard.
Hoffmann, Daniel. 1978. *Poe Poe Poe Poe Poe Poe Poe*. New York: Avon Books.
Hohmann, Hanns. 2001. "Stasis." In *Encyclopedia of Rhetoric*. Edited by Thomas O. Sloane, 741–45. Oxford, New York: Oxford University Press.
Horace. (1926) 1945. *Satires, Epistles and Ars Poetica*. Edited by H. R. Fairclough. The Loeb Classical Library. Cambridge, MA: Harvard University.
Horace. 1836. *Works*. Edited by C. Smart. 2 vols. Philadelphia: Joseph Whetham.
Horn, Mirjam. 2010. "Authorship as a Key Issue in Literary Theory: Concepts and Reconceptualisations." In *Schlüsselthemen der Anglistik und Amerikanistik: Key Topics in English and American Studies*, edited by Sonja Altnöder, Wolfgang Hallet, and Ansgar Nünning, 321–344. Trier: Wissenschaftlicher Verlag Trier.
Horn, Mirjam. 2015. *Postmodern Plagiarisms: Cultural Agenda and Aesthetic Strategies of Appropriation in US-American Literature (1970–2010)*. Berlin, Boston: De Gruyter Mouton.
Horner, Winifred Bryan. 1988. *Rhetoric in the Classical Tradition*. New York: St. Martin's Press.
Horner, Winifred Bryan. 1993a. "Introduction." In *Rhetorical Memory and Delivery: Classical Concepts for Contemporary Composition and Communication*. Edited by John F. Reynolds, ix–xii. Hillsdale, NJ: Erlbaum.
Horner, Winifred Bryan. 1993b. *Nineteenth-Century Scottish Rhetoric: The American Connection*. Carbondale: Southern Illinois University Press.
Horstmann, Ulrich. 1975. *Ansätze zu einer technomorphen Theorie der Dichtung bei Edgar Allan Poe*. Frankfurt am Main: Peter Lang.
Höss, Tilman. 2003. *Poe, James, Hitchcock: Die Rationalisierung der Kunst*. Heidelberg: Winter.
Hovey, Kenneth Alan. 1987. "Critical Provincialism: Poe's Poetic Principle in Antebellum Context." *American Quarterly* 39 (3): 341–354.
Howard, Leon. 1972. "Poe's Eureka: The Detective Story That Failed." *The Mystery and Detection Annual*, 1–13.
Howell, Wilbur Samuel. 1971. *Eighteenth-Century British Logic and Rhetoric*. Princeton, NJ: Princeton University Press.

Howells, William Dean. 1894. "My First Visit to New England." *Harper's New Monthly Magazine* 89 (531): 441–452.
Hubbell, Jay B. 1972. "Edgar Allan Poe." In *Eight American Authors: A Review of Research and Criticism*, edited by James Woodress, 3–36. Revised ed. New York: Norton.
Hungerford, Edward. (1930) 1993. "Poe and Phrenology." In *On Poe*. Edited by Louis J. Budd and Edwin H. Cady, 1–23. Durham, NC: Duke University Press.
Hurh, Paul. 2012. "'The Creative and the Resolvent': The Origins of Poe's Analytical Method." *Nineteenth-Century Literature* 66 (4): 466–493.
Hurh, Paul. 2015. *American Terror: The Feeling of Thinking in Edwards, Poe, and Melville*. Stanford: Stanford University Press.
Huss, Bernhard. 2013. "Demosthenes." In *Historische Gestalten der Antike: Rezeption in Literatur, Kunst und Musik*. Edited by Peter v. Möllendorff, Annette Simonis, and Linda Simonis, 351–360. Stuttgart, Weimar: Metzler.
Huxley, Aldous. (1930) 1969. "Vulgarity in Literature." In *The Recognition of Edgar Allan Poe: Selected Criticism Since 1829*, edited by Eric W. Carlson, 160–166. Ann Arbor: University of Michigan Press.
Irwin, John T. 1992. "Reading Poe's Mind: Politics, Mathematics, and the Association of Ideas in 'The Murders in the Rue Morgue'." *American Literary History* 4 (2): 187–206.
Irwin, John T. 1994. *The Mystery to a Solution*. Baltimore: Johns Hopkins University Press.
Iser, Wolfgang. 1980. *The Act of Reading: A Theory of Aesthetic Response*. Baltimore: Johns Hopkins University Press.
Iser, Wolfgang. 1993. *The Fictive and the Imaginary: Charting Literary Anthropology*. Baltimore: Johns Hopkins University Press.
Jacewicz, Ewa, Robert A. Fox, and Joseph Salmons. 2007. "Vowel Duration in Three American English Dialects." *American Speech* 82 (4): 367–385.
Jackson, Leon. 2008. *The Business of Letters: Authorial Economies in Antebellum America*. Stanford: Stanford University Press.
Jackson, Leon. 2010. "'The Italics are Mine': Edgar Allan Poe and the Semiotics of Print." In *Illuminating Letters: Typography and Literary Interpretation*. Edited by Paul C. Gutjahr and Megan L. Benton, 139–162. Amherst: University of Massachusetts Press.
Jacobs, Robert D. 1958. "Rhetoric in Southern Writing: Poe." *Georgia Review* 12: 76–79.
Jacobs, Robert D. 1969. *Poe: Journalist and Critic*. Baton Rouge: Louisiana State University Press.
Jakobson, Roman. 1981. "Language in Operation." In *Selected Writings III: Poetry of Grammar and Grammar of Poetry*. Edited by Stephen Rudy, 7–17. The Hague: Mouton.
Jakobson, Roman. 1987a. "Linguistics and Poetics." In *Language in Literature*. Edited by Krystyna Pomorska and Stephen Rudy. 2, 62–94. Cambridge, MA: Belknap Press of Harvard University Press.
Jakobson, Roman. 1987b. "Two Aspects of Language and Two Types of Aphasic Disturbances." In *Language in Literature*. Edited by Krystyna Pomorska and Stephen Rudy. 2, 95–114. Cambridge, MA: Belknap Press of Harvard University Press.
James, Henry. 1969. "Comments." In *The Recognition of Edgar Allan Poe: Selected Criticism since 1829*. Edited by Eric W. Carlson, 65–67. Ann Arbor: University of Michigan Press.
Jameson, Fredric. 1978a. "The Symbolic Inference: Or, Kenneth Burke and Ideological Analysis." *Critical Inquiry* 4 (3): 507–523.
Jameson, Fredric. 1978b. "Ideology and Symbolic Action." *Critical Inquiry* 5 (2): 417–422.

Jameson, Fredric. 1981. *The Political Unconscious: Narrative as a Socially Symbolic Act.* Ithaca, NY Cornell University Press.
Jannaccone, Pasquale. (1895) 1974. "The Aesthetics of Edgar Poe." Translated by Peter Mitilineos. *Poe Studies* 7 (1): 1–13.
Jannidis, Fotis, Gerhard Lauer, Matías Martínez, and Simone Winko, eds. 1999. *Rückkehr des Autors: Zur Erneuerung eines umstrittenen Begriffs.* Tübingen: Niemeyer.
Jannidis, Fotis, Gerhard Lauer, Matias Martinez, and Simone Winko, eds. 2000. *Texte zur Theorie der Autorschaft.* Stuttgart: Reclam.
Jeffrey, Francis. 1814. "Review of The Excursion, By William Wordsworth." *Edinburgh Review* 24 (47): 1–30.
Johnson, Nan. 1991. *Nineteenth-Century Rhetoric in North America.* Carbondale: Southern Illinois University Press.
Jones, Buford, and Kent Ljungquist. 1976. "Monsieur Dupin: Further Details on the Reality Behind the Legend." *Southern Literary Journal* 9 (1): 70–77.
Kennedy, George A. 1999. *Classical Rhetoric and its Christian and Secular Tradition from Ancient to Modern Times.* 2nd ed. Chapel Hill: University of North Carolina Press.
Kennedy, George A. 2005. "The Contributions of Rhetoric to Literary Criticism." In *The Eighteenth Century.* Edited by Hugh B. Nisbet, George A. Kennedy, and Claude Rawson, 349–364. The Cambridge History of Literary Criticism 4. Cambridge: Cambridge University Press.
Kennedy, George A. 2007. "Introduction." In *On Rhetoric: A Theory of Civic Discourse.* Edited by George A. Kennedy. 2nd ed., 1–26. New York: Oxford University Press.
Kennedy, J. Gerald. 2001. "Edgar Allan Poe, 1809–1849: A Brief Biography." In *A Historical Guide to Edgar Allan Poe.* Edited by J. Gerald Kennedy, 19–62. Oxford: Oxford University Press.
Kennedy, J. Gerald. 2013. "Introduction." In *Poe and the Remapping of Antebellum Print Culture.* Edited by J. Gerald Kennedy and Jerome J. McGann, 1–12. Baton Rouge: Louisiana State University Press.
Kennedy, J. Gerald. 2016. *Strange Nation: Literary Nationalism and Cultural Conflict in the Age of Poe.* New York: Oxford University Press.
Kennedy, J. Gerald, and Jerome J. McGann, eds. 2013. *Poe and the Remapping of Antebellum Print Culture.* Baton Rouge: Louisiana State UP.
Kennedy, J. Gerald, and Liliane Weissberg. 2001. "Introduction: Poe, Race, and Contemporary Criticism." In *Romancing the Shadow: Poe and Race.* Edited by J. Gerald Kennedy and Liliane Weissberg, xi–xviii. Oxford: Oxford University Press.
Kerr, Lucille. 1992. *Reclaiming the Author: Figures and Fictions from Spanish America.* Durham, NC: Duke University Press.
Kidd, Robert. 1857. *Vocal Culture and Elocution: With Numerous Exercises in Reading and Speaking.* Cincinnati: Van Antwerp, Bragg and Co.
Knape, Joachim. 2000a. *Allgemeine Rhetorik.* Stuttgart: Reclam.
Knape, Joachim. 2000b. *Was ist Rhetorik?* Stuttgart: Reclam.
Knape, Joachim, ed. 2005. *Medienrhetorik.* Tübingen: Attempto.
Knape, Joachim. 2013. *Modern Rhetoric in Culture, Arts, and Media.* Berlin: de Gruyter.
Kolodny, Annette. 1994. "Inventing a Feminist Discourse: Rhetoric and Resistance in Margaret Fuller's *Woman in the Nineteenth Century.*" *New Literary History* 25 (2): 355–382.
Kopley, Richard. 2008. *Edgar Allan Poe and the Dupin Mysteries.* New York: Palgrave Macmillan.

Kopley, Richard. 2013. "Introduction." In *Poe Writing/Writing Poe*. Edited by Richard Kopley and Jana Argersinger, xiii–xvii. New York: AMS Press.

Kopley, Richard, and Kevin J. Hayes. 2002. "'The Raven' and 'Ulalume'." In *The Cambridge Companion to Edgar Allan Poe*. Edited by Kevin J. Hayes, 191–204. Cambridge: Cambridge University Press.

Kopperschmidt, Josef, ed. 1994. *Nietzsche oder "Die Sprache ist Rhetorik."* München: Fink.

Krutch, Joseph W. 1965. *Edgar Allan Poe: A Study in Genius*. New York: Russell and Russell.

Kyora, Sabine, ed. 2014. *Subjektform Autor: Autorschaftsinszenierungen als Praktiken der Subjektivierung*. Bielefeld: Transcript.

Labov, William, Sharon Ash, and Charles Boberg. 2006. *The Atlas of North American English: Phonetics, Phonology, and Sound Change*. Berlin, New York: de Gruyter Mouton.

Larsen, Elizabeth. 1993. "Re-Inventing Invention: Alexander Gerard and 'An Essay on Genius'." *Rhetorica* 11 (2): 181–197.

Lausberg, Heinrich. 1973. *Handbuch der literarischen Rhetorik: Eine Grundlegung der Literaturwissenschaft*. 2nd ed. 2 vols. München: Hueber.

Lausberg, Heinrich. 1998. *Handbook of Literary Rhetoric: A Foundation for Literary Study*. Edited by David E. Orton and R. D. Anderson. Leiden: Brill.

Lee, Maurice S. 2010. "Edgar Allan Poe (1809–1849)." In *A Companion to Crime Fiction*. Edited by Charles J. Rzepka and Lee Horsley, 369–389. Oxford: Wiley-Blackwell.

Lemprière, John. 1839. *A Classical Dictionary: New Edition*. London: Cadell.

Levine, Caroline. 2015. *Forms: Whole, Rhythm, Hierarchy, Network*. Princeton: Princeton University Press.

Liddell, Henry George, Robert Scott, and Henry Stuart Jones, eds. 1940. *A Greek-English Lexicon*. Oxford: Clarendon Press.

Lindberg-Seyersted, Brita. 1968. *The Voice of the Poet: Aspects of Style in the Poetry of Emily Dickinson*. Uppsala: Almqvist and Wiksell.

Liszka, James Jakób. 1996. *A General Introduction to the Semeiotic of Charles Sanders Peirce*. Bloomington: Indiana University Press.

Liszka, James Jakób. 2000. "Peirce's New Rhetoric." *Transactions of the Charles S. Peirce Society* 36 (4): 439–476.

Livingston, Paisley. 2005. *Art and Intention: A Philosophical Study*. Oxford: Clarendon Press.

Ljungquist, Kent. 1997a. "'Raising More Wind': Another Source for Poe's 'Diddling' and Its Possible Folio Club Context." *Essays in Arts and Sciences* 26: 59–70.

Ljungquist, Kent. 1997b. "'Valdemar' and the 'Frogpondians': The Aftermath of Poe's Boston Lyceum Appearance." In *Emersonian Circles: Essays in Honor of Joel Myerson*. Edited by Wesley T. Mott and Robert E. Burkholder, 181–206. Rochester, NY: University of Rochester Press.

Lobkowicz, Nikolaus. 1967. *Theory and Practice: History of a Concept from Aristotle to Marx*. Notre Dame: University of Notre Dame Press.

Lobsien, Eckhard. 2008. *Zeit der Imagination: Das Imaginäre (in) der englischen Romantik*. Heidelberg: Winter.

Loesberg, Jonathan. 2005. *A Return to Aesthetics: Autonomy, Indifference, and Postmodernism*. Stanford: Stanford University Press.

Love, Harold. 2002. *Attributing Authorship: An Introduction*. Cambridge: Cambridge University Press.

Lowell, James Russell. 1848. *A Fable for Critics*. New York: Putnam.

Luhmann, Niklas. 2009. "Wahrheit und Ideologie: Vorschläge zur Wiederaufnahme der Diskussion." In *Aufsätze zur Theorie sozialer Systeme*. 8th ed., 68–82. Wiesbaden: Verlag für Sozialwissenschaften.

Lundberg, Christian O. 2012. *Lacan in Public: Psychoanalysis and the Science of Rhetoric*. Tuscaloosa: The University of Alabama Press.

MacDowell, Douglas M. 2009. *Demosthenes the Orator*. Oxford: Oxford University Press.

Machor, James L. 2011. *Reading Fiction in Antebellum America: Informed Response and Reception Histories, 1820–1865*. Baltimore: Johns Hopkins University Press.

Mack, Peter. 2011. *A History of Renaissance Rhetoric, 1380–1620*. Oxford: Oxford University Press.

Mahon, M. Wade. 2001. "The Rhetorical Value of Reading Aloud in Thomas Sheridan's Theory of Elocution." *Rhetoric Society Quarterly* 31 (4): 67–88.

Mailloux, Steven. 2000. "Disciplinary Identities: On the Rhetorical Paths between English and Communication Studies." *Rhetoric Society Quarterly* 30 (2): 5–29.

Manning, Susan. 2002. *Fragments of Union: Making Connections in Scottish and American Writing*. Basingstoke: Palgrave.

Manning, Susan. (1990) 2009. *The Puritan-Provincial Vision: Scottish and American Literature in the Nineteenth Century*. Cambridge: Cambridge University Press.

Manning, Susan. 2013. *Poetics of Character: Transatlantic Encounters, 1700–1900*. Cambridge: Cambridge University Press.

Martin, Meredith. 2012. *The Rise and Fall of Meter: Poetry and English National Culture, 1860–1930*. Princeton, NJ: Princeton University Press.

Martin, Terence. 1961. *The Instructed Vision: Scottish Common Sense Philosophy and the Origins of American Fiction*. Bloomington: Indiana University Press.

Martínez, Matías. 2008. "Autorschaft, historische Modelle der." In *Metzler-Lexikon Literatur- und Kulturtheorie*. Edited by Ansgar Nünning. 4th ed., 45. Stuttgart: Metzler.

Matthiessen, Francis O. (1941) 1968. *American Renaissance: Art and Expression in the Age of Emerson and Whitman*. Oxford: Oxford University Press.

McCorkle, Ben. 2012. *Rhetorical Delivery as Technological Discourse: A Cross-Historical Study*. Carbondale: Southern Illinois University Press.

McGann, Jerome J. (1983) 1999. *The Romantic Ideology: A Critical Investigation*. Chicago: University of Chicago Press.

McGann, Jerome J. 2013a. "Poe, Decentered Culture, and Critical Method." In *Poe and the Remapping of Antebellum Print Culture*. Edited by J. Gerald Kennedy and Jerome J. McGann, 245–259. Baton Rouge: Louisiana State University Press.

McGann, Jerome J. 2013b. "Poe: The Politics of a Poetry Without Politics (Part I)." *Literature Compass* 10 (11): 871–884.

McGann, Jerome J. 2014a. *A New Republic of Letters: Memory and Scholarship in the Age of Digital Reproduction*. Cambridge, MA: Harvard University Press.

McGann, Jerome J. 2014b. *The Poet Edgar Allan Poe: Alien Angel*. Cambridge, MA: Harvard University Press.

McGill, Meredith L. 2001. "Reading Poe, Reading Capitalism: Review of Edgar Allan Poe and the Masses: The Political Economy of Literature in Antebellum America. By Terence Whalen." *American Quarterly* 53 (1): 139–147.

McGill, Meredith L. 2003. *American Literature and the Culture of Reprinting, 1834–1853*. Philadelphia: University of Pennsylvania Press.

McGurl, Mark. 2009. *The Program Era: Postwar Fiction and the Rise of Creative Writing.* Cambridge, MA: Harvard University Press.

McKeon, Richard. 1973. "Creativity and the Commonplace." *Philosophy and Rhetoric* 6 (4): 199–210.

McKeon, Richard. (1971) 2005. "The Uses of Rhetoric in a Technological Age: Architectonic Productive Arts." In *Selected Writings of Richard McKeon: Volume 2. Culture, Education, and the Arts.* Edited by Zahava K. McKeon and William G. Swenson, 197–214. Chicago: University of Chicago Press.

McLuhan, Herbert Marshall. 1944. "Edgar Poe's Tradition." *Sewanee Review* 52 (1): 24–33.

McMullen, Bonnie Shannon. 2010. "'A Desert of Ebony': Poe, Blackwood's, and Tales of the Sea." *Edgar Allan Poe Review* 11 (1): 70–78.

Meizoz, Jérôme. 2007. *Postures littéraires: Mises en scène modernes de l'auteur.* Geneva: Slatkine.

Mill, John Stuart. (1833) 1981. "Thoughts On Poetry And Its Varieties." In *Autobiography and Literary Essays.* Edited by John M. Robson and Jack Stillinger, 341–365. Collected Works of John Stuart Mill 1. Toronto: University of Toronto Press.

Mill, John Stuart. (1843) 1974. *A System of Logic Ratiocinative and Inductive: Being a Connected View of the Principles of Evidence and the Methods of Scientific Investigation. Books 1–3.* Edited by John M. Robson and R. F. McRae. Collected Works of John Stuart Mill 7. Toronto: University of Toronto Press.

Milton, John. 2007. *Paradise Lost.* Edited by Barbara K. Lewalski. Malden, MA: Blackwell.

Minnis, Alastair J. 1984. *Medieval Theory of Authorship: Scholastic Literary Attitudes in the Later Middle Ages.* London: Scolar Press.

Minturno, Antonio S. 1559. *De poeta libri VI.* Venice.

Moldenhauer, Joseph J. 1968. "Murder as a Fine Art: Basic Connections Between Poe's Aesthetics, Psychology, and Moral Vision." *PMLA* 83 (2): 284–297.

Moreland, Sean, and Devin Z. Shaw. 2012. "'As Urged by Schelling': Coleridge, Poe and the Schellingian Refrain." *Edgar Allan Poe Review* 13 (2): 50–80.

Moritz, Karl Philipp. (1785) 2012. "An Attempt to Unify All the Fine Arts and Sciences under the Concept of That Which Is Complete in Itself." *PMLA* 127 (1): 94–100.

Morrison, Toni. 1992. *Playing in the Dark: Whiteness and the Literary Imagination.* The William E. Massey Sr. Lectures in the History of American Civilization 1990. Cambridge, MA: Harvard University Press.

Moss, Ann. 2001. "Commonplaces and Commonplace Books." In *Encyclopedia of Rhetoric.* Edited by Thomas O. Sloane, 119–124. Oxford: Oxford University Press.

Moss, Sidney P. 1963. *Poe's Literary Battles: The Critic in the Context of His Literary Milieu.* Carbondale: Southern Illinois University Press.

Moss, Sidney P. 1978. "Poe's 'Two Long Interviews' with Dickens." *Poe Studies* 11 (1): 10–12.

Most, Glenn W. 2010. "Horace." In *The Classical Tradition.* Edited by Anthony Grafton, Glenn W. Most, and Salvatore Settis, 454–460. Cambridge, MA: Belknap Press of Harvard University Press.

Muller, John P., and William J. Richardson, eds. 1988. *The Purloined Poe: Lacan, Derrida and Psychoanalytic Reading.* Baltimore: Johns Hopkins University Press.

Müller, Wolfgang G. 1993. "*Ars rhetorica* und *ars poetica:* Zum Verhältnis von Rhetorik und Literatur in der englischen Renaissance." In *Renaissance-Rhetorik: Renaissance Rhetoric.* Edited by Heinrich F. Plett, 225–243. Berlin, New York: de Gruyter.

Müller, Wolfgang G. 2001. "Style." In *Encyclopedia of Rhetoric*. Edited by Thomas O. Sloane, 745–757. Oxford, New York: Oxford University Press.
Murdoch, James E., and William Russell. 1845. *Orthophony or Vocal Culture*. Boston: William D. Tichnor and Co.
Murphy, James J. 1974. *Rhetoric in the Middle Ages: A History of Rhetorical Theory from Saint Augustine to the Renaissance*. Berkeley: University of California Press.
Murray, Lindley. 1808. *An English Grammar*. A new ed. York.
Newbury, Michael. 1997. *Figuring Authorship in Antebellum America*. Stanford: Stanford University Press.
Nietzsche, Friedrich Wilhelm. 1995. *Vorlesungsaufzeichnungen (WS 1871/72 – WS 1874/75)*. Edited by Fritz Bornmann and Mario Carpitella. Werke II.4. Berlin: de Gruyter.
Niiniluoto, Ilkka. 1999. "Abduction and Geometrical Analysis: Notes on Charles S. Peirce and Edgar Allan Poe." In *Model-Based Reasoning in Scientific Discovery*. Edited by Lorenzo Magnani, Nancy J. Nersessian, and Paul Thagard, 239–254. New York: Kluwer Academic.
Nygaard, Loisa. 1994. "Winning the Game: Inductive Reasoning in Poe's 'Murders in the Rue Morgue'." *Studies in Romanticism* 33 (2): 223–254.
OED = The Oxford English Dictionary. 2000–. 3rd ed. online. Oxford: Oxford University Press. <http://www.oed.com/> [last accessed 27 October 2016].
"On the Utility of Poetry." 1835. In *Selections from the Edinburgh Review*. Edited by Maurice Cross. 6 vols, 111–120 1. Paris.
Ong, Walter J. (1958) 2004. *Ramus, Method, and the Decay of Dialogue: From the Art of Discourse to the Art of Reason*. Chicago: University of Chicago Press.
Ong, Walter J. 2010. "From the Foreword to the 1990 Edition." In *The Present State of Scholarship in the History of Rhetoric: A Twenty-First Century Guide*. Edited by Lynee L. Gaillet and Winifred B. Horner. 3rd ed., 1–6. Columbia: University of Missouri Press.
Ong, Walter J. 2013. *Orality and Literacy: The Technologizing of the Word*. London: Routledge.
Pahl, Dennis. 1996. "De-Composing Poe's 'Philosophy'." *Texas Studies in Literature and Language* 38.
Parker, Edward G. 1857. *The Golden Age of American Oratory*. Boston: Whittemore, Niles, and Hall.
Parks, Edd Winfield. 1964. *Edgar Allan Poe as Literary Critic*. Athens: University of Georgia Press.
Parrington, Vernon L. (1927) 1987. *The Romantic Revolution in America: 1800–1860*. Main Currents in American Thought 2. Norman: University of Oklahoma Press.
Peeples, Scott. 2002. "Poe's 'Constructiveness' and 'The Fall of the House of Usher'." In *The Cambridge Companion to Edgar Allan Poe*, edited by Kevin J. Hayes, 178–190. Cambridge: Cambridge University Press.
Peeples, Scott. 2004. *The Afterlife of Edgar Allan Poe*. Rochester NY: Camden House.
Peirce, Charles Sanders. 1991. "A Neglected Argument for the Reality of God." In *Peirce on Signs: Writings on Semiotic*. Edited by James Hoopes, 260–278. Chapel Hill: University of North Carolina Press.
Peirce, Charles Sanders. 1992. "Deduction, Induction, and Hypothesis." In *The Essential Peirce (1867–1893)*, 186–199. Selected Philosophical Writings 1. Bloomington: Indiana University Press.
Peirce, Charles Sanders. 1998a. "Of Reasoning in General." In *The Essential Peirce (1893–1913)*, 11–26. Selected Philosophical Writings 2. Bloomington: Indiana University Press.

Peirce, Charles Sanders. 1998b. "On the Logic of Drawing History from Ancient Documents, Especially from Testimonies." In *The Essential Peirce (1893–1913)*, 75–114. Selected Philosophical Writings 2. Bloomington: Indiana University Press.

Peirce, Charles Sanders. 1998c. "[Pragmatism as the Logic of Abduction]." In *The Essential Peirce (1893–1913)*, 226–241. Selected Philosophical Writings 2. Bloomington: Indiana University Press.

Peirce, Charles Sanders. 1998d. "[Sundry Logical Conceptions]." In *The Essential Peirce (1893–1913)*, 267–288. Selected Philosophical Writings 2. Bloomington: Indiana University Press.

Peirce, Charles Sanders. 1998e. "[The Maxim of Pragmatism]." In *The Essential Peirce (1893–1913)*, 133–144. Selected Philosophical Writings 2. Bloomington: Indiana University Press.

Peirce, Charles Sanders. 1998f. "The Nature of Meaning." In *The Essential Peirce (1893–1913)*, 208–225. Selected Philosophical Writings 2. Bloomington: Indiana University Press.

Perelman, Chaïm, and Lucie Olbrechts-Tyteca. (1958) 1969. *The New Rhetoric: A Treatise on Argumentation*. Notre Dame: University of Notre Dame Press.

Perkins, David. 1991. "How the Romantics Recited Poetry." *Studies in English Literature 1500–1900* 31 (4): 655–671.

Perkins, Leroy, and Joseph A. Dupras. 1990. "Mystery and Meaning in Poe's 'X-ing a Paragrab'." *Studies in Short Fiction* 27 (4): 489–494.

Perry, Dennis R., and Carl H. Sederholm. 2012. *Adapting Poe: Re-imaginings in Popular Culture*. New York: Palgrave Macmillan.

Person, Leland S. 1990. "Poe's Composition of Philosophy: Reading and Writing 'The Raven'." *Arizona Quarterly* 46 (3): 1–15.

Person, Leland S. 2001. "Poe and Nineteenth-Century Gender Constructions." In *A Historical Guide to Edgar Allan Poe*, edited by J. Gerald Kennedy, 129–166. Oxford: Oxford University Press.

Pfeiffer, K. Ludwig 1994. "The Materiality of Communication." In *Materialities of Communication*. Edited by Hans U. Gumbrecht and K. Ludwig Pfeiffer, 1–12. Stanford: Stanford University Press.

Phelan, James. 1996. *Narrative as Rhetoric: Technique, Audiences, Ethics, Ideology*. Columbus: Ohio State University Press.

Phelan, James. 2010. "Imagining a Sequel to Wayne C. Booth's *The Rhetoric of Fiction*: Or A Dialogue on Dialogue." *Comparative Critical Studies* 7: 243–255.

Phillips, Elizabeth. 1996. "The Poems: 1824–1835." In *A Companion to Poe Studies*, edited by Eric W. Carlson, 67–88. Westport, CT: Greenwod Press.

Phillips, Philip Edward. 2013. "Poe's 1845 Boston Lyceum Incident Reconsidered." In *Deciphering Poe: Subtexts, Contexts, Subversive Meanings*. Edited by Alexandra Urakova, 41–52. Lanham: Lehigh University Press.

Plett, Heinrich F. 2004. *Rhetoric and Renaissance Culture*. Berlin, New York: de Gruyter.

Plett, Heinrich F. 2010. *Literary Rhetoric: Concepts, Structures, Analyses*. Leiden: Brill.

Poe, Edgar A. 1902. *The Complete Works of Edgar Allan Poe*. Edited by James A. Harrison. 17 vols. New York: Sproul. (referred to in the text as MTC)

Poe, Edgar A. 1969. *Poems*. Edited by Thomas O. Mabbott. Collected Works of Edgar Allan Poe 1. Cambridge, MA: Belknap Press of Harvard University Press. (= PMS)

Poe, Edgar A. (1978) 2000. *Tales and Sketches*, volume 1: 1831 – 1842 and volume 2: 1843 – 1849. Edited by Thomas O. Mabbott. Collected Works of Edgar Allan Poe 2 and 3. Urbana: University of Illinois Press. As reprints of the original edition published by Harvard, these two volumes are continuously paginated (vol. 1, 1–713; vol. 2, 715–1451). (= T&S)

Poe, Edgar A. 1981–1997. *The Collected Writings of Edgar Allan Poe 1–5*. Edited by Burton R. Pollin. New York: Gordian. (While also reprinted by Gordian, vol. 1 was originally published by Twayne Publishers in Boston in 1981). (= CW)

Poe, Edgar A. 1986. *Writings in the* Broadway Journal. *Nonfictional Prose. Part 1, The Text*. Edited by Burton R. Pollin. The Collected Writings of Edgar Allan Poe 3. New York: Gordian. (= CW 3)

Poe, Edgar A. 1986. *Writings in the* Southern Literary Messenger. Edited by Burton R. Pollin. The Collected Writings of Edgar Allan Poe 5. New York: Gordian. (= CW 5)

Poe, Edgar A. 1984. *Essays and Reviews*. Edited by G. R. Thompson. New York: Library of America. (= E&R)

Poe, Edgar A. 2004. *Eureka*. Edited by Stuart Levine and Susan F. Levine. Urbana: University of Illinois Press. (= ERK)

Poe, Edgar A. 2008. *The Letters of Edgar Allan Poe: Revised, Corrected, and Expanded*. 3rd ed. Edited by John W. Ostrom, Burton R. Pollin, and Jeffrey A. Savoye. Staten Island: Gordian. 2 vols. The letters are consecutively numbered. (= LTR)

Poe, Edgar A. 2009. *Critical Theory: The Major Documents*. Edited by Stuart Levine and Susan F. Levine. Urbana: University of Illinois Press. (= CT)

Polaschegg, Andrea. 2002. "Diskussionsbericht." In *Autorschaft: Positionen und Revisionen*. Edited by Heinrich Detering, 310–323. Germanistische Symposien-Berichtsbände 24. Stuttgart: Metzler.

Pollin, Burton R. "'The Living Writers of America': A Manuscript by Edgar Allan Poe." *Studies in the American Renaisssance* 1991: 151–200.

Polonsky, Rachel. 2002. "Poe's Aesthetic Theory." In *The Cambridge Companion to Edgar Allan Poe*. Edited by Kevin J. Hayes, 42–56. Cambridge: Cambridge University Press.

Pope, Alexander. 1961. *Pastoral Poetry and An Essay on Criticism*. Edited by Émile Audra and Aubrey L. Williams. London: Methuen.

Porter, Dennis. 1981. *The Pursuit of Crime: Art and Ideology in Detective Fiction*. New Haven: Yale University Press.

Porter, Ebenezer. 1827. *Analysis of the Principles of Rhetorical Delivery as Applied in Reading and Speaking*. New York: J. Leavitt.

Poulakos, John. 2007. "From the Depths of Rhetoric: The Emergence of Aesthetics as a Discipline." *Philosophy and Rhetoric* 40 (4): 335–352.

Pound, Ezra. 1971. *The Selected Letters of Ezra Pound: 1907–1941*. 2nd ed. New York: New Directions Publishing.

Prown, Katherine H. 1993. "The Cavalier and the Syren: Edgar Allan Poe, Cornelia Wells Walter, and the Boston Lyceum Incident." *New England Quarterly* 66 (1): 110–123.

"Public Lectures." 1834. *Scientific Tracts and Family Lyceum* 1 (1): 33.

Pue, Hugh A. 1841. *A Grammar of the English Language: In a Series of Letters, Addressed to Every American Youth*. Philadelphia: F. Turner.

Purcell, William M., and David Snowball. 1996. "Style." In *Encyclopedia of Rhetoric and Composition: Communication from Ancient Times to the Information Age*, edited by Theresa Enos, 698–703. New York: Garland.

Putnam, George Palmer. 1845. *American Facts*. London, New York: Wiley and Putnam.
Quinn, Arthur H. (1941) 1942. *Edgar Allan Poe: A Critical Biography*. New York: Appleton-Century.
Quinn, Patrick F. (1957) 1971. *The French Face of Edgar Poe*. Carbondale: Southern Illinois University Press.
Quintilian. 2001a-e. *The Orator's Education: Books 1–2; 3–5; 6–8; 9–10; 11–12*. Edited by Donald A. Russell. The Orator's Education 1–5. The Loeb Classical Library. Cambridge, MA: Harvard University Press.
Railton, Stephen. 1991. *Authorship and Audience: Literary Performance in the American Renaissance*. Princeton, NJ: Princeton University Press.
Ray, Angela G. 2005. *The Lyceum and Public Culture in the Nineteenth-Century United States*. East Lansing: Michigan State University Press.
Renza, Louis A. 2002. *Edgar Allan Poe, Wallace Stevens, and the Poetics of American Privacy*. Baton Rouge: Louisiana State University Press.
"Review of The Songs of Scotland, Ancient and Modern, by Allan Cunningham." 1828. *Edinburgh Review* 47 (93): 184–204.
Reynolds, David S. (1988) 2011. *Beneath the American Renaissance: The Subversive Imagination in the Age of Emerson and Melville*. New York: Oxford University Press.
Rhetorica ad Herennium (Ad C. Herennium de ratione dicendi). 1964. Edited by Harry Caplan. The Loeb Classical Library. Cambridge, MA: Harvard University Press.
Rhodes, Neil. 2008. "From Rhetoric to Criticism." In *The Scottish Invention of English Literature*. Edited by Robert Crawford, 22–36. Cambridge: Cambridge University Press.
Richards, Eliza. 2000. "Women's Place in Poe Studies." *Poe Studies* 33 (1–2): 10–14.
Richards, Eliza. 2004. *Gender and the Poetics of Reception in Poe's Circle*. Cambridge: Cambridge University Press.
Richards, Eliza. 2005. "Outsourcing 'The Raven': Retroactive Origins." *Victorian Poetry* 43 (2): 205–221.
Richards, I. A. (1936) 1971. *The Philosophy of Rhetoric*. The Mary Flexner Lectures on the Humanities 3. Oxford: Oxford University Press.
Ricoeur, Paul. 1996. "Between Rhetoric and Poetics." In *Essays on Aristotle's Rhetoric*. Edited by Amélie Rorty, 324–384. Berkeley: University of California Press.
Ricoeur, Paul. 2003. *The Rule of Metaphor: The Creation of Meaning in Language*. Translated by Robert Czerny, Kathleen McLaughlin, and John Costello. London: Routledge.
Ridgely, Joseph V. 1992. "The Authorship of the 'Paulding-Drayton Review'." *Poe Studies Association Newsletter* 20 (2): 1–3, 6.
<http://www.eapoe.org/papers/misc1921/JVR19921.htm> [last accessed 27 November 2016].
Ritivoi, Andreea D., and Richard Graff. 2008. "Rhetoric and Modern Literary Theory." In *Rhetorik und Stilistik: Ein internationales Handbuch historischer und systematischer Forschung*. Edited by Ulla Fix, Andreas Gardt, and Joachim Knape, 2 vols, 944–958 1. Berlin, New York: de Gruyter.
Rolston, David L. 2010. "Traditional Fiction Commentary." In *The Columbia History of Chinese Literature*. Edited by Victor H. Mair, 940–952. New York, Chichester: Columbia University Press.
Rose, Mark. 1993. *Authors and Owners: The Invention of Copyright*. Cambridge, MA: Harvard University Press.

Rosenheim, Shawn, and Stephen D. Rachman, eds. 1995. *The American Face of Edgar Allan Poe*. Baltimore: Johns Hopkins University Press.
Rosenthal, Bernard. 1974. "Poe, Slavery, and the Southern Literary Messenger: A Reexamination." *Poe Studies* 7: 29–38.
Russell, William. 1844. *The American Elocutionist: Comprising 'Lessons in Enunciation,' 'Exercises in Elocution,' and 'Rudiments of Gesture.'* Boston: Jenks and Palmer.
Savoye, Jeffrey A. 2011. "[[Exordium]]." <http://www.eapoe.org/works/essays/exordm.htm> [last accessed 13 November 2016].
Savoye, Jeffrey A. 2014. "'The Murders in the Rue Morgue': Historical Texts." <http://www.eapoe.org/works/info/pt030.htm>. [last accessed 24 November 2016]
Schaffrick, Matthias, and Marcus Willand, eds. 2014. *Theorien und Praktiken der Autorschaft*. Berlin: de Gruyter.
Schirren, Thomas. 2008. "Rhetorik des Textes: Produktionsstadien der Rede." In *Rhetorik und Stilistik: Ein internationales Handbuch historischer und systematischer Forschung*. Edited by Ulla Fix, Andreas Gardt, and Joachim Knape, 2 vols, 620–630 1. Berlin, New York: de Gruyter.
Schlegel, August Wilhelm von. 1833. *A Course of Lectures on Dramatic Art and Literature*. Philadelphia: Hogan and Thompson. Translated from the Original German by John Black.
Schlutz, Alexander. 2008. "Purloined Voices: Edgar Allan Poe Reading Samuel Taylor Coleridge." *Studies in Romanticism* 47 (2): 195–224.
Schmitt, Arbogast. 2008. "Einleitung." In *Poetik*. Edited by Arbogast Schmitt, 45–127. Aristoteles – Werke in deutscher Übersetzung 5. Berlin: Akademie Verlag.
Scott, Donald. 1983. "The Profession that Vanished: Public Lecturing in Mid-Nineteenth-Century America." In *Professions and Professional Ideologies in America*, edited by Gerald L. Geison, 12–28. Chapel Hill: University of North Carolina Press.
Shakespeare, William. 2005. *The Oxford Shakespeare. The Complete Works*. Edited by Stanley Wells, Gary Taylor, John Jowett, and William Montgomery. Oxford: Clarendon Press.
Sheridan, Thomas. 1775. *Lectures on the Art of Reading: Second Part: Containing the Art of Reading Verse*. London.
Sheridan, Thomas. 1780. *A General Dictionary of the English Language: One Main Object of which, is, to establish a plain and permanent Standard of Pronunciation; to which is Prefixed A Rhetorical Grammar*. 2 vols. London: Dodsley.
Short, Bryan C. 1992. *Cast by Means of Figures: Herman Melville's Rhetorical Development*. Amherst: University of Massachusetts Press.
Shucard, Alan. 1990. *American Poetry: The Puritans Through Walt Whitman*. Amherst: University of Massachusetts Press.
Sidney, Philip. 2011. *An Apologie for Poetrie*. Edited by Evelyn S. Shuckburgh. Cambridge: Cambridge University Press.
Silverman, Kenneth. 1991. *Edgar A. Poe: Mournful and Never-Ending Remembrance*. New York: HarperCollins.
Skinner, Quentin. 1996. *Reason and Rhetoric in the Philosophy of Hobbes*. Cambridge: Cambridge University Press.
"Slavery: Review of Slavery in the United States, by J. K. Paulding; and the South Vindicated from the Treason and Fanaticism of the Northern Abolitionists." April 1836. *Southern Literary Messenger* 2 (5): 336–339.
Sloane, Thomas O., ed. 2001. *Encyclopedia of Rhetoric*. Oxford: Oxford University Press.

Sloane, Thomas O. 2013. "From Elocution to New Criticism: An Episode in the History of Rhetoric." *Rhetorica* 31 (3): 297–330.
Smith, Andrew. 2013. *Gothic Literature*. New ed. Edinburgh: Edinburgh University Press.
Smith, Sydney. 1820. "Review of Statistical Annals of the United States, by Adam Seybert." *Edinburgh Review* 33 (65): 69–80.
Spalding, William. 1839. "Treatise on Rhetoric." In *Treatises on Poetry, Modern Romance, and Rhetoric: Being the Articles under those Heads, Contributed to the Encyclopaedia Britannica, Seventh Edition*, 275–381. Edinburgh: Black.
Spoel, Philippa M. 1998. "The Science of Bodily Rhetoric in Gilbert Austin's 'Chironomia'." *Rhetoric Society Quarterly* 28 (4): 5–27.
Stecker, Robert. 2005. "Interpretation." In *The Routledge Companion to Aesthetics*. Edited by Berys N. Gaut and Dominic Lopes. 2nd ed, 321–334. London: Routledge.
Stillinger, Jack. 1991. *Multiple Authorship and the Myth of Solitary Genius*. New York: Oxford University Press.
Stoneman, Richard. 1976. "The 'Theban Eagle'." *Classical Quarterly* 26 (2): 188–197.
Stovall, Floyd. 1930. "Poe's Debt to Coleridge." *Studies in English* (10): 70–127.
Suderman, Jeffrey M. 2001. *Orthodoxy and Enlightenment: George Campbell in the Eighteenth Century*. Montréal: McGill-Queen's University Press.
Sutton, Jane. 1986. "The Death of Rhetoric and its Rebirth in Philosophy." *Rhetorica* 4 (3): 203–226.
Tally, Robert T. 2014. *Poe and the Subversion of American Literature: Satire, Fantasy, Critique*. New York: Bloomsbury Academic.
Tate, Allen. 1952. "The Angelic Imagination: Poe and the Power of Words." *The Kenyon Review* 14 (3): 455–475.
Taylor, Bayard. 1849. *Rhymes of Travel: Ballads and Poems*. 2nd ed. New York: Putnam.
"The Utility of Letters of Recommendation to Young Men Visiting Paris." 1825. *The European Magazine, and London Review* 87: 514–517.
Theile, Verena, and Linda Tredennick, eds. 2013. *New Formalisms and Literary Theory*. Basingstoke: Palgrave Macmillan.
Thomas, Dwight, and David K. Jackson. 1987. *The Poe Log*. Boston: Hall.
Thompson, G. R. 1973. *Poe's Fiction: Romantic Irony in the Gothic Tales*. Madison: University of Wisconsin Press.
Thompson, G. R., ed. 1974. *The Gothic Imagination: Essays in Dark Romanticism*. Pullman: Washington State University Press.
Thompson, Roger. 2007. "'Habit of Heat': Emerson, Belletristic Rhetoric, and the Role of the Imagination." *College English* 69 (3): 260–282.
Thoms, Peter. 2002. "Poe's Dupin and the Power of Detection." In *The Cambridge Companion to Edgar Allan Poe*. Edited by Kevin J. Hayes, 133–147. Cambridge: Cambridge University Press.
Thorpe, Dwayne. 1996. "The Poems: 1836–1849." In *A Companion to Poe Studies*, edited by Eric W. Carlson, 89–109. Westport: Greenwod Press.
Till, Dietmar. 2004. *Transformationen der Rhetorik: Untersuchungen zum Wandel der Rhetoriktheorie im 17. und 18. Jahrhundert*. Tübingen: Niemeyer.
Todorov, Tzvetan. 1977. "Typology of Detective Fiction." In *The Poetics of Prose*, 42–52. Oxford: Blackwell.
Toulmin, Stephen E. (1958) 2003. *The Uses of Argument*. Updated ed. Cambridge: Cambridge University Press.

Treffert, Darold A. 2009. "The Savant Syndrome: An Extraordinary Condition. A Synopsis: Past, Present, Future." *Philosophical Transactions of the Royal Society of London. Series B, Biological sciences* 364 (1522): 1351–1357.
Uhlig, Stefan H. 2012. "The Long Goodbye to Rhetoric." In *Mobility in Literature and Culture, 1500 – 1900*. Edited by Ingo Berensmeyer, Christoph Ehland, and Herbert Grabes, 237–264. REAL Yearbook of Research in English and American Literature 28. Tübingen: Narr.
Van Leer, David. 1990. "Nature's Book: The Language of Science in the American Renaissance." In *Romanticism and the Sciences*. Edited by Andrew Cunningham and Nicholas Jardine, 307–322. Cambridge: Cambridge University Press.
Varro, Marcus Terentius. 1938. *On the Latin Language*. Edited by Roland G. Kent. The Loeb Classical Library. Cambridge, MA: Harvard University Press.
Vatz, Richard E. 1973. "The Myth of the Rhetorical Situation." *Philosophy and Rhetoric* 6 (3): 154–161.
Vickers, Brian. 1984. "Figures of Rhetoric/Figures of Music?" *Rhetorica* 2 (1): 1–44.
Vickers, Brian. 1988a. "The Atrophy of Modern Rhetoric, Vico to De Man." *Rhetorica* 6 (1): 21–56.
Vickers, Brian. 1988b. *In Defence of Rhetoric*. Oxford: Clarendon Press.
Vickers, Brian. 1996. "Bacon and Rhetoric." In *The Cambridge Companion to Bacon*, edited by Markku Peltonen, 200–231. Cambridge: Cambridge University Press.
Vines, Lois D., ed. 1999. *Poe Abroad: Influence, Reputation, Affinities*. Iowa City: University of Iowa Press.
Voelz, Johannes. 2010. *Transcendental Resistance: The New Americanists and Emerson's Challenge*. Hanover, NH: University Press of New England.
Voloshin, Beverly R. 1996. "The Essays and 'Marginalia': Poe's Literary Theory." In *A Companion to Poe Studies*. Edited by Eric W. Carlson, 276–295. Westport: Greenwod Press.
Walker, Jeffrey. 2000. *Rhetoric and Poetics in Antiquity*. Oxford: Oxford University Press.
Walker, Jeffrey. 2008. "Pathos and Katharsis in 'Aristotelian Rhetoric': Some Implications." In *Rereading Aristotle's 'Rhetoric.'* Edited by Alan G Gross and Arthur E Walzer, 74–92. Carbondale: Southern Illinois University Press.
Wall, Brian. 2013. "Narrative Purpose and Legal Logic in 'The Tell-Tale Heart'." *Edgar Allan Poe Review* 14 (2): 129–143.
Walzer, Arthur E. 2003. *George Campbell: Rhetoric in the Age of Enlightenment*. Albany: SUNY Press.
Warren, James Perrin. 1999. *Culture of Eloquence: Oratory and Reform in Antebellum America*. University Park: Pennsylvania State University Press.
Watson, Walter. 2001. "Invention." In *Encyclopedia of Rhetoric*. Edited by Thomas O. Sloane. Oxford: Oxford University Press.
Weiner, Bruce I. 1986. "'That Metaphysical Art': Mystery and Detection in Poe's Tales." In *Poe and Our Times: Influences and Affinities*. Edited by Benjamin F. Fisher, 32–48. Baltimore: The Edgar Allan Poe Society.
Weiner, Bruce I. 1990. "Poe and the Blackwood's Tale of Sensation." In *Poe and His Times*. Edited by Benjamin F. Fisher, 45–65. Baltimore: Edgar Allan Poe Society.
Webster, Noah, ed. 1848. *An American Dictionary of the English Language*. Revised and Enlarged by Chauncey A. Goodrich. New York: Harper and Brothers.

Welch, Kathleen E. 2001. "Delivery." In *Encyclopedia of Rhetoric*. Edited by Thomas O. Sloane, 217–20. Oxford, New York: Oxford University Press.

Welch, Kathleen E. 2013. *The Contemporary Reception of Classical Rhetoric: Appropriations of Ancient Discourse*. Hoboken: Taylor and Francis.

Wellek, René. (1955) 1970. *The Romantic Age*. A History of Modern Criticism 2. London: Cape.

Wellek, René. (1965) 1966. *The Age of Transition*. A History of Modern Criticism 3. London: Cape.

Wess, Robert. 1996. *Kenneth Burke: Rhetoric, Subjectivity, Postmodernism*. Cambridge: Cambridge University Press.

West, William N. 2001. "Memory." In *Encyclopedia of Rhetoric*. Edited by Thomas O. Sloane, 483–493. Oxford: Oxford University Press.

Wetherbee, Ben. 2015. "Jameson, Burke, and the Virus of Suggestion: Between Ideology and Rhetoric." *The Henry James Review* 36 (3): 280–287.

Whalen, Terence. 1992. "Edgar Allan Poe and the Horrid Laws of Political Economy." *American Quarterly* 44 (3): 381–417.

Whalen, Terence. 1999. *Edgar Allan Poe and the Masses: The Political Economy of Literature in Antebellum America*. Princeton, NJ: Princeton University Press.

Whately, Richard. 1828. *Elements of Rhetoric*. 2nd ed. Oxford.

Whately, Richard. (1828) 1963. *Elements of Rhetoric*. Edited by Douglas Ehninger. Carbondale: Southern Illinois University Press, reprint 2010.

White, Hayden. 1997. "The Suppression of Rhetoric in the Nineteenth Century." In *The Rhetoric Canon*. Edited by Brenda D. Schildgen, 21–32. Detroit: Wayne State University Press.

White, Hayden. 1973. *Metahistory: The Historical Imagination in Nineteenth-Century Europe*. Baltimore: Johns Hopkins University Press.

Williams, Michael J. S. 1988. *A World of Words: Language and Displacement in the Fiction of Edgar Allan Poe*. Durham, NC: Duke University Press.

Williams, Raymond. 1985. *Keywords*. 2nd ed. New York: Oxford University Press.

Wilson, Raymond J. 1989. *Figures of Speech: American Writers and the Literary Marketplace from Benjamin Franklin to Emily Dickinson*. Baltimore: Johns Hopkins University Press.

Winko, Simone. 2002. "Autor-Funktionen: Zur argumentativen Verwendung von Autorkonzepten in der gegenwärtigen literaturwissenschaftlichen Interpretationspraxis." In *Autorschaft: Positionen und Revisionen*. Edited by Heinrich Detering, 334–354. Germanistische Symposien-Berichtsbände 24. Stuttgart: Metzler.

Wirth, Uwe. 1995. "Abduktion und ihre Anwendungen." *Zeitschrift für Semiotik* 17: 405–424.

Wirth, Uwe. 2008. "Abduktion." In *Metzler-Lexikon Literatur- und Kulturtheorie*. Edited by Ansgar Nünning. 4th ed, 1. Stuttgart: Metzler.

Wolosky, Shira. 2010. *Poetry and Public Discourse in Nineteenth-Century America*. New York: Palgrave Macmillan.

Woodlief, Annette M. 1975. "The Influence of Theories of Rhetoric on Thoreau." *Thoreau Journal Quarterly* 7: 13–22.

Woodmansee, Martha. 1984a. "The Genius and the Copyright: Economic and Legal Conditions of the Emergence of the 'Author'." *Eighteenth-Century Studies* 17 (4): 425–448.

Woodmansee, Martha. 1984b. "The Interests in Disinterestedness: Karl Philipp Moritz and the Emergence of the Theory of Aesthetic Autonomy in Eighteenth-Century Germany." *Modern Language Quarterly* 45: 22–47.

Woodmansee, Martha. 1994. *The Author, Art, and the Market.* New York: Columbia University Press.

Woodmansee, Martha, and Peter Jaszi, eds. 1994. *The Construction of Authorship: Textual Appropriation in Law and Literature.* Durham, NC: Duke University Press.

Wordsworth, Jonathan. 1985. "'The Infinite I AM': Coleridge and the Ascent of Being." In *Coleridge's Imagination: Essays in Memory of Pete Laver,* edited by Richard Gravil, Lucy Newlyn, and Nicholas Roe, 22–52. Cambridge: Cambridge University Press.

Wordsworth, William. 1991. "Preface to Lyrical Ballads (1802)." In *Lyrical Ballads.* Edited by R. L. Brett and Alun R. Jones. 2nd ed, 233–258. London: Routledge.

Wordsworth, William. 1974. "Essay Upon Epitaphs, III." In *The Prose Works of William Wordsworth,* edited by Warwick J. B. Owen, 80–96 2. Oxford: Clarendon Press.

Wright, Tom F., ed. 2013. *The Cosmopolitan Lyceum: Lecture Culture and the Globe in Nineteenth-Century America.* Amherst: University of Massachusetts Press.

Wylder, Edith. 1971. *The Last Face: Emily Dickinson's Manuscripts.* Albuquerque: University of New Mexico Press.

Yates, Frances A. (1966) 1999. *The Art of Memory.* Selected Works 3. London: Routledge.

Zimmerman, Brett. 2001. "Frantic Forensic Oratory: Poe's 'The Tell-Tale Heart'." *Style* 35 (1): 34–49.

Zimmerman, Brett. 2005. *Edgar Allan Poe: Rhetoric and Style.* Montreal: McGill-Queen's University Press.

Index of Names

Abernethy, John   107
Abrams, M. H.   38, 43, 58, 69, 89, 95, 99, 209
Adams, John   81
Adams, John Quincy   12, 81, 106, 108, 117f., 149, 164–166, 179
Allen, Michael L.   77, 82
Alterton, Margaret   10, 82, 131–133
Anderson, Benedict   49, 99
Aristotle   13, 26, 28, 33f., 36–38, 42–46, 48, 58, 61, 67–69, 78, 96, 99f., 130f., 135, 151, 156, 158
Auerbach, Erich   26f.
Austin, Gilbert   49, 179, 214–216
Austin, J. L.   29

Bacon, Francis   66, 101, 135, 156
Barthes, Roland   21, 23–25, 35, 55
Bate, Jonathan   94f., 109.
Bate, Walter Jackson   71f., 110, 112, 115–117
Baudelaire, Charles   2, 6, 78, 129, 177
Baumgarten, Alexander Gottlieb   63, 120f.
Bennett, Andrew   11, 23, 56f.
Berensmeyer, Ingo   8, 23, 25, 53
Berlin, James A.   11f., 59, 63f.
Bialostosky, Don H.   65, 179
Bitzer, Lloyd F.   30
Blair, Hugh   12, 66, 79f., 82, 85f., 119f., 134, 178f., 189
Booth, Wayne C.   21, 23, 28, 39, 43, 61
Bristed, Charles Astor   93, 118
Bronson, Cotesworth P.   172, 181f., 184f.
Brown, Goold   188f.
Bryant, William Cullen   16, 37, 65, 67, 73f., 76, 86, 101, 136f., 202, 224
Bühler, Karl   14, 37–39
Burke, Kenneth   14, 28, 30f., 45, 53, 91, 137f., 145
Burke, Seán   23f., 31, 56, 224
Butler, Samuel   106–109, 118

Campbell, George   10, 12, 16f., 36f., 65–73, 75f., 80, 82, 85f., 103, 106, 116, 118, 133f., 136f., 143, 163, 178f., 189

Charvat, William   77f.
Cicero, Marcus Tullius   26, 28, 37, 39, 42, 45, 48, 210
Clark, Gregory   1, 11f., 79
Coleridge, Samuel Taylor   16, 35, 92–95, 100f., 103f., 109–114, 116, 118, 120, 132f., 153f., 209
Combe, George   152f.
Comstock, Andrew   211
Culler, Jonathan D.   29f.

Dayan, Colin (Joan)   4, 209
De Quincey, Thomas   16, 65, 68–70, 75f.
Demosthenes   41, 48, 210–212, 217
Dern, John A.   10, 221
Detering, Heinrich   23, 25, 91, 139–141
Dickens, Charles   2, 17, 50, 103, 124–126, 128–131, 137f., 141–144, 147, 151, 199f.
Doyle, Arthur Conan   160
Dryden, John   58, 115, 117

Eagleton, Terry   32–34, 63, 118
Eco, Umberto   160, 163, 168
Eliot, T. S.   1, 6, 172
Elmer, Jonathan   3, 6, 8, 27, 175
Engell, James   65, 80, 110, 112, 115–117
Epicurus   100, 117, 160

Fauvel-Gouraud, Francis   210
Felman, Shoshana   1, 5
Foucault, Michel   24, 35, 55–57

Genette, Gérard   1, 21, 32–34, 126–128, 146, 199f.
Gerard, Alexander   66, 71, 122
Godwin, William   17, 124–126, 128, 141–146
Gorgias of Leontinoi   28, 105, 176f.
Greenblatt, Stephen   13
Griswold, Rufus   2, 201f.

Halloran, S. Michael   1, 11f., 79
Hayes, Kevin J.   2, 7, 102, 130, 183–186, 189

Horace 16, 49, 89, 91f., 96–101, 103f.
Horner, Winifred Bryan 1, 28, 41f., 81
Howell, Wilbur Samuel 12, 28, 49
Howells, William Dean 105, 173–175
Hume, David 66, 71, 116, 122
Hurh, Paul 5, 151, 168, 214
Huxley, Aldous 5, 183, 187

Irwin, John T. 5, 150, 160
Iser, Wolfgang 140

Jackson, Leon 3, 78, 219
Jakobson, Roman 28f., 37, 91, 129
James, Henry 200
Jameson, Fredric 9, 31
Jannidis, Fotis 22–24
Jeffrey, Francis 54, 93, 110
Johnson, Nan 1, 11f., 49, 64, 80, 151, 178
Johnson, Samuel 58, 119

Kennedy, George A. 11, 28, 46, 224
Kennedy, J. Gerald 1, 3–5, 8f., 77, 172, 201, 224
Knape, Joachim 11, 28f., 36f., 39f., 59
Kopley, Richard 6, 8, 130, 159, 183–186

Lacan, Jacques 4f., 151
Lausberg, Heinrich 33, 36, 43–47, 106
Liszka, James Jakób 163f.
Ljungquist, Kent 170, 199, 203
Love, Harold 15, 23, 41, 224
Lowell, James Russell 7, 9, 203

Manning, Susan 1, 12, 81f.
Martin, Meredith 189f.
Matthiessen, Francis O. 6, 177
McGann, Jerome J. 1, 4, 6, 8, 10, 60, 90, 94f., 104, 113, 117, 172f., 180, 184, 186f., 193
McGill, Meredith L. 1f., 8, 77, 92, 202–205
McKeon, Richard 13, 28, 34
Mill, John Stuart 16, 29, 37, 64f., 67f., 70–76, 106, 132, 175, 180, 187, 224
Milton, John 67, 69, 97
Minturno, Antonio S. 37
Moritz, Karl Philipp 57, 111
Morrison, Toni 3, 35

Moss, Sidney P. 124, 203f.
Müller, Wolfgang G. 37, 46, 178
Murray, Lindley 189–191

Newbury, Michael 26, 77f.
Nietzsche, Friedrich Wilhelm 27f., 117

Ong, Walter J. 11, 43, 51, 218

Pahl, Dennis 5, 91, 139, 141
Parker, Edward G. 11, 79
Parrington, Vernon Louis 2
Peeples, Scott 2–6, 152, 176
Peirce, Charles Sanders 17, 149, 151, 154–156, 159, 162–166, 171, 225
Person, Leland S. 4, 91, 129, 139
Phelan, James 28, 39
Plett, Heinrich F. 45, 47
Pollin, Burton R. 196
Pope, Alexander 58, 67, 115, 202
Porter, Ebenezer 82, 138, 218
Pound, Ezra 174f.
Pue, Hugh A. 189
Putnam, George Palmer 86, 192

Quinn, Patrick F. 6, 172, 176
Quintilian 13, 26–28, 33f., 36f., 41f., 45f., 48–51, 58, 69, 74f., 134f., 174, 186, 209–211

Reynolds, David S. 117
Richards, Eliza 3f., 130
Richards, I. A. 28
Ricoeur, Paul 44, 61
Rose, Mark 56–58
Russell, William 11, 49f., 179, 214

Savoye, Jeffrey A. 120, 152
Schlegel, August Wilhelm von 119, 131–133, 143
Shakespeare, William 59, 164, 184, 196, 213
Shelley, Percy Bysshe 113, 117, 122
Sheridan, Thomas 49, 179, 189–191, 194
Sidney, Philip 35, 37, 58, 69
Silverman, Kenneth 4, 205
Skinner, Quentin 65

Sloane, Thomas O.   49 f.
Spalding, William   54, 64
Stillinger, Jack   23, 41
Stovall, Floyd   109

Tally, Robert T.   2, 209
Tate, Allen   5, 45 f.
Taylor, Bayard   105–107, 187
Thompson, G. R.   6 f., 112, 119, 131
Thoms, Peter   159, 168
Till, Dietmar   61
Todorov, Tzvetan   160, 162
Toulmin, Stephen E.   28
Tucker, Nathaniel Beverley   3

Varro, Marcus Terentius   26
Vickers, Brian   28 f., 134 f.

Walker, Jeffrey   43 f., 49, 96,
Walker, John   48, 179, 190 f., 194
Warren, James Perrin   1, 11, 74 f., 79
Webster, Daniel 79, 202
Webster, Noah   121, 134 f., 195

Weiner, Bruce I.   84, 150
Wellek, René   69 f., 90, 93, 113
Whalen, Terence   2 f., 77, 158, 192 f.
Whately, Richard   12, 16, 65, 68–70, 75 f., 80, 82, 86, 106, 108 f., 123, 138 f., 163, 178 f.
White, Hayden   28 f., 60–64, 73, 75 f., 100
White, Thomas Willis   3
Whitman, Sarah Helen   2
Whitman, Walt   175, 177
Williams, Michael J. S.   5, 208 f., 220
Williams, Raymond   10, 60–62, 64, 76
Winko, Simone   24
Wirth, Uwe   154, 163
Wolosky, Shira   177
Woodmansee, Martha   11, 23, 56, 58, 111
Wordsworth, Jonathan   111 f., 116
Wordsworth, William   16, 58, 69, 72, 92 f., 95, 100, 103, 111, 116, 178 f.

Yates, Frances A.   51 f.

Zimmerman, Brett   10, 41, 46, 104, 175, 184

Index of Subjects

Acting 48, 209–214, 216–218
Aesthetics 16f., 54, 59, 63f., 73, 76, 89–93, 98, 101–104, 109, 113f., 118, 120–123, 126, 128, 140f., 147, 177
Anastatic printing 218–220
Arrangement 14, 16, 22, 24f., 35, 40–43, 45, 47, 52, 73, 115, 135, 157, 219f.
– Author as arranger 16, 40, 46f., 118
– *Dispositio* 14, 16, 40–43, 45f., 52, 115, 118, 135, 157
Autheme 15, 41, 46f., 50, 52, 118, 135, 147, 149, 163f., 196, 220
Autocommentary 17, 126–130, 138f., 141f., 145–147
Autonomy 4, 10, 13, 25, 27, 45f., 53, 57, 83, 91, 111, 127f., 139f., 144–147, 150, 171, 193, 205, 216, 222–224

Beauty 4, 47, 63, 67, 94, 97f., 113f., 116f., 121, 135–137, 165, 177f., 180, 185, 193, 201, 212, 217
Blackwood 16, 41, 47, 68, 76f., 82–85, 120, 132f., 208, 213

Capitalism 2, 49, 57, 60, 62, 77, 99
Class 6, 24, 62, 77, 153
Commonplace 28, 44, 51f., 57, 84, 92f., 97f., 106, 108, 110, 135, 173, 205
Common sense 71, 82, 84, 119, 121, 123
Communication 11, 37, 39, 41f., 50, 60, 66–68, 70, 76, 80, 106, 225
Composition 15, 17, 41, 45, 50, 57, 67f., 70, 81, 84, 91, 93, 105, 111, 113, 120, 123–139, 141, 144, 146–148, 151, 164, 168, 173, 179f., 187, 195f., 203, 209, 217, 220f., 223
Constructiveness 152f., 158
Critic 1, 9–10, 16, 34, 37, 46, 72, 91f., 99, 102f., 105, 121–123, 126, 129f., 141, 147, 187, 196, 201, 212, 223
Culture of eloquence 11, 79
Culture of rhetoric 1, 9, 11–13, 16, 53, 64, 68, 74, 76, 79, 86, 136, 164, 170, 172, 197, 214, 218, 222–225

Deconstruction 2, 5, 29, 32, 214
Delectare 14f., 35–37, 39f., 47, 66, 71, 74, 89, 98f., 101, 135f.
– Author as entertainer 35, 40, 101
Delivery 16, 18, 35, 42–44, 48–50, 52, 84, 169, 179f., 187, 196–200, 202–221
Detective fiction 46, 160, 162, 166, 170f., 223
– Detective 5, 9, 17, 34, 46, 138, 148–151, 153, 156–163, 165f., 168–171, 223
Docere 14f., 35–37, 39f., 47, 66, 71, 74, 89, 99, 101, 135f.
– Instruction 35, 62f., 83f., 89, 98–101, 198
– Author as instructor 39f., 101
Dupin, Chevalier C. Auguste 5, 17, 29, 40, 92, 98, 102, 148–150, 153–155, 159–161, 163, 167–171

Edinburgh Review 54, 82, 85, 93, 100f., 197
Elocutionary movement 10, 12, 17, 49f., 55, 81, 172, 178–181, 214, 218
Elocutionist 9, 34, 49f., 172f., 176, 181–187, 189–191, 193–195, 210–212, 214, 216f., 223
Eloquence 11, 18, 51, 54, 64–66, 69–74, 76, 79, 133, 172, 174, 189, 224
Eloquence, Market of 18, 197, 205–208
Emergence of literature 9, 11, 55, 61f., 64f., 76, 223
Empiricism 66, 115f.
Ethos 36–38, 205, 207

Faculties 17, 42, 47, 66, 71, 74, 80, 94, 113f., 136f., 153, 157
Fancy 10, 67, 91, 104, 109–118, 150, 152–154
Figuration 3, 15, 17f., 27–32, 47, 91, 107, 126, 152, 161f., 170, 188, 197, 212, 219, 223f.
Figures of the author 1, 8f., 13–17, 22, 25, 27, 31–34, 76, 223f. and passim
Figures of the author, performative 1, 13f., 17, 22, 40, 47–53, 101, 149, 172f., 178, 180, 187, 192, 194, 196f., 218, 222–224

Figures of the author, poetical 13–17, 33, 40–47, 90f., 149–152, 161, 163, 166, 169–171, 223f.
Figures of the author, theoretical 13f., 15, 17, 22, 29–40, 72, 75, 89–92, 103, 118, 122, 127, 141, 145, 147, 152, 223f.

Gender 3f., 6, 22, 24, 78, 198
Genius 4, 7, 9, 17, 22, 25, 31, 34, 41, 57–59, 66, 72, 76, 78, 86, 91f., 94f., 102–104, 108f., 118, 121–124, 126, 128, 141, 146f., 165, 223
Gesture 4f., 16–22, 42f., 48, 50, 78, 117, 120, 188, 199f., 211–217
Gothic 7, 45, 54, 82f., 85, 105, 167, 177, 180, 184, 186

Heroes of consciousness 150, 171
Heteronomy 4, 13, 25, 27, 38, 45f., 53, 57, 72, 91, 127, 139f., 144f., 147, 150, 205, 216, 223
Histrio 196, 208f., 213, 217–219, 222, 223
Holmes, Sherlock 160

Imagination 10, 27, 36f., 46, 52, 61, 66f., 71f., 74, 91, 95, 101, 104, 109–117, 124, 136f., 150, 152f., 156f., 164, 166, 213
Inference 17, 29, 44, 137, 149, 151, 154–157, 160–167, 171, 223
– Inference, abductive 17, 151, 154–157, 160–164, 166, 168
– Inference, deductive 17, 154–156, 160, 166
– Inference, inductive 17, 69, 154–157, 166, 169
Intentionalism 23
Invention 14–17, 22, 25, 35, 40, 42–45, 47, 51f., 62, 66, 80, 115f., 119, 122, 142f., 149, 157, 161, 163–165, 169–171, 186, 210, 219, 223
  Inventio 14, 16, 40f., 43f., 116, 135, 157, 161, 163f., 169, 171
Inventor 5, 16f., 40, 44, 47, 138, 148, 161f.
Irony 5, 7, 28f., 207

Jingle-man 17, 105, 173–176, 187, 222f.

Lecturing 1, 10f., 18, 34, 51, 73, 79f., 82, 86, 106f., 117, 128, 131, 133, 149, 152, 172f., 181, 189, 197–203, 197, 223
Lecturer 10, 18, 82, 173, 198–203
Letter of recommendation 101–103
Logos 36f.
Lyceum 11, 18, 53, 79, 182, 193, 197f., 201, 203–208, 216f.

Madness 4, 45f., 126, 139f., 144, 205
Magazine 2f., 9, 21, 27, 68, 77, 79, 82f., 85f., 96, 98, 100–103, 109, 112, 119, 121f., 124f., 132, 134, 146, 189, 193, 197, 201, 207, 207f., 219f.
Market 2, 18, 2656f., 77f., 82, 101f., 122, 196, 197, 201, 205–209, 222f.
Mass culture 2f., 6, 27, 77
Memory 14–16, 22, 35, 42, 47f., 51–53, 111, 135, 153, 172, 174, 180, 186, 197, 199, 209f., 217
– Memoria 14, 16, 40f., 51f., 209
Metaphor 4, 26, 28f., 32, 44, 46, 61, 70, 78, 117, 138, 165, 178f., 208f.
Mimesis 43f., 61
Modernism 5f., 12, 128, 180
Movere 14f., 35–37, 39f., 47, 66, 71, 74, 99, 135f.
– Author as agitator 40, 101

Narrator 45f., 56, 83, 140, 153f., 160f., 167–170, 208–210, 212f., 221
Nation 3f., 11, 62, 81, 190
Neoclassicism 39, 57f., 60, 69, 80, 101, 115, 132, 179
Novel 3, 34, 57, 124–126, 128, 141–146, 153, 162
Novelty 113–115, 166

Oedipus 150, 158, 162
Orator 28, 37, 39–42, 48f., 51, 66f., 73–75, 79, 82, 108, 117f., 133, 165f., 170, 178, 196–198, 201, 205, 207f., 211, 218, 222
Oratory 10f., 41–43, 48, 67, 70, 79, 117, 134, 177, 211
Originality 9, 56, 58, 60, 117, 126, 146, 178, 206f., 210

Index of Subjects

Passion   36 f., 59, 66 f., 71 f., 74 f., 135 – 137, 165, 202 f., 212
Pathos   36 f.
Performance   3, 11, 14 – 17, 22 f., 32, 35, 42, 47 – 53, 78 f., 127, 139, 172 f., 177 – 180, 182, 185 – 188, 190, 193, 195, 197 – 202, 204 – 208, 213 – 220, 222 – 224
Actio   14, 16, 40, 48, 50, 178 f.
Author as performer   18, 173, 186 f., 207 – 209, 212 – 214, 216 f.
Persuasion   15, 27 – 32, 36, 68, 74, 107, 126, 136, 165, 185, 223 f.
Philosophy   22 f., 29, 61, 66, 68, 82, 94, 97, 100, 113, 116, 127, 130, 133 f., 163, 166, 220
Plagiarism   35, 77, 116, 130, 203
Pleasure   69, 93, 98 – 101, 103, 114, 134, 159, 175 f., 212
Poet-critic   9, 16, 34 f., 37, 91 – 93, 95, 99, 103, 122 f., 130, 141, 147, 175, 187, 223
Poetics   14 f., 26, 32, 34 f., 40, 43 f., 47, 53, 61, 70, 76, 79, 81, 95 f., 99 – 101, 103 f., 115, 126, 128, 136, 138 – 141, 143 – 145, 147, 205, 210, 223
Poetry   4 – 6, 10 f., 16 f., 34, 37 f., 44, 47 – 49, 54 f., 58 – 61, 63 – 65, 67 – 70, 72 – 76, 86, 89, 93 f., 96 – 101, 103 – 106, 108, 117, 119, 125, 130, 132, 134 f., 164 f., 172 --- 188, 190 f., 193, 195, 198 – 203, 205 – 208, 222 – 224
Pragmatism   29, 163, 166, 170
Print culture   1 – 4, 8 f., 11, 49 f., 54 f., 61, 77 f., 85 f., 102, 172, 209, 214
– Culture of reprinting   2, 8, 77, 83, 92, 146, 206, 216
Pronuntiatio   16, 40 f., 48, 178 f., 209
Prosody   188 f., 191, 193 f., 200
Psychoanalysis   2, 4 f., 129

Race   3, 6, 191 f.
Ratiocination   17, 44 f., 138 – 140, 148 f., 156, 160 f., 163 – 167, 169
Remediation   218, 220 f.
Rhetoric of authorship   13 – 15, 21 f., 25, 27, 31 f., 34, 47, 53, 90, 149, 223
Rhetoric, belletristic   12, 55, 120, 178, 189, 223 f.

Rhetoric, death of   21, 44
Rhetoric, dispersal of   11 f., 54, 64 f., 85 f., 90, 104, 141, 147, 177, 223 f.
Rhetoric, elocutionist   12, 49 and see entry on elocutionary movement
Rhetoric, epistemological   12, 55 and see entry on George Campbell
Rhetoric, New   12, 16 f., 28, 32, 50, 64, 68, 80, 82, 90, 93, 116, 137, 154, 163, 178, 223
Rhetoric, suppression of   61 f., 64, 73, 100
Rhetorical criticism   30, 95, 99, 118
Rhetorical effect   12 – 17, 35 – 39, 131 – 140 and passim
Rhetorical situation   28, 30 – 32, 173, 205
Rhetoricianism   109
Rhetoricity   10, 105, 174 f.
Romantic author   9 f., 12, 16, 31, 54, 57, 59, 71, 95, 111, 152 f., 178
Romantic ideology   10, 60, 72, 76, 90
Romanticism   5 f., 12, 16, 58, 60 f., 65, 69 f., 83, 90, 92, 95 f., 103, 127 f., 145, 147, 178
Romanticism, High   60, 92, 178

Satire   18, 67, 83, 168, 199, 204, 209, 223
Semiotic   21, 32, 38, 92, 163
Slavery   3, 167, 192, 206
South, American   2, 9 f., 79, 167, 188, 192 f., 195, 198, 206
Style   10, 14 – 17, 22, 30, 35 f., 40, 42 – 44, 46 f., 60, 68, 76, 84, 105 f., 108 f., 114, 122, 124, 135, 175, 177 – 180, 183, 187, 202, 206, 211, 213, 216, 219 f.
– *Elocutio*   14, 16, 40 f., 43, 46, 135, 177 – 180, 187
– Author as stylizer   16, 41, 47
Sublime   46, 74, 105, 116, 212

Tale   2, 4 f., 7, 10, 16 f., 34, 40, 44 – 46, 51, 54, 82 – 85, 98, 102, 124, 131, 138 – 140, 143, 148 f., 156, 160 f., 163 – 166, 168 f., 172, 192, 197, 208 – 210, 212, 217 f., 220 f.
Topos   44, 52 f., 75, 109, 157, 159, 196, 213
Transatlanticism   1, 6, 9, 11 f., 16 – 18, 28, 34, 54 f., 77, 80 – 85, 89, 91, 102 f., 120, 123, 145, 194, 196, 200, 223 f.

Truth 9, 17, 39, 43, 54, 58, 67–69, 93, 106f., 114, 118, 132, 135–137, 155, 162, 164f., 176, 192f., 198, 203

Utility 69, 73, 98, 100–102

Versification 49, 118, 134, 188, 190, 193

Voice 23, 31, 39, 42f., 48, 50, 81, 90, 139f., 154f., 169, 179, 183, 190, 196, 200, 202, 204f., 208f., 211f., 214–216

www.ingramcontent.com/pod-product-compliance
Lightning Source LLC
Chambersburg PA
CBHW030615230426
43661CB00053B/2000